FAR FROM MECCA

FAR FROM MECCA

Globalizing the Muslim Caribbean

ALIYAH KHAN

The University of the West Indies Press

Jamaica • Barbados • Trinidad and Tobago

The University of the West Indies Press
7A Gibraltar Hall Road, Mona
Kingston 7, Jamaica
www.uwipress.com

A catalogue record of this book is available from the National Library of Jamaica.

ISBN: 978-976-640-804-6 (paper)
978-976-640-805-3 (Kindle)
978-976-640-806-0 (ePub)

Cover photograph: Moulvi Azeez giving the Eid al-Fitr sermon at Louisa Row masjid,
Georgetown, Guyana, mid-1960s. Author's family archives.
Cover design by Richard Rawlins

Printed in the United States of America

To my parents, Jan and Salima Khan, and
my grandfather, Imam Mohamed Rasheed

CONTENTS

FAR FROM MECCA

INTRODUCTION

Muslims in / of the Caribbean

My grandfather was a Muslim
And my daddy was a Rasta.

—Khāled Siddīq

I was entitled to the feast of Husein, to the mirrors and crepe-paper temples
of the Muslim epic.... The palms and the Muslim minarets are Antillean
exclamations.

—Derek Walcott

Not every Muslim in the Caribbean is East Indian.[1] As British Jamai-
can singer and YouTube star Khāled Siddīq sings to a reggae beat in "My
Grandfather Was a Muslim," his Afro-Jamaican grandfather or enslaved ancestors
past could have been Muslims, even if his real or metaphorical father became a
Jamaican Rastafarian.[2] Similarly, Jamaican Muslim artist Sayeed Tijani (Tijani
Concious [sic]) sings an ode to the "Fulani Woman" as the ideal African and
Afro-Jamaican Muslim woman.[3] Siddīq and Tijani emphasize that Islam in Jamaica
and the Caribbean is as religiously linked to Africa as are syncretic polytheistic
Caribbean religions like Santería and Obeah. They suggest that Afro-Caribbean
Muslims like them are not converts but, rather, reverts to ancestral African Islamic
lineages lost to the Middle Passage. Tijani takes as a name the epithet "Tijani,"
denoting a follower of North African Sufi reformist leader and mystic Ahmad al-
Tijānī (1737–1815). In "Baye Niasse (Boom Baye)," Tijani also follows in the musical footsteps of famed Senegalese singer Youssou N'Dour to call on Emir Baay
Ibrahim Niasse (1900–1975), founder of the West African Ibrāhīmiyyah branch of
the Sufi Tijāniyyah *tarīqa* brotherhood, to solve the social ills of, in this case,
Jamaica.[4] Of his Muslim grandfather and Rastafarian father, Siddīq sings, "They
were searching for the truth / And the Qur'an it gave the answer." Anticolonial, Old
Testament– and Ethiopian history–influenced Rastafarianism is one step toward
the liberation of the African diaspora in the New World, but the final answer to the
Caribbean search for African roots and spiritual truth, Siddīq implies, is Islam.

That the legacy of Africa in the Caribbean includes Islam is history worth emphasizing when Caribbean Muslims are commonly assumed to be all descendants of South Asian Indian indentured laborers, particularly in Guyana, Trinidad, Jamaica, and Suriname, the countries in which those Hindu, Muslim, and Christian descendants are a relatively cohesive ethnic community. The St. Lucian writer Derek Walcott frames his 1992 Nobel Prize in Literature lecture with an account of the Hindu Indo-Caribbean villagers of Felicity, Trinidad, preparing their costumes and *murtis*—representations of the gods—to perform the *Ramleela*, the dramatization of the epic *Ramayana*. He invokes Asia as an unfolding temporal, material, and historic space not *in* the Caribbean, but *of* the Caribbean. The *Ramleela* is not the "visual echo of History" he had expected, nor a fragment of lost memory, nor "degenerative mimicry," but a "dialect" that was "not a distortion or even a reduction of its epic scale."[5] In this large-scale performance of a Hindu epic on a field, under the open sky, Walcott sees not simply the static preservation and remembrance of a religious tradition, but an ongoing reconstitution of Hinduism and the relocation of mythic Asia to the Caribbean. On the strength of the players' faith and conviction—they are named true believers, rather than theatrical actors or "amateurs"—the *Ramleela*, performed in a field that may have once been a cane field in which the worshipers' indentured ancestors and enslaved Africans toiled, becomes part of the Caribbean landscape. The *Ramleela* also reminds Walcott that there are other non-African, non-Indian migrant cultural forces at work in the Caribbean: English, Jewish, Chinese, and Lebanese.[6] The indigenous remain annihilated and unmentioned, though they still live in ecologically compromised circumstances with little state power in countries dominated by people of African and Indian descent in Guyana, Suriname, and Dominica.

The *landscape* of Walcott's Caribbean difference is exemplified by the "Muslim minaret," tall as a palm tree and just as at home against the Antillean sky. The more obvious architectural visual referent to Islam, the round central dome of a mosque, is ignored in favor of the alliterative Muslim minaret, the corner pillar from which the muezzin delivers the five-times-daily Islamic call to prayer. Through both its visual markers and its distinctive soundscape, Islam writes itself and the Qur'anic Word of God onto the islands (and continental Guyana and Suriname). We do not learn directly from Walcott the specific identity of the people of the minaret the way we learn about the Hindus performing the *Ramleela*. The Levantine Arabs he mentions, who migrated to the Caribbean and the United States from the late nineteenth century through the interwar period of the twentieth century, were predominantly Christian Orthodox, Maronite, and Melkite. There is a clue, however, in Walcott's realization that as a Caribbean writer, the cultural field of Islam open to him includes the "feast of Husein" and the "crepe-paper temples of the Muslim epic." These are references to the Muslim Indo-Caribbean festival of Hosay, the originally Shi'a Muslim commemoration of the martyrdom of the Prophet Muhammad's grandson Hussein. Hussein gives his name to Hosay in Trinidad and Hussay in Jamaica, though in Guyana and Suriname the festival is called Tadjah and Taziya, after the commemorative model tombs carried in Hosay processions and the Arabo-Persian term *ta'zīya*, meaning grief-comfort or condolence. Tellingly, Walcott thinks of Islam in the context of an Indian Hindu festival, implying that for him Islam in the Caribbean is Indian, not African.

In 1970, the number of Muslims in Guyana peaked at 9.1 percent and in Trinidad at 6.26 percent of the population. These numbers have decreased as a result of migration to England and North America.[7] Muslims represented 13.5 percent of Surinamese in 2004 (this percentage includes Javanese and Indian Muslims), and a statistically negligible 0.04 percent of Jamaicans in 2001.[8] Approximately 543,700 Indian indentured laborers were brought to the Caribbean between 1838 and 1917, following the end of African slavery in the British Caribbean colonies. Estimates of the number of these who were Muslim vary between 6 and 14 percent. The vast majority of Muslim migrants were Sunni, with small numbers of Shi'a. The Sunnis were generally of the Hanafi *fiqh*, the largest school of Sunni Muslim jurisprudence whose adherents span the Indian subcontinent, Turkey, Eastern Europe, Egypt, and China.[9] Though they gave nineteenth-century Caribbean Islam its defining public ritual celebration of Hosay, there are very small numbers of practicing Shi'a in the Caribbean today. From the early twentieth century onward, international missionary activity has resulted in the Ahmadiyya reformist sect becoming the most vocal minority Muslim sect in the Caribbean, in contrast to its current persecution and disenfranchisement in Pakistan, where it originated in the late nineteenth century and where it was in 1974 declared doctrinally non-Muslim by the state.

The Islam that Walcott recognizes as Caribbean, the religion of most mosques and minarets in Trinidad, is a heavily subcontinental Sunni one, with Shi'a influence and Ahmadi visibility: an intrareligious, intersectarian, syncretic Caribbean faith. But that iteration of hybrid, migrant Caribbean Islam that nonetheless remains Indian, does not account for a number of factors: the history of enslaved Africans' Islam in the New World, Caribbean Islam's relationship to Hinduism, the place of the Caribbean Muslim in contemporary global narratives of terrorism and religious citizenship, and a global Muslim religious identity that is continuously and now more visibly disaggregating from race and place. The "new" Caribbean Muslim of the twenty-first century can be a "born" Indo-Caribbean Muslim or an Afro-Caribbean convert, a local, or a transnational person living between the Caribbean and North America or Europe. Beginning in the 1970s, Caribbean Muslims have also contended with worldwide revivalist *tajdīd* and reformist *islah* Islamic projects, and a growing Islamization of local religious practices deemed "cultural," a movement loosely termed in the Saudi and Egyptian contexts the Islamic Revival or Awakening (*as-Sahwa al-'Islāmiyyah*), which Saba Mahmood identifies as including both "the activities of state-oriented political groups" and the development of a fairly conservative, piety-oriented "religious ethos or sensibility" in majority Muslim countries.[10] Charles Kurzman quantifies the triple forces at work in the last two centuries of worldwide Muslim debates over Islamic praxis as customary Islam, revivalist Islam, and liberal Islam, the latter of which "calls upon the past in the name of modernity, while revivalists might be said to call upon modernity . . . in the name of the past."[11] These conflicting and overlapping forces manifest in the Muslim Caribbean in multiple ways discussed in this book: as conflicts between perceived traditional "Indo-Iranian" Islam and various types of Islamic "orthodoxy" influenced by missionizing from and education in Libya, Egypt, and the Gulf States; as suspicions that Indo-Caribbean Islam is untowardly influenced by Hinduism; as assertions that Islam is not rightfully a religion of African diaspora people in the Americas, and that when they convert, they have violent fundamentalist leanings mysteriously linked to Malcolm X and the Nation of Islam; and that Caribbean Muslims' regional belonging and citizenship is superseded by their allegiance to global Islam.

There is no Muslim country or Muslim society per se in the Caribbean. Yet Caribbean Muslims have always had a sense of themselves as part of the global *ummah* (community), whether as displaced branches of South Asian or African Islam, or, now, as people who look to the Arab world for a sense of cultural and religious origin and political orientation, in a time of ongoing U.S. imperialist military action in the Middle East. This book argues, above all, that the Caribbean Muslim subject, whom I call by the Guyanese term for a Muslim of any race, the "fullaman," has never been fixed or static. Furthermore, the long-standing presence of Muslims and shifting negotiations of Muslim identity in the Caribbean demonstrate the fruition of a process that the United States and European countries with large numbers of Muslim migrants and refugees have only recently begun to acknowledge: that Islam always functions as a racial category. Islam has been racialized from medieval European crusader imaginings of the Saracen, to the colonial Arab and Turkish harems of orientalist fantasies, to stereotypes of Salafi European immigrant men radicalized into the Islamic State on the Internet, to its Indo-Caribbean minarets against the Antillean sky.

Through analysis of literary texts and music by and about Caribbean Muslims, this book makes three central arguments: first, that the Muslim subject in the Caribbean, the *fullaman* (from, as I will discuss, the African tribal name Fulani), is a temporal figure that traverses the path of the racialized Caribbean labor subject from premodern, non-European, native "savage" Caliban, to modernity's African plantation slave, to late colonialism's Asian indentured laborer. The colonial fullaman begins as the "Eastern" savage infiltrator in the New World, the Arab or North African Moor or *Morisco*, who enters the early Spanish colonies as an illegal migrant or slave at a post-Reconquista time when "the term *Moor* did not connote racial characteristics as much as cultural, specifically Islamic, ones."[12] The entry of Moors, Jews, Protestants, and "Gypsies" into Spanish colonies was barred or limited up to the twentieth century; many of the *Moriscos* who none-theless entered in the early colonial era were women, and the figure of the *Morisca* became racially conflated with the mixed-race, brown-skinned *mulata*.[13] After the Moor and *Morisco*, the colonial American fullaman, specter of Islam in the New World, inhabited the enslaved Muslim West African from the regions of Guinea, Senegal, Nigeria, Mali, and Côte-d'Ivoire, then the "Mahometan Hindoo" indentured laborer from British India.[14] Caliban, the deformed island man who is taught to speak and forced into servitude by the European magician Prospero in Shakespeare's *The Tempest*—a play that was influenced by colonial fantasies of Americas hurricanes' force and geographic and climatological alienness—became a literary metaphor for the "hybrid" Caribbean man with Roberto Fernández Retamar's 1979 privileging of Caliban over earlier Latin American and U.S. figurations of Ariel the sprite as embodiment of the Americas.[15] Caliban has been taken up by Edward Kamau Brathwaite, Aimé Césaire, David Dabydeen, Paget Henry, and other Caribbean writers as the representative Caribbean (post)colonial. As Jodi Byrd argues, however, "the translocation of indigeneity from the prior Ariel to Caliban and his mother, Sycorax, enacts the machinations of settler discourses that detach indigeneity from the original inhabit-ants of the Americas and relocate it on settlers and arrivants themselves."[16] The dan-ger of "overdetermined" Caliban "is that every time a claim to Caliban is made from within or without empire . . . colonization is maintained with a difference."[17] I show that rather than being another iteration of Caliban that elides indigeneity, the Muslim fullman is interpellated into Caribbean postcolonial citizenship through the same indigenous signification that produces settlers, the Afro-Caribbean, and Caliban himself as native. Still, Caliban retains direct affiliation with the fullaman not only because both have been dehumanized, forced laborers in the Americas, but because the origins of Caliban and his witchy mother, Sycorax, lie in Algiers: the exotic, villainous Muslim Others of Shakespeare's Elizabethan England transmogrified into the amoral, hybrid monsters of the New World. The fullaman transgresses the colo-nial legacy of racialized Caribbean labor categories through a shifting engagement with global Islamic modernity and the worldwide *ummah*, as defined later.

Second, the book shows that the figure of the fullaman neither resists nor fully enters discourses of creolization and syncretism that are fundamental to postco-lonial nationalisms in the Caribbean. The fullaman simultaneously deconstructs essentialist ideas of the religious Muslim and provides an alternative iteration of the Caribbean "mimic man" of Trinidadian novelist and literary Nobel Prize winner V. S. Naipaul. The mimic man, in Caribbean postcolonial parlance, is the former slave or indentured laborer who has lost his ancestral culture and language, and poorly imitates the tongue, cultural practices, and governmental structure of the European colonizer, dooming him to personal and national failure after colonial independence. Naipaul's work, as shown here, contains the genesis of both the Caribbean mimic man and the specific iteration of the Muslim Caribbean mimic man. The Muslim mimic man appears in Caribbean literature in the form of a postcolonial person who looks to the Middle East, rather than to Britain or Europe, as his or her metropolitan cultural referent.

Third, this book demonstrates that the Caribbean Muslim fullaman is a fluid, *performative* identity. For the fullaman, as perhaps for a person of any faith, religious identity is often performative, in the sense that ongoing ritual, sartorial, and other private and public actions may change social and material reality and perceptions of and by the adherent and religious community. The fullaman's form and boundaries shift. For women, there is a double performativity of gendered religion. Muslim theater may be performed by pious women, for example, through ritual prayer (*salah* or *namāz*) that requires specific dress and emotional and intentional affect. Saba Mahmood identifies this as "rehearsed spontaneity" in Egypt: women rehearse behavior and *feeling*, and produce pious Islamic belonging through dress, thought, and material practices, until "Muslim" affect becomes natural to their bodies.[18] Rehearsed spontaneity may be viewed as doctrinal or customary. Talal Asad, identifying the problematics of an "anthropology of Islam" in 1986, points out that the customary scholarly opposition between "Great" (orthodox) and "Little" (nonorthodox) religious traditions is in fact orientalist, reifying distinctions between "East" and "West" and ignoring the fact that both scriptural orthodoxy and local religious customs are highly variable in Islam.[19] As an object of study, Islam, Asad argues, "should be approached as a discursive tradition that connects variously with the formation of moral selves, the manipulation of populations (or resistance to it), and the production of appropriate knowledges."[20] Fluid performances of Muslim religiosity contradict a common view of both Caribbean Muslims and Indo-Caribbean people as racialized, static, and religiously saturated. Viranjini Munasinghe argues that Indians in the colonial Caribbean were considered "culturally saturated," with "[b]iologization of East Indian [cultural] traits, which are viewed as immutable, ingrained in nature."[21] Fullaman identity is always in the process of becoming, in relation to other Muslims and to non-Muslims, and its momentary fixity and locus of enunciation in any time and place are often determined by the dress and "moral" behavior of Muslim women.

My methodology is one that combines archival, historiographic, and ethnographic framing with cultural studies and postcolonial theory in the analysis of literature. The core is literary analysis. Each chapter, with the exception of the fourth, which blends analysis of a novel and music, is a literary diptych preceded by the aforementioned framework, a structure I have chosen because there is not enough analysis or common contextual knowledge of lived Islam in the Anglophone Caribbean to proceed solely with relatively abstract literary readings, even when those readings act as much-needed supplements to the archive. My position is that when it is not widely known that a people even exist, their historical journey must first be acknowledged, but not defensively so. In the diptych structure, I begin with an older literary work or works that shed light on a newer one, and bolster the argument that Islam has been in the Caribbean a long time, under many ethnic and sectarian guises. The settings of the older works of the diptychs in each chapter are in chronological order with each other. The works in the fourth chapter, on the 1990 Jamaat al Muslimeen attempted government coup in Trinidad, are literature and music, so I have interwoven them in counterpoint to each other. Two significant interviews anchor my ethnographic work on Islam in the Caribbean: one with Yasin Abu Bakr, leader of the Trinidadian Jamaat al Muslimeen, who occupies the imagined place of the originary Caribbean Muslim "terrorist" in the view of both Trinidadians and the U.S. government; and the other with Anesa Ahamad, the Trinidadian medical doctor who, in 1995, was the first Muslim woman to give a Friday *Jumu'ah khutbah* sermon in a Caribbean mosque. Also instructive were my interactions with calypsonians from Trinidad, including David Rudder, Cro Cro (Weston Rawlins), G. B. (Gregory Ballantyne), and Vincentian Brother Ebony (Fitzroy Joseph), who generously allowed me to quote their songs on Muslims, race, and the Muslimeen coup in Trinidad. I spent significant time in the National Archives of Guyana perusing the *Voice of Islam*, the colonial-era Indo-Muslim newspaper of British Guiana, and the *Clarion*, the Muslim Black Nationalist revolutionary newspaper of 1960s British Guiana (as of independence in 1966, Guyana). All in all, there is slippage in field positioning in this ostensibly literary academic book. Traces of my own Caribbean fullaman life are also woven throughout, in the inspirational spirit of Audre Lorde's biomythography, a subaltern genre of producing a literary and experiential whole by simultaneously writing the self and the story of one's people. The genre is inspired by Lorde's own Grenadian, Carriacou, and Bajan (Barbadian) Caribbean heritage, originating in her resistance to the silencing of queer Afro-Caribbean *zami* women.[22] My interdisciplinary methodology is a purposeful, field-establishing choice in the understudied, undertheorized nascent field of Muslim and Islamic Caribbean Studies. "Muslim," in this formulation, refers to adherents and their cultural and other lived practices, also acknowledging that, as Junaid Rana says, "the Muslim" can be "a unit of analysis that is central to the examination of Islamic societies, cultures, and communities," even as the figure "is also a transmigratory, global figure that enters and exits multiple terrains."[23] By contrast, "Islam" here indicates religious and doctrinal concerns that do not always overlap with cultural practices or identity formulations.

I focus on the Muslim literature of the Anglophone Caribbean nations of Guyana, Trinidad, and Jamaica. Suriname, a former Dutch South American colony, is home to the largest population of Muslims in South America and the Caribbean, and has produced one very important regional Muslim text: *Jeevan Prakash*, the recently translated autobiography of Munshi Rahman Khan (1874–1972), a Muslim Indian indentured laborer in Suriname.[24] *Jeevan Prakash* is a masterwork of the Munshi's (teacher's) autobiographical and poetic literary ability, and holds important documentation of the shifting and surprisingly conciliatory relationships between Hindu and Muslim indentured laborers in the region before and after the British Partition of India. It is important, however, to be thoroughly conversant with Dutch, Sranan Tongo, Javanese, and Sarnami Hindoestani literature and culture in order to do the work of examining formulations of the Surinamese Muslim, and including that figure in a book that is primarily on the Anglophone Caribbean would not do it justice. However, I pay equal or more national attention to Guyana, which has the second-largest population of Muslims in the Caribbean, and which is significantly understudied in comparison to Trinidad and Jamaica. The latter two countries are simply more accessible to more scholars, particularly English-speaking scholars, for socioeconomic, educational, linguistic, and geographic reasons. I discuss Muslims and the development of Islamic identities in countries that offer comparative Muslim histories of African slavery and Indian indentureship; as such, I do not address the growing and also understudied Muslim communities in Hispanophone Caribbean countries like Puerto Rico and the Dominican Republic, and in Brazil, Mexico, and other countries in the American hemisphere.

This book is a literary complement to existing Islamic and Caribbean studies work in anthropology, history, gender studies, Indo-Caribbean studies, and, recently and problematically, security studies. Before the late twentieth century, there was but a small body of literature by and about Caribbean Muslims, not enough for drawing any major conclusions, and most of the groundbreaking work on Caribbean Islam and Muslims was produced by anthropologists and historians, including Edward E. Curtis, Sylviane Diouf, Michael A. Gomez, Paul Lovejoy, and Maureen Warner-Lewis on the Afro-Muslim Caribbean, and Raymond Chickrie, Gabrielle Hosein, Halima Sa'adia Kassim, Aisha Khan, Frank Korom, and Patricia Mohammed on the Indo-Muslim Caribbean. The divisions are notably ethnic. I, however, take a comparative approach that looks at Afro-Caribbean and Indo-Caribbean Muslims together, as they are the two largest historical and contemporary groups of Muslims in the Anglophone Caribbean, and they have intersected and shared space and social and political concerns since the Indo-Caribbean community came into being in 1838.

I conceive of the field of Muslim and Islamic Caribbean studies as falling primarily within the postcolonial and area studies discipline of Caribbean studies. Muslim and Islamic Caribbean studies is concerned with the general Caribbean studies field issues of racial identities, postcolonial citizenship, cultural creolization and hybridity, and economic neo-imperialism in the region. Still, Muslim and Islamic Caribbean studies necessarily has a lateral relationship with critical Muslim *American* studies—itself broadly conceptualized as a transnational and hemispheric discipline with a U.S. focus. In particular, I wish to decenter the place of the United States in the study of Islam in the Americas. Muslim and Islamic American studies cannot be defined as the study of twentieth- and twenty-first-century Arab, South Asian, Persian, Turkish, West African, and other Muslim immigration to the United States and Canada, with its temporal pivot point as September 11, 2001, when the story of Muslims in the Americas began in the colonial era with enslaved Iberian-Maghrebi *Moriscos* and the transatlantic African slave trade.

There is significant controversy over some historians' recuperation of narratives of enslaved Caribbean African Muslims, because there are so few verifiable written records of them. Particularly in the case of Jamaica, Maureen Warner-Lewis notes issues with historiographic scholarly works by Sultana Afroz that read as though they challenge Caribbean historical scholarship with the political agenda of "the promotion of Islam," utilizing "extravagance of assertion, leaps in assumptions, and glib transitions from probability to dogmatism," as well as "attribution of causation to the conjuncture or correlation of event, behaviour or custom."[25] That is to say, all scholars write from their own biases, but some recurring assertions, for example that Jamaican Maroons lived in mostly Muslim communities, are stretches unsupported by data or literature. This book revolves around finding the elided Muslim in Caribbean history and literature, and I have significant personal and academic sympathy for that cause; but the missing Muslim in the archive cannot be produced simply by desire. As such, I agree with Warner-Lewis and have omitted seemingly shaky historiographies from my research—though I have noted some of the texts bibliographically.

Much of Caribbean studies and Caribbean literature, including the Indo-Caribbean literature that provides one gateway into the lives of regional Muslims, has been concerned with questions of trauma, loss, and recuperation—an inevitability given the depredations, displacement, and suffering caused by African slavery and, later, Indian indentureship. The recovery of Africa, for example, was a central artistic and political concern of the pan-Africanist Négritude movement of the 1930s—a movement spearheaded by Francophone Afro-Caribbean intellectuals including Martinican Aimé Césaire and French Guianese Léon Damas. Indo-Caribbean literature also begins with the varied positioning of ancestral India as lost, never-lost, or always in a process of recovery, and in the Naipaulian tradition, by fixing the Indo-Caribbean person as mimic man or permanent exile. The primary subject of Indo-Caribbean studies and literature, as identified by Miriam Pirbhai, Sean Lokaisingh-Meighoo, Peggy Mohan, Brinda Mehta, and others, is the *jahaji bhai* or *jahaji bahin*, "ship brother" or "ship sister," the familial, fraternal shipboard relationship of indentured Indians, whose subjectivity is formed by the rupture from India and the geocultural loss of caste and culture caused, in nineteenth-century Hinduism, by the physical act of crossing the *kala pani*, the "black water" of the ocean. Mourning, recuperation, and a preoccupation with the intersections of the remnants of "lost" ancestral cultures with European imperialist legacies are central to Caribbean postcoloniality. I adhere to Gayatri Spivak's vision of subaltern studies in which "a nostalgia for lost origins can be detrimental to the exploration of social realities within the critique of impe-rialism."[26] This is not a project of nostalgia or traumatic loss.

I take the foundational position that *the Caribbean Muslim exists, and is both Caribbean and Muslim.* This is a necessary statement in light of the gross general-ization of the touristic "Caribbean" ethos as one involving sun, sand, sex, reggae, revelry, and rum—the opposite of the generalization of the straitlaced, pious Mus-lim. The assertion that a Caribbean Muslim subjectivity exists is also a response to the deep identitarian and existential insecurity, and internalized racial and cul-tural self-hatred, of some postcolonial Caribbean literature, writers, scholarship, and national discourse. To wit, as Naipaul said in *his* 2001 Nobel Prize in Litera-ture lecture, his choices of subject are the "areas of darkness" that surrounded him as a child in Trinidad, a place where people "inquired about nothing," were "not yet capable of self-assessment," and were "perhaps not pretending, perhaps only feeling, never formulating it as an idea—that [they] had brought a kind of India with us."[27] Of Trinidad Muslims Naipaul recalls not Walcott's soaring minaret, but a ramshackle shop run by a man called Mian, of whom Naipaul knew naught else but his name, as "We knew nothing of Muslims," and "This idea of strangeness, of the thing to be kept outside, extended even to other Hindus."[28] Religion as an unpleasant "strangeness" is a recurring theme of Naipaul's. His is the project of recovery and identification of the past, and critique of the inadequate present. Wal-cott's is the future-oriented but nostalgic project of recognition of the historical expanse. My project is neither; I identify the Caribbean Muslim fullaman as both *a literary and a political subject.* While recuperative historicizing is contextually nec-essary, I am more concerned with the ongoing and shifting positionality of Caribbean Muslims—whom I take as a diverse but established presence—in con-temporary narratives of, first, Caribbean citizenship, and second, global Islam.

Caribbean fiction writers including Willi Chen, David Dabydeen, Brenda Fla-nagan, Wilson Harris, Ismith Khan, Rooplall Monar, Sheik Sadeek, Ryhaan Shah, and Jan Lowe Shinebourne; poets including Faizal Deen, Abdur-Rahman Slade Hopkinson, and Rajiv Mohabir; autobiographers including Munshi Rahman Khan, Muhammad Kabā Saghanughu, and Abū Bakr al-Siddīq; and many calyp-sonians and musicians have all contributed to a canon of Muslim Caribbean lit-erature and lyricism. Here I acknowledge, as have ethnomusicologists of the Caribbean, including Mark Brill, Peter Manuel, Tejaswini Niranjana, and Tina K. Ramnarine, that music remains an integral part of community self-identification and formation in the Caribbean, including—despite the fact that some Muslims frown on music and dance—for Caribbean Muslims. From medieval Sufis to con-temporary Indonesia and Iran, there are centuries' worth of debate from every major Muslim society, sect, and school on the permissibility of various types of music (the possible irony is that the Arab, Asian, African, and Eurasian societies that are majority Muslim have extremely rich, complex, and alive indigenous music and dance traditions, and are at the forefront of global fusion music).[29] Muslims who believe that all or some music is *harām* (prohibited) generally do so on the basis of *hadīth*, and *fiqh* juridical reasoning on the Prophet Muhammad's intent concerning the emotional and morally actionable effects of playing musical instruments and singing (instrumentation and vocalization are often treated separately). The Qur'an has nothing explicit to say about music, though some scholars argue that a Qur'anic reference to the pitfalls of idle talk and entertaining speech in the form of "distracting tales," as opposed to mindful Qur'anic recitation, is a reference to music.[30] I suggest, however, that even without reference to the musical inclinations of Sufi dervishes and mystics, Islam in practice is suffused with music. The aforementioned recitation and traditional chanting of the Qur'an, which is written in classical Arabic rhyming verse, is an internationally competitive high art form called *tajwīd* (elocution). Even the grotesque martyrdom videos of one of the greatest of contemporary Islamic music-haters and ironically professional media producers—the Islamic State—are often accompanied by a cappella *nasheeds* (devotional chants) that function as liturgical background music. In the Caribbean, the first Trinidadian recordings of "sacred Mohammedan chants," Moulood Sharif songs for the Prophet's birthday, were also the first recordings of Indo-Caribbean music, performed by vocalists S. M. Akberali and Gellum Hossein and recorded by the American Victor Talking Machine Company in Trinidad in 1914.[31] Limitations on music, as I will show, remain an unpopular idea among the majority of Muslims in the Caribbean.

THE CARIBBEAN MUSLIM FULLAMAN: FROM ENSLAVED WEST AFRICAN TO INDENTURED INDIAN

From the West African tribal name Fula/Fulani/Fulbe, "fullaman" in Anglophone British Guiana once literally meant an enslaved "Fula man"; but in contemporary common usage, it is a mildly insulting slang word for a Muslim of any race.[32] The similarly derived term "Mandingo" or "Madinga," from Mandé/Mandinka, occupies the same linguistic and social place in Trinidad: an African tribal name that now denotes any Muslim. I use the Guyanese term because, unlike "Mandingo," which has a number of non-Caribbean contemporary associations, including the African tribal group and, derogatorily, a sexualized black man, "fullaman" is a word that evolved in the Caribbean and has no contemporary associations other than "Muslim." In addition, the word without question now indicates a Muslim of any ethnic background. As such, I extend it to indicate any Muslim in the Caribbean.

I have noted that "fullaman" can be used in an insulting manner. It does not reach the extremity of an ethnic slur. I make this assertion as a person against whom the word has been deployed in the Caribbean, and who grew up around its regular usage by Muslims and non-Muslims. My project here is not to politically recuperate or rehabilitate the word for Caribbean Muslims, but rather to explore it and extend its meaning. This is a different goal than that of Gaiutra

Bahadur, David Dabydeen, Rajiv Mohabir, Rajkumari Singh, and Khal Torabully, who have in various ways sought to recover the labor-based racial slur for Indians in the Caribbean and other diasporic regions of indentureship, "coolie."[33] Indeed, many Indo-Caribbean people, particularly youths in the North American diaspora, already use "coolie" freely in speech and music without the benefit of academic discourse. To my knowledge, there are no other scholars or writers engaging with recuperation or deep exploration of the word "fullaman," which is far more obscure than "coolie," and perhaps more difficult to quantify. "Coolie" is a dysphemism and "fullaman" a cacophemism. The latter definition allows for a humorous tone to the slur; "fullaman" can be deployed in affectionate or biting jest by Muslims and non-Muslims, and when it is used as a religious insult, the sting is less than with the racist use of "coolie." In my experience, "fullaman" is indeed used jokingly, but in a spectrum of Anglophone Caribbean wit and jokery that ranges from affection to stinging criticism and dismissal. Both Muslims and non-Muslims tend to use "fullaman" when they criticize Muslims for being *too* Muslim (i.e., for being too religious or manifesting the visual, mostly sartorial signifiers of Islam in public in a way that compromises belonging in the "Western" Caribbean postcolonial nation-state). None of this is to say that the word should be easily spoken in a scholarly context without specifying its local usages and history. But it is an instructive term for Islam in the Caribbean.

The etymology of "fullaman" is complex and full of suppositions. The Fulani and the Mandinka are linguistically discrete and very large ethnic groups with many subgroups that overlap across West Africa and the Sahel. The majority of members of both groups are historically Muslim. The Fulani are divided into discrete urban and pastoral groups, with the *gidah*/Toroodbe "town Fulani" leading several West African eighteenth- and nineteenth-century *jihāds* to establish anticolonial Islamic theocracies across West Africa. The Fulani call themselves Fulbe, and were named "Fulani," the more widely used term in and outside Africa, by the Hausa.[34] It is not implausible that the Hausa would have called one of their closest neighbors in and around Nigeria the Arabic-language equivalent of "those men." The Hausa are also Muslim, and the use of Arabic as a liturgical, governmental, and commercial language across Muslim West Africa has a history spanning ten centuries. The Arabic word فلان (*fulān*), meaning "so-and-so" or "what's-his-name," occurring in the storytelling name Sayyid Fulan or "Mister X," has cognates with similar meaning in languages including Persian and Turkish, and has lent itself to the Spanish and Portuguese term *fulano*, meaning "this man" or "that guy," picturesquely used in Latin American, Spanish Caribbean, and European Spanish colloquial formulations like "Fulano, Mengano, y Zutano" (Tom, Dick, and Harry), and "fulano de tal" (John Doe). The dictionary of the Real Academia Española cites the origin term *fulān* as having even older roots in Ancient Egypt, and there are possible cognates in Aramaic and at least one use of the word in the Qur'an: the symbolic polytheist wrongdoer, regretting his actions on the

Day of Judgment, cries: "Woe is me! If only I had not taken *so and so* as a friend" (emphasis added).[35] "Fula-" is a self-reflexive term for the Other that has conservatively retained form and meaning across time and place: it denotes "that one over there," a proximal person whose name is unknown and whose affiliation may be distrusted. Though the term is present in both the Anglophone Caribbean and the Hispanophone/Lusophone Caribbean, in the former—because it was indirectly introduced by the African Muslim people called Fulani—it has come to mean "Muslim," rather than signifying an unknown person. I suggest, however, that the implicit meaning of "someone else" is still present in the application of "fullaman" to *any* Muslim in Guyana and the Caribbean.

It is impossible to determine how many African Muslims were enslaved in the Americas. As Diouf, Rudolph Ware, Ivor Wilks, and others show, from the fifteenth century onward, male and female literacy and Qur'anic literacy were highly valued in the Muslim theocracies of West Africa. Enslaved people from Timbuktu (Mali) and Futa Jallon (Guinea), for example, were likely Muslims who read and wrote in both Arabic and *'ajamī*, the generic name for West African languages, including Fulani and Hausa, that were transliterated into Arabic script.[36] Islamic schools, *madrassas*, were and are widespread in West Africa. Ware argues that Islam must be understood as "an integral and authentic part of the African historical experience," one in which the often-Sufi West African religious approach was an *embodied* practice in which knowledge and deeds, following the examples of the Prophet Muhammad's life, were considered inseparable.[37] The Jamaican singer Tijani Concious's spiritual mentor Baay Ibrahim Niasse was one of four West African scholarly founders of, says Zachary Wright, "the largest Muslim communities in West African history. Together, they command the allegiance of a majority of Muslims in the region to this day—and are at least partly responsible for the continued flourishing of Sufism in Africa when it has sometimes become marginalized elsewhere in the Muslim world."[38] The other West African Muslim community–founding scholars are Ahmadu Bamba, 'Umar Tai, and 'Uthman bin Fudi or Dan Fodio, founder of the Sokoto Empire, the largest state in nineteenth-century sub-Saharan Africa, spanning modern-day Nigeria, Niger, and Chad.[39] Dan Fodio, as I will discuss further in the first chapter of this book, was a politician who led with scholarly literary and spiritual writings. Baay Niasse wrote specifically of how in *Bilād as-Sūdān*, the historical Arabic denotation of "Lands of the Blacks," "poetry and love for the Prophet were something special by which black African Muslims had demonstrated their scholarly authority in Islam."[40] West African Islam has always been in close conversation with Middle Eastern Arab and Asian Islam, but Baay Niasse here emphasizes its particular history of literacy and embodiment of the Prophetic example.

Accordingly, African Muslims distinguished themselves partly by their literacy in the Americas. The academic study of enslaved African Muslims in the Americas often focuses on two Afro-Muslim communities and incidents: the Malê

Revolt, an 1835 African Muslim uprising during Ramadan in Bahia, Brazil, that was the largest slave rebellion in the Americas; and the legacy of enslaved West African Bilali Muhammad, his descendants, and his Gullah Muslim community on Sapelo Island, off the Georgia coast of the United States. Both sets of Muslims have what most other enslaved Africans lacked: existing documentation of their origins written in their own hands. The Malês in Brazil were numerous enough to hold informal Islamic schools to teach Arabic and the Qur'an. The U.S. Bilali Muhammad Document, or the Ben Ali Diary, is Muhammad's still-existing hand-written treatise on West African Islamic law. In the Caribbean and North America, racial typologizing of Africans combined with Muslim literacy produced in white plantation society a belief that the Fulani and Mandinka were racially superior by dint of their alleged straighter hair, "less glossy black" skin, and proposed North African/Iberian Moorish Arab admixture.[41] Gomez reports the case of British Jamaican planter Bryan Edwards, who wrote in 1794 of his slaves knowing the "Alcoran," and who considered the Muslim Fulani racially superior to other Africans, and therefore "not well adapted for hard labour."[42] Such attitudes sometimes resulted in better treatment for enslaved African Muslims on plantations. Diouf writes that Muslims "distinguished themselves among the rest of the enslaved population more frequently than their numbers alone could have warranted. There is some indication that the Muslims succeeded in the slave structure, that they were promoted and trusted in a particular way."[43] These "successes" belonged to men. The historical record of black Muslims in the Americas consists primarily of planter and administrative references to and fragments of writing by enslaved and free African Muslim men. There are almost no records of enslaved African Muslim women, and none extant in their own voices. As I will show in the first chapter, rather than religion or the strength of religious belief itself, it is literacy, and planters' racist beliefs in the inherent superiority of the "Arab" African over the sub-Saharan African, that were key to some Muslim men's modest successes in plantation societies.

Europeans conceived of enslavement as the entrée of the premodern "cannibal" Carib and "savage" African into a biopolitical modernity that construed them as labor by stripping them of the human ability to reason.[44] Fullaman African Muslims and their relationship to literacy and a literary religious practice troubled this vision of voiceless Caliban that encompassed the indigenous, all Africans, and at times in the Caribbean, Europeans considered nonwhite, like Portuguese indentured laborers. Educated African Muslims could not fit comfortably into the linear grand narrative of racialized "progress" framed by European superiority. "Fullaman," Muslim, is a state of exception that exists in what I will borrow from Trinidadian calypso and describe in the fourth chapter as "Muslim time": a construct of state emergency that may inevitably be the rule, as Walter Benjamin points out, but at the very least teaches us that "Muslim" is always a racialized, nonlinear temporal category.[45]

"Fullaman" has thus outlasted the tribal "Fulani" as an ethnoreligious identity in Guyana by almost 200 years. It survived by waiting for new Muslims to begin arriving in 1838, and attaching itself to them, as enslaved African Muslims left no Guyanese Muslim descendants. The first ships transporting Indian indentured laborers to the Caribbean, the *Whitby* and the *Hesperus,* which both reached British Guiana from Calcutta on May 5, 1838, carried 94 Muslim passengers, 3 of whom were adult women, out of a total of 424 migrants.[46] The *Whitby* also transported the first Caribbean Indian Muslim convert to Christianity: one Nertha Khan, who opportunistically converted soon after landing in Guiana to curry colonial administrative favor, as Indian Christian converts were looked upon more favorably than the majority who remained Hindu or Muslim.[47]

The bodily signifiers of Islam in the Caribbean are almost entirely sartorial, but the raiment has changed. Until the 1990s, "Muslim" garments consisted mostly of "Indian" dress: at religious and "cultural" functions, Indo-Caribbean Muslim women wore and still wear *salwar kameez,* and loosely covered their heads to distinguish themselves from sari-wearing Hindus—though older Indian women of both religions wore *ohrnis* draped around their heads for reasons of modesty. A Muslim man might wear a *kufi* (skullcap) and a long, loose *kurta* shirt. Nowadays, Muslim Caribbean dress also includes, for men, the option to wear an Arab *thobe* and cultivate what Muslims around the globe, sometimes darkly, sometimes humorously, refer to as a "Salafi beard," a long beard sans mustache that can symbolize patriarchy, political conservatism, strict adherence to the *hadīth* sayings of the Prophet that advise not trimming the beard, or just generic Muslim. For women, the new, more conservative options include modern *hijabs* (or *khimar* in Guyana, headscarves that often have a second, inner, hair-covering piece), *niqabs* (full-face veils), and *chador* cloaks. It is a relatively new phenomenon to see Muslims dressed "Arab style" in the Caribbean, and, as I will discuss in the fourth and fifth chapters, not everyone is happy with this change.

Urdu is Indo-Caribbean Muslims' traditional liturgical language, outlasting in children's religious educational *madrassa* (a place for studying) and *maktab* (a place of writing) schools its spokenness, but it has been replaced by Arabic in those schools over the course of the twentieth century.[48] I learned strictly the Arabic alphabet and religious terms at my Georgetown, Guyana Sunni Sad'r Islamic Anjuman madrassa (see fig. I.1) in the 1980s and 1990s, whereas my mother's generation learned the Urdu alphabet and a mix of Urdu and Arabic Islamic terms in Georgetown in the 1960s.[49] We girls were moved away from sitting on the same floor as boys and lost access to more highly trained male Islamic teachers in the late 1980s, when young Guyanese men educated in Egypt and the Gulf returned to their home mosques with Islamic revivalist ideas. The linguistic shift is perhaps more inevitable than the change in dress for two reasons: except in Suriname, the majority of Indo-Caribbean people have not spoken their ancestral languages for at least three or four generations, depending on when their families

FIGURE I.1 Guyana United Sad'r Islamic Anjuman Masjid and author's childhood madrassa. Kitty, Georgetown, 2018. (HAM Photo Services.)

migrated, and the revealed language and encouraged study language of the Qur'an is classical Arabic.[50]

ISLAM, CREOLIZATION, AND HYBRIDITY

The *difference* that Caribbean Islam—envisioned by most Caribbean people as a religion of indentured Indians—has traditionally posed to the Caribbean, that postcolonial space par excellence of creolization and hybridity, is one of a particularity ontologically identifiable in two ways by what it is not: first, it is not Hindu, and second, and more importantly, it is not black. Neither of these defining attributes, particularly the latter, is accurate. The *Ramleela* of Walcott's observation represents not only Hinduism but the entirety of the Indo-Caribbean. Caribbean Muslims are first represented in the historical record by the colonial British as a subset of Indian/Hindu, first as "Hindoo" without distinction, then as "Mahometan Hindoo," and sometimes as "Mussulman."[51] Alexander Rocklin argues that Hinduism did not become a collective religious construct until comparatively quantified by British colonial authorities, Christian missionaries, and Indian elites in the nineteenth century in India, and that correspondingly, "Hinduism in Trinidad was discursively produced and performatively enacted with urgency and fervor by a range of actors beginning only in the early twentieth century."[52] Islam cohered differently in different places but usually around at least an idea—if not practice—of monotheism, belief in the Prophet Muhammad's importance, and the text of the Qur'an itself; as I will show, some enslaved African Muslims certainly thought of themselves as Muslim followers of a religion called Islam, and indentured Indian Muslims, though mostly unlettered, sought to build mosques and find knowledgeable imams who knew enough Qur'an to lead them in ritual prayer from early on in their Caribbean colonial history. Even before a drive toward unification of religious practice, Hindus, it must be noted, also sought pandits and built *kutias*, small places of worship, on the plantations. As Peter van der Veer and Steven Vertovec observe, "Hindus may not need caste, but even in the case of the West Indies they seem to need Brahmans as their religious specialists"—perhaps *especially* in the case of the West Indies, as Brahmins, like plantation and village imams, provided religious legitimacy and structure in places where there was little to no state or social validation of Hinduism and Islam.[53]

The most important historical Indo-Caribbean group identifier is not religion but race and the seeming purity thereof: "Indianness" posed in opposition to both "Africanness" and mixed-race "Creoleness." As Henry argues, Caribbean creolization is coterminous with the forces of Old World African, Asian, and Arab "purisms" in an oscillating "pure/creole binary" that never reconciles or resolves.[54] In popular regional conception, national discourses of citizenship, and Indo-Caribbean academic analysis, the postcolonial group identity "Indo-Caribbean" is extrapolated through moral judgments of women's roles and behavior that are conceptualized in large part through Hinduism. As Sherry-Ann Singh has argued and I will discuss in the second chapter, all Indo-Caribbean women are subject to the Ramayanic Sita ideal of the faithful Indian wife and mother.[55] Caribbean Hindus and Muslims also often intermarry and participate in each other's familial and neighborly religious occasions, including the historic celebration of Hosay.

The vast majority of the Indo-Caribbean is indeed Hindu, adhering to both the traditional Sanatan Dharma, with the significant Caribbean difference of the historical breakdown of caste divisions, and to the reformist, anticaste, monotheistic Indian Arya Samaj movement. Strict caste strictures could not be maintained, nor were they particularly desired, on the ships of indenture or on plantations, when the Indian migrant population was relatively small and heavily derived from *ahir* (cowherd), *chamar* (leatherworker), and other laboring castes of Bihar, Uttar Pradesh, Punjab, Lahore, a few other north and northwestern Indian regions, and Madras in the south. Indentureship contracts and embarkation and disembarkation registers listed each contractee's caste and subcastes, but most migrants were illiterate. It is an old running joke in the Caribbean that many were the newly minted, self-declared Brahmins who emerged from British ships onto the shores of Guiana and Trinidad, seeking opportunity. The large number of Indian laborers brought to French Guadeloupe and Martinique are now predominantly Catholic and have diverged in culturally and demographically significant ways from their Anglophone and Néerlandophone brethren. Hinduism, in its Caribbean noncaste form, became emblematic of the large historic Indo-Caribbean populations in Trinidad, Guyana, and Suriname, and smaller communities in Jamaica, Grenada, St. Lucia, St. Vincent, and other islands. As I argue, however, the Caribbean Muslim subject is not fixed as a racial-religious Indian.

Both Afro- and Indo-Caribbean communities find themselves in the position of defining their postcolonial identities as "native" when they are not autochthonous to the Caribbean: the aforementioned problem of Caliban's elision of the indigenous. Afro- and Indo-Caribbean people must become "native" in order to prove their sovereign rights to land of which they are not the original inhabitants, in such a way as to also revoke the claim of the colonizer. Shona Jackson calls this particularly Caribbean nativization, which occurs at the expense of indigenous tribal peoples who still live in Dominica, Guyana, and other continental American locales, "creole indigeneity."[56] Munasinghe argues that in Trinidad, Creoles—a category that conflates Afro-Caribbeans with people who are racially mixed but never only Indo-Caribbean—are through a narrative of mythicizing "impurity" produced as rightful inheritors of the postcolonial island.[57]

Hybridity and creolization are sometimes used loosely and interchangeably in Caribbean literary and national discourses, but they are different ways of conceptualizing the "mixing" of peoples and cultures. José Martí in 1891 begins a discussion of Caribbean and Latin American hybridity as a counterpoint to monocultural "authenticity" in "nuestra América Mestiza."[58] Retamar in 1979 describes Caribbean and Latin American hybridity as exceptionalist, arguing that revolution and decolonization in "nuestra América Mestiza" would only be successful if the colonized identify as mestizo (racially "mixed").[59] In its Latin American guise, hybridity insufficiently describes the Anglophone Caribbean for at least two reasons: the vast majority of the latter's people do not identify as mestizo or mixed-race, and they are likely to take umbrage at the idea that they possess a history and cultural practices that do not privilege ties to Africa or India. The British strategy of colonization in the Caribbean also did not include major European settlement and racial intermixing; in the region, theirs was an overseas empire.[60] This system of colonial governance is different from that practiced in the settler colonies of Hispanophone and Lusophone Latin America, where theories of Caribbean hybridity and creolization originate. Rather than hybridity, Shalini Puri says, a multiplicity of local concepts of mixing, including "*mestizaje*, creolization, douglarization, *jibarismo* . . . keep visible the specificities and histories of each term. In contrast, the umbrella term 'hybridity' enacts a dehistoricizing conflation."[61] "Creolization" is a broader term than most of the others. In Trinidad, its usage is specific to mixed-race and Afro-Trinidadian "Creole" identity, as Munasinghe describes, but the word's earliest Latin American and Caribbean application was to colonial whites born in the Americas.[62] In the context of religion, syncretism is a type of creolization, signifying "the malleability and mutability of various beliefs and practices as they adapt to new understandings of class, race, gender, power, labor, and sexuality," and "is one of the most significant phenomena in Caribbean religious history."[63] The term "creolization" is overdetermined in the Caribbean. The fullaman of Caribbean literature, I show, is a figure who experiences the *process of creolization*, in that the Muslim in the Caribbean contends with a host of cultural traditions, political ideologies, and religious theologies, but who does not become a fully hybridized, creolized Americas "native" who is the sum of his parts. Instead, the Muslim literary fullaman experiences an ongoing, antiessentialist process of becoming in response to local and global pressures.

THE MUSLIM "RACE(S)" AND HOSAY

From medieval and Crusader depictions of the monstrous Saracen idolater, to nineteenth-century orientalist paintings of women in Ottoman harems, to contemporary media representations of turbaned terrorists, Muslims and Islam have always been racialized by Europeans and their white North American cultural inheritors. Racialized Muslims, embodied by the amorphously brown-skinned, vaguely "Middle Eastern" man and his veiled female counterpart, have become a regular feature of the global mediascape after September 11, 2001. Evelyn Alsultany, Mustafa Bayoumi, Sylvester Johnson, Erik Love, Rana, and others have written about the racialization of Muslims in the United States and abroad. As Rana says,

> Race is tied to terror and migration precisely through the conjuring of an enemy. The foe is defined in relation not only to democracy and freedom but also to the moral precepts of the ideologically motivated formation of a Christian subject that argues for just war as an obligation of secularity and imperialism. That this enemy is crafted as a religious entity, albeit a radically militant one, does not obscure the racial nature of the construction. . . . The figures of the terrorist and the migrant are woven together in the figure of "the Muslim" as a racial type; as such, they are historically, ethnologically, and contemporaneously bound to each other.[64]

As Muslims are always racialized enemies of the state, they fit neatly into Johnson's definition of race in the African American religious milieu as "a state practice of ruling people within a political order that perpetually places some within and others outside of the political community through which the constitution of the state is conceived."[65] Bayoumi writes that "Religion determines race. At least in 1942," when, in December 1942—during World War II and after the Immigration Acts of 1917 and 1924 that enforced bans and quotas on migration from Asia and other "nonwhite" regions—Yemeni Muslim immigrant Ahmed Hassan lost his petition for citizenship in Michigan District Court on the basis of his "dark brown" color.[66] The vicious conflation of religion and race and the imputed questionable social and citizenship status of Arabs and Muslims is ongoing. Ethnic Arabs and the phenotypically brown-skinned people mistaken for them, religious

Muslims, and an imagined geography of the "Middle East" that reaches into Asia, Africa, and immigrant neighborhoods in Europe and North America, constitute an enduring nexus of orientalist orientation coded generically as "Muslim." Simply put, 9/11 was hardly the first engagement of Europe or the United States with the "otherness" of the Muslim. The current moment of hysteria over the specter of the Muslim is partly a result of the fact that, in a world of around-the-clock news reporting, social media, easy intercontinental travel, and intensive technological surveillance of the public, there is, especially in the case of Muslim women who are often called upon to represent all Muslims because of their identifying hijabs, simply more coverage. Media images and surveillance of Muslims in the United States and Europe remain racialized: Louise Cainkar and Sunaina Maira write of "flying while Muslim" and the racial profiling and criminalization of Muslim travelers; Alsultany identifies film, television, and news "simplified complex representations" of Muslims that masquerade as "post-race," but in fact justify racist and exclusionist policies by conflating all Muslims and Arabs.[67] Jasbir Puar further complicates the U.S. racialization of Muslims by pointing out that post-9/11, "Muslim = Islam = Arab. Religion, in particular Islam, has now supplanted race as one side of the irreconcilable binary between queer and something else."[68] In Puar's homonationalist United States, normative queerness is incompatible with the racial Other, but also the religious Other: the very existence of queer Muslims becomes irreconcilable with both queer Western secularity and the historical vastness that is Islamic theology.

Describing Muslims in racialized terms is not a phenomenon limited to the United States and other countries with growing populations of migrant Muslims. Muslims arrived in visible numbers in the Caribbean at the same time as they did in the United States, with the transatlantic slave trade. In Trinidad and Guyana, the countries with near-even numbers of Afro- and Indo-Caribbean people, Muslims have passed through, as I will explore, at least three stages of racial-religious conflation. First, during the transatlantic slave trade, African Muslims of all tribes and cultures were deemed fullaman (Guyana) or Mandingo (Trinidad). Second, from the nineteenth century to the 1990s, the common belief in both countries was that all Muslims were Indian, and Islam was part of an Indian ethnocultural heritage; and third, contemporary national discourses suggest that while all "born" Muslims are still Indo-Caribbean, there are more Afro-Caribbean converts now, and both groups are prone to national and transnational violence.

There is one exceptional historical case of Islamic religious creolization in the Caribbean: Walcott's "festival of Husein," or Hosay. In the nineteenth century, indentured Muslim Indians in Trinidad, Guiana, Jamaica, and Suriname transformed the Shi'a subcontinental and Persian commemoration of Muharram into the festival of Hosay, Hussay, Tadjah, or Taziya (see figs. I.2 and I.3). In Mauritius, another major site of the Indian labor diaspora, the transplanted Muharram processional festival is called Yamsé.[69] According to Mohammed, "The earliest

FIGURE 1.2 Hussay East Indian Muslim festival with *tadjah* model tombs and diverse participants and spectators in colonial Westmoreland, Jamaica. (Courtesy of the National Library of Jamaica.)

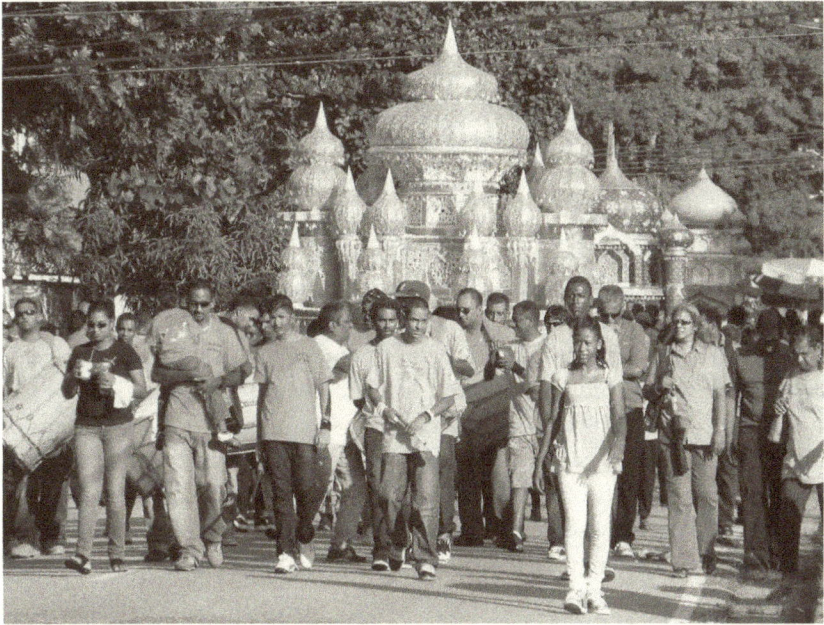

FIGURE 1.3 Hosay procession on Hayes Street, St. Clair, heading west into St. James in Port of Spain, Trinidad. From left to right: Ghulam Hussein, Balma, and Bis *tadjahs*, accompanied by *tassa* drummers and spectators. December 17, 2010. (Courtesy of Nicholas Laughlin.)

observance of Hosay in Trinidad has been traced to 1854, eleven years after the first set of indentured laborers arrived from India."[70] Hosay was—and is, in its remaining historic bastions of St. James and Cedros in Trinidad, and in revived festivities elsewhere—a multiday religious celebration featuring a public procession of large and small model tombs (tadjahs), a red model of the crescent moon and a green model of the moon representing the brothers Hussein and Hasan, respectively, flags, singing, dancing, drumming, and, in earlier days, stick-fighting (gatcar) and fire dancing (fire pass).[71] The tadjahs are carried toward a mythic, extranational "Karbala" and usually into the sea to be submerged—a gesture sometimes criticized as "Hindu," though Mohammed points out that the submergence "symboliz[es] both the violence of this moment in Islamic history and the transience of life."[72]

It was of especial concern to colonial authorities in the Caribbean that Hosay was one of the few times and spaces in which blacks and Indians, who were pitted against each other in the colonial labor economy, congregated and celebrated together.[73] In Trinidad, Hosay belonged to all Trinidadians even more than did the Ramleela. Though "an ostensibly Muslim ritual commemoration, [it] was the only 'Indian' holiday Trinidadian laborers officially had off from work, regardless of religious identification."[74] As Bridget Brereton says, Hosay "became the major Indian festival in Trinidad. It soon lost its special religious meaning as a commemorative rite . . . and became almost entirely secular. Most of the participants were Hindus, not Moslems, and Creoles participated enthusiastically until 1885."[75] Afro-Caribbean people found Hosay's street festival aspect familiar and "began to take a more respectable part in the procession as drummers for which they were paid in rum or cash," and sometimes carried the taziyas.[76] Rocklin points to the fact that even the first novel of Indo-Guiana, the anti-indenture English lawyer and politician John Edward Jenkins's 1877 colonial romance Lutchmee and Dilloo: A Study of West Indian Life, describes the Tadjah festival.[77] Jenkins, who observed Tadjah upon his visit to the colony to report upon the living conditions of the indentured, wrote that the festival often erupted in violence that caused planters to demand its prohibition, and that "Corresponding to the Mohammedan Feast of the Mohurrun, in India, it is nevertheless but a hybrid and foreign imitation of it. All the Coolies, of whatever denomination, join in celebrating it, as a sort of holiday, or rather of carnival."[78] Creolized religious culture, in this colonial moment, was a "hybrid and foreign imitation" of legitimate Old World religious practice. Jenkins was also savvy enough to describe an indentured Indian Sepoy soldier named Ramsammy—some Sepoys were forcibly relocated to the colonies after mutinying against the British East India Company in 1857—as "at best a Wahabee, wild and violent."[79] Here Jenkins demonstrates his worldly orientalist awareness of goings-on in the farthest reaches of Empire, namely the eighteenth-century development of Muhammad ibn 'Abd al-Wahhab's puritanical Islamic Wahhabism and his collusion with the political aims of Muhammad ibn Saud, progenitor of the House of Saud, that eventually led to the unification of the Kingdom of Saudi Arabia in 1932. In 1877, the Muslim in the Caribbean was already associated with religious violence stemming from the Arabian Peninsula that gave birth to Islam, and even the Hindu Sepoy Ramsammy's anticolonial rebelliousness—all rebelliousness against Christian domains—was coded as Muslim.

Jenkins associates Hosay/Tadjah with carnival revelry. In Trinidad, says Korom, the festival became "carnivalized . . . so that it takes on aspects of observances occurring during periods of carnival in the Caribbean."[80] As such, it was a way for Indians to "participate in Creole culture, but they also reassert their own Indian ethnic identity by performing a tradition that is perceived to have come to Trinidad from India in an unaltered state."[81] David Wood, though, points out the differences between Hosay and Trinidad Lenten Carnival: while "revelry and uninhibited behavior," were a feature of both, "[t]he Saturnalian aspects of Carnival, the wearing of disguise, the assumption for two days pf the status and roles of other people, the mocking of the foibles and pretensions of the powers-that-be, were absent in Hosein."[82] Afro-Trinidadians were not the first non-Muslims to ever occupy the position of Hosay drummers: in India, Hindu *Chamar* were hired to play drums during Muharram processions.[83] Hindus also participated in Hosay in Trinidad.[84] Chamars are *Dalits*, so-called untouchables who traditionally occupied a position outside of the Hindu caste system, and as such may have been more likely to accept work in a Muslim religious celebration. Many Chamars migrated to the Caribbean as indentured laborers, so the idea that non-Muslims could serve as Hosay drummers was not forgotten.

Though the Indo-Muslim origins of the rite can be observed clearly in Trinidad, as Korom shows, the ritual performance went through a lengthy process of indigenization.[85] It is Caribbean, but Aisha Khan argues that it "may appear an opposite contrast to other Caribbean 'creole' or 'syncretic' religions, not the least reasons being the centrality of public performance (at the same time that the Muslim preparatory rituals connected to its culminating procession are considered sacred and hence restricted to observant Muslims); its possessing a name (it is one ritual situated within a recognized religion, Islam); its capacity to have participants who are not necessarily practitioners; and its written documentation in colonial Caribbean history, which has been more consistent than other religious traditions whose histories are significantly, or at times entirely, based on oral historiographies."[86] Hosay is a past challenge to Henry's Caribbean creolization-purity binary: Indian Muslims saw themselves as *participating in creole practices though reenacting their own purity*. Rather than hybridity, this singularity that exists comfortably within difference is the hallmark of Caribbean Islam, making Hosay a metonym of Caribbean Islam.

The working-class Afro-Caribbean transition from Hosay partygoer to participant was even more pronounced in colonial British Guiana, where Afro-Guianese also began as festival porters and drummers, but then started up their own parallel Good Friday festival of Black Tadjah. Black Tadjah was a product of Afro-Guianese desires to "assert power and another excuse for rowdy behavior. . . . Others were attracted simply because of the spectacle and loudness of the event."[87] Simply gathering in the streets and celebrating was a challenge to colonial authority, as all Tadjah and Hosay participants undoubtedly understood. The British moved quickly to curtail the festival in the Caribbean.

Tadjah was suppressed in British Guiana with colonial Ordinance No. 16 of 1869, which stipulated that "No 'Tadjah' processions will be permitted to enter the precincts either of the city of Georgetown or of the town of New Amsterdam," and imposed a host of other restrictions on pain of imprisonment and hard labor.[88] As Georgetown was the country's capital and New Amsterdam its second-largest town—they are the places where blacks and Indians interacted most—that was the festival's first death knell in Guiana. In Trinidad, in an 1884 event that came to be known as the "Muharram Massacre," colonial police read the Riot Act to Hosay processions entering the town of San Fernando in defiance of an 1882 government ordinance, then opened fire on the defiant but unarmed crowd, killing 16 and wounding scores more.[89] These killings, not the 1882 ordinance—which was less restrictive than British Guiana's—were what signaled the decline of the festival and Afro-Trinidadian participation in Trinidad. What remained of Hosay in early twentieth-century Trinidad and Guiana after colonial restrictions and the "uncompromising hostility" directed toward the festival by Presbyterian missionaries, then fell out of favor with Sunni Muslims who looked down on the event's Shi'a origins, and the festive irreligiousness and alleged idolatry of *taziadari*, the model tomb procession.[90]

At its colonial height, Hosay was an intriguingly "flexible arena for interracial and interreligious participation," providing an early Muslim avenue for cultural exchange between black and Indian residents of the Caribbean.[91] The festival has undergone somewhat of an interethnic twentieth-century revival in Trinidad, as an adjunct celebration similar in mood to Carnival itself. Some Muslims still call Hosay "un-Islamic," while others still believe "Afro-Trinidadian participation has turned Hosay into a fete."[92] Michael Goring, an elder who has been building *tadjahs* in St. James since he was seven years old, and who was born into a Muslim family but became Anglican, bemoans that "the older heads have not taught the younger ones and the younger ones are doing it for show."[93] Contemporary perceptions of the festival vary, but as Khan describes, many non-Muslim Trinidadians do know that Hosay is a Muslim celebration, and can describe why, in general terms.[94] Muslims have lived in the Caribbean and been of the Caribbean for a long time; they have been an uncontested and visible part of the multicultural fabric of postcolonial Trinidad, Guyana, Suriname, and Jamaica.

PERFORMING THE GLOBAL CARIBBEAN MUSLIM

As political entities produced and sustained by creolized race and culture, Caribbean nation-states idealize their ability to incorporate and enfold all difference. Muslims are framed in Guyana as equal national participants, as evidenced by the fact that they, Hindus, and Christians have been allotted two public holidays each: Muslims get Youman Nabi (Mawlid an-Nabi, the birthday of the Prophet Muhammad) and Eid al-Adha; Hindus get Phagwah (Holi) and Diwali; and Christians— or really everyone, Guyana being a former British Anglican colony where people of all faiths engage in the festivities of Christian holidays—get Easter and Christmas. Schoolchildren are taught about the celebrations of each of the three major settler religions of the nation. Muslims, though, number far fewer than Hindus or Christians, and there are small numbers of adherents of other faiths, notably Obeah and Bahá'i, present. Unlike Trinidad, Guyana does not legally recognize Orisha, or any African-derived faiths; and indigenous Amerindian cosmologies rarely enter the discussion. Christianity in the Anglophone Caribbean also encompasses minority groups that are not mainstream Protestant (here the mainstream is mostly Anglicans, Lutherans, Methodists, Presbyterians, and Baptists): notably, Catholics, Jehovah's Witnesses, Seventh-day Adventists, and growing numbers of North American–missionized evangelicals.

The Caribbean capacity to encompass difference elides and flattens particularity, but the repressed returns in myriad ways. While the Muslim *presence* in the Caribbean is indisputable and acknowledged by most, Muslim *citizenship* in the Caribbean nation-state has not been equally uncontested. In the fourth chapter, I discuss the 1990 Muslimeen Islamic coup in Trinidad and court cases in Guyana in which the fitness of Muslims to be counted as citizens and the compatibility of Islam with Caribbean politics were called into question. These cases show that in the Caribbean, as elsewhere, Muslims are adjudged by their fellow citizens to be more visible and vociferous than their demographic numbers would suggest. Their religion seems to have an outsized impact on their politics, and they seem somehow more intense and extreme than other people in their ideological purity and conservatism. These traits appear incompatible with creole Caribbean citizenship, especially if one assumes the Caribbean is fundamentally a laid-back tourist destination. But the Caribbean barely conceals the festering wounds of slavery, and the majority of its inhabitants are, amidst their Carnival celebrations, religiously conservative and fairly patriarchal people: regardless of their specific faith or ethnicity, there is very little disagreement among members of the Anglophone Caribbean general public over issues that are considered simultaneously moral, social, and legislative—like homosexuality, marriage, abortion, and gender roles.[95] Sexual acts between men, for one, remain illegal under inherited colonial "buggery" statutes in most of the former British Caribbean colonies, with the notable exceptions of the Bahamas (1991) and Trinidad (2018). Muslims, on the whole, are no more or less tolerant or engaged with social issues than other Caribbean people.

There are reasons why Muslims are perceived as "different" wherever they live in majority non-Muslim countries. It is not because they are natural extremists or even a different species of human being, as some Islamophobes suggest.[96] First, some Muslims are more visible because of their religious dress, especially when in the present day they pattern their clothing after traditional Saudi and Arabian Gulf garments. Second, the Islamic combination of holy book (Qur'an); the Prophet's and his *sahābah* companions' words and deeds by which one is to live one's life (*hadīth*); the *sunnah* traditional practices of the early Islamic community; multiple bodies of canonical legal opinions (*shari'a*) derived from centuries of *fiqh* jurisprudence; and varied regional traditions, together produce a recognizable common religious framework that nonetheless has no single authority, voice, or leader—there is, so to speak, no pope, or more accurately, no agreed-upon caliph. Frustratingly for some, no one source can with any legitimacy "speak for the Muslims" to explain, apologize, or temporize when world events involve Muslims. Third, the hajj pilgrimage to Mecca and other transnational engagement with the global ummah, the Muslim worldwide community, produces in 1.8 billion Muslims the sense of being part of a prescribed and named community even while they are extremely different in culture and religious practice. "Ummah" occurs sixty-two times in the Qur'an "in the sense of religious community, as well as instances where it means 'fixed term' . . . and communities of animals like unto human groups."[97] There is also "a chronological development of the meaning of *umma* from generic application to religious communities to a more focused reference to the emerging Muslim community," and "throughout Islamic history the *umma* has usually been thought to possess final authority (under God) with respect to overseeing the leadership of the Muslims. The consensus has favored a unified *umma* as an ideal that transcends a particular period's limitations and divisions. Colonialism's challenge instigated a great renewal of *umma* awareness among Muslims."[98] In the ideal ummah, language, culture, ethnicity, and even ideological and sectarian markers of difference would be irrelevant. Calling oneself a Muslim who believes in the Islamic *Shahādah* creed (for Sunnis, "There is no God but God. Muhammad is the [final] messenger of God") is the only technical requirement for ummah community entry. But one implication of the ummah overseeing its own leadership is that it can be invoked as a disciplining and regulatory body, a problem when some strains and cultures of Islam, from Sunnis to Saudis, occupy hegemonic positions.

The Caribbean is included in the reach of contemporary global Islam, which I define as the manifestations of the ummah in postmodernity that include the following:

- Mass voluntary and involuntary migrations and diasporas
- 24/7 Internet, social media, and other peer-to-peer digital connectivity
- "Tradition" and "modernity" framed as oppositional forces, with, as Khan points out, tradition representing "abiding customs that carry the force of unspoken law," and, as I will discuss, the heavily weighted Islamic principle of *bid'a* (innovation) determining which forms of modernity are allowable and which are not[99]
- A conflation of ethnicity with religion that reinscribes Edward Said's orientalist construct of "[brown] Islam versus the [white] West" by transforming "Muslim" into a racial category[100]
- What Jamaican-British theorist of cultural studies Stuart Hall calls "global mass culture," particularized for Muslims as the combination of English-privileging news-dissemination technologies and visually Islamized homogenization of cultural representation[101]
- The paradoxical concentration of capital in social, economic, and political forms that signify, again following Hall, a reactionary "return to the local" as a response to globalization[102]
- A global linking of Islam with contemporary political iterations of terrorism, fundamentalism, radicalism, extremism, and other -isms that are often used interchangeably and confusingly to denote religious conservatism and revivalism linked to the potential for the use of violence to achieve an ideological goal that is often viewed as anti-imperialist

Islam, like all diaspora religions spread beyond their origins, is a faith that is simultaneously local and global. In Trinidad, N. Fadeke Castor has similarly framed diasporic Ifá/Orisha religion as linked to global black internationalism in "transnational spiritual networks" that produce a multilayered, scalar "spiritual citizenship."[103] This is different from Caribbean Muslim belonging in a preexisting, theological ummah. But the models of Caribbean diasporic religion are teleologically related, as in both Caribbean Ifá/Orisha and Caribbean Islam, "National citizenship does not preclude or compete with spiritual citizenship; rather, it is one facet within the entanglement of belonging."[104] All Muslims orient themselves directly or indirectly toward Mecca. This global engagement poses a distinct difficulty for local citizenship formulations in non-Muslim-majority countries—though *not usually for Muslims themselves*, the majority of whom find their national and spiritual citizenships relatively compatible. It is mostly non-Muslim fellow citizens who question the state loyalty of Muslims. The real local-global difference ascribed to Islam, in the present moment, is the figuring of Muslims as a singular global group linked to antistate violence.

Muslims from the Anglophone Caribbean and Suriname occupy a unique local space within global Islam. They have become, Khan says, "*of* the West and not simply *in* the West" (emphasis in original).[105] They are not "Westernized" Muslims or contemporary immigrant Muslims to the Americas or Europe. They are native, hemispheric American Muslims who nonetheless have a connection to the rest of the global ummah, with its geographic center in the Arab world, and retain yet other links to ancestral India or Africa. Caribbean countries' reach is not politically confined to the Americas. During the reign of the socialist Linden Forbes Sampson Burnham in Guyana from the 1960s to the 1980s, for example, Guyana, though geographically far away from Africa and India, established close diplomatic ties with the global Non-Aligned Movement of countries that viewed themselves as outside of Cold War divisions and European and North American concerns— and this, as I will discuss in the final chapter, is how Arab (Libyan) Muslim missionaries and proselytization first came to Guyana. Partly as a result of its own demographics, Burnham's Guyana viewed itself as an especially close ally of Jawaharlal Nehru in India and Kwame Nkrumah in Ghana. Caribbean Muslims are people with multiple origins and cultural points of reference (i.e., they are typical Caribbean people).

The Caribbean Muslim fullaman is usually depicted in Caribbean literature as a "cultural" Muslim who as a result of enslavement or indentureship knows very little about doctrinal Islam. The postcolonial question for the literary fullaman is inevitably whether, in a bid to avoid the fate of the "mimic man" imitator of colonial culture, he or she will choose creolized Caribbean culture or the religious Islamic "purity" that is associated either with the Arab world or with the same ancestral African and Indian origins creolization ironically invokes. This book reads the Afro- and Indo-Muslim Caribbean together to suggest that it is not necessary, in the Caribbean, to choose an origin or a future in any more than a temporarily strategically essential way. It is more necessary to acknowledge, know, and live with difference without fear.

Islam, Robert Young says, "was not a major preoccupation of postcolonial studies as a whole in its first twenty or so years of existence" (with the exception of Said's work), as the field of postcolonial studies was "[d]eveloped out of the secular tradition of Marxism, in which religion was deemed to merit little serious attention."[106] As such, "While an intense interest in postcolonial theory has developed in Islamic countries, in 2001 Islam was just as unreadable for most postcolonial theorists in the West as for everyone else."[107] This gap in the postcolonial theorization of Islam has been recently filled by the work of Sadia Abbas, Hadi Enayat, John Erickson, Anouar Majid, Esra Mirze Santesso, Salman Sayyid, and Jamie Scott, among others. Anticolonial liberation projects in the Muslim world have always engaged with Islam: witness the religiously oriented 1979 Iranian Revolution against a U.S.-backed monarchy, and Frantz Fanon's chronicling of the Algerian Muslim liberation war from France in *A Dying Colonialism* (1959) and *The Wretched of the Earth* (1961). Abbas asserts that, "according to the religious turn initiated by [Talal] Asad, literature has taken over the functions once performed by religion and, at the same time, has targeted religion for criticism, indeed, for insult and parody. Even as literature continues to perform this category-confusing, attack-and-mirror maneuver, it is misunderstood as stably secular."[108] The Caribbean fiction, poetry, and music I discuss here are colonial or postcolonial, and decidedly not secular. Majid points out that "the term *secularism* cannot avoid its unmistakable cultural origins" in late eighteenth- and early nineteenth-century Enlightenment Europe as "a classical liberal philosophy whose goal was nothing less than the recalibration and redefinition of human morality to adjust it to a new social calculus that excluded traditional religious commitments (irrational as these might have been)."[109]

There is no reason why the literary and cultural production of the postcolonial Anglophone Caribbean need aspire to European secularism, which naturalizes "Christian" values as secular. Though adherence varies wildly, Caribbean people are steeped in Anglicanism, Lutheranism, Presbyterianism, Evangelism, Hinduism, Islam, Rastafarianism, and a host of syncretic Afro-Caribbean religions deriving from Catholicism and Yoruba, Kongo, and other sub-Saharan African religions. M. Jacqui Alexander, Brathwaite, Harris, Lorde, and other theorists and writers have long insisted on the importance of the sacred and the spiritual in Caribbean postcoloniality, with particular reference to the African diaspora. Alexander advocates for "pedagogies of the sacred" in which "the designation of the personal as spiritual need not be taken to mean that the social has been evacuated for a domain that is ineluctably private"; the benefits are that we "take the lives of primarily working-class women and men seriously, and it would move us away from theorizing primarily from the point of marginalization."[110] Walter Mignolo similarly acknowledges that in the project of decoloniality, "Secularization is not by itself a safe place . . . secular modernity has its own politics, which do not necessarily coincide with the needs, visions, and desires of everyone on the planet."[111] Secularism can be arrogant and neocolonial in its sometimes fearful dismissal of the way people in the postcolonies live their spiritual lives, and disingenuous in its blindness to its own Europeanness and Christianity. Saidiya Hartman says that "history is how the secular world attends to the dead."[112] Caribbean diasporic and indigenous peoples require a full historical and spiritual accounting of their dead and their living.

The interplay between religious knowledge, religious custom, national belonging, and global belonging is ever shifting, and performed differently by the same individuals at different times, in different social contexts. The fullaman is always becoming, nonstatic, cyclical, and resistant to permanent hybridization in the manner of the dominant temporal and spatial metaphors of Caribbean *nature-culture*: Brathwaite's tidalectics, which rejects Hegelian dialectical synthesis in favor of "the movement of the water backwards and forwards as a kind of cyclic . . . motion, rather than linear"; Édouard Glissant's submerged "submarine roots," which "float . . . free, not fixed in one position in some primordial spot, but extending in all directions in our world through its network of branches"; Harris's "limbo gateway" of the Middle Passage; and Marina Carter and Torabully's diasporic "coolitude" of labor diasporas.[113] There is drift and recall, ebb and flow, in the often-maritime metaphors of Caribbean identities, including Muslim Caribbean identities; I emphasize here that Muslims in the Caribbean are *not* different from other Caribbean people in their negotiations with culture and place.

The ongoing becomings of models of Caribbean identity emphasize that it is important to avoid formulating the Caribbean Muslim fullaman as either a rigid ideological fanatic for whom Islam always takes precedence over national and regional belonging, or a secular, "cultural Muslim" marked by loss. Khan says that Hosay processions in Trinidad are watched by "non-Muslim on-lookers as well as nonobservant Muslims, locally termed 'Muslims in name only.' These groups tend to stand along the sidelines and watch the *tadjahs*, drummers, and flag bearers march by, theirs being a secular orientation that might be associated with a parade. Some among them may consume alcohol or dance to the rhythms of the drums."[114] Religious parade-watcher—spectator—is not a nonparticipating role. And does the empty signifier of "Muslim in name only" exist as real, when parade-goers recognize unspoken markers of community in the nonobservant? There are many reasons why an individual might prefer to watch, rather than participate in, a parade—religious or otherwise. Religiosity is a matter of actions performed in public, actions performed in private, and personal belief, and the latter is particularly important in religions—including Islam—that encourage personal relationships with the divine. People's degrees of religious observance and their opinions of religions that they are born or convert into fluctuate, especially when their families, and perhaps partners, remain observant. There are many daily sites of Muslim negotiation, extending far beyond larger sectarian belonging. Does one fast for Ramadan every year, and if so, how much? Does a woman don the hijab, and if so, to what degree and in which settings? Does that woman go to a mosque or pray at home? Does the mosque have a parallel prayer space for women where they can see the imam, or does the mosque house them in, as is often the case, a basement or second floor? Does one engage in a civil marriage alongside the Islamic *nikkah* ceremony? Does the groom pay a *mahr* (bride price), and if so, is it symbolic or material wealth? Does the community follow the doctrine that Muslim men can marry all female "People of the Book," ('*Ahl-al-Kitāb*—Jews, Christians, Sabians) without conversion? At what ages and how are children indoctrinated into particular beliefs and practices? Does one drink alcohol? Listen to instrumental music, or only vocal singing? Pray the required five times a day? Pray the optional daily prayers? Go on the *umrah*, the optional, non-hajj pilgrimage to Mecca? The resolution of these quotidian questions depends on personal, familial, and cultural preferences, as well as sometimes contradictory juridical opinions and theological doctrines. In the Caribbean, "Muslims in name only"—a term that may be used in jest, in coreligionist affection, or in derision by those who believe their own religious performance denotes greater observance, though it is less derisive than "fullaman"—are likely to have at least been married by an imam, and to have gone to mosques with their extended families to mark the major holidays of Eid al-Adha and Eid al-Fitr, whether they pray, observe, participate, or occupy any combination of subject positions. Religiosity is not linear. It is discursive, partially submerged, tidal, and held in limbo, and the performance of it changes.

That Walcott focuses on the minority Indian cultural inheritance of the Caribbean, rather than the majority Afro-Caribbean history, culture, and postcolonial identity formation that is the backbone of his literary work, is an inclusive gesture—though there is a hint of Indians being unable to creolize. I suggest that Walcott may offer a third choice appropriate to fullaman religiosity that is neither the (re)constitution of cultural purity that never existed, nor a turn to the dominant tropes of Caribbean creolization and hybridity that tend to fix identities and cultures. Instead, the *Ramleela* performance as a fully realized product of both India and the Caribbean implies a model of Caribbean culture in which coterminous radical differences are bisected by what Glissant names "transversality."[115] A transversal line crosses at least two other lines on the same plane and can be used in geometry to determine whether those lines are parallel. Islam is the transversal; the points of crossing are the moments that can be identified as nodal African and Indian fullaman roots, before the fullaman flows off again on any line.

Walcott's early observation of the *Ramleela* set as it was being assembled is a desultory "Deities were entering the field. . . . Costumed actors were arriving. Princes and gods, I suppose." When he comes to understand the particularity and historical significance of the play, he wryly observes of his initial reaction that "'Gods, I suppose' is the shrug that embodies our African and Asian diasporas."[116] The gods of the world—indigenous American, African, Asian, European, Middle Eastern—rode their human horses, *chwal* (cheval), in the godly possession process of Haitian vodou, across land and sea routes to the Americas. As Sylvia Wynter says, the Caribbean postmodern, postslavery project of "the re-writing of knowledge . . . must necessarily entail the un/writing of our present normative defining of the secular mode of the Subject."[117] As previously argued, the Caribbean subject, regardless of ancestral origin, is never a secular one. The Americas contain almost too many gods in various states of remembrance and metamorphosis; yet more deities at first merit a shrug—until, as Walcott comes to understand, what seems to be "theatre" is in actuality "faith," and what seems to be the "visual echo of History" is "a delight of conviction, not loss."[118] "Faith" in Caribbean diasporic communities with their histories of slavery and indentureship means religious faith, faith in community persistence, faith in personal existence, faith in being without fear of becoming. To have faith—the struggle of the fullaman— is to attempt to reconcile one's simultaneous existence as a Muslim, a person of African, Indian, both, or other descent, a citizen of a particular country or countries, a regional Caribbean person, and a participant in the global Islamic ummah. The fullaman, as I show, therefore exists in many iterations and in different proportions of local and global resonance, all of which resist the figure of the essentialized Muslim.

SUMMARY OF CHAPTERS

This book is arranged in roughly chronological order, as specified earlier. Each chapter, excepting the fourth, begins with Muslim Caribbean historiographic contextualization of the literary diptych that follows.

The first chapter, "Black Literary Islam: Enslaved Learned Men in Jamaica and the Hidden Sufi Aesthetic," first examines the nineteenth-century autobiographical and religious texts of the original fullamen of the Muslim Caribbean: two West African Muslim men enslaved in Jamaica in the early 1800s, Abū Bakr al-Siddīq of Timbuktu and Muhammad Kabā Saghanughu. What these men had in common other than their material circumstances was that they were literate and educated in the Qur'an (they also corresponded with each other). Together they give voice to the peculiar lament of the educated religious person who has become a bonded laborer: fallen very far, a long way from home, and having not much in common with either whites or other enslaved Africans. I argue that by virtue of their Islamic education, they nonetheless managed to secure better lives for themselves, and that recitation and invocation of the Qur'an provided solace and a way to remember their identities and even attempt to propagate their Islamic beliefs in religious and seemingly nonreligious forms. Both men came from West African Sufi families and traditions. I link them to the Sufi postcolonial Guyanese poetry of Abdur-Rahman Slade Hopkinson, whom I call the poet laureate of the Muslim Caribbean, and whose thematically "Muslim poems" I examine in the second half of the chapter. I argue that Afro-Caribbean literary Islam is suffused with a Sufi aesthetic that bridges the time and place of the enslaved men and Hopkinson's Guyanese twentieth century.

The second chapter, "Silence and Suicide: Indo-Caribbean Fullawomen in Post-Plantation Modernity," examines two Guyanese writers' works that are set primarily in the interwar period and mid-twentieth century, when former indentured Indian laborers, their children, and grandchildren began to leave the sugar estates and grapple with changing religious, racial, gender, and class norms. I read Ryhaan Shah's novel *A Silent Place* (2005) and several of Rooplall Monar's short stories written in the 1980s and 1990s to show that, much as the Indo-Caribbean defines itself in opposition to the Afro-Caribbean through the former's positing of Indian women as properly submissive to patriarchal values, so too do Indo-Caribbean Muslims position themselves as the proper Other of the Hindu majority through insistence on the properly Islamic "moral" behavior of Muslim fullawomen. I document the 1995 first Friday *khutbah* sermon given by a Muslim woman in a mosque in the Caribbean (Trinidad), and illustrate the Indo-

Caribbean *jahaji bahin* "ship sister" narrative that rejects the erasure of indentured women's histories on the moral margins of Indian society and their replacement with sanitized domestic narratives of gendered normativity.

The third chapter, "The Marvelous Muslim: Limbo, Logophagy, and Islamic Indigeneity in El Dorado," considers the relevance of the Cuban writer Alejo Carpentier's persistent literary genre of the Caribbean marvelous real, with its concerns over the integration of the postcolonial-to-be into the natural environment, to the fullaman and Muslim Caribbean. I read two Guyanese texts, David Dabydeen's novel *Molly and the Muslim Stick* (2008) and Wilson Harris' novella *The Far Journey of Oudin* (1961), which are set primarily during and after World War II in the preindependence colonial period—though *Molly* continues on into the present—as texts that integrate Islam and Muslims into the complex landscape of the Caribbean marvelous real through the temporally nonlinear, mimetic functions of limbo and doubling, and also through curiously similar incidents of what I call "logophagy," the literal eating of words. I argue that both texts interpellate the Muslim into the Caribbean through negotiation with Amerindian indigeneity and environmental space, showing that Islam—unlike, traditionally, the Indo-Caribbean—does not require mediation through the Afro-Caribbean in order to be naturalized as Caribbean.

In the fourth chapter, "'Muslim Time': The Muslimeen Coup and Calypso in the Trinidad Imaginary," I argue that as a result of a 1990 attempted coup d'état in Trinidad by the primarily Afro-Trinidadian Muslim group the Jamaat al Muslimeen and its leader Yasin Abu Bakr, whom I interview, Trinidad's postcolonial engagement with contemporary Americas discourse on terrorism and the Muslim Other is filtered through coup-influenced nationalism, rather than solely through the lens of historical Indo-Trinidadian Islam. I examine the historical fiction novel *Allah in the Islands* (2009) by Trinidadian writer Brenda Flanagan—the younger sister of Abu Bakr—alongside 1991 postcoup Carnival calypso music on Islam and the insurrection, to show how Afro- and Indo-Trinidadian racial tensions are troubled by the advent of contemporary "new" fullaman Afro-Caribbean conversion to Islam, a religion that is usually associated with and believed "owned" by the Muslim Indo-Caribbean.

The fifth and final chapter, "Mimic Muslim and Ethnorientalist: Global Caribbean Islam and the Specter of Terror," brings the fullaman fully into the contemporary moment of the figure of the global "Muslim terrorist." I explore the application of V. S. Naipaul's figure of the "mimic man," with his aping of the colonizer in service of the postcolonial nation-state, to the globalized Muslim Caribbean. I argue that in the Guyanese writer Jan Lowe Shinebourne's novel *Chinese Women* (2010), the Indo-Guyanese fullaman protagonist attempts and to some extent fails to resist Caribbean cultural mimicry with Islamic particularity when his metropolitan referent shifts post-9/11 from the British colonizer to the idealized Arab Salafist, and he begins to imagine himself as not merely dressing and thinking "Arab," but as possessing the imagined typical racial characteristics of Middle Eastern people. Postcolonial Caribbean creolization discourse, I conclude, is generally troubled by the Muslim in its midst because the local fullaman Muslim forces engagement with contemporary global concerns and exposes the limitations of hybridity and diaspora.

In the conclusion, I summarize the major interventions of the book and suggest further related fields of Caribbean and Latin American Muslim regional inquiry, in addition to further exploring the humor and pathos of the stereotyped figure of the Muslim in contemporary literature, music, and politics.

1 · BLACK LITERARY ISLAM
Enslaved Learned Men in Jamaica and the Hidden Sufi Aesthetic

Imagine, said Magistrate R. R. Madden in 1837 Jamaica, the "stealing away of a person . . . as much a nobleman in his own country as any titled chief is in ours . . . for example, educated at Oxford. . . . Fancy the poor youth marched in the common slave coffle to the first market-place on the coast. He is exposed for sale: nobody inquires whether he is a patrician or a plebeian: nobody cares whether he is ignorant or enlightened."[1] Madden was an Irishman sent to Jamaica to enforce the 1833 Slavery Abolition Act that set the stage for Emancipation Day on August 1, 1834, and the later near-slavery "apprenticeship" scheme that did not end until 1838. He was an abolitionist who believed slavery was "the misfortune of Jamaica, the crime of the mother-country."[2] But Madden's imagination, like those of some white Europeans and North and South Americans in the eighteenth and nineteenth centuries, was captured not by the degraded human circumstances of the average enslaved, illiterate black "plebeian," but by the written narratives and "Moorish" physiognomies and dress of a type of person to whom whites could relate: the literate, enslaved African Muslim in the Caribbean, Brazil, and the United States, the originary fullaman.

This chapter traces a genealogy of Muslim writing and poetics in the Anglophone Afro-Caribbean, from the autobiographical and religious writings of Muhammad Kabā Saghanughu and Abū Bakr al-Siddīq—both Islamically educated West African Muslims enslaved in early nineteenth-century Jamaica—to, after a gap of a century and a half, the poetry of Afro-Guyanese Muslim Muhammad Abdur-Rahman Slade Hopkinson (1934–1993), in his collection *Snowscape with Signature* (1993).[3] Paul Lovejoy and translator Yacine Daddi Addoun dub Kabā's unnamed ca. 1820 Arabic autobiographical and theological treatise the *Kitāb al-salāt* (The Book on Praying), as the work shows the influence of the traditionalist Qādiriyya and pacifist Sūwarī brotherhood's Islamic Sufi teachings.[4]

The earliest version of Abū Bakr's autobiography and the one he translated from the Arabic is a fragment within Madden's *A Twelvemonth's Residence in the West Indies, During the Transition from Slavery to Apprenticeship* (1835), and notes Abū Bakr's Islamic training. Hopkinson's poems in *Snowscape with Signature* invoke medieval Sufi mystics and the late eighteenth-century Moroccan teacher Shaykh Mawlāy al-ʿArabī ad-Darqāwī, who gave his name to the ascetic Darqāwā branch of the Shādhilīyyah brotherhood.[5]

The story of Black Muslim Caribbean poetics and religious and aesthetic inspiration is deeply rooted and perpetuated in the literary traditions of Sufism, the so-called mystical strain of Islam, and Sufi *tarīqa* (order) brotherhoods in West Africa. I show that in its defining aesthetic and religious engagement with tensions between the spiritual and the material, the sacred and the profane, and superficial and hidden truths, a Sufi sensibility pervades the texts and worldview of this chapter's African and Afro-Caribbean Muslim writers, whether they openly identified themselves as Sufi or not. My underlying argument is that in the Islamic Afro-Caribbean literature discussed here, Sufi-influenced emphases on the idea of hidden truth (*bātin*) and literary practices that encourage union (*tawhīd*) with the love and oneness of the Beloved/Allah provide ways of articulating and surviving enslavement and its legacy, the omnipresent Caribbean agony of traumatic loss of freedom, bodily autonomy, and cultural and religious knowledge. In addition, the common Sufi emphasis on brotherhood and the teaching of Islam and the Sufi path of enlightenment to one's followers and countrymen is present in most of the works discussed here (Hopkinson's poetry appears more ascetic and individualist, but he too has a pedagogical Islamic project). I will not delve into the lengthy religious history of global Sufism, but rather into the way the works and writers discussed show the influence of both classical Arab and Persian Sufi literature and later political-religious African Sufism.

The distinction of being the first Muslims in the Americas does not fall to those Africans forcibly relocated by the transatlantic slave trade. As noted in the introduction, the first likely Muslims whose New World presence can be substantiated were *Moriscos*, enslaved Iberian and North African Moors on Spanish missions of exploration and conquest to the Americas. The most famous of these was the enslaved Moroccan adventurer Estevanico, a survivor of the 1527–1536 Narváez expedition, whose story was recorded in Álvar Núñez Cabeza de Vaca's 1542 account of the expedition.[6] Hisham Aidi also notes the colonial literary transmission of the legendary Iberian *a moura encantada* (the enchanted Mooress) from sixteenth-century Iberian folktales to Cuban poetry and Brazilian fiction, and, far less poetically, King Ferdinand's 1512 order to send *Moriscas* as prostitutes to the Americas to prevent sexual relationships between Spanish colonists and indigenous women.[7] Migration of *Moriscos* to the New World was otherwise restricted.[8] Like the later wave of enslaved Africans in the Americas, none of the *Moriscos* left Muslim descendants.

In the era of the transatlantic slave trade, Sylviane Diouf suggests that though followers of Islam were a religious minority, there may have been "hundreds of thousands of Muslims in the Americas."[9] In estimating the numbers of Muslims brought to the United States, historians including Michael Gomez and Edward Curtis find "tens of thousands" (or 10 percent) more persuasive.[10] As difficult as it is to estimate the numbers of Africans who embarked upon slave ships and did or did not survive the Middle Passage, it is impossible to know how many enslaved Africans might have been Muslim, even with some knowledge of how many slave ships departed Muslim-majority areas. What we do know is that, though a continental minority, there were many Muslims of many ethnicities and tribal affiliations in West Africa, particularly in the Senegambian and Guinean slave-trading regions. Nehemia Levtzion shows that Islam first entered Africa with traders, through an eastern Indian Ocean coastal route that dates from 780 C.E., and a northern Sahara Arab route that began much earlier but reached a critical mercantile mark in the tenth century.[11] Clerics came after merchants. Literary Islam reached a height in the fifteenth and sixteenth centuries, with 150–180 predominantly Sunni Mālikī Qur'anic schools in Timbuktu and international engagement with Sunni Shāfi'ī Egyptian scholars and the Mecca Arabian hajj.[12] Maghrebian Sufism arrived in Timbuktu in the fifteenth century.[13] Rudolph Ware emphasizes that Islam is as historically African as it is Arab or Asian, and that Senegambians' approach to Islamic education emphasizes bodily disciplinary practices and memorization of the Qur'an, thereby possessing and embodying the Word of God and the Prophetic example "as a kind of inalienable spiritual good."[14]

For Kabā and Abū Bakr, Islam and Sufi tarīqas constituted the large part of the religious landscapes into which they were born. Through the actions of charismatic leaders and marabout holy men and scholars, Sufi brotherhoods grew in the Maghreb from the seventeenth century onward and in West Africa throughout the eighteenth and nineteenth centuries, encouraging literacy and Islamic learning as well as military jihāds against polytheism, monarchy, and corruption. The jihāds resulted in the founding of Islamic states in Nigeria and the Sahel, and the capture and enslavement in the Americas of Hausa, Yoruba, and other West African Muslims.[15] Like many other contemporary Afro-Caribbean Muslims, however, Hopkinson converted to Islam. At the beginning of their Muslim lives, the two continental Africans did not choose Islam; they were born Muslims with centuries of familial and literary relationships to Islam. But choice is involved in the incomprehensibly hard work to retain one's cultural and religious heritage under conditions of chattel slavery. As Addoun, Lovejoy, Gomez, and Magistrate Madden himself have pointed out, the writings of enslaved Muslims in Jamaica show possible feigned or partial syncretic conversion and dissimulation to hide adherence to Islam. The primary means of selecting for an audience of fellow enslaved Muslims and hiding the content of writing from missionaries and slaveholders was to write in Arabic.[16] I will return to this discussion, but first wish to properly name the Islamic survival tactic of religious dissimulation: it is *taqīyyah* (prudence), an Islamic theological and jurisprudential concept permitting hiding one's religion if there is a threat to one's life. The doctrinal and juridical guidelines for *taqīyyah* are loose, and, other than bigotry and misunderstanding, that is one reason why the concept has received traction in contemporary anti-immigrant U.S. circles as proof of Muslim migrants constituting a fifth column. Historically, *taqīyyah* is a tactic most commonly known for its use by minority Shi'a under threat by Sunni majorities, and by Muslims during the Reconquista of the Iberian Peninsula, but I suggest it is also appropriate to enslaved Africans hiding their Islam in the New World.

Kabā and Abū Bakr, the first fullamen, were engaged in a project of preservation and to a lesser extent propagation of West African Islam, including its Sufi leanings, in the Caribbean. Hopkinson finds in Islam and Sufi poetry spiritual and artistic inspiration. Their works add Muslim answers to Afro-Caribbean questions of lost ancestral histories that are often imagined through the syncretic Afro-Caribbean and African American religious and spiritual practices evolving from Yoruba, Fon, Ewe, Akan, Kongo, Bantu, and other polytheistic African religions—most featuring ancestor veneration—and sometimes their interaction with Christianity and particularly Catholicism. The African diaspora religions include Santería (Regla de Ocha or Ifá, Lucumí), Candomblé, Umbanda, vodou, Obeah, Myal, Hoodoo, Conjure, and others (Rastafarianism has a different and more recent anticolonial Jamaican history).[17] These religions have become postcolonial metonyms for Afro-Caribbean identity, in service of an articulation of modernity that places the slave trade as the beginning of history for the African diaspora in the Americas. Colin Dayan, citing African Islam, critiques the way in which, in Paul Gilroy's seminal work on the Middle Passage that articulates the tropes of the Black Atlantic, Black Modernity, and the slave ship as chronotope, "the slave experience becomes an icon for modernity; and in a strangely magical way, the Middle Passage becomes a metaphor, anchored somewhere in a vanishing history."[18] That pre-Middle Passage history is not lost to the mists of time and racial brutality, and it exists for historiographic encounters: African Muslims were transnational empire builders before they unwillingly migrated to the United States, the Caribbean, and Europe, bringing their educations and skills with them.

In the Americas, African Muslims left several written texts. Ware documents that Qur'an schools in the same West African traditions that produced Kabā and Abū Bakr still exist. These facts may be construed as representing an erudite Muslim global cosmopolitanism, but Aisha Khan argues that cosmopolitanism in the Caribbean "marginalizes or elides Islam," and "both defines the Caribbean (with its emphasis on modernity and creolization) and invites an eliding of African Islam—despite Islam's being historically approached as cosmopolitan in ways not typically employed in discussions of Vodou."[19] Thus Afro-Caribbean Muslims' "Muslimness recedes into their Africanness (their race)," and Indo-Caribbeans'

"Indianness reced[es] into their Muslimness (their religion)," while simultaneously their "Muslimness is not construed as possessing cosmopolitan attributes, or those attributes make no contribution to the cosmopolitan character of the Caribbean."[20] The Afro-Caribbean Muslim is defined more by race than by religion, and Indo-Caribbean Muslims occupy a particularly exclusionary category where they are outside of the majority Hindu Indo-Caribbean *and* their Islam is not part of the creolized cosmopolitan Caribbean, even as Islam is framed as cosmopolitan else-where. I will address the distinctions between Caribbean Muslims of African and Indian descent in subsequent chapters.

This chapter does the work that Dayan and Khan imply is necessary: establish-ing Islam and the literary production of Muslims as part of the historical inheri-tance and contemporary religious and artistic practices of the Afro-Caribbean. Colonial Christianity, the syncretic polytheistic faiths, and Hinduism together make up most of the religious story of the Caribbean, but they are not all of it. In addition, elision of African Islam neglects the interaction of Muslims and non-Muslims before and during the transatlantic slave trade. I take the position that Afro-Caribbean Muslim history and identity begin before the slave ship, in Africa. Thus I begin by tracing the African origins and Caribbean history of the Jamaican Muslim manuscripts, performing brief readings of the literary and religious senti-ments of the authors. I then present a literary analysis of the Guyanese Hopkin-son's religious poetry. While other scholars as noted earlier have addressed the (relatively brief) writings of Kabā and Abū Bakr as historical and religious docu-ments, the poetry and plays of Hopkinson—a contemporary and friend of Derek Walcott's—are occasionally praised but very little analyzed. His work is not well known outside of mid-twentieth-century Guyana. I am arguing that there is a body of Afro-Caribbean Muslim literature that is just as Muslim as it is African and Afro-Caribbean, that it is suffused with a Sufi historical and aesthetic sensibil-ity, and that Abdur-Rahman Slade Hopkinson is no less than its poet laureate.

'ULAMĀ IN SERVITUDE: KABĀ, ABŪ BAKR, AND HIDDEN *BĀTIN* IN JAMAICA

'Ulamā (singular *'ālim*) means in Arabic "learned men," a general term for male scholars trained in the Qur'an and Islamic law, traditionally under respected elder scholars and now usually at *madrassa* religious schools. Along with their lineages and schooling, Kabā's and Abū Bakr's abilities to write in Arabic and repeat Islamic principles make it reasonable to accord them that title, especially in the New World. The suffering of such erudite Africans, it seemed to Magistrate Madden and his European contemporaries in the Americas, was magnified, more compre-hensible, and worthier of sympathy than that of an illiterate person, a stereo-typical African savage. Imagine, as Madden did, that the enslaved *'ālim* could have been born into the privilege of a noble and educated at the equivalent of Oxford

in Africa! Conversely, the *'ālim* could also pose a greater threat to race-based hierarchical systems of enslavement. The difference between whether the fallen
Muslim African "patrician" was deemed sympathetic figure or threat depended
on if there were a few unique cases, as in the United States or the Caribbean, or if
there was a large, politically active community of literate Africans, as in Brazil. In
the United States, in 1826 Mississippi, Abd ar-Rahman Ibrahima (ca. 1762–1829)
became known to the public as the "Muslim Prince" when he criticized Christianity and wrote, among other documents, a letter in Arabic to his father in Futa
Jalon in present-day Guinea, pleading for help to secure his release from enslavement. That letter reached the U.S. Consulate in Morocco and slave-owning U.S.
Secretary of State Henry Clay, who advocated for Abd ar-Rahman's release and
eventual transport with his wife and some of his children to Liberia.[21]

As scholars of the historical Muslim African Americas Curtis, Diouf, Kambiz
GhaneaBassiri, Gomez, Lovejoy, and Richard Brent Turner have documented,
there were other literate Muslim Africans whose stories were known to their contemporaries in the United States. The enslaved Senegambian teacher and trained
theologian Omar ibn Said (sometimes Sayyid, 1770–1864) became the "Arabian
Prince" to the U.S. public with his "appealing Orientalist variation on the already
popular genre of the Indian captivity narrative," *The Life of Omar Ibn Said, Written by Himself* (in Arabic in 1831).[22] Ibn Said's manuscript was obtained by the U.S.
Library of Congress and digitized with supporting historical documents in early
2019, and is enjoying renewed scholarly and popular attention.[23] Mahommah
Gardo Baquaqua's (b. ca. 1830) account of his enslavement and life in the United
States, Canada, Brazil, and Haiti was published in 1854. The biography of Ayuba
Suleiman Diallo, alias Ayuba Boon Salumena Jalo, alias Job Ben Solomon
(ca. 1701–ca. 1773), Fulbe son of an imam from Bundu, Senegal, was published in
1734 by Maryland judge Thomas Bluett. An 1819 portrait by Charles Willson Peale
of Muhammad Yaro, alias Yarrow Mamout (ca. 1736–1829), a Guinean Fulbe
who became a landowner and financier in Georgetown, Washington, D.C., hangs
in the Philadelphia Museum of Art.[24] The first nonautobiographical Muslim religious text in the United States was written by Bilali Muhammad, alias Ben Ali
(ca. 1760–1859), of Timbo, Futa Jallon, later of Sapelo Island, Georgia: his "First
Fruits of Happiness," also known as the "Ben Ali Diary," is an instructional Islamic
manual derived from the tenth-century Tunisian Mālikī *fiqh* legal text *ar-Risāla*
(the Message) by ibn Abī Zayd al-Qayrawānī.[25] The Arabic language and Islamic
prayer, dietary, clothing, festival, and other religious practices of Bilali Muhammad and Salih Bilali, leaders of the small nineteenth-century African Muslim
community of Sapelo Island and St. Simon's Island, Georgia, were memorial-
ized by their descendants, who were interviewed by the Works Progress Administration in the 1930s.[26]

In several cases, notably those of Abd ar-Rahman, ibn Said, and Suleiman
Diallo—who, like Abd ar-Rahman, wrote to his own father for help—freedom

and its necessary funding were procured as a direct result of wealthy individuals' or politicians' sympathy arising from the vision of "patrician" enslavement.[27] The U.S. white public was not particularly aroused by the potential of individual non-Christian, literate threats to slavery; the enslaved African Muslims were curiosities. Timothy Marr argues that Joel Chandler Harris's use of Bilali Muhammad's story to create his titular character Aaron in *The Story of Aaron (So Named): The Son of Ben Ali* (1896) and its prequel *Aaron in the Wildwoods* (1897), was an abandonment of "African-American storytellers Uncle Remus and African Jack in favor of an Arab slave whose cultural power was both more globally resonant and less politically threatening," thus "negotiat[ing] the ambivalence of racial identity by exoticizing its difference as a resource for social stability at the same time that he dramatized the hidden and supernatural sources of an underappreciated African power."[28] The enslaved Oriental, Eastern "Arab"—invoking the popular European and American eighteenth- and nineteenth-century translations of *One Thousand and One Nights*—and the mystic, savage "African" were familiar, globalized colonial and literary tropes that salved the consciences of white Americans by embracing racial "difference" while providing a respite from heated domestic political debates over the enslaved American Negro and abolitionism.[29] Any Muslim, even an African one enslaved in the United States, was subject to a "deterritorialized Muslim otherness," what Marr calls "islamicism—the transcultural orientalism ascribed to Islam by those uninformed by its actual ethos."[30] A single literate Aladdin or one of the Romantic poets' childlike African natives capable of writing was an exotic oddity, not a threat to the financial futures of slavers and plantation owners.

Brazilian slave society, however, understood that a critical mass of literate Africans could be a problem. The major role in the 1835 Bahia Uprising, the largest urban slave revolt in the Americas, was played by the widely literate Malê Muslim African community. Those predominantly Yoruba Nagô and Hausa Muslims went to war on the streets on January 25, 1835, a day that was both the 27th day of Ramadan and the Bonfim feast day of Nossa Senhora da Guia. They wore *tiá* (Yoruba *tira*) amulets containing Qur'anic *sūras*, and white *abadá* (Yoruba *agbada*) caftans, usually worn only at home, that colonial police came to call "war garments."[31] About seventy Africans were killed during the rebellion and five hundred executed, deported, or otherwise punished.[32] After the rebellion, writing slates and scores of documents and amulets written in Arabic were confiscated, and the wearing of *abadás* and writing in Arabic were banned by, as João José Reis writes, a society in which many whites were illiterate and found it hard to accept the existence of African Muslim literacy and Islamic practices.[33] The mass suppression of Islam and related African cultural practices meant that despite its relative size, the Malê community did not survive the era of slavery as a discrete African Muslim cultural group in Bahia. Some cultural Muslim remnants, notably the practice of giving *saraka* (alms) in the form of food or charitable offerings at celebratory events, were adopted by other people of African descent and persisted throughout the Americas.[34]

In the Anglophone Caribbean, the recovered writings of enslaved Muslims include the Jamaican manuscripts written in Arabic and a short 1817 Trinidadian compendium of "infidel peoples," admonitions, prayers, and authorship notes, written primarily in Hausa but in Arabic script.[35] The latter 'ajamī document was written, as recorded on its exterior, by "Private Philip Finlay—Grenadier Company 3d WI Regiment—(an Arabian Priest) Trinidad," and commissioned "Nov[ember] 21st 1817 for James B [Lenon]. Assist[ant] Surgeon, 3rd W[est] I[ndian] Reg[iment]."[36] In the manuscript the "Arabian Priest" *imam* author records his Muslim name as "Muhammadu A'ishatu Hausa [from] Gobir."[37] This document recalls that in addition to Yunus Muhammad Bath's nineteenth-century group near Port-of-Spain, another significant African Muslim community in Trinidad consisted of decommissioned soldiers from the 3rd West Indian and (less so) 5th West Indian regiments, men who after 1807 had been pulled off of slave ships and freed upon agreeing to fight for the British in the Napoleonic wars.[38] David Trotman and Lovejoy write that "a significant minority of the soldiers in the Regiments were Muslims," partly as many may have come from ships traveling from the Bight of Benin in the Gulf of Guinea.[39] Some discharged soldiers were given land and settled in Manzanilla, northern Trinidad, building what may be "the first documented consecrated mosque in the western hemisphere" around 1819.[40] The first known mosque built by indentured Indian Muslims in Trinidad was constructed half a century after, in 1868, in Iere Village, south Trinidad.[41]

Nikolay Dobronravin's assessment of Muhammadu A'ishatu's Trinidadian document reveals the curious fact that while its text "is undoubtedly Islamic . . . it does not include some very common words such as Allah, Qur'an, or Islam, even though the Muslims are mentioned as *jama'a* or *j[a]m[a]' [a]' l—m[u]sl[i]min[a]* ([Muslim] community) and *Musulmīna* (Muslims)."[42] "Allah" and "Islam" are similarly referred to by euphemisms, respectively including *'ā'l-rabī* (*Ar-Rabb* means Lord, Master, a denotation of Allah), and variants on *ad[d]ini* (religion) for Islam.[43] Dobronravin argues that the imam used euphemisms "maybe because the text was written for a Christian who could do harm even touching the paper with such words. The absence of any Qur'anic quotation in the manuscript may be explained by the same considerations. It cannot be the result of an attempt to conceal the religion of the scribe, as his Muslim identity was known to the addressee."[44] Providing a superficial gloss while withholding the mysteries, I suggest, comes under the auspices of *taqīyyah*. The manuscript may have been written at the behest of a curious military surgeon, but as it was written in 'ajamī, he may not have been its true audience. Perhaps Muhammadu A'ishatu was writing for himself and the memory of who he was in Gobir; perhaps, as an imam, he was writing for the Muslim African congregational community, the *Jamā'a al-Muslimīna* in Trinidad who could read and understand his words.

FIGURE 1.1 Muhammad Kabā Saghanughu's *Kitāb al-Salāt* Arabic manuscript, Jamaica, ca. 1820s. These opening pages (read right to left) begin with the *basmalah* Islamic invocation. (Courtesy of Paul Lovejoy/The Harriet Tubman Institute.)

In the same vein, thrice at the beginning of his Jamaican manuscript Muhammad Kabā Saghanughu calls upon the *Jamā'atu 'l-muslimīna wa 'l-muslimāt* (Muslim men and Muslim women of the community) to heed his words on submission, eschatology, and prayer that make up the first of two parts of his manuscript.[45] The *Kitāb al-Salāt* was written around 1820, when Kabā was in his sixties, in a Baptist Missionary Society notebook, in a "colloquial" West African Arabic dialect (see fig. 1.1).[46] The second part of the manuscript cites the books of *hadīth* of Muslim and Bukhārī, and delivers further lessons on Islamic eschatology and warnings to Muslims, after which, "[a]pparently as a symbol of legitimacy, he states that he finished the book on a Friday," the day of Muslim congregational *Jumu'ah* prayer.[47]

The Qur'an itself was present in Jamaica, but the *Kitāb* was a collection of Sufi Qādiriyya teachings.[48] As verification of his identity, Kabā writes in his manuscript that people whom he identifies as "Jews" referred to him by his Muslim name, Muhammad Kabā Saghanughu.[49] This third-person signature, in Arabic and Persian Sufi writing and poetry, is called a *takhallus*, a concept to which I will return in discussing Hopkinson's poetry. Addoun and Lovejoy provide a translation and thorough assessment of Kabā's document, the use of Arabic writing in Jamaica, and a history of Kabā's life in a number of works. Muhammad Kabā Saghanughu, alias Dick, Robert Peart, Robert Tuffit, Mahomed Caba, and "the Mahometan," a native of Bouka in northern Côte d'Ivoire, arrived in Jamaica in 1777 at the age of about 21 and died in 1845, still enslaved in Jamaica.[50] The patronymic "Kabā" suggests that he was likely a member of the Senegambian Mande

Jakhanke merchant and clerical diaspora, and the "Saghanughu were an important clerical family noted for teaching the Islamic sciences and associated with the tradition of scholarship founded by *shaykh* Sālim al-Sūwarī in the late fifteenth century."[51] Ivor Wilks and other historians of West Africa describe the Sūwarīan tradition as a learned, "pacificist and quietist" one that after the seventeenth-century decline of the Muslim-led Mali Empire embraced "an ideology of pluralism" and coexistence for Muslims living in non-Muslim lands.[52] Important principles included characterizing "kufr, unbelief, as ignorance rather than wickedness," and not advocating conversion through proselytization.[53] In the 1800s, the Sūwarīans were affiliated with, though not completely a part of, the Sufi Qādiriyya brotherhood. In an effort to remain strictly monotheist, though, they "venerated the founders of their various lineages, they did not make shrines of their tombs, nor did they perform ecstatic dhikr chanting or dancing and singing. . . . What the Suwarians did take from Sufism was batin, the occult aspect of Islam, and this indirectly brought them closer to indigenous African religion."[54] *Bātin* (the inner, the hidden) included the making of amulets containing Qur'anic and other sacred texts, numerology, and on occasion the ritual use of plants.[55] Kabā's textual Islamic references, however, "suggest a standard Islamic education as instituted by the Qādiriyya in West Africa," and he identifies his father as "Abon loo de Kadri," possibly "'Abd al-Qādiri, clearly connecting Kabā with the Qādiriyya."[56] Following Wilks, Addoun and Lovejoy note that "[i]n the western Sudan the Qādiriyya was associated both with the jihad movement and with a quietest, pacifist tradition. . . . The Kabā were associated with the quietest faction" (i.e., the Sūwarīans).[57] In sum, Kabā was born into the Sūwarī-Qādiriyya West African Sufi Islamic tradition that was relatively peaceful and oriented toward surviving in non-Muslim regions.

There is no way of knowing whether Kabā's understanding of his accommodationist natal Islamic tradition allowed him to convert to Christianity in Jamaica. He was baptized as a Moravian in 1813—*before* he wrote the *Kitāb*.[58] Kabā reported mystic prophesying dreams—Sufi *bātin*—that drove his Christian conversion; perhaps he then felt that Allah endorsed his *taqīyyah*.[59] Once known as "Dick" and always a leader on his Spice Grove coffee estate, he adopted the name of his dead master Robert Peart when he was baptized.[60] He was never freed, and he was involved and well regarded in the Moravian mission.[61] In considering Kabā's conversion to Christianity and theorizing his nonetheless continued adherence to Islam, I emphasize that the *Kitāb*, essentially a manual on practicing Islam, was written at least seven years after his Christian baptism; that Kabā was a Sūwarī-Qādiri West African Muslim from a tradition revolving around accommodation in a non-Muslim society but surviving through literary propagation; and that finally, his own words suggest that he was grieved by the material *and* religious circumstances in which he found himself. In addition to his initial exhortations to the Jamā'atu 'l-muslimīna wa 'l-muslimāt Muslim community speaking as *one of them*, the closest the Jamaican Muslim community had to an ālim, empowered by his knowledge to give the Muslim community the religious guidance that followed in the text, he concludes Part I with a wrenching sentiment: "The book is finished. The last day of writing by the hands of the *'abd* . . . is Friday. The Jews refer to the name of the one who owns the writing as Muhammad Kabā Saqanuqu. . . . I am Muhammad Kabā Saqanuqu. I do not know anything of the knowledge of *al-Bahr*. My memory . . . is corrupted. I am not finding science. I have started asking for pardon day and night. I ask for pardon for every situation."[62] The last two lines may be read as a *du'ā'*, an invocation and prayer; asking for pardon or asking for forgiveness is a common closing formulation in Islamic prayer and poetry. *'Abd* is usually translated as "slave," including in the sense of Islamic submission to Allah (it is also a racist antiblack slur in the Arabic-speaking world). Kabā implies that he is a slave within (by choice, to Allah) and without (by force, to whites in Jamaica). *Al-Bahr* also has a double meaning: it "literally means sea but refers specifically to any man of science, or one who displays a wide range of knowledge."[63] When Kabā says that he does "not know anything of the knowledge of *al-Bahr*," it is not because he never did, but because, after decades of enslavement, his "memory . . . is corrupted" and he is not "finding science." His knowledge of the Sūwarī-Qādiriyyah West African Muslim way, his birthright, has become fragmented, but he nonetheless attempts to set it on paper for posterity. Of whom is he then asking pardon "day and night"? He subsequently mentions his teachers by name; he is also perhaps asking religious pardon for his forgetting of religious knowledge and for his conversion, but this lament also carries the sense of asking God and the very universe itself for both answer and forgiveness for the hardships of his existence. Kabā is already an old man, thinking of and welcoming death. He writes to the Muslim community: "This world is a house for the one who does not have a place in paradise. This world is carrion, who asks for it is like a dog. The things of this world are insignificant; they are [the objects of] vanity; for people who have illusions. The afterworld is the place of happiness. Do not hold this world on your heads."[64] For an enslaved man, it is no surprise that the "world is carrion," filled with "insignificant" and vain things and illusions. The only escape Kabā envisions is in death, "the place of happiness." This formulation is a Muslim (and Christian) one; the endgame for the human being is not life and struggle on earth, but the reward of the afterlife paradise—in Islam *Jannah*, the garden of the righteous, filled with surprisingly material delights. In order to assure "a place in paradise" in the Muslim worldview, one must be a Muslim. Kabā does not exclude himself from reaching paradise, and continues to ask pardon so that he might reach it; he is still a Muslim in essence. His conversion to Christianity may have been *taqīyyah* or even partly true; but he has not given up on his desire to finally rest in a paradise that he explicitly describes in the text as being reachable after the Islamic eschatological process of Judgment Day and the end of the world. In no way can Kabā be judged for his conversion by any Islamic religious standard that does not allow for the horror of chattel slavery. He did far more to preserve his Islam than most could have.

Magistrate Madden recorded the names of and his theological discussions with a number of educated enslaved and free African Muslims in Jamaica, stumbling upon "a small Muslim community that had existed in Jamaica since at least the end of the 18th century and which identified itself as Mandingo."[65] Kabā corresponded with the Muslim in whom Madden took the greatest interest, helping to secure that man's freedom: Abū Bakr al-Siddīq of Timbuktu, alias Edward Donlan (Donellan). Madden recorded Kabā's and Abū Bakr's letters to each other, offering proof of both men's diffident conversions. Kabā first "writes a letter, in Arabic, to Donlan, and states . . . that the purport of the letter is to convert Donlan from Mahometanism to the Christian faith; and for this purpose the old African requests of me [Madden] to be the medium of communication between them."[66] Madden, no fool, exclaims, "But what is my surprise at finding the letter of the old man, who is so anxious to convert his countryman from the Mussulman creed, commencing in these terms, 'In the name of God, merciful and omnipotent, the blessing of God, the peace of his prophet Mahomet!' So much for the old African's renunciation of Islamism."[67] As an amateur Orientalist with an Islamic fascination, Madden correctly identified the *basmalah* that precedes each *sūra* of the Qur'an and, customarily, correspondence and other writings with Islamic religious content. He facilitated contact between the two Muslims, and Kabā wrote to Abū Bakr that he had heard of the other man in the paper, and that "This is from the hand of Mahomed Caba, unto Bekir Sadiki Scheriffe. . . . I am glad to hear you are master of yourself, it is a heartfelt joy to me, for Many told me about your character. I thank you to give me a good answer, 'Salaam aleikoum.'"[68] Of note is not just Kabā's joy that Abū Bakr was free but that he introduced himself as one Muslim does to another, with *As-salāmu 'alaykum* (peace be upon you). In addition, Kabā was careful to call Abū Bakr by "Scheriffe," his *sharīf* title, indicating that Abū Bakr was from an important Muslim family claiming Prophetic descent. Abū Bakr replied and introduced himself in 1834 to Kabā with "my name, in Arabic, is Abon Becr Sadiki, and, in Christian language, Edward Donlan, I born in Timbuctoo, and brought up in Geneh; I finished read the Coran in the country of Gounah, which place I was taken captive in war."[69] He continued at length with praise for his master and Madden, but then concluded with "Whenever you wish to send me a letter, write it in Arabic language, then I will understand it properly."[70] Countryman comprehension was one reason to write in Arabic; concealment was another. Madden and the vast majority of Europeans in Jamaica would not have understood or been able to record any correspondence in Arabic.

Abū Bakr also wrote that he "finished read the Coran," which is a very particular way of quantifying his Islamic education; a person who has completed reading or reciting the entire Qur'an has performed a celebrated milestone, the *Khatm al-Qur'ān*. This achievement speaks to the extent of Abū Bakr's Islamic education.

In order for Kabā to understand who Abū Bakr was, Abū Bakr's Muslim title and educational credentials were necessary. After obtaining his freedom, Abū Bakr asked two clergymen for copies of the Bible in Arabic, as well as "a prayer-book, the psalms, and an Arabic grammar—*also a copy of the Alcoran*" (emphasis in original).[71] Madden wryly and correctly noted, once again, that "the latter part of the request, I think, looks like the yearning of one who was not quite weaned from the recollections of his old religion."[72] Though Madden was convinced of Christian theological superiority—"I still prefer my own" religion, he said, as "mine was intended, by its founder, to apply to the whole human race"—he never attempted to proselytize his Muslim objects of fascination.[73]

Abū Bakr's main written work is an autobiographical fragment written in Arabic, of which there are two existing versions—a third was lost aboard ship. Abū Bakr gave Madden the first in Arabic and translation to record in 1834. The second was written in Arabic in England, dated August 29, 1835, and published in translation by G. C. Renouard.[74] The British Africanist Wilks writes that "[T]here is little doubt that Renouard's translation, obviously made by a competent Arabist, is preferable to that of Madden in collaboration with Abu Bakr himself."[75] However, I prefer to use the earlier version Abū Bakr translated himself, rather than that of an overcorrecting, Orientalist "competent Arabist" of the nineteenth century. Abū Bakr relays an expanded account of his noble patrilineal *sharīf* background in Timbuktu and Djenné, the story of his capture, and an account of the pillars of Islam and methods of worship practiced by his family: five times daily prayer, polygamy, male circumcision, fasting in Ramadan, charity, meat and alcohol restrictions, and the hajj; nonassociation with idol worshipers, blasphemers, murderers, bearers of false witness, and other morally suspect persons; and an account of his teachers and the state of education in his native lands.

Abū Bakr's account, dated September 20, 1834, in Kingston, is almost solely that of his life in Africa, which he had left thirty years previous and to which he indeed returned after he was freed with the assistance of Madden. It is as though his life in bondage, the circumstances in which he unwillingly found himself, was of no import to his identity as an African, a Muslim, and a human being. He kept the books in Arabic for the slaveowner Alexander Anderson, who deemed him so valuable that he refused initial offers by Madden and others to secure Abū Bakr's freedom.[76] Anderson was much praised in the English letter to Kabā but is not important in Abū Bakr's account of his own true self and history. The autobiography is not a religious text, but Abū Bakr is clear about his Muslim familial identity. Abū Bakr's conclusion is very similar to Kabā's *du'ā'* lament: he fears that enslavement has caused him the loss of himself, his education, and his religion, and he begs God's pardon and understanding. He says, "My parents' religion is of the Mussulman. . . . They fight for their religion. . . . They are particularly careful in the education of their children, and in their behaviour, but I am lost to all these advantages: since my bondage I am become corrupt; and I now conclude by begging the Almighty God to lead me into the path that is proper for me, for he alone knows the secrets of my heart and what I am in need of."[77] Both Abū Bakr and Kabā used the word "corrupt" to describe themselves in an enslaved state: Abū Bakr to describe himself "since my bondage," and Kabā to describe his loss of memory and science. "Corrupt" suggests that enslavement does not just result in *loss* of the "advantages" of careful parental education and behavioral training Abū Bakr and Kabā enjoyed, but causes an unwarranted feeling of guilt over coercion: the men were forced into behaviors and circumstances they actively believed to be wrong, immoral, and antithetical to their upbringing and religious training. Perhaps Abū Bakr is also saying that he should have fought harder for his religion, as his forefathers did; but that would have been nearly impossible in colonial Jamaica. But if, as he says, God "alone knows the secrets of my heart" and needs, he acknowledges that he has kept an interior part of himself an African Muslim. And so, like Kabā, he does not exclude himself from deserving the help of "Almighty God," and begs God to show him his path. Unlike Kabā, however, he does not seem to seek the afterlife as the only possible alternative to the sufferings of the world. For Abū Bakr, return to Africa was possible.

The other main religious reference in Abū Bakr's autobiography alludes to enslavement as a burden he has to bear. After relating the tale of his capture and three-month journey to Jamaica (whereupon the Jamaican part of the story begins and ends), he says: "I have none to thank but those that brought me here. But, praise be to God, who has every thing in his power to do as he thinks good, and no man can remove whatever burden he chooses to put on us. As he said, 'Nothing shall fall on us except what he shall ordain; he is our Lord, and let all that believe in him put their trust in him.'"[78] Audra Diptee reads this autobiographical section and his statement that he was sold to "Christians" as proof that "by Abu Bakr's understanding, slavery was sanctioned by Islam," that his "view on slavery was informed by his religious beliefs," and that even though he suffered, it was important that "he saw his enslavement as 'ordained' and part of a divine plan."[79] In my view, it cannot be proven that Abū Bakr believed his or anyone else's enslavement was sanctioned by Islam; that is not what he says. What Abū Bakr is doing is quoting the Qur'an on carrying the burdens of life, not making his own statement about enslavement as Islamically justified or as fate. "Praise be to God, who has everything in his power to do as he thinks good," "no man can remove whatever burden," and "Nothing shall fall on us except what he shall ordain" paraphrase an oft-quoted section of the Qur'an, the end of Sūra al-Baqarah, the second and longest chapter of the Book: "He has power over all things. . . . God does not burden any soul with more than it can bear: each gains whatever good it has done, and suffers its bad—'Lord, do not take us to task if we forget or make mistakes. Lord, do not burden us as You burdened those before us. Lord, do not burden us with more than we have strength to bear. Pardon us, forgive us, and have mercy on us. You are our Protector, so help us against the disbelievers.'"[80] The closing *duʿāʾ* asking pardon here is the model for Abū Bakr and Kabā's stylistic choices of ending their writings by asking pardon of God; it is a rhetorical closing device in Sufi and Muslim prayer, poetic writing, and oratory, as I will discuss further in the case of Hopkinson's poems. This invocation is about shouldering any burden in life, not specifically about enslavement. "God does not burden any soul with more than it can bear" does not necessarily mean any evil is fated, or that the speaker believes enslavement is divinely justified. Rather, the verse and Abū Bakr's call focus on acquiring divine help to survive.

It must be noted, however, that while Abū Bakr's theological opinions on slavery cannot be discerned, many Arab and African Muslims profited off of slavery. David Robinson writes that in the context of Muslim Africa, "Islam recognized slavery and the legitimacy of enslavement, as long as it occurred across the basic divide . . . between the *Dar al-Islam* and the *Dar al-Kufr*, between the faithful people of Islam and the 'pagans' who were still in ignorance and darkness."[81] There were at least three systems of trans-African slave trading implicating Arab and African Muslims as slavers and displacing sub-Saharan Africans: the trans-Saharan slave trade, which "existed for about 1,000 years and 'fed' people from the Sahel, woodlands, and forests of Africa to owners in the Sahara, North Africa, and other parts of the Mediterranean"; the similarly lengthy "Northeast African trade, which channeled people to the Arabian peninsula, the Middle East, and as far as India"; and a later, eighteenth- and nineteenth-century "East African trade to ports and consumers around the shores of the Indian Ocean."[82] These slave systems used the enslaved mostly as domestic servants and in some cases allowed slave soldiers to become rulers, though these are not justifications.[83] There is evidence that some Muslims in the slave trade were concerned on moral grounds, and the issue was addressed by scholars. But elite Islamic scholars in states that profited from slave trading tended to render opinions that justified slavery "because the Sahelian societies that were identified as Muslim, whether city-states in Hausaland such as Kano and Katsina or larger states such as Bornu and Songhay, usually had the power to enslave rather than be enslaved."[84] It is true that following the Prophetic example, Islam encourages the freeing of slaves, particularly if they convert to Islam. The case of the Ethiopian or Abyssinian Bilāl, who after being freed in Mecca became a companion of the Prophet and the first Muslim muezzin, and from whom some Africans, including the rulers of imperial Mali, later claimed descent, is often cited in my observation as a primary example of Islam's generosity to slaves and inherent antiracism—a citation sometimes used to absolve the speaker of attending to the material conditions of discrimination.[85]

Racism and colorism in Islam, historically and now, are extremely complex. The following can be summarized: there are differing juridical opinions on whether and under what conditions Islam permits slavery; Islam gives Qur'anic and Prophetic examples for owning and freeing slaves, including female concubines; some Arab and African Muslims did enslave Africans for profit over the course of centuries; the majority of that enslavement was not chattel slavery; there is a long history of racism by "white" Arabs against black Africans in Muslim North and Northwest Africa; and Islamic religious wars in West Africa resulted in the capture and subsequent enslavement of unknown numbers of Muslims in the Americas. In addition, an important factor in understanding Muslim involvement in the transatlantic slave trade is that newly abolitionist nineteenth-century Europeans used the intra-African slave trades to blame Arabs and Islam for slavery, frame themselves as more humane, and justify the European colonization and missionizing of Africa.[86]

Abū Bakr al-Siddīq and Muhammad Kabā Saghanughu, educated West African Muslim 'ulamā, were victims of the transatlantic slave trade in the early nineteenth century, near its end in the Caribbean. That is one reason why their writings survived; by then, sympathetic abolitionist whites like Madden understood Abū Bakr to be Muslim and recorded his biographic details and writings, and Baptist missionaries preserved Kabā's Kitāb rather than destroying it as their predecessors might have. It has been less than two hundred years from Kabā's and Abū Bakr's time of writing to now. The men left no identifiably Muslim descendants, but they left written proof of their identities and Sufi-informed formal Islamic knowledge to substantiate the Muslim part of the African legacy in Jamaica and the Caribbean. Ware says in his study of West African Islam that "knowledge in Islam does not abide in texts; it lives in people."[87] This is true and not true; Kabā and Abū Bakr possessed and lived Islam in their bodies, which were the only material possessions allowed them from Africa, but they acquired and transmitted their knowledge via texts. Islam has been both a literary and an oral religion from its inception: IQRĀ'! (which means both "read" and "recite") is the imperative commandment the angel Jibrīl (Gabriel) gives the Prophet Muhammad upon the event of the first Qur'anic revelation in the Cave of Hirā'. Even as oral recitation of Qur'anic verses is held in high regard, much of the transmission of Islamic knowledge is textual, revolving around the Qur'an, collections of juridical opinions and exegesis, and accounts of the words and deeds of the Prophet and his companions and successors. Kabā, Abū Bakr, and their African Muslim contemporaries both embodied and transmitted by text the first wave of Islam in the Caribbean.

THE GUYANESE SUFI POET: ABDUR-RAHMAN SLADE HOPKINSON

Mystical verse emerged in the seventeenth and eighteenth centuries as the earliest Islamic vernacular literature in East Africa and Asia.[88] By the late eighteenth century, reformers in West Africa composed and disseminated pious poetry in Fulfulde and Hausa for political and pedagogical purposes.[89] Shaykh 'Uthman bin Muhammad bin 'Uthman bin Salih (1754–1817), known most popularly as Dan

Fodio in Hausa, was the Fula leader of the early nineteenth-century *jihād* against polytheism and peasant oppression that resulted in the establishment of the Islamic Sokoto Caliphate, the largest state of its time in sub-Saharan Africa.[90] Dan Fodio was also a Qādiri Sufi scholar who produced legal, political, and spiritual writings, and set his call to arms to poetry, in a *qasīda 'ajamiyya qādiriyya,* "mystical verse [that] had a hypnotic effect upon devotees on the eve of the jihad."[91] Mystical verse and Islamic verse have been intertwined from the Arab and Persian beginnings of oral and written verse tradition by people who identified themselves as Muslim. As later discussed, "mystical verse" here signifies poetic appeals to the divine and to love, and an affective spirituality linked to Sufi ecstatic practices, without necessarily including explicit Islamic religious references in lyrical form or content.

When 'Uthman Dan Fodio the Qādiri called for an African Islamic revolution through mystical poetry, and Kabā the Qādiri perhaps thought of his education in African Sufi bātin (hidden) teachings to conceal his religion when enslaved in Jamaica, they called into being an ancestral African Sufi literary tradition for the descendants of Africans in the Caribbean. It is the simultaneous appeal to love of every kind, a divine savior, a prescriptive religion, and a non-European tradition that drew Afro-Guyanese poet, playwright, and actor Muhammad Abdur-Rahman Slade Hopkinson to study and write poems in the Islamic mystical tradition of classical Sufi poets.

Hopkinson, father of award-winning speculative fiction writer Nalo Hopkinson, was a Caribbean poet of the Brathwaite-Walcott independence and postcolonial generation, but his work is far less well known and studied than that of most of his contemporaries. In my view, the reasons for his lack of recognition include that he did not publish prolifically, partly because he did not wish to publish his poems; he suffered from serious renal disease for the last decades of his life; Guyanese poets, hailing from a unique Anglophone South American postcolonial space, have generally received less recognition in the Anglophone Caribbean than "island" poets; and Hopkinson's national contributions have been overshadowed by those of another of his contemporaries, the Guyanese poet of anticolonialism Martin Carter—his cousin, and one of those to whom he dedicates the collection *Snowscape with Signature* in its first poem "These Poems Are . . .".[92] Hopkinson first published a book of poetry, *The Four and Other Poems,* in 1954, followed by a series of plays. The Guyanese Ministry of Education and Social Development published his secular Caribbean poetry collection *The Madwoman of Papine* (named for its titular poem, his most famous) and the religious and philosophical collection *The Friend* in 1976.[93] Though they were published at the same time, the former was released under the name Slade Hopkinson, and the latter under Abdul-Rahman.[94] *Snowscape with Signature* collects many of his poems from 1952 to 1992 and was published in 1993 shortly after his death, though he chose the poems therein.

The Jamaican poet and critic Mervyn Morris writes in his introduction to Hopkinson's *Snowscape* that Hopkinson's religious poems are "perhaps his most distinctive contribution to West Indian poetry."[95] Peepal Tree Press, the collection's Caribbean and Black British literary publisher, notes that Hopkinson wrote "some of the finest religious poetry to come from the Caribbean."[96] Hopkinson's work is usually briefly listed in histories of Caribbean poetry as displaying a formal "educated thoughtfulness and stylistic discipline" similar to his more famous contemporaries, including Edward Kamau Brathwaite, Morris, and Derek Walcott; his acting in Walcott's theater workshop is usually noted; his most famous poem "The Madwoman of Papine" may be mentioned; and the review will conclude with a general word about his religion and religious poetry, in the vein of his entry in Edward Baugh's "A History of Poetry" in *A History of Literature in the Caribbean* (2001): "He became a convert to Islam, and the poems that come out of this development are distinguished by a near-mystical sweetness and light and provide yet another current in the stream of Caribbean poetry."[97] To put it plainly, Caribbean literary critics do not know what to do with Hopkinson's religious poetry, as it explicitly engages with a religious "current"—Islam—that seems foreign to the Caribbean and its majority Christian and African syncretic religions. So the critics defer analysis. As Morris observes of the glossary of Caribbean and Islamic words at the back of *Snowscape*, "for many readers, perhaps, the necessary notes are those that help us with Muslim allusions."[98] "Us" suggests that the readers who need help with Muslim allusions, but not with Caribbean ones, are Caribbean. But there are people who are both Muslim and Caribbean, who may not need a glossary for either Islamic or creole words. Lack of knowledge of references leads to hesitant readings; I disagree with Baugh's perception that the poems engaging with Islam display "a near-mystical sweetness and light." The poems are in fact thoroughly mystical, and when Hopkinson begins his most formally striking "Islamic" poem "Azan" with the line "A minaret coruscates in screaming light," one might infer there is much light but no sweetness.[99]

The sensibility of the Islamic poems, I show, is an introspective and at times spiritually tormented one. Hopkinson never strays from formal, deliberate lyrical construction. As mentioned, there is little scholarly study of any of Hopkinson's work, and no in-depth literary analysis of his religious poetry. My aim here is to do a first reading of some of Hopkinson's religious poems as Islamic and Caribbean poems, with attention to the poet's technique and stated Sufi literary influences. I show that Hopkinson brings Islam into Caribbean literary discourse by engaging with traditional Sufi poetic technique and themes and Sufi methods of worship, namely *dhikr*—rhythmic repetition of one or more of the names of Allah or a brief prayer, sometimes accompanied by dancing, *raqs*. Paul Thifault in his analysis of the secular poems in *Snowscape* argues that the "tension between aesthetics and politics . . . . [is] an organizing principle in Hopkinson's poems," and that even Hopkinson's religious poetry displays his "persistent fascination with mapping the fault lines between harsh socioeconomic realities and the pursuit of a sublime aesthetic; albeit, in these poems it is the monotheistic God that fills the space that various abstractions on art and perception had occupied in earlier work."[100] I do not read Hopkinson's poems as displaying "fault lines" or "tension" between aesthetic and socioeconomic or political considerations. I argue that artistic and spiritual abstraction are not separable in his work, nor do they operate in opposition to materiality, and that Hopkinson's project is to reach for the sublime hidden truth (bātin) behind suffering and degraded material conditions through art and aesthetic form. Adherence to certain rules of traditional Arabic-Persian Islamic prosody, as medieval Sufi poets and Hopkinson understood, is a way to reach the hidden freedom of spiritual unity with God/the Beloved. Caribbean diaspora poets, including Guyanese American Rajiv Mohabir and Guyanese Canadian Faizal Deen have written about Islam, but Hopkinson in his pan-Caribbean immersion and singular religious focus is *the* Muslim Guyanese and Anglophone Caribbean poet.

Hopkinson converted to Islam in 1964. Asked in 1977 what led to his conversion, he replied, "That's like asking what led to my poetry. I don't know. I really don't know. In '64 I became a Muslim. Shortly after that I lapsed. Not in belief, but in practice. But always retaining the conviction. And coincidental with my illness, I returned. But I had never really mentally left."[101] He pointed to his interest in what he characterized in Islam as the "perpetual exercise of the intellect," "the scientific spirit," and an obligatory search for knowledge.[102] What is more interesting than the reasons why Hopkinson (or anyone) converted—a problematic question to ask when the "authenticity" of the religious practice of converts is sometimes challenged—is that when asked how he identified, he replied "Muslim. Muslim, Muslim, not a Black Muslim." This disavowal of a racialized Muslim identification can be read in at least three ways: as distancing Hopkinson from the Black Muslims associated in 1977 in the Americas with the radical Nation of Islam; as adhering to the Islamic insistence that the major distinction between people is between believers and unbelievers, with the aforementioned Bilāl story "proving" that Africans were part of the Islamic origin story; or in the Guyanese context, as Hopkinson distancing himself from racial African / Indian strife and identification of only Indo-Caribbean people with Islam. Regardless of what Hopkinson meant—and I do not believe he was in any way disavowing blackness itself—it is clear that "Muslim" for him was a religious and intellectual category of spiritual and artistic exploration, not a racialized identifier. Nonetheless, he is an Afro-Guyanese writer who engages deeply with the legacy of colonialism, and he occupies a crucial place in the development of African Caribbean Muslim literature.

Hopkinson was born into a middle-class life in New Amsterdam, Berbice, British Guiana, in 1934. But he was many times a Caribbean and North American migrant: from Guyana to Barbados in 1947 when he was twelve years old; to Jamaica from 1952 to 1961 to attend the (then) University College of the West Indies and work in the theater; to Trinidad from 1961 to 1965; to the United States to attend Yale University School of Drama, where he did not finish his degree but returned to Guyana as a university lecturer in 1966; back to Trinidad as a teacher in 1968; to Jamaica for Guyanese government-funded medical treatment in 1973; and eventually to Canada as a Guyanese diplomat in the late 1970s.[103] He also traveled with Walcott's Trinidad Theatre Workshop from 1962 onward, but he broke with Walcott and formed the Caribbean Theatre Guild in 1970.[104] He is a poet who truly knew the expanse of the twentieth-century Anglophone Caribbean but always thought of himself as Guyanese. As he said in the comprehensive 1977 interview, there remained

> a conflict in my emotions between the continental landscape and problems of Guyana ... between Guyana pictorially, aesthetically and politically; and the islands, which are surrounded by the blue Caribbean Sea, et cetera, and which are sandy or of limestone and have a different quality of vegetation and have a different kind of inhabitant.... I have lived in two different areas which are, although for purposes of geography and cricket, are labelled the West Indies, nevertheless present two different kinds of geographical, and therefore cultural, being.... I alternately hanker for the forested, tropical richness and difficulty of Guyana, on the one hand, and on the other for the more delicate beauty of the islands.[105]

Cricket acts as a regional West Indian unifier, as Hopkinson says—both because sports fandom unites and because cricket is a metaphor for British colonialism and its subversion, as described by the Trinidadian Marxist historian C.L.R. James in his semiautobiographical cricket classic *Beyond a Boundary* (1963). Hopkinson's engagement with landscape, distinction between island and continent, and suggestion that geography produces distinct cultural "being" are typical positionalities of Caribbean writers. But as I will discuss in the third chapter, Guyanese writers like Hopkinson, David Dabydeen, and Wilson Harris are particularly drawn to the anticolonial, nation-building symbolism offered by Guyana's diverse continental jungle, savanna, and riverine landscapes in which indigenous tribal people still live. The continental Guyanese landscape is characterized by "forested, tropical richness and difficulty" and a coastal Atlantic Ocean that is rather more muddy than the blue of the Caribbean Sea surrounding the islands and their archipelagic soil, vegetation, and people. Hopkinson's pan-Caribbean experiences and differentiation between the continental and island landscapes are reflected in his poems, which he says "reflect two parochialisms. There are the Guyanese poems and there are the West Indian poems ... they are different because the landscapes in which they are set are different."[106] There is a third distinct grouping of Hopkinson's poems that is different from the other regional two, as it is about his own soul-searching and only sometimes engages with questions of Guyanese or broader West Indian postcolonial identity: his Sufi-inspired religious verse.

Hopkinson was explicit about his engagement with the most famed Sufi poets. He named as some of his influences "Omar Khayyam in the serious translation by Robert Graves. Not in the misguided and unfortunate translation by Edward Fitzgerald. There is the brilliant poet and author Ferid-ud-Deen Attar. There is the poet Jalaludin Rumi. A lot of these are perhaps not well known in the West Indian world. They are Muslim Sufi poets in whom I've recently taken a profound interest."[107] Khayyām (1048–1141) was a Persian mathematician and astronomer known to European and North American readers for the quatrains of his Rubā'iyāt, so named in the freewheeling translation in 1859 by Edward FitzGerald. Whether Khayyām wrote all or even some poems attributed to him is as debatable as whether he was a skeptic or a mystic.[108] The latter question revolves around the tone and accuracy of various translations. Hopkinson is clearly aware of the differences, though it is interesting that he picks the Graves translation, which as J.T.P. de Bruijn observes was later proven to be based on "forged materials."[109] Whether Hopkinson knew of the Graves discrediting is uncertain, but why that translation appealed is perhaps clearer: FitzGerald's was known to be much his own Victorian creation—for Hopkinson raising the specter of European colonial appropriation—and Graves's was a "mystical interpretation" opposed to FitzGerald's framing of Khayyām as a disillusioned skeptic.[110] Hopkinson posed in his 1977 interview "a meditative, or a religious poet, or a love poet, or a lyrical poet" who "writes for some critical intelligence of one," in opposition to "dramatic poets" and "satirical poets" who write for a public audience.[111] He clearly thought of himself in the former category of solitary meditative, religious, lyrical, and perhaps love poet when asserting that "I do not need anybody to tell me which are my good poems, I know. . . . My poetry is an act of communication between me and myself."[112] And so the "mystic" Khayyām, more concerned with the spiritual than the material, prevailed in influence. The second influential Sufi poet Hopkinson cites, Farīd ad-Dīn 'Attār (d. ca. 1220) is known for his religious animal parable Mantiq-ut-Tayr (Conference of the Birds) and Ilāhii-Nāma (The Book of the Divine).[113] The third, Jalāl ad-Dīn Rūmī (1207–1273), is famed for his massive collection of Sufi ghazal mystic love poetry, Dīwān-i Kabīr (The Great Divan).[114]

As Hopkinson noted, these Muslim poets were "perhaps not well known in the West Indian world." Even if Rūmī's and perhaps Khayyām's poetry were known to some in the Caribbean by way of Victorian English orientalism, a preindependence colonial education in poetry taught Hopkinson only the sonnets and other European poetic forms he deployed so well. He ends the second poem of Snowscape, "Intro," with the couplet

And I, ex-slave from sugar's golden times,
Choose my own irons; these free, linked English rhymes.[115]

In this poignant declaration Hopkinson signals the Afro-Caribbean writer's ambivalence over the use of the colonizer's English and its literary forms. Brathwaite famously responds to this dilemma by positing Creole languages as deriving from Europe, Africa, and elsewhere, but becoming new, local "nation languages" in the Caribbean.[116] Hopkinson, however, acknowledges that though he is a descendant of people enslaved in an English colony, he chooses to use "English rhymes"—but those rhymes are chains that can be linked and free. His poetic form is interlinked word patterns tied to colonialism, but in his mouth and from his pen the effect is freedom. This approach to language puts Hopkinson in the company of the medieval Sufi poets who found their prosodic confines the surest way to achieve ecstatic spiritual unity with the Divine. Hopkinson says the Sufi poets were his own adult reading, and he was likely entirely self-taught in the formalities of Arabic-Persian Sufi poetry. This literary interest was interwoven with his religious identification as a Muslim. For Hopkinson, being a Muslim who was a poet meant that he had to trace his inseparable religious-poetic lineage to the classical Muslim poets.

The *Snowscape* poems I will focus on here are "Ahad," "Zikr," "Soul," and "Azan." The untitled fourth section of the collection contains most of the poems with Islamic or Sufi poetic allusions. Other than the aforementioned four poems, the religious poems include "Prayer," "Neither Fog Nor Flight," "Respite for a Businessman," "The Friend," "Auto-Bio," "Snowscape with Signature," and "His Light Is Rationed." Only "Neither Fog Nor Flight," an existential poem that describes the night, the stars, and the search for truth, and employs an apostrophic appeal to "O Breath" that is life-sustaining oxygen and God, begins with the *basmalah* prayer invocation, "Bismillāh-ir-Rahmān-ir-Rahīm," (In the Name of God, the Most Gracious, the Most Merciful).[117] The poems on which I focus revolve around Islamic and Sufi religious practice, poetic technique, or both. The compositions are different in form, and at six verses "Azan" is the lengthiest and most well developed, but each poem calls upon God by apostrophe or in the second person as an all-knowing force who can answer questions of mortal existence and especially material and spiritual suffering. None of the poems is long enough to qualify as a panegyric *qasīda*; they are instead more similar to the shorter *ghazal* poetic form. I am not arguing that Hopkinson's poems fit the dictates of the major forms of Arabic-Persian Sufi poetry. He does not follow the strict prosodic rules that make a poem a qasīda, a ghazal, or any other recognizable Sufi poetic form—rules that resulted in the stereotyping of that poetry by European Orientalists as "atomistic," "molecular," static, and lacking in the individual "personal expression," spontaneity, and emotion of "Western" poetry even when the latter was also governed by formal rules.[118] Hopkinson writes sonnets and other European poetic forms, pays strict attention to rhythm and meter, and employs the metaphor, allegory, irony, and typical figurative devices of the "Western tradition" in his secular poetry.[119] In his religious poetry, he *experiments* with the poetic rules and conventions of the longer qasīda, which usually describes a heroic sufferer's journey, and the ghazal, most commonly a lyrical love poem.

The qasīda has its beginnings in Persian courtly poetry but became primarily a Prophetic and (for Shi'a) Imamate religious praise medium, elevated to a precise high art by Persian Sufi mystic poets between the eleventh to twelfth centuries and the late nineteenth century.[120] There are four main formal types of pretwentieth-century Arabic and Persian mystical Islamic poetry that were adapted to subcontinental Indian, Turkish, African, and other literary and musical traditions in the Muslim world: the rubā'ī quatrain, the qasīda panegyric ode, the ghazal secular-sacred love poem, and the epic masnavī.[121] Mystical poetry in the Muslim world begins not with the qasīda, but with the love poetry of Bedouin and other poets in Iraq, Egypt, and the Arab world in the first millennium c.e., and originally secular Persian love poetry in Persian in the tenth and eleventh centuries.[122] Persians dominated the religious forms after the tenth century. Those early forms of love poetry are closest to shorter ghazal poems, with their theme of divine and romantic mystic love, but as de Bruijn explains, "The theme of love is so pervasive that it touches all other forms of mystical poetry," and the "connection between profane and mystical love" has been an "openly expressed" feature of poetry in the Islamic world from the time of "medieval Persian writers who were knowledgeable about this process of sublimation by their own experience."[123] Islamic mystical poetry, particularly in its most well-developed Persian Sufi philosophical and aesthetic forms that influenced its expression everywhere else, is strongly characterized by metonymic and metaphorical relationships between divine and profane love, and the spiritual and material worlds. These relationships are not always oppositional binaries. The most important way in which Hopkinson does not follow the conventions of the qasīda and ghazal forms is, with very few exceptions, in their shared required rhyme scheme of distichs, either a-a/b-a or a-a/a-a.[124] There are poetic stanzas in which he follows this convention, but in his religious poetry, the rhyme scheme tends to shift within single poems. In addition, Hopkinson rarely refers explicitly to the Sufi bread-and-butter of love, either love for the Divine or for a mortal. The exception is in the poem "Prayer," when the speaker refers to "my love for you [God]," and says of God that "He is love," a capaciousness of feeling reflected by the many blue and green hues of the sea.[125] Prayer is equated with love, or love is prayer. Otherwise, Hopkinson is almost hesitant to approach love, speaking more of spiritual torment or ecstatic feeling without love.

I examine here Hopkinson's use of the poet's takhallus (self-naming in a signature verse), which is a characteristic device of transition or closure dating from tenth-century Persian poetry; the sound patterns of his poems; and Sufi philosophy and rituals like dhikr and bātin that underlie his poetry's form and content.[126] The collection is titled Snowscape with Signature after one of its poems. The title poem "Snowscape with Signature" finds in the observation of a wintry landscape

... a Countenance
That gazes back upon you; there is a signature
On star, and starry snowflake.[127]

Those lines hark back to Qur'an 2:115; in the Yusuf Ali translation given in the book's glossary, "W[h]ithersoever ye turn, there is the Presence (literally, 'face') of God."[128] In the poem, that signature belongs to the landscape designer "Him"—presumably God, from the capitalization. The poet finds the signature of God in nature, everywhere he looks. But it is also his desire to add his own signature to his creations. Hopkinson's takhallus signature occurs in the poems "Ahad," "Zikr," and "His Light Is Rationed." In "Ahad," one of Allah's names meaning the monotheistic "One," Hopkinson repeats in each of the first three verses the words "drumming" or "drummed" and "Your Name" when describing calling out to God, thus performing in verse the Sufi musical dhikr of repetitively chanting a name of God to achieve oneness with Him. The fourth, penultimate stanza is

You give Abdur-Rahman
The heart to call on You,
And that is enough
To make him a poet.[129]

The insertion of the poet's name is a striking personal interruption to the rhythmic religious drumming achieved by the poem, and to the repetition of "Your [God's] Name" as the important poetic Name. But it is a clear and proper use of the takhallus self-naming poetic device. The takhallus appends the signature of the poet near the end of a ghazal poem. The device blurs the line between speaker and poet in a manner perhaps uncomfortable for the connoisseur of traditional English-language poetry. There are times here in which I will refer interchangeably to the speaker's voice and poet's voice, because in this style of poetry, the poet has named himself, and thus he is the speaker (there is little evidence of disingenuousness). Hopkinson has also said, as noted, that his poems are "an act of communication between me and myself." A. J. Arberry, the British Orientalist noted for his translations of the Qur'an and Rūmī that introduced the latter to Anglophone audiences, identified the takhallus as a "clasp" theme—as in the closing of a necklace—from the famed ghazals of the Persian poet Hāfez (1315–1390). It is a device that initiates closure of the poem, but also brings the narrative back to the desire and invocation of the poet who began the poem. The clasp, or rather, takhallus, likely originates in the qasīda panegyric as the naming of the patron marking a poetic transition, and it became a standard device of ghazal poetic closure between the tenth and twelfth centuries.[130] The ghazal takhallus was often the poet's pen name and usually occurred in the penultimate or final *bayt* (the

Arabic-Persian poetic line, divided into two *shatr* isometric hemistichs that may or may not be written as a couplet).[131] Rūmī, one of Hopkinson's Persian poetic influences, was a great user of the takhallus clasp, though he often named his mystical inspiration and love object Shams ad-Dīn Tabrīzī in that poetic position.[132] Unlike the rest of the poem, Hopkinson's takhallus verse in "Ahad" is structured as a two-shatr bayt, drawing particular attention to itself by its Arabic-Persian conventionality in self-naming and metrical arrangement. It is the poet's declaration that though as a Caribbean Muslim poet he may not follow all the poetic and religious conventions of the Arab and Persian Muslim world, he well knows what they are. Naming himself to Allah is also a declaration of himself as a Muslim, subject to Allah's judgment. The takhallus verse attributes the poet's artistic ability to God. Being given "The heart to call on You" is what "make[s] him a poet," implying in Sufi fashion that calling on God is what poetry is. Julie Meisami writes that the takhallus was often combined with other closure devices, thus functioning more as an "additional sentential or epigrammatic cap," and that though it identifies the poet "both as the author of the ghazal and its principal focus, it can often serve at the same time to distance him from it, in particular when such references are made in the second or third person, thus achieving a degree of ambiguity."[133] In the final stanza of "Ahad," Hopkinson distances himself from the material practice and reception of poetry—even after crediting God with his poetic ability. He writes:

> But if I am Yours
> It matters not
> Whether men call me poet,
> Or dimwit, gibbering
> The One and Only
> Number he knows.[134]

His being a Muslim, and belonging to God rather than to his worldly audience, is most important. The "poet/dimwit" bayt rhyme in which "gibbering" is then attached to the second hemistich is an instance of *radīf* construction in ghazal, in which a morpheme, the radīf "gibbering," is added to the end of the second rhyming half-line.[135] The graphic physicality of "gibbering" separates it from mystical allusions and godly invocation and emphasizes the unstructured madness of poetry that includes the ecstatic verbal worship of dhikr. The repetition of "One" and the poem "Ahad" itself are simultaneously religious and poetic practice, even if only God knows.

In Hopkinson's poem "Zikr" (a transliteration of "dhikr"), the Name repeated is simply "Allah": "'Allah! Allah!' with awe."[136] Each verse is a bayt written in two lines as a couplet, not always end-rhyming but often alliterative and containing repeated words. The takhallus appears in the final verse:

A landscape of garbage and warehouses?
Abdur-Rahman sees the wide green, gold-flecked.[137]

Preceding this is the penultimate bayt

Do I walk through a workaday city?
No. I stand at the harbour, elated.[138]

When the speaker-poet ends by standing at a harbor, his back to the "workaday city" and "garbage and warehouses," seeing instead the "wide green, gold flecked" expanse of a body of water, I see a rare instance of juxtaposition of Hopkinson's spiritual and postcolonial Guyanese concerns. The moment of the takhallus, the self-naming, is when Hopkinson introduces Caribbean references into his religious poems "Zikr" and "His Light Is Rationed." As Abdur-Rahman, a Guyanese Muslim poet, has been named, it is only right that the poems then envision Abdur-Rahman in a Guyanese landscape. In the case of "Zikr," green and gold are the primary colors of the Guyana flag, the colors most often seen in Guyanese heraldry, and certainly the colors associated with its jungles, gold, and sun. Should one stand at the end of the Demerara Harbor Bridge in Georgetown, Guyana, which when it was built in 1978 was the longest span of floating bridge in the world, one would see the Demerara River reflecting the sunlight and surrounded by green. Perhaps Hopkinson stood there, as I have, with the Georgetown capital's conspicuous garbage of colonialism and governmentally uncollected domestic waste behind him, and found in the landscape something with which to be "elated." In "His Light Is Rationed," the takhallus occurs when the poet tells God at the end of the first of two sections that he is "Abdur-Rahman, bound-coolie, your ward."[139] "Bound-coolie" in the Caribbean is a reference to Indian and Chinese indentured "coolies," a term that is now racially pejorative when applied to Indo-Caribbean people. Here Hopkinson is referencing the historical word when he describes earlier in the poem his spiritual torment and how heeding the Word of God is difficult. He is bound, in this moment, not entirely voluntarily. Fullaman-style, he is also making common cause with other groups in the Caribbean; the terms "fullaman" and, here, "coolie," do not belong only to the ethnic labor groups with whom they originated.

The beginning of the poem "Zikr" is devoted to asking who the speaker is becoming now that he is taking the Sufi path: "Is my body becoming a dancer's" is the first line, followed by lines like "does my heart begin drumming" and "Have I turned furious drunkard."[140] The bodily movement of ecstatic, rhythmic Sufi dancing and the physical and spiritual drumming of the heart are emphasized by the adjacent end of the second line of the fourth bayt and end of the first line of the fifth: "rib-cage" and "heart-beat," respectively. This construction is repeated at the end of the poem with "gold-flecked." The hyphenated pause for breath in the words links the body of the dancing poet, just mentioned by name in the takhallus, to the "gold-flecked" landscape of Guyana: Abdur-Rahman, the Sufi Muslim dancing in Guyana. The antinomian theme of drunkenness and wine is less apparent in Hopkinson's poetry than in classical Sufi works, but it appears in poems in which Hopkinson mentions Sufi poets by name. In "Auto-Bio" the speaker says that his needs include

... wine for my soul,
Drunk from Fariduddin's and Rumi's bowl.[141]

The "wine" drunk from the bowls of the Sufi poet greats is both literal and figurative, but it is in every respect a companionable activity.

In "Zikr," the aforementioned line "No. I stand at the harbour, elated" is preceded two bayts before, as noted, by "Do I linger behind Manzoor, the Elated, / Despite workaday destinations?" With the repetition of "elated" as the emotion experienced by both the poet and Manzoor the Elated, Hopkinson is again placing himself in the spiritual and literary company of the great Sufi poets. In the poem "In One Swift Year," Hopkinson also refers to "Dearest Manzoor, the pivot of our circle."[142] This elated and important Manzoor is most likely the Persian Sufi mystic Mansūr al-Hallāj (the Wool-Carder, ca. 858–922). Mansūr was arrested for heresy, crucified, and violently executed, but was revered by his Sufi contemporaries and later famed Sufi poets like Farīd ad-Dīn 'Attār, from whom Hopkinson drew inspiration.[143] Edward Granville Brown, a historian of Arberry's British Orientalist generation, chronicled Mansūr's life and the most striking sin for which Mansūr was celebrated and killed in Abbasid Baghdad: his *shath*, an ecstatic, outrageous utterance that may be blasphemous. Says Brown, "In a state of ecstasy he cried, 'Ana 'l-Haqq' ('I am the True One,' or 'the Fact,' i.e. God)."[144] "Anā 'l-Haqq," "I am the Truth," was regarded by al-Hallāj's supporters as a gnostic utterance of *bātin*, and "at most, say they, his crime was only that he revealed the secret."[145] By contrast, the authorities seem to have regarded the declaration as the sin of *shirk*, the idolatrous association of oneself or another party with the monotheistic God. The poem's speaker who "linger[s] behind Manzoor" and then names himself Abdur-Rahman literally and figuratively follows Mansūr into an ecstatic unity with God that is so complete it is heretical. Hopkinson's work seeks the truth of how close he can come to God through his Sufi poetic and religious practice. He ends the poem "Zikr," though, by surveying the Guyanese natural land- and waterscape, raising the ecotheological question of whether that is where Allah is already to be found in the Caribbean.

"Soul" is a brief five-line poem that reflects upon the teachings of a more recent Sufi teacher than the aforementioned classic poets: the Moroccan Shaykh Mawlāy al-'Arabī ad-Darqāwī (d. 1823), founder of the Darqāwiyyah *tarīqa* (school, path) of the Shādhilī order. Ad-Darqāwī's *The Darqawi Way: Letters from the Shaykh to*

the *Fuqara* (1981 translation) is the most important collection of his work still cir-
culated among his followers. *Fuqarā*, better known to English speakers in its
singular form *faqīr* (fakir), are poor or needy men, but in a religious context Sufi
ascetics who "need" only God. In "Soul," both title and subject of the poem, the
speaker wrestles with the near-universal religious question of distinction between
ego-self and soul. The poem begins:

> Ego must die, so that the soul may be born;
> But ego is identical with the soul.[146]

The speaker calls the ego/soul differentiation

> Ad-Darqawi's mystery:
> You built it into the soul's architecture.[147]

In the middle of the poem, the Beloved is called upon to reconcile the conflict
between ego and soul, though the resolution is inbuilt in the soul. The Beloved
"You" here is God, as in this poem there is no mortal foil. Ad-Darqāwī's mystery
of the soul belongs in the Islamic and Sufi theological schools that identify a distinction between the *rūh* (immortal soul-self) and *nafs* (ego, psyche, seat of
worldly desires). These exist together in the living person, and the *jihād* of life is
the struggle between them, and the fight to keep the nafs—of which there are also
many dimensions—in check. Ad-Darqāwī Letter 52 on the subject informs Hopkinson's poem. The learned *shaykh* writes:

> The ruh (spirit) and the nafs (self) are the same luminous thing from the world of
> light. . . . it is not two different things even though it has two descriptions: purity
> and turbidity. The root is purity and the branch is turbidity. . . . as long as the ruh
> retains its purity, excellence, radiance, beauty, nobility, height and elevation, then
> only the name "ruh" is true for it. When it leaves its original purity, excellence, radi-
> ance, honour, height, and elevation, and becomes turbid by leaving its homeland
> and relying on other than its loved ones, then it is true to call it "nafs."[148]

Ad-Darqāwī's contribution to "Soul" is the paradox that ego (nafs, turbidity) must
be sublimated to soul (*rūh*, purity), but that they are in fact branch and root,
respectively, of "the same luminous thing from the world of light." The "soul's architecture" designed by God already contains this answer. The faqīr seeking the
metaphysical "homeland from which you came"—the luminous realm of God—
is enjoined by ad-Darqāwī to "strip yourself of the world of impurity" and turbidity.[149] Hopkinson the poet is the seeker, the faqīr, attempting to resolve material
and spiritual desires and coming to the understanding that the former, though it
must be managed, is not evil, but part of the same tree of being. Ad-Darqāwī ends

this letter to his followers—who perhaps include Hopkinson—with a Sufi conundrum: "It is said that the nafs has a secret and that that secret did not manifest itself to any of Allah's creation except for Pharaoh. That is why he said, 'I am your Lord Most High.'"[150] It seems the shath of the Pharaoh who battled the Abrahamic Mūsa/Moses is the same uttered by Mansūr al-Hallāj: "Anā 'l-Haqq," "I am the Truth" or "True One," i.e., God or the "Lord Most High." What secret does the nafs hold that only the pagan ruler who competed with God and fought His chosen prophet knew? Another Sufi paradox, flirting with heresy to arrive at hidden truth.

Hopkinson's struggle to reconcile the material and the spiritual is most visceral in the poem "Azan." This poem is titled after the *adhān* or *azān*, the five-times-daily Islamic call to prayer, typically performed by a muezzin—inheritor of the mantle of Bilāl—from a minaret. I argue that, though significantly shorter than a traditional qasīda, "Azan" displays the thematic structure of the qasīda and the chiastic ring composition often found in the ghazal and shorter lyric forms.[151] In addition, the poem attends in part to the qasīda's and ghazal's shared rhyme scheme. Hopkinson's rhythmic poem, its namesake call to prayer, and the Sufi poetic forms that inspire it are also all musical: early Persian ghazals were oral compositions that were sung, and "even 'literary' ghazals retain many of the characteristic features associated with song."[152] Qasīdas are often set to music in their subcontinental adaptations in India, Pakistan, and as a result the Caribbean; and the *adhān* call to prayer is musical, if not music.

A classical panegyric qasīda generally has three main parts: the *nasīb* and *rahīl*, which constitute the exordium, and the *madīh*. There is also a landscape setup at the beginning, and often a *du'ā'* for closure at the end.[153] According to the normative definition given by the ninth-century Abbasid Islamic scholar Ibn Qutayba, the poet of the qasīda begins with a description of deserted landscapes marked by loss and lament, followed by the nasīb, which "complains of the force of his passion, the pain of separation, and the excessiveness of his longing and desire, so as to incline hearts towards him and attract interest, and gain an attentive hearing."[154] The audience thus sympathetically engaged, the poet continues with the rahil, "traveling by camel" on a wearying desert journey in search of justice and reward. This is followed by the madīh, in which the patron is praised and urged toward generosity.[155] In the ghazal, as described, the takhallus is the poet's self-naming. In the qasīda, the takhallus is the transition point between exordium and madīh, when the praiseworthy patron is first named as the destination of the camel journey.[156] Hopkinson's "Azan" is a qasīda story. It begins with a description of a wasted landscape, in which a muezzin on his "exalted balcony" is contrasted with the deserted seeming aftermath of violence below: "Streets ripped by picks and spades," "Dust left to parch and blow / Into our faces," and "our wastes and deserts."[157] The second verse is a nasīb, mourning loss and separation from a woman and seeking the empathy of the audience. The speaker has lost his young sister:

Seven months ago
Chill seized my sister's heart. She screamed and died.
So I was told.
She was on the green side of twenty-five.[158]

The rahīl, comprising the third to fifth verses, is a temporal and spiritual journey—camel journeys would be an odd reference for a Caribbean poet. The journey to Islam and to the wasteland in which the speaker finds himself has already been six months: "It is six months since I was called to prayer," he says.[159] The speaker is coughing from dust in the street, surrounded by bones, and physically disintegrating of "ague, chill and fear"—"ague" most often refers to the shivering fever of malaria, a disease endemic to tropical Guyana.[160] His hair is falling out. The third verse ends with two end-rhyming bayts, "brain/vein" and "fear/hair," emphasizing the visceral degradation of the speaker's physical and mental faculties.

This du-baytī, internal quatrain of sorts, is followed by a radīf end-rhyming with the latter bayt: the aforementioned line "It is six months since I was called to prayer."[161] The radīf sheds new light on why the speaker is suffering: he has been called to prayer (i.e., Islam). The seriousness of the spiritual conflict is marked by his observing a man hanging upside down from the minaret, bleeding and dying from a jugular vein slit by a "pious knife." It may be the speaker himself, as he has been losing his hair and this man's "carcass" is "as good as bald," which contradicts his youth. The man is a sacrifice whose blood "quench[es]" the dusty world below him. Hopkinson employs an alternate end-rhyme at the conclusion of the fifth verse to describe what happens to the dying man:

His wrinkling hide begins to strip and peel.
There he hangs
Parody of a legal meal.[162]

Here the man's sacrifice is compared to legal Islamic slaughter and food, that is, zabīha (dhabīhah) ritual slaughter and halāl, "permissible" food (especially meat). Human sacrifice, suicide, or murder is not Islamically permissible or legal. The man is thus a parody of a halāl meal, but still the speaker is unsure about whether self-sacrifice is required for conversion, as will become clear at the end of the poem. The beginning of the sixth and last verse is when the rahīl journey is complete, and so several lines, words, and the end-rhymes of the bayts employed in the third verse, when the journey began, are repeated: "fear/overhear/prayer/hair" (in the a-a/a-a second most common structure of a Persian quatrain).[163] Hopkinson's "Azan" thus displays circular rhyming composition. Chiastic ring composition or a loose circularity is "frequent in the [Persian] short lyric," including ghazals.[164] The repetitive structure of the poem also recalls that of the adhān itself, which in its Sunni iteration has a ring form: it begins with the takbīr ("Allāhu akbar," "God is great(est)") and the complete *Shahādah* declaration of Muslim faith, each repeated twice. In the middle the faithful are told to hasten to prayer and salvation. The *takbīr* and the first half of the *Shahādah* pertaining to the oneness of God (the second half declares Muhammad the Messenger of God) are repeated at the end. Hopkinson's work displays a virtuoso interplay of multiple poetic and religious references from all of his traditions.

As the madīh is reached at the end of the sixth and last verse of "Azan," the takhallus of the patron is finally invoked by apostrophe. The patron is God himself:

> O my God, "Closer than the jugular vein,"
> Whose truth includes
> Spawning jungle and sterile desert—
> I must know, tell me:
> Did You require this of them, and of me?[165]

The effusive, embellished praise of the patron normal to the qasīda is missing here. Instead, God is simply given due credit as creator of both fertile land and the wastes. The final two lines, however, are characteristic of the *du'ā'* invocation for closure. Meisami argues that the *du'ā'* "can provide a key to the poem's meaning" by either "recapitulating certain important topics or suggesting others relevant to the circumstances of the poem but not stated elsewhere."[166] In "Azan," the final appeal asks God to shed light on the speaker's suffering. The speaker's and Hopkinson's journey is conversion to Islam, being "called to prayer." The *du'ā'* summarizes the poem by asking whether the mental and physical suffering experienced on the journey—that may involve the independence-era violence of Guyana, and the poet's own medical sufferings as a result of his kidney disease—is required to reach the hidden truth of being a Muslim. Help, intervention, and answers from God are required to stay on the path of Islam—just as Kabā and Abū Bakr asked for in their *du'ā's* imploring God to give them succor and the strength to privately remain Muslim while enslaved.

REVELATION: AFRO-CARIBBEAN LITERARY ISLAM

As noted, the first line in "Azan" is "A minaret coruscates in screaming light," followed by an implied critique of the idea "that mere habit is holy," and at the end of the first verse, "The crier's voice, in rusty quavers, / Proclaims God great, / Not from that exalted balcony, / But the back of the hall, ground floor."[167] The initial distressing personification of "screaming" light from a "coruscating," too-bright and flashing minaret recalls Sufi poems like those of the great Egyptian Sufi mystic Ibn al-Fārid (1181–1234), in which there is play between light-related words with the same root but opposed meanings: *barq* (lightning, but also the flashing light of Sufi realization) and *barāqi'* (veils, connoting bringing into darkness).[168] Light and its symbolic meanings, as seen in ad-Darqāwī's reference to the luminosity and radiance associated with the immortal "pure" soul, is a common Sufi poetic theme. Sufi *barq*, the light of revelation, is sought after but painful to the eyes and the soul. The search for truth/Islam being spiritually rewarding at its end but inherently and contradictorily painful in the journey is a thread that runs through "Azan." The poem is full of paired, opposing images: the holy, light-filled mosque contrasted with the deserted streets, wastes, and deserts; the nobility of the muezzin's role belied by his "rusty quavers" of a voice; God's "[s]pawning jungle and sterile desert"; and the hanging man contrasted with a "legal meal," to name a few. Hopkinson the poet was concerned with the contradictions of faith, and the struggles between materiality and spirituality, ego and soul, divine and profane, and ecstasy and suffering. A search for the truth, the real, and enlightenment was his hallmark in life and work.

Hopkinson was not easy on those who obfuscated truth. In the Caribbean, he was a cutting critic of what he called the "pallid approval" of educated, bourgeois audiences of his and Walcott's plays in "more developed" nations like Barbados and Jamaica. Unlike audiences in the Small Islands, he wrote, they refused engagement with the concept of what was really "home" in the West Indian postcolony.[169] In 1979 he wrote a letter to the editor of the Toronto *Globe and Mail*, condemning the newspaper and two Canadian Muslim leaders for appearing to endorse polygamy and forced conversion. In his argument he cited the Qur'an and concluded, "In Canada, where perhaps a majority of people hold views on Islam that are based on ignorance, hearsay, and ancient, entrenched prejudice, a great deal of harm can be done by glibness, and a lack of accuracy. It behooves us all to be strict and fastidious with the details of the truth about Islamic doctrine."[170] Hopkinson would likely never call himself an *'ālim* like his Sufi poet inspirations were, but he assumed that role here and in the way his poetry "teaches" Islam to Caribbean audiences by locating it in their milieu. Being strict and fastidious about Islamic doctrine and politics in general, though, was always for Hopkinson about seeking bātin, the hidden, real truth behind what words seem to say: the *niyyah* (intention) is a crucial doctrinal and juridical concept in Islam. "Mere strict habit," as "Azan" points out, is not "holy." In Hopkinson's religious poetry, he entertains Sufi teachings that suggest apparent binary oppositions ought instead to be reframed as having the same root and source in the divine realm where the truth lies. The poems never quite come to a spiritual or material resolution or peace; the state of being seeker and observer, in transit to unity with the divine, is paramount. Hopkinson said in 1977 that his illness had given him a "consciousness of death" with which he was living "[q]uite comfortably" and "beyond terror." Writing poems had become for him primarily "an act of spiritual clarification."[171] Kabā and Abū Bakr, as older men who had been enslaved for most of their adult lives, also faced their mortality, made offerings of their words, and sought spiritual clarification in their writings. Hopkinson's poetry and engagement with Sufism provides a continuity of Afro-Caribbean literary Islam that reaches across a century and a half to assure Kabā and Abū Bakr that though they left no direct Muslim descendants, Islam, practiced by the descendants of Africans, was and is a religion of the Caribbean.

2 · SILENCE AND SUICIDE

Indo-Caribbean Fullawomen in
Post-Plantation Modernity

In the previous chapter, I argued that enslaved West African Muslim men in Jamaica who were educated in Qur'anic traditions alleviated their material labor conditions and gained community status through their literacy and transmission of Islamic knowledge. But what of the vast majority of Muslim and non-Muslim Caribbean enslaved and indentured laborers who were not literate, but nonetheless managed to transmit religious knowledge: their Yoruba *orisha* or Kongo *loa* deities, their Hindu cosmologies, their Qur'anic *tajwīd* (elocution)? Though this chapter focuses on the transmission of Islam among Indo-Caribbean indentured laborers and their descendants, with attention to gendered differences, the significant methods of community perpetuation of each tradition in the Caribbean are the same: memorization, ritualized oral transmission during community events and religious functions, and the verbal instruction of children.[1] Though Islam is the "the book religion par excellence," as William Graham argues, "the oral, recited Qur'ān has retained its primacy despite being written down as well as transmitted orally."[2] But with a few notable exceptions, including in fiction, Caribbean Muslim women's voices are barely recorded in the archives and the mosque.

Dr. Anesa Ahamad was the first Muslim woman to give a *khutbah* sermon at Friday *Jumu'ah* prayers in the Caribbean. On June 21, 1995, at the Fireburn *masjid* (mosque) of the Ahmadiyya Anjuman Ishaat-i-Islam in Freeport, Trinidad, Ahamad, an Indo-Trinidadian medical doctor in her thirties, trained at the University of the West Indies at Mount Hope, delivered a sermon that, as the BBC reported when it picked up the story and interviewed her, made "[t]he small Caribbean island of Trinidad . . . hit the headlines in the Muslim world."[3] The khutbah's delivery by a woman and its encouragement by the doctrinally controversial Ahmadiyya community was criticized as un-Islamic innovation (*bid'a*) by the major Trinidadian Sunni organization the Anjuman Sunnat-ul-Jamaat Association and others at home and abroad, but as Halima-Sa'adia Kassim explores, the event happened in the context of, most prominently, Dr. Amina Wadud performing a khutbah in South Africa by 1994 and (much later) in the United States in 2005.[4] Some in Trinidad saw Ahamad as following in the footsteps of Indrani Rampersad, who became the first Trinidadian Hindu *pandita* in 1994.[5] Both of Ahamad's grandfathers had been imams at the mosque at which she gave her khutbah. Ahamad says, "It was in the Caribbean. For the majority of cases Islam is not a radical religion. It's a practical religion and the way I was taught it is to use the principles to apply to your life . . . [it's] not necessarily that the religion dictates your life, because our lives are so different in whichever country you might be."[6] For Ahamad, there is no question of contravening Islamic principles; women's participation in the mosque is a matter of interpretation and context.

Twenty-three years later, I interviewed Ahamad at the University of Miami, where she is now an oncologist, about her famous khutbah. At her own masjid, says Ahamad, "The reaction at the mosque was very positive, and they were proud. I took the time and I read and ensured, double-checked my references to ensure everything I was saying could be corroborated; and once I did it the community was very happy, both men and women. They were very proud. The elder men were very proud."[7] Ahamad was asked to give the sermon by imam and Ahmadi leader Mustapha Kemal Hydal, who is regularly quoted on Muslim issues in Trinidad media and involved in controversies with majority Sunnis and the government. Ahamad believes that community leaders viewed her as an educated person "who would look at the Qur'an and understand it, and believe it, and interpret it for her own local community in a way they understand . . . [to which] they would pay attention."[8] The community benefit was explicitly linked to gender concerns, as "Maybe perhaps they thought the novelty of a female doing it may also draw more attention to the idea," but "two decades ago a small island in the Caribbean was able to interpret the Qur'an to say and . . . writ[e] extensively that the Qur'an is a proponent for gender equality . . . they wanted to promote gender equality, but they did not want to do it for its own sake."[9] There is some suggestion here that the mosque wanted to be the first in the Caribbean to have a woman give a khutbah, but there was more importantly a commitment to Islamically justified ideas of gender parity.

It is telling that what some Trinidadian Muslim opponents to the khutbah protested was that Ahamad was not dressed appropriately for speaking in front of men and women at the mosque, not that she had no right to give the sermon on account of being a woman. Ahamad says she was wearing "a long black gown, and I covered my head but I wasn't wearing a burqa. . . . I wore just a head scarf, but I don't think my neck was covered. So, there was a big protest for that, about I was inappropriately dressed and very disrespectful to the mosque for me to speak like that because I didn't have a burqa on."[10] Until the mid-1970s, when praying, most Indian Muslim women in the Caribbean usually wore on their heads

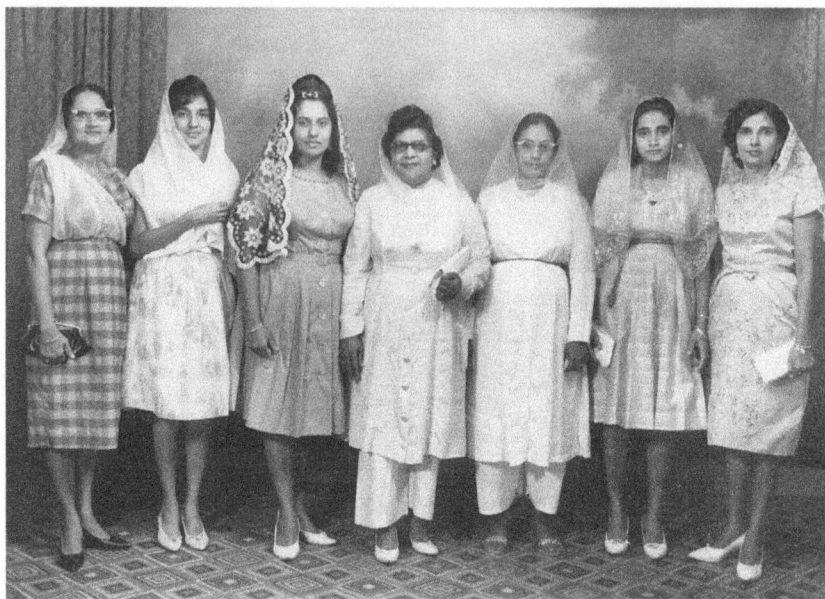

FIGURE 2.1 Muslim women's fashion in 1964 British Guiana: the executive body of the Ahmadiyya Anjuman Women's Auxiliary, Louisa Row, Georgetown. (Author's family archives.)

loosely draped Indian *ohrnis* similar to those of their Hindu counterparts (see fig 2.1).[11] The hijab is most common now, though it took at least two decades to filter through all Muslim Caribbean communities. Nasser Mustapha links the changes in dress to global Muslim youth awareness of and pride in the 1979 Iranian Revolution, though there are also other factors at work, including Libyan, Egyptian, Saudi, and other Gulf-sponsored proselytization and funding.[12] Ahamad gave the sermon in 1995, precisely when Caribbean Muslims had gained a greater awareness of and were navigating their place in the global *ummah*, as I discuss in chapter 5.

Ahamad's khutbah was particularly striking in light of the fact that in Trinidad, as Kassim points out, "Muslim women did not attend the *masajid* until 1928 when they joined the 'Eid-ul-Adha (Feast of Sacrifice) prayers in St. James."[13] Mosque attendance and facilities for women across the Caribbean—and the world— remain uneven, controversial, and dependent on mosque and sect, as Rhoda Reddock has explored.[14] There is little open discussion of the most controversial idea of Muslim women leading mixed-gender prayers. Ahamad's khutbah was a first but fairly singular event. A few women have given talks and khutbahs in Trinidadian Ahmadi mosques since then, but in the Caribbean as elsewhere, the practice remains exceedingly rare. At least one woman, Farida Mohammed, has also graduated from the Ahmadi Institute for Imamaat Training; and there are now female Muslim Marriage and Divorce Officers in Trinidad.[15] These Caribbean Muslims are fullamen too, but the point is that they are not men.

In this chapter, I identify the particularity of the Indo-Caribbean Muslim "fullawoman" (the word "fullaman" is not gendered in speech and can refer to a woman or a man). Study of this fullawoman must first contend with the major identitarian trope of Indo-Caribbean identity and literature, the historical *jahaji bhai*—the "ship brother" fraternal relationship developed onboard the ships of indenture—which becomes, in the contemporary academic and community recovery of Indo-Caribbean women's stories, the *jahaji bahin* (ship sister). The jahaji bahin, however, is usually articulated as a Hindu woman in the Caribbean, and so work must be done to clarify the positionality of the multi-minority Muslim jahaji bahin, or fullawoman. It is important to note, however, that Indo-Islam partly sustained itself in the Caribbean through the marriages of Hindu women to Muslim men, and their conversion to Islam; proportionately fewer Muslim women migrated to the Caribbean. I examine two Guyanese writers' works that are set mainly in the interwar to mid-twentieth century period, when former indentured Indian laborers, their children, and grandchildren began to leave the sugar estates and grapple with changing religious, racial, gender, and class norms: Ryhaan Shah's novel *A Silent Life* (2005) and Rooplall Monar's 1980s–1990s short stories "Hakim Driver" from *Backdam People* (1985), the local magazine story "Pork Eater" (1990), and "Infidel" and "Big People Story" from the collection *High House and Radio* (1991). I argue, first, that the Indo-Caribbean defines itself in opposition to the Afro-Caribbean through the former's positing of Indian women as properly submissive to patriarchal values. The mechanism through which this happens is the eliding of jahaji bahin narratives of indentured women's histories on the moral margins of Indian society, and their replacement with sanitized domestic narratives of gendered normativity made possible by a "generational skip" wherein the first generation of Indian women born in the Caribbean enjoyed much *less* freedom than their indentured mothers. Second, I show that Indo-Caribbean Muslims then position themselves as the Other of the Hindu majority through insistence on the *performance* of properly "Islamic" moral behavior by Muslim women. As Gabrielle Hosein says in a discussion of women's electoral participation in Trinidadian mosque leadership, "Indo-Muslim women cannot engage in . . . creolization without conveying irreverence, misinterpretation, and failure to fulfill appropriate forms of womanhood associated with Islamic authenticity and piety. For these women, to be creole is to be like non-Muslim women, and men, and to risk a damaging reputation, which is associated with a lack of respectability."[16] An educated, respectable "modernity" is what Hosein argues "offers an alternative to tradition as a source of honor."[17] This is the mode of *A Silent Life*'s protagonist's initial escape from her cultural and religious strictures. In the case of Monar's short stories, where it is nearly impossible for anyone to "modernize" or change their social place, humor and Creole language deployed by women and men function as markers of cultural authenticity *and* postcolonial becomings.

JAHAJI BAHIN: BETWEEN SITA AND *RAND*

Indian indentureship in the Caribbean lasted from 1838 to 1917. Like Hindus, indentured Muslims were allocated caste identifications in indenture documents. Those indenture caste identifications were often variants of "Musulman" or "Mohammedan," but were sometimes other types of religious, ethnic, and professional identifiers: "Musulman, Mosulman, Musalman, Sheik Musulman, Mahomedaan, Syed, Sheik, Jolaba, Mughal, Pathan, Pattian, and Musulman (Pathan)."[18] "Syed," "Sayyid," "Sharif," or "Sidi" denotes a lineal descendant of the Prophet Muhammad. "Sheik(h)" is an honorific for a royal, a cleric, a leader, a scholar, or an upper-class trader, depending on location in the Muslim world. The most common names among the early Hindustani Muslims were Mohammed and Ally (Ali).[19] Muslim (Afghan) Pathans, many of whom were dissidents against British rule in India who were imprisoned and exiled during the Indian Rebellion or Sepoy Mutiny of 1857–1858, were sent to Guiana and Suriname and had an outsize impact on early Indo-Islam in Guyana: in 1895, Gool (Gul) Mohammad Khan, a Nasruddin Khel tribal Afghan from Dir, who arrived in the colony as an indentured immigrant at age 16, initiated the building of the Queenstown Jama Masjid, the first mosque in Guyana's capital of Georgetown.[20] By 1891, there were about twenty-nine mosques and thirty-three temples in British Guiana. By 1917, the last year of Indian indentureship, there were about forty-six mosques and forty-four temples.[21] This is a striking comparative number, when Muslims originally amounted to 20 percent of Indian migrants, declining later to about 10 percent through, mostly, remigration—Gool Mohammad Khan himself returned to India.[22] Muslims were heavily invested in preserving their religious practices during indentureship.

Indian indentured laborers' Islam and Hinduism were not in principle suppressed on a wide scale in the Anglophone Caribbean, but there were limitations: religious gatherings like Hosay that posed a threat to colonial authority were monitored and forcibly limited by governments and militias. Anglican and later Canadian Presbyterian proselytization, complemented by promises of schooling and upward class mobility, was encouraged in Indian communities by the British. Marriages solemnized by Hindu pandits and Muslim imams (locally, in the Urdu Muslim tradition, *moulvis* and *majees*) were not legally recognized in British Guiana until the early 1960s preindependence premiership of Indo-Guyanese Cheddi Jagan.[23] Trinidadian law still incorporates four separate marital acts for Muslim, Hindu, Orisa, and general Christian and civil marriages: in Trinidad, Muslim marriages were not recognized as legal—affecting inheritance rights and the legitimacy of children—until 1935; Hindu marriages, colloquially stigmatized as "marriage under bamboo" (marriages solemnized under the *maro* bamboo-pole tent) became legal only in 1946.[24] Notoriously, until a parliamentary amendment in September 2017, while all other girls were required to be a minimum age of 18 years old at the time of marriage, Muslim girls could be married at the age of 12, and Hindu girls at the age of 14, in deference to alleged community norms in Trinidad. In all cases, boys were required to be 18 years old.

For indentured Indian female migrants and their immediate descendants, the intersection of religion, law, and racialized, prescribed gender roles produced a gendered subalternity wherein their material circumstances were dictated by a colonial government of white men and community leadership of Indian men. As Gayatri Spivak says, if, in the course of the epistemic violence of the production of the colonial Other, "the subaltern has no history and cannot speak, the subaltern as female is even more deeply in shadow."[25] "Silence" is the key archival operating term when "the relationship between woman and silence," determined by everyone but women themselves, transcends race and class.[26] As I describe elsewhere, it is not that women do not appear in the historical records of Indian indentureship, or that they never occupied positions as community and even plantation strike leaders.[27] It is that the archives and narratives of Indian indentureship are *structured* by the absence of women's voices. Women lurk at the margins of official and unofficial archival production of the Indo-Caribbean community, even while the policing of their movements and bodies creates the differentiating identities of that community. In her novel of the Indo-Trinidadian family *The Swinging Bridge* (2003), Ramabai Espinet writes: "If you happen to be born into an Indo-Caribbean family, an Indian family from the Caribbean, migratory, never certain of the terrain, that's how life falls down around you. It's close and thick and sheltering, its ugly and violent secrets locked inside the family walls. The outside encroaches, but the ramparts are strong, and once you leave it you have no shelter and no ready skills for finding a different one."[28] The physical and metaphorical "sheltering" ramparts and walls of home especially keep Indo-Caribbean women inside the domestic sphere, silencing the movement of their bodies and the telling of their diverse stories in an attempt to stabilize the terrain of migrancy. Postcolonial fiction and poetry by and about Indo-Caribbean women directly address familial secrecy, attempting to lift violent and violating silences. What Spivak identifies as women's "minimal predication as indeterminate . . . available to the phallocentric tradition" is thereby refashioned through literature into the radical difference of determinate, distinct individuals who share community histories but not daily lives.[29]

Jahaji bhai describes the bond formed between mostly male indentured Indian shipmates bound for the New World. One founding oceanic myth of the Indo-Caribbean is the decline of caste strictures precipitated by the *kala pani* "black water" voyage, which, according to the nineteenth-century Hinduism of Indian indentured migrants, produced a loss of caste identity and the inability to return home. The sea-crossing, as explored by Rosanne Kanhai, Brinda Mehta, and other scholars of the Indo-Caribbean, was not only a physical voyage away from home. Hindus understood that they were also incurring the painful possibility of adharmic religious exile. Some migrants, however, voluntarily and immediately—at the Calcutta and Madras departure depots—stripped themselves of the markers and strictures of religion, including upper-caste migrants ridding themselves of forehead *tikka, janeu* masculine sacred threads, *kanthi mala* necklaces, and *juthaa* food purity taboos. That desire for reinvention, argue Raymond Chickrie and Bibi Halima Khanam, may also have contributed to the close Hindu-Muslim relations produced by racial solidarity.[30] The jahaji bhai bond was sustained in the early generations of indenture and sometimes beyond, when men, and later their families, attempted to maintain relations with those "relatives" dispersed to distant plantations. I argue elsewhere that "Indo-Caribbeans are thus maneuvered into the hybrid, ocean-crossing paradigms of Caribbean area studies because the jahaji bhai suffered a 'Middle Passage' voyage too."[31] In pursuit of an Indo-Caribbean origin myth, the jahaji bhai narrative erases Indo-Caribbean women's agency, nonmarital romantic and sexual relationships, and friendships with other women, in order to rehabilitate the women's nonnormative origins and banish the specter of *shame* that is a recurring trope in fictional and nonfictional narratives of indentured women.[32]

The figure of the jahaji bahin, the Indo-Caribbean woman, represents, I argue, a continuum between two Hindu Indian poles: the domestic ideal of the Ramayanic Sita and the sexual danger of the *rand* or *randi*, a Hindi (Hindustani, on the estates) word that originally meant "widow" or "woman," but that in India, before indenture, tellingly came to mean "prostitute."[33] It is the specter of this rand that results in the eliding of the diverse histories of Indo-Caribbean women. The term signified, in the Caribbean plantation era, a widow, harlot, both, or simply an Indian woman of allegedly loose morals.[34] Mehta and Patricia Mohammed argue that indentured Hindu men, having already been disenfranchised in India by the upper castes, had much to gain from emigration. Nonetheless, says Mehta, Hindu women "had the most to gain by crossing over to different lands because their confinement within Hindu patriarchal structures in India made them victims of abusive family and communal traditions."[35] As Gaiutra Bahadur shows in her archival history of indentured women on Guianese plantations, the first Hindu and Muslim women migrants found themselves with theretofore-unknown freedoms, notably an extensive choice of sexual and marital partners. Indian women in the Caribbean thus acquired from both Indian men and the colonial British an early reputation for having "loose morals."[36] Every Indian woman was automatically assumed to be a rand.

Between Sita and rand, Indo-Caribbean Muslim women in close living, marital, and other domestic proximity with Hindus were subsumed under their Indianness. Sita also applied to them. Jahaji bahin is the uncomfortable synthesis of

Sita and rand, in which Indo-Caribbean women are idealized but always under sexual suspicion; what I want to do here is to frame this dialectic as Caribbean *dialectic*, recovering the multiplicity of gender performances of Indo-Caribbean women that are creolized dialects of Indianness and Caribbeanness. In the Indo-Caribbean, the wifely ideal was and to some extent still is Sita of the *Ramayana*: Sherry-Ann Singh writes that "the essentially patriarchal family system that developed during the early post-indenture period held Sita—chaste, submissive, faithful, and loyal to her husband—as the highest ideal of womanhood."[37] Valmiki's ancient epic *Ramayana* and Tulsidas's sixteenth-century Ramayanic *bhakti* (devotional) poetic retelling of the *Ramcharitmanas*, the epic story of the exile of Lord Rama, his brother Lakshmana, and wife Sita from Ayodhya, constitute the most important texts in Caribbean Hinduism. After being kidnapped by the demon king Ravana, Sita throws herself on a burning pyre to prove her fidelity to her god-avatar husband Rama. Sita has been the perfect wife, following her husband into exile and living in his forest hut performing domestic tasks even though she is a princess and then a queen. Humility and deference to her husband are her ultimate virtues, even though she is shown to be very brave.

In addition to individual and group devotion, the *Ramayana* is celebrated in the Caribbean through the *Ramleela* play observed by Derek Walcott, and the Bhojpuri folksong-style practice of "singing *Ramayana*," which is often done by women. The *Ramayana* assumes importance in Caribbean Hinduism as a function of its central theme of exile from home, and its multiple incidences of characters overcoming material, familial, and spiritual hardships. Indentured Hindu women, facing separation from natal and marital families, were, like Sita, kidnapped by foreign demons and in the greatest sexual and spiritual danger. Like Sita, they were also expected to return to pious purity as soon as possible, even on pain of death. Singh argues that Hindus in the Caribbean diaspora accounted for the seemingly unjust behavior of Rama, avatar of the god Vishnu, toward his wife Sita—testing her virtue and banishing her—by explaining that "Rama's status as a king duty-bound to his subjects took precedence over his role as a husband."[38] The Sita ideal of Indo-Caribbean women persisted until at least the 1970s, and it is never entirely absent from discussions of Indo-Caribbean women's public and private behaviors that continue to frame the community's self-perceptions at home and abroad.[39] For Muslim and Hindu Indo-Caribbean women, following Sita's example means privileging their roles in the domestic sphere—certainly not giving khutbahs and leading services in mosques and temples.

Following Fatima Mernissi and Leila Ahmed, Mohammed suggests the wealthy and self-sufficient Khadijah, eldest first wife of the Prophet Muhammad, as a model and symbol for Indo-Caribbean Muslim women.[40] That idea has yet to gain traction in Caribbean literature or criticism. Another option is that of Aisha, Muhammad's youngest and most erudite wife, and daughter of the first Muslim Caliph Abu Baker. Both women are considered by some Muslims to have modeled ideal feminine behavior. Aisha, whose personality is depicted in the *hadīth* as a loving contrarian, rigorous scholar, and advocate for women's education, is perhaps the more well-rounded choice than Khadijah, who is noted for her business ability, her support of the Prophet, and for being the first convert to Islam. Aisha was also herself a warrior who led men in battle. Together, they and his other wives are referred to as Mothers of the Believers (*Ummahāt al-Muʾminīn*). There are some barriers, I suggest, to the ascendancy of either woman to symbolic Indo-Caribbean Muslim fullawoman. First, these historical women's stories are not integral to the Qur'an itself, as storied Sita is to the *Ramayana*. They are mentioned in the Qur'an, but most information on their lives comes from *hadīth* and *tafsīr* (Qur'anic exegesis). The Qur'an is not a cohesive single story or collection of emplotted narratives (neither are the sacred epics and texts of Hinduism). Second, the feminist Aisha is a favorite of Sunnis—but not of Shiʿa, who partly blame her for the religious schism that produced the two sects. Third, and most importantly, though they face various trials and Aisha has military prowess, neither Muslim woman's story contains the dominant elements of exile, loss, suffering, purity testing, and recuperation of gendered morality that are truly necessary for identification with the female Indo-Caribbean or Afro-Caribbean labor diasporas. Those traits are necessary for a Caribbean Muslim heroine or female role model, as it is a journeying and captivity-surviving New World ancestress who is required, not a woman whose life was honorable and modeled desirable community values. The Prophet Muhammad is, overall, depicted in Muslim tradition as an exemplary and peaceful husband who often sought the opinions of his wives. I do not believe it is necessary to search for (and force) a symbolic cultural heroine that fits every identity category of a community, particularly in the Indo-Caribbean milieu, where racialization as *Indian* has always superseded religious identification; but if it must happen, Aisha, in her ability to fight, her recorded concern for women's issues, and her repeated, educated questioning of her husband and his followers, is perhaps the better choice for the Muslim jahaji bahin and fullawoman.

In a postcolonial context that privileges racial concerns over gender, Indo-Caribbean women's specific issues and the recovery of the jahaji bahin has been a neglected priority for Caribbean scholars, as argued by Caribbean feminists. Beginning with the work of Rawwida Baksh (Soodeen), Nesha Haniff, Mohammed, Reddock, and others, and culminating recently in Gabrielle Hosein and Lisa Outar's groundbreaking edited collection *Indo-Caribbean Feminist Thought: Genealogies, Theories, Enactments* (2016), feminist scholars of the Indo-Caribbean have shown that in Trinidad and Guyana, the bodies of Indo-Caribbean women function as the loci and repositories of Indianness, contra Africanness, in both colonial and postcolonial national rhetoric. Postcolonial pan-Caribbean feminism itself both privileges Afro-Caribbean female subjectivity and creates a space in which Indo-Caribbean feminism can emerge. But the early tendency of the discourse was to assume an umbrella set of Caribbean women's concerns that is dominated by the majority Afro-Caribbean experience and that "imposed certain themes, objectives and discursive spaces that Indo-Caribbean women found too confining, repressive, and culturally inappropriate."[41] Implied and overt claims that Afro-Caribbeans have greater Caribbean "authenticity" and privilege are often rooted in statements of greater comparative racial suffering, as I have described—a narrative that extends to the experiences of women.[42] Systemic historical analyses of Indian women's experiences on Caribbean plantations do exist, in the work of Bahadur, Gayatri Gopinath, Madhavi Kale, Mehta, Mohammed, Hugh Tinker, and a few others. There are not many *scholars* who argue that Indian indentured women suffered en masse under the same abusive sexual and labor conditions as enslaved African women. Indo-Caribbean and Indian feminist critics typically take an approach that emphasizes both commonalities and differences. Mehta points out that "African and Indian women in the Caribbean share a common history of geographical and cultural displacement, forced labour, economic enterprise, resistance and familial dispersal."[43] It is usually politicians who advance the narrative that the experiences were either the same or completely different. Such statements are symptomatic of the type of impassioned and educated racism that has negatively impacted postcolonial nation-building in Guyana and Trinidad. The depth to which racialized arguments can extend—comparing, for example, how many African women were raped versus how many Indian women were raped, even in the context of the transport of millions more African women than Indian women to the Caribbean—has foreclosed open debate over national presents and futures in favor of painful pasts.

From the beginning of Indian indentureship, Indian women and African women were pitted against each other in articulating the ideal models of the colonial woman and the postcolonial woman-to-be. In some discourses, the idealized colonial woman was the docile Indian, whereas the postcolonial ideal was the liberated African woman. In British colonial literature, the focus remained on white men who, against their wills, fell victim to the wiles of Indian women. Such literature is exemplified by the early twentieth-century British Guianese colonial romances of Edgar Mittelholzer, who was of mixed European and African heritage himself. During Indian indentureship in the nineteenth century, British Orientalists like Charles Kingsley, surveying the pulchritude of their feminine colonial subjects, contrasted the masculine, "superabundant animal vigour and the perfect independence of the younger [African] women" to "the young Indian woman 'hung all over with bangles, in a white muslin petticoat . . . and gauze green veil; a clever, smiling, delicate little woman, who is quite aware of the brightness of her own eyes.'"[44] British colonial literature found the Indian woman to be less doomed and more dangerously seductive even in her docility. "Loose" Indian women on the plantation were and are accorded a different sort of negative valorization in comparison with Afro-Caribbean women: "as the very antithesis of African female resilience and self-sufficiency," they "have been confined to inhibiting paradigms of docility, passivity and subservience" and located "solely within the limitations of victimhood and subjugation."[45] In the Caribbean, the postslavery feminine contrast to the "delicate" Indian indentured woman was "the African woman, the ex-slave, the *jamette* of Carnival whose sexuality was othered, and sought to be regulated, by the European ruling class" and later by the emerging middle class.[46]

The frightening independence of the *jamette* and the anarchic possibilities of Carnival called for the imagining of the Indian woman as the Afro-Caribbean woman's docile opposite: to (re)create this paragon of domesticity, "'Indian tradition' was invoked by different groups, and the lack of conformity of indentured women to the virtuous ideal of Indian culture was deplored."[47] After the first few years of indentured immigration, Muslim, Hindu, and later Christian Indian women's sexual freedoms were quashed by a "nationalism created by the jahaji bhai bonds of fraternity on the ships of indenture and Hinducentric ideals of femininity."[48] Both the general social push for creolization and the Indo-Caribbean community insistence on unbroken Indian-Caribbean lineages trade on women as agents without agency. Neither social movement acknowledges that Indo-Caribbean women may in fact be capable of retaining a desired cultural discreteness and living as full citizens of a multiethnic nation. Invoking the jahaji bahin past, rather than hiding it to perform a dislocated subcontinental Indian normativity in the manner of jahaji bhai nationalist narratives, opens up a space for an ongoing Indo-Caribbean feminist becoming.

Within the genre of Indo-Caribbean writing that focuses on the domestic and social sphere, there is an emerging canon of "women's narratives," written mostly by Indo-Caribbean women themselves, but also by male writers like Rooplall Monar, that act as supplements to the nation-centric model of the Indo-Caribbean novel. As scholars and writers including Joy Mahabir, Mohammed, Peggy Mohan, and Mariam Pirbhai show, such women's narratives call implicitly for a jahaji bahin gender politics commensurate with the heterosexual jahaji bhai migrant story that functions, Sean Lokaisingh-Meighoo argues, as the originary Indo-Caribbean familial relationship, and thus as a totalizing historical narrative of all Indo-Caribbean people.[49] Indo-Caribbean women writers like Espinet and Shani Mootoo were last on the literary scene, behind Caribbean men and then Afro-Caribbean women. With the notable exception of Guyanese Rajkumari Singh, who was active as a poet and playwright from the 1940s to the 1970s, most did not begin writing until late in the twentieth century.[50] Mehta argued in 2004 that it is therefore "impossible to speak either of an identifiable genre or of a canon of Indo-Caribbean women's writing: these writers are still fighting for a legitimate place and authority within the larger domain of anglophone Caribbean literature."[51] This is no longer true. Shah's *A Silent Life*, as I will discuss, is characteristic of women's literature written primarily by Indo-Guyanese and Indo-Trinidadian women at home and abroad, that challenges traditional androcentric, exilic models of the Indo-Caribbean novel promulgated by writers like V. S. Naipaul, Samuel Selvon, and David Dabydeen. Narratives that instead center the lives and experiences of Indo-Caribbean women include fiction from the 1970s onward by Trinidadian writers like Espinet, Lelawattee Manoo-Rahming, Mootoo, and Lakshmi Persaud, and Guyanese Ryhaan Shah and Narmala Shewcharan; plays by Guyanese Paloma Mohamed; and poetry by Trinidadians Vahni Capildeo, Rajandaye Ramkissoon-Chen, and Shivanee Ramlochan, and Guyanese Mahadai Das, Lakshmi Kallicharran, and Rajkumari Singh.

The postcolonial Indo-Caribbean novel modeled by male writers like V. S. Naipaul—so influential and foundational is the only Indo-Caribbean Nobel Prize in Literature winner that he cannot be escaped or ignored—responds to twentieth-century Caribbean national struggles with the despair of the embittered man who is either emasculated and isolated at home (as typified by Naipaul's *A House for Mr. Biswas*, 1961), or dislocated in permanent geographic exile in the cosmopolitan colonial center (as exemplified by nearly all of Naipaul's works except his earliest, most humorous writings, such as the collection *Miguel Street*, 1951). The exile is emotionally and physically separated from his natal family, rarely returns to his homeland, and he and the novel offer little hope for an uncorrupt Caribbean political future. There is often an implied disavowal of the Indian indentured ancestor by his nominally civilized, urban Indo-Caribbean descendant, and "country coolies" are typically portrayed as still living in the ignorance and poverty of the village or plantation. By contrast, narratives that revolve around the lives of Muslim and Hindu Indo-Caribbean women center the past in a familial, gendered way: women protagonists tend to remain embedded in their families regardless of whether they live or travel abroad, and women's stories almost always contend with the figure of the migrant ancestress and the intersection of her perceived sexual morality with Indo-Caribbean community (re)formation. Indo-Caribbean women's writing has always had a more migrational, transnational focus than men's writing: the "women's stories" tend less to feature permanent exile and more to explore the possibilities of crossing back and forth between psychic and physical locations.[52] Even after colonialism, Indo-Caribbean women experience a continuous reshaping of their history as it changes to accommodate shifting national myths of origin and community perseverance. The jahaji bahin was not always a sainted wife and mother like Sita or a (highly unlikely but romantically) down-and-out royal, but possibly a widow, maybe a bazaar dancer or prostitute rand, perhaps a runaway or victim of abuse—a woman on the moral margins of Indian society who nonetheless had her own agency.

PORK-EATING AND OTHER INFIDELITIES: ROOPLALL MONAR'S "MUSLIM" STORIES

Rooplall Monar's short stories, poems, and novel of preindependence Indo-Guianese life on plantations, villages, and "housing scheme" planned settlements—established by the Guiana government from the 1940s onward to house the former indentured and their descendants—tell the stories of that community in their own Guyanese "Creolese" language, through their own situational humor and Caribbean wordplay.[53] The world of Monar's short stories is insular, but as Shona Jackson proposes, in their isolation his rural Indo-Guianese characters define a "black water," "*kala pani* modernity," a nonsubaltern, anticapitalist, aesthetic "mode of Indian indigenization through both labor and cultural creolization that does *not* necessarily have to be ethno-teleological."[54] Even while it "chronicles both the labor experience of indentured workers and their eventual transition off the sugar plantations and into village communities"—in other words, the trajectory of Creole modernity—Monar's work displays a unique Indo-Caribbean working class aesthetic that is characterized by Creole language usage, but that nonetheless turns away from nationalism and the postcolonial ideal of state creolization.[55]

Monar is a poet, short story writer, and novelist who often sets his work in the first and second generation after indenture (i.e., the 1920s to the early 1960s) on Indo-Guianese sugar estates like Lusignan, where he was born in 1945, or in Annandale, the rural, majority-Indian housing scheme where he was raised. He is most well-known for his story collection *Backdam People* (1985), which describes the lives of Indo-Guyanese residents of Annandale. His many other works include the poetry collections *Meanings* (1972), *Patterns* (1983), and *Koker* (1987); the short story collections *Estate People* (1994) and *High House and Radio* (1991); and the novel *Janjhat* (2003). *Backdam People* and *Koker* earned him the Judges' Award in the 1987 Guyana Prize for Literature competition. Monar's work usually features Hindu protagonists. The four stories I will briefly consider here, however, constitute the majority of his realist attempts at depicting the lives of rural Indo-Guianese Muslims. With the exception of "Hakim Driver" (*Backdam People*, 1985), which describes a central Muslim figure and his pretensions to religious leadership and power on an unnamed sugar estate, the stories—"Pork Eater" (*Bim* and *Kyk-Over-Al* magazines, 1990), and "Infidel" and "Big People Story" (*High House and Radio*, 1991)—all revolve around Muslim conflict with Hindus in the period after indenture but before Guyanese independence in 1966. There is little direct engagement with Afro-Guianese, as the characters live in mostly Indian-only areas.

Monar's short stories often revolve around relationships between men and women, and Jackson argues that in them "patriarchy . . . lingers in the fact that women in the stories still reproduce culture in the economy of gendered signs."[56] While it is true that women in the stories do not *overcome* Indo-Caribbean patriarchy, I argue here that Monar critiques it, and that the reproduction of gendered signs sets up a quotidian that is thoroughly undermined by humor. As Frank Birbalsingh notes, Monar's tone is comic.[57] Monar's stories are deeply, subversively funny and clever, but they require a good working knowledge of Guyanese Creolese language, proverbs, and racial, religious, and class stereotypes to fully enjoy. The stories trade upon the assumption that the reader knows the archetypes, the "people like these," as well as their classic conflicts—in this case, the biblical brotherly yet murderous rivalries between Hindus and Muslims in Guiana, informed by their reluctant understanding that they are far more similar to each other than they are to anyone else (i.e., Afro-Guianese). But the nascent Indo-Guianese, who were to become over half of the Guyanese population, cannot remain isolated in a postcolonial nation whose epithet is "Land of Six Peoples" but whose slogan is "One People, One Nation, One Destiny." In the end, I show, it is the young fullawomen of Monar's stories who provoke and drag their communities into the uncomfortably creolized national future—contra their appointed role as jahaji bahin preservers of Indian culture.

In his study of the Indo-Caribbean short story, which he defines in its simplest form as "short fiction either by Indo-Caribbean authors or about Indo-Caribbean experience," the Guyanese critic and pioneering scholar of the Indo-Caribbean Birbalsingh argues for four stages of its development.[58] The first stage includes observational, sometimes thinly fictionalized writing by late nineteenth-century British visitors and Canadian missionaries, as well as early Creole writers like A.R.F. Webber from Trinidad and Tobago. Birbalsingh critiques these missives as promulgating stereotypes of Indians as laboring brutes, "a slightly strange minority not yet fully integrated into creole culture and society."[59] The second stage of the Indo-Caribbean short story is Indians' own mid-twentieth-century writing, which Birbalsingh characterizes as "occasional, amateurish, generally of slender quality," until the writing of *The Adventures of Gurudeva and Other Stories* (1943) by Seeparsad Naipaul, father of V. S. Naipaul.[60] Seeparsad Naipaul's collection frames Indians as isolated Hindu peasants whose customs are nonetheless being slowly infiltrated by urbanized black Christianity.[61] The third short story stage encompasses the 1970s, 1980s, and mass migration of writers to Britain and North America, with their nostalgic, exilic preoccupations.[62] Birbalsingh allocates Monar's work to this stage of short story development because Monar is chronologically a writer of the 1970s onward, but I believe Monar's work more accurately straddles this and the earlier second stage that focuses on rural locations and customs. Monar always invokes the past of his childhood, and his concerns are local and heavily intra-Caribbean—he does not write of exile. In the fourth stage of Indo-Caribbean literary short story development Birbalsingh includes writing by Mootoo and other diasporic scions of the Caribbean who were born outside of it or emigrated as children. This generation's work "is notable for characters who are alienated by differences of skin color and culture" from whites,

Afro-Caribbeans, and Indian immigrants from India in their new homelands.[63] By contrast, Monar's concerns remain nondiasporic, and he does not stray from extensive use of colloquial Creolese: his audience is Guyanese.

Monar's stories are linear, written in the third person, and relatively brief. "Hakim Driver" explores the trials and tribulations of the corrupt Hakim, estate driver (cane-cutting gang boss, a privileged position) and son of the first *majee* (imam) on an unnamed Guianese estate. After the Muslims pool their money to build a mosque on the estate, they ask permission of "Big Manager," the estate manager, to make Hakim's *baap* (father) imam, as "he could read the Koran in Arabic, and he could officiate at Muslim ceremony, which he been learn from an old Mussulman who come from India to wuk in canefield."[64] This backstory reveals that not all the Indian workers on the estate are the first generation of indentured laborers, but their preindependence children and grandchildren who are not indentured but who are nonetheless generationally employed for meager wages in cane-cutting occupations on sugar plantations. The workers must still ask the white estate manager for permission to build the mosque and appoint their religious leader. In the story, religious knowledge among Muslims on the estate is partly passed down through word of mouth by nonliterate people, fullaman-style, rather than by formal independent or apprentice study of the Qur'an and religious tradition. The most common way that Muslims in Guyana read the Qur'an in Arabic is by sounding the syllables without knowing the meaning of the words. In the colonial era, indentured Muslims either spoke the same languages of their Hindu brethren, or Urdu, then a register of Hindustani. A few indentured Afghan Pathans may have spoken Pashto and related languages. As John Rickford and other Guyanese linguists have pointed out, Indians likely first acquired Creole English—Creolese—from Afro-Guyanese on and around sugar estates, rather than from the white British. This Creolese existed alongside but eventually superseded Guyanese Bhojpuri, called Hindi or Hindustani, a koine of related Bihari and Hindi dialects, including Urdu.[65] The imam in the story and in the historical Indo-Caribbean is the man who knows the most about Islam, and authenticity, at least in the early days, was conferred by degree of direct lineage and ancestral connection to Muslim India (see figs. 2.2 and 2.3, on the importance of imam lineage in my own Indo-Guyanese family).

In Monar's "Hakim Driver," as soon as Hakim's baap becomes a full-time imam, "slow-slow Hakim baap and them backra [white] man come thick-thick like konky," and he becomes their intermediary when they have grievances with the manager over their labor conditions.[66] "Konky," usually rendered "conkie," is a very dense, pudding-like Guyanese dish consisting of pumpkin, cornmeal, lard, coconut, sugar, and other seasoning ingredients wrapped and boiled together in a banana leaf. Conkie is also considered a food with African roots and is associated with Emancipation Day celebrations—showing that the Indo-Guyanese laborers may already be familiar with non-Indian foods and with the proverbs of Cre-

FIGURE 2.2 Hajj passport photo ca. 1958 of Imam Meer Abdur Rahman, imam of the Queenstown Jama Masjid in British Guiana. His family from Lucknow, India, settled first in Jamaica, then migrated to Guiana. Author's great-grandfather. (Author's family archives.)

olese. Any comparison to conkie also invokes the Guyanese saying "Me and you conkie can't boil"—we can't get along. This raises the question of whether Hakim's baap and Big Manager really are "thick-thick like konky." When people come to him with work conditions and pay grievances, Hakim's baap's advice is, "Don't invoke the wrath of the All Merciful Allah. . . . Get more faith, and Allah shall grant

FIGURE 2.3 Imam Mohamed Rasheed with his pupils at the Windsor Forest, Demerara, Islamic madrassa in British Guiana, January 1960. Son of Imam Meer Abdur Rahman. Author's grandfather. (Author's family archives.)

you your reward, me brother."[67] When the situation is especially dire, Hakim's baap talks like he "possess with Allah spirit while he quoting one-two Koranic injunction," and he "does kneel down and pray in the mosque to show them men he really concern bout them welfare."[68] The people then kiss his finger and leave. The token ritual performance of Islam is enough for him to retain his position as community leader even though he is actually terrified of Big Manager and never mentions the people's concerns. He fears that "if he come too disgusting, Big Manager might want send he back to backdam which he frighten more than jail," and he would have to "quit the logie" ("disgusting" means "bothersome" in Creolese).[69] Hakim's baap, allegedly thick like konky with Big Manager, is still afraid of the overseer. It is not that he does not want to help his people; he is instead most concerned with saving himself from backbreaking cane-cutting labor and not losing his *logie* barracks quarters on the estate. The fullaman people, respectful of learning that they do not have, are pacified with "one-two Koranic injunction," witnessed prayer, and empty assurances that Allah will provide. Hakim's baap betrays them; on the sugar estate, Monar suggests, it is every man for himself. And so, the generational corruption of religious hypocrisy, of some Muslim leaders preying on Muslims, begins.

When Hakim's baap dies, Hakim, who refuses to follow in his baap's footsteps as imam but still accepts the privileged position of driver, associate of Big Manager, and fixer for the estate workers, also becomes the most prolific adulterer on the estate, exchanging work favors for sexual ones. When men become ill from over-work, he finds them the medicine—if their wives have sex with him. When women want to save their daughters from manual plantation labor and get them jobs cooking or cleaning instead, the women have sex with him. Women's value on the estate is measured only in the labor, sexual or otherwise, that they can per-form, and their bodies are the only commodities they possess. One Muslim man, Khan, "sickly through backdam wuk and too much rum drinking," knows and accepts that his wife is exchanging sexual favors for his medicine.[70] But the story ends when another man known only as "Jamela daddy" (like "Hakim baap" privi-leging in his identity the fact that he has fathered a child) catches Hakim with his wife and "prappa chop cross he belly," wounding Hakim and causing him to lose his virility.[71] In losing his vigor, however, Hakim finds his virtue: "No matter how much praying he doing, still he private weak. Hakim feel is God punishment. Then to them people surprise Hakim come majee just after one year. After that he come one very good man, and people say he always doing fasting and praying."[72]

The story's narrator directly addresses the reader as "pardna" (partner) through-out, emphasizing the conversational nature of the dialogue, and the story's position as a morality tale. Creolese, after all, is spoken, not usually written. Birbalsingh writes that originary orality and an "anecdotal, episodic structure" that reflects that orality are also features of the Indo-Caribbean short story.[73] Like Afro-Caribbean Anansi tales, the Indo-Caribbean has its own trickster tradition in the form of the oral folktales of a seemingly simple yet devious boy named Sakchu-lee and other usually human "trickster figures who start off as underdogs but, through deviousness or ingenuity, outmaneuver their rivals in the end."[74] Hakim outsmarts everyone temporarily, but gets his comeuppance. In Sakchulee tales, everyone gets their just desserts. Birbalsingh suggests that Indo-Caribbean short stories may also function as morality plays in "the homiletic tradition of Indian puranas—stories from Hindu mythology—which inculcate practical, moral les-sons in accounts of gods or divine figures intervening in human affairs."[75] The deep intertwining of Hindu and Muslim Indo-Caribbean experiences—and families—allows for such a connection in literature by and about Muslims.

That Hakim gets chopped for adultery, effectively loses his "manhood," and becomes an imam to atone for his sins—though one wonders who exactly he is "fasting and praying" for—is highly ironic, even funny. "Humor," says Birbalsingh, "is probably the most striking feature of the Indo-Caribbean short story."[76] Birbals-ingh is critical of the lack of "moral earnestness, depth and exhaustiveness" of Monar's writing as compared to that of other writers, partly because "Monar's pre-sentation is altogether less stark, softened principally by humor and a lightness of touch that makes for a bitter-sweet tone of reluctant, if not complicit, accep-tance," and because his amoral, quarrelsome, and violent characters sometimes "collaborate in their own victimization" and the victimization of their own communities.[77] Nonetheless, "the unethical behavior of Monar's characters [is] relieved by our awareness of their victimization and a prevailing comic tone."[78] I am less convinced that works that appear light and comic and feature characters lacking "moral earnestness" also lack seriousness. What is implied here is that it may be the obligation of a writer—particularly a postcolonial writer or a writer of color—to present an ideal view of his or her community if the community lacks representation in literature. As I will show in subsequent chapters, David Daby-deen, V. S. Naipaul, and Jan Lowe Shinebourne demonstrate that no writer is so obliged. Monar's work, I suggest, reproduces humorous Indo-Caribbean arche-types of the sort that one finds in Naipaul's early comic works like *The Mystic Masseur* (1957) and *Miguel Street* (1959): the mimic of "Indian" culture, the incompe-tent bumbler, the greedy religious hypocrite, the racist, the violent patriarch, the wayward daughter, the pathetically long-suffering wife. These characters are famil-iar and persist in general Caribbean and Indo-Caribbean literature because they evoke real types of people and ways of life in the Caribbean. Crucial to the par-ticular brand of often dark and ironic Indo-Guyanese humor is the way in which language is employed.

Monar, as demonstrated in "Hakim Driver," is a master at using Guyanese Anglophone Creolese in his work; his short stories are almost entirely written in it. Jackson points out that Monar's use of Creolese is both an instance of Barba-dian poet Edward Kamau Brathwaite's "nation language" and "a commitment to depicting in that language the material, cultural, and spiritual realities of Indo-Caribbean peoples."[79] Brathwaite's exhortation for Caribbean writers to write Afro-Caribbean "nation language" also applies to the Indo-Caribbean, whose cre-ole language *is* Afro-Caribbean, with some additions. Brathwaite defines nation language in contrast to dialect. Nation language is derived from the oppressed cul-tures and sensibilities of the people, and from their oral tradition.[80] Dialect, by contrast, is a linguistic form that is "pejorative," associated with "bad English," "from the plantation," and, most damningly, "Caricature speaks in dialect."[81] Rick-ford argues that Creolese—the proper name of Guyana's Anglophone Creole—exists as a "creole-standard continuum," rather than a dialect or a Creole distinct from a standard form.[82] As such, Creolese fits Brathwaite's conditions for a "nation language." Monar's Indo-Guyanese speakers tend most to speak in what Rickford and others identify as the Creolese basilect, the Creole language forms usually associated with rural speakers, as distinct from the mesolect, the common medial form spoken by primarily urban Georgetown residents, and the acrolect, the Stan-dard (British) English learned in schools. The landscape of the Creolese contin-uum, though, is thick with speakers' own disavowals of their modes of speaking. There are various ways in which Guyanese define their own Creolese English as "bad English": saying that one "talks Broken" (with "Broken" used variously as a noun, dialect name, and adjective) is perhaps the most self-deprecating of them. The irony is that the tongue is least broken and most facile when speaking in one's native idiom. Rickford points out that what native speakers mean when they say "Creolese" is often narrower than what linguists mean. For example, "Georgetown speakers sometimes decry the use of 'Creolese' while themselves using mesolectal forms; when this apparent contradiction is pointed out, it becomes evident that they consider their mesolectal forms a variant of 'English,' and by 'Creolese' intend the basilectal forms."[83] Language politics linked to class aspirations matters. One indicator in Monar's work that his Indo-Guianese speakers' language is basilectal is that they do not really code-switch between forms, even when speaking to Big Manager and others not from their community. They have not been placed in (usually educational) contexts that force them to learn how to switch between their native basilects, mesolect, and acrolect.

Monar's nation language writing is humorous and his characters often venal, but he does not mock them; he uses humor to critique the material conditions and cultural conflicts that created them. In "Big People Story" he relays the angst of greedy little (Hindu) boys who sneak into a Muslim wedding specifically to eat mutton curry, an exercise for which they have been training for days by drinking castor oil to purge their stomachs, and of which their vegetarian Hindu parents would highly disapprove. Their scheme is thwarted by the mean men in charge of serving the food. Still, it would be unthinkable to not feed a guest at a "wedding house," so they are served—in a terribly miserly way. Their disappointment is bitter. Rendered in Creolese, "Is then them worms does crawl in we belly, and we teeth does turn sharp to attack the mutton curry. But we face does come like dull flower in nightfall soon as Taj and Noor throw one spoonful mutton curry on we plate. Is sheer mutton bone. Not one piece of mutton flesh self. And the bone does sound clatang in we plate. Eh-eh! Talk about vexness? It does show in we face while we cursing down Taj and Noor in we mind, eating the roti for sheer spite because we can't get the meat."[84] The sheer outrage of the hungry boys at this injustice is palpable and visceral in the Creolese descriptions of "belly-worms," "dull flower" faces, resentful roti-eating and clattering meatless bones. Their "vexness" is also humorous because they are not really hungry; they are little boys sneaking into a wedding reception to eat their fill of forbidden mutton. The local idiomatic and Creolese attention to vivid onomatopoeia (clatang!) allow them to emphasize the youthful joy of crashing the Indian wedding-house, where "Is food to burn and dance to kill."[85] The story's narrator, one of the boys, tells the tale just as everyone in it speaks. Rickford says that Guyana exhibits the worldwide "stereotypical association of creole with humor and gossip—as if this were all that nonstandard varieties were good for."[86] Creolese, he argues, is used in literature and newspapers mostly for dialogue.[87] Brathwaite and younger poets like the Guyanese American Rajiv Mohabir use their Creolese extensively in their poetry, but Rickford's assertion is still mostly true of fiction, though writers like Monar and Mootoo have attempted narratives that are written entirely in Creole. Monar's stories, though, read as oral tales entirely in dialogue; his speakers directly address readers and draw them in with jokery. Roger Abrahams draws a masculine Caribbean distinction between the Creole oral humor of the "broad talker," a man who takes license with the basilect to satirize the everyday, "bringing the vernacular creole into stylized use, in the form of wit, repartee, and directed slander," and the "sweet talker," who demonstrates "abilities in Standard English, but strictly on the elaborate oratorical level."[88] Implied is that the Anglophone Caribbean greatly values witty talk, but in different registers at different times. The young wedding-house boys are basilectal sweet talkers-in-training, hilariously "cursing down" the miserly food servers and the culinary slim pickings.

The reason the boys receive mere bones to eat, though, is less funny. The miserly Taj and Noor, it seems, are "kingpin feedman at most Muslim wedding house in the Scheme and they going Masjid every nightfall, wearing white cap and white kurta, greeting people with *Assalam wali kum*, looking as if they just talk with Allah. Is why this hate in Taj and Noor eye at we Hindu small boy when them men does talk to they Muslim God, when Hindu people and Muslim people living nice-nice? Is why?"[89] The "kingpin feedmen's" stinginess is juxtaposed with their ostentatious religious performance, and here Monar uses Creolese to paint a portrait of simmering conflicts between Muslim and Hindu Indo-Guyanese. The boys find out that the real "big people story," the adult story, is an unfunny one of religion and politics and sex. The Muslim kingpin feedmen Taj and Noor, who are brothers, treat the Hindu boys stingily—"scravenly" in Creolese—because their sister Bibi ran away with a Hindu named Ram. "Me neva trust one Hinduman ever since them kill them Muslim people in India," Noor says, roaming the street at night with a cutlass looking for Ram, and "India belong to Muslim people. Not to Hindu people."[90] Though they leave India before the Partition of India, (West) Pakistan, and Bangladesh (East Pakistan), Indians in the Caribbean hear of it; and though their information about Partition is incomplete, the news fuels antagonism between Hindus and Muslims. In Guyana, however, that antagonism was mostly limited to verbal vitriol and insults. Chickrie and Khanam argue that even though Partition "ushered in a new era of Muslim awareness" in the Caribbean, "Guyana's history does not reflect Hindu-Muslim communalism."[91] Hindus and Muslims intermarried during indenture and continue to do so, the retention of a cohesive Indian racial identity being in the end more important than religious differences. It is also, of course, darkly funny for Noor to claim that India belongs to Muslims and not Hindus, given the divisions of Partition and contemporary *Hindutva* Indian politics, and to imagine him powerlessly roaming the street waving a cutlass.

When interreligious Indian antagonism does arise, as shown, it is often precipitated by parental disapproval of romantic relationships between their offspring. Women shoulder the heavier burden of shame, recrimination, and violence. The plots of Monar's "Pork Eater" and "Infidel" are very similar to each other: both stories feature a single Indo-Muslim family that includes an irate and repressive

Muslim father; his oppressed wife, whom he frequently beats; and a daughter who is chafing at her lack of freedom, characterized by her forbidden love for a Hindu boy. Both fathers try and fail, even with violence, to stop their daughters from fulfilling their romantic desires. In "Pork Eater," a Muslim man known only as (another) "Jamila's father" feels himself on the verge of ultimate shame when he finds out a Hindu boy nicknamed "Crabbe" is pursuing Jamila. The girl is beaten by her father, the boy is beaten by his father, she is sent away to family in a neighboring village, and the boy ultimately realizes he can still visit her there. In "Infidel," Alim (his name, as noted in the first chapter, ironically means a Muslim "learned man") is faced with the prospect of his school-aged daughter Naimoon's budding sexuality. He beats her, he beats his wife Bibi to whom he had been married when he was eighteen and she fourteen, he tries to pull the daughter out of school and find a Muslim boy for her to marry, and he still fails to stop the girl from eloping with a Hindu boy named Sharma. As on the plantation, and perhaps as a legacy of that indenture experience, violence against women and youths is endemic in these stories. The family patriarch has the power to do what he wills to any member of his family, and to any male threatening his power. Women are the enemy of family and community cohesion even while they produce it: in "Infidel," "mother and daughter like enemy in front Alim."[92] For her part, his wife Bibi thinks "Man is a terrible people, she been tell she self."[93] Though there is no reference to the doctrine in Monar's work, it must also be noted here that some Muslims believe the Qur'an permits a type of token "moderate," chastising wife-beating, as per various *hadīth* and two Qur'anic verses, the precise meanings and translations of which are highly debated and interpreted in a multitude of regional and sectarian ways in *fiqh* jurisprudence.[94] But domestic violence is an endemic problem in the entire Indo-Caribbean and indeed, the entire Caribbean, with its legacies of slavery, indentureship, indigenous genocide, and the extreme violences of colonialism.

In Monar's stories, the madder and more violent a man becomes, the more of a Muslim fullaman the Hindu villagers believe him to be. The Hindu boy Crabbe is told in "Pork Eater," "You better keep away from Jamila daddy. That man have real Arab blood in he. And you know them Arab quick fo murder? Rememba the hackia stick?"[95] Crabbe's mother tells her husband, "You not see that fullahman mad! God shoulda never give he one daughta. And he have the hackia stick."[96] Jamila's daddy carries a hackia stick, the symbol of his fullaman violence that may erupt at any moment. The Hindu boy Crabbe is beaten by his own Hindu father, and there are plenty of beatings to go around in the story's entire Indo-Guyanese community. The specter of the Muslim fundamentalist, though, is already present, in the form of Hindus' lack of knowledge and fear of Islam, as well as the Indian Muslim association with "real [hot] Arab blood." None of them know any Arabs; Arabs are just simply, in the popular imagination, the most Muslim of all, and even in this rural Guianese place, reputedly violent. Jamila's father is also depicted as engaging in the stereotypical rhetoric of the violent extremist when he is reported as saying "me is true born mussulman. Me blood run straight to Mecca. And pork-eater is infidel, de lowest of all nation."[97] The use of the words "blood," "Mecca," "infidel," and the casual slur "pork-eater" for non-Muslims show that even while he refers to himself in the old Indian (and colonial British) way, as a "Mussulman" rather than a "Muslim," Jamila's father engages with the discourses of fear of contemporary global Islam. He fears the encroachment of postindependence creolization and religious syncretism on the already tenuous Islam of a barely literate Muslim minority, declaring: "Is since this country get Independence all this confusion come . . . is how you could be one people when this country have black-man, Chineseman, Putagee man, coolie man? Is the damn Independence thing, and the Christian bottom-house causing all this corruption. . . . Is important, me commonsense tell me, that you hold-on tight-tight on you religion if you want walk in the road with you head showing high high."[98] The thrust of both "Pork Eater" and "Infidel" is that "confusion" of customs will come, want it or not: The young Indo-Muslim girls of the new generation have agency, and cannot be controlled by their ignorant fathers in the coming postcolonial nation.

"Pork Eater" humorously details the way Jamila and her rebellious teenage female friends act with each other, with boys, and with their families. They refuse to cover their heads, go to a mosque, or greet their elders with the traditional *Assal-amu alaikum.* Instead, they dress up in high heels, lipstick, and Avon perfume, talk about men and gossip about other women, and declare, "Tink we uncivilize? This is different time. Hindu and Muslim is one people, and we have to tink ahead. Be in the style . . . we not living in India or Pakistan. We live in a modern country where people speaking English, you hear."[99] Being "in the style" is rather an amazing way to frame Hindu-Muslim unity. It is civilized modern style, commensurate with their dress and speech, they say, to ease religious tensions with an eye to intraracial unity. The suggestion that they are in a "different time" of Hindu-Muslim unity and a different place that is neither India nor Pakistan but "a modern country where people speaking English" is both true and an excuse to do whatever they want, and so, the speaker implicitly mocks the girls. Though they say they are speaking English, "This time, them girls can't spell A to bullfoot properly, but whenever they talking to strangers, winking-winking they eye, you going to believe all to God they been to College. True! The English word in they mouth more crispy than salt biscuit: 'I has a beautiful dress. You looks good.'"[100] The girls are, in short, teenagers, but they take public liberties, talking and dressing in a way that their mothers do not. They take themselves very seriously, but as is typical with all pretentious persons in Monar's work, they are rather comic: they have pretensions to the Queen's English, and even though their verbal delivery is "more crispy than salt biscuit," they have not had much or any schooling, and muddle their acrolectal subject-verb agreements. "I has a beautiful dress" and "You looks good" are typical of the comedic wordplay offered by the Indo-Caribbean mimic man's imitative speech in V. S. Naipaul's work. Naipaul's *The Mystic Masseur* (1957) ends with the revelation that onetime schoolteacher-turned-mystic-turned-colonial statesman Ganesh Ramsumair (who, along with his fellow Trinidadian country Indians, fetishizes literacy and initially measures the import of books by the inches of space they occupy), has renamed himself "G. Ramsey Muir," Trinidad Parliamentarian.[101] Jamila and her friends are different from Ganesh Ramsumair; they are young, and they are female. Control of their bodies, sexuality, and marriages is linked to the future of the Indo-Guianese racial community, and to the individual futures of Muslim and Hindu religious communities. For the original indentured laborers, life in plantation logies made marital privacy impossible, and in this context, the public-private performance of marriage was privileged over intimacy: men policed men and women policed women in the proper conducting of marital roles. After indenture, the Indian man's audience for the public performance of heteronormativity did not shift from his jahaji bhai: that male community simply grew larger, with Jamila's daddy, Noor, and Hakim baap roaming the estates and housing schemes looking for a target and an audience. Somehow, in this milieu, the rand had to become a wife again. The redemption of the Indian woman from prostitute and widow to Indo-Caribbean wife and mother, whether Muslim or Hindu, was accomplished by erasing many of their origins, but Monar's stories show that becoming the Sita ideal was not the final act in Muslim or Hindu Indian women's becoming Caribbean.

A SILENT LIFE: KILLING MEN, SUICIDE, AND SILENCE

As in Monar's short stories, in Ryhaan Shah's novel *A Silent Life*, Indo-Guyanese women's social behavior is extrapolated to define the community internally and relationally on the political stage. Shah's novel, which won the 2007 Guyana Prize for Literature first book award, displaces the importance of jahaji bhai ties and legacy in favor of inventing and incorporating the jahaji bahin into the story of Indo-Caribbean, but emphasizes that the maternal ancestral legacy must be both recognized and resisted in the pursuit of contemporary Indo-Caribbean women's self-development. Unlike Monar's stories, Shah's novel is cosmopolitan; set in Guyana and in London in the second half of the twentieth century, it exhibits the characteristic Caribbean literary engagement with London or North American exile, as established by an earlier generation of male novelists, including George Lamming, Naipaul, and Samuel Selvon, as well as Afro-Caribbean women writers, such as Jamaica Kincaid and Paule Marshall.

A Silent Life follows the life of Muslim protagonist Aleyah Hassan, who leaves British Guiana as a young adult on the eve of independence in 1966 to study in London; she is a "modern" postcolonial fullawoman-to-be. She stays and marries a well-off Indo-Guyanese man in England, but she is continually haunted by the life and secrets of her grandmother Nani ("maternal grandmother"), to whom she had been very close as a child. These hauntings occur in a series of temporally disrupted, nonlinear dreams and interludes of "madness," in which the life histories of Aleyah's maternal ancestresses intrude into her heteronormative life. She begins to chafe at her own matrimonial bonds and oppressive husband, and eventually experiences a stereotypically hysterical feminine nervous breakdown. The breakdown causes her to divorce her husband and leave her children to return to Guyana in the 1990s, when the nation too is experiencing a time of political turmoil and transition: in 1992, after twenty-eight years of rule amidst allegations of fraudulent voting and rigged elections, the Afro-Guyanese-dominated People's National Congress lost the national election to the Indo-Guyanese-majority People's Progressive Party. Upon Aleyah's return to Guyana, her grandmother Nani divulges the secrets of her own and her female indentured ancestress's lives, then dies. The structuring, familial "violent secret" of Shah's novel A Silent Life is that the Indo-Guyanese woman Nani, by dint of her anticolonial labor organizing and participation in public life, caused not simply the death, but the suicide of her husband, cursing her female descendants to a life of gendered unhappiness.

Marriage is of primary importance in A Silent Life. Aleyah's entire female lineage is haunted by her grandmother Nani's inability to be a community-approved "proper wife," and Aleyah herself, in leaving her emotionally abusive husband, acquires the same stigma. But A Silent Life is not a Caribbean story that simply memorializes community suffering; instead, the novel suggests, among other feminisms, that Indo-Caribbean women's historical plantation labor activism is a precursor to their descendants' long-awaited political participation in and leadership of the postcolonial nation. I show, overall, that A Silent Life is a jahaji bahin—ship sister—narrative predicated on a rejection of Indo-Guyanese heterosexist morality and the concomitant remembrance of the Indian ancestress as she was: not the Ramayanic Sita ideal of sainted mother and submissive wife adopted by Indo-Caribbean migrants, but a labor leader, or a sex worker, or any number of other identities, including wife and mother.[102] I argue that there is a "generational skip" in the fullawoman jahaji bahin's ability to enter the public sphere: the indentured woman had much more freedom of movement, relationships, and sexuality, than did her daughter and even granddaughter who were charged with reforming the Indo-Caribbean domestic sphere and community through chaste and silent performance as wife and mother. It is only in the generation around independence—the 1960s and after—that Indo-Caribbean granddaughters and great-granddaughters like Aleyah begin to attempt to reenter the cultural and political public sphere. I also argue that through the telling of the women's jahaji bahin stories, A Silent Life attempts to move beyond static memorialization of a jahaji bhai Indo-Caribbean community. As Judith Mizrahi-Barak writes, though A Silent Life revolves around "the disjunction and conjunction of voice and silence" in the hidden history of the subaltern, the "reconstruction of self is also made possible through the written word of the text."[103] Shah's novel, in the tradition of Caribbean writers like Brathwaite, Audre Lorde, Walcott, and many others, is a historicizing text that tells the submerged, unwritten story of a community created by colonialism, violence, and displacement: characters in *A Silent Life* draw together orally recovered fragments to recount and therefore (re)create female ancestral Indo-Caribbean history as they imagine it happened, as it may well have happened—and the identification of a multiplicity of possible subaltern histories constitutes Caribbean truth and authenticity.

Indo-Caribbean women's novels, such as Shah's *A Silent Life*, Espinet's *The Swinging Bridge* (2003), Mootoo's *Cereus Blooms at Night* (1996) and *Valmiki's Daughter* (2009), and Persaud's *Raise the Lanterns High* (2004), episodically move back and forth in time and place among colonial, postcolonial, and even ancient locales. Shah's later novels *Weaving Water* (2013) and *A Death in the Family* (2014) also focus on Indo-Guyanese women's stories; the former engages with Hindu indentured women's marital and labor struggles aboard ship and on the plantation, and the latter returns to one minor theme in *A Silent Life*: the interweaving of Islam and Indo-Caribbean family identities in the present day.

Not much is known of the Indian indentured ancestress Gaitree (the Vedic Gayatri is the Brahmic consort and mother of all) in *A Silent Life*, with the exception of the fact that she had, against her will, committed the cardinal sin of motherhood: abandoning her children to save her own life. Still, for Aleyah, she is a worthy progenitor *because* she saved her own life. The legacy that Gaitree leaves to her female descendant is courage. But the courage always skips generations. Aleyah describes the first generation of her family born in British Guiana as a weeder and a cane-cutter on Plantation Leonora, West Coast Demerara, who had a hard life but accepted it with a sort of resignation that, rather than bravery, becomes the Indo-Caribbean inheritance. The history of the Hassan family is tied to Leonora, a traditional locus of female sugar worker resistance. As I have described elsewhere, Leonora was the site of the killings of female striker Sumintra in 1939, and Kowsilla, who became a martyr to the causes of Indo-Guianese sugar worker rights and national independence, in 1964.[104] Though their indentured Indian progenitors were initially sent to Plantation Versailles, the first female member of the Hassan family born in British Guiana ends up married, as a weeder and a cane-cutter, at Leonora; that woman is described as one who had a hard life but accepted it with a sort of resignation that, rather than bravery, becomes the Indo-Caribbean female inheritance. So Aleyah theorizes that her grandmother Nani got her spirit from the progenitors who actually made the ship journey, as "[t]hat would take spirit and daring—to stand at the stern of a sailing ship and watch the land of your ancestors disappear from view, possibly forever. It had to be their blood that made fists of their hands and placed the fight in her shoulders."[105] Once on the estates, the intrepid migrants revert and turn inward, raising their children to be quiet and keep their heads down. Aleyah describes her natal Indo-Guyanese township of Victorine in semirural West Demerara—the family has not moved very far from where they were indentured—as the kind of place where people "accept everything that comes their way with a minimum of fuss: births, deaths, newcomers, new laws, higher taxes. Everything is tacked on accommodated, absorbed. . . . All that happens is God's will and they thank the heavens for life and everything that goes with it."[106] This type of fatalism is a common Muslim and Indian stereotype, though Shah does not suggest directly that their behavior is a product of being Indian; rather, it is a product of wanting to survive. When the first indentureds and the first generation born in Guyana died, says Nani, "so they lived, and so they died, and the old world went with them."[107] But not really. In Indo-Caribbean literature, the old world always reasserts itself: as a veiled historical imaginary and an ever-present yearning for roots.

In *A Silent Life*, Gaitree's marriage to Calcutta Muslim Janki Khan takes place while the migrants wait for their ship to arrive at the Calcutta depot. The "bored" female migrants dress her up in their own clothing and jewelry and "danced around her as they took her out into the yard to present her to her husband. When Janki looked upon her, he saw a rich Hindu bride."[108] This dancing foreshadows *matikor*, the ribald, prewedding, women-only dance in which an Indo-Caribbean Hindu bride is "initiated" into sex by dint of highly suggestive songs and dancing by older women. Mohammed, following Kanhai, names matikor, in lieu of jahaji bahin, the trope that is "perhaps the most dominant and potentially useful one for defining an Indo-Caribbean femininity."[109] Matikor is certainly an early ritual performance of that femininity and sexuality, but jahaji bahin, I argue, casts a wider net, encompassing all Indo-Caribbean women, regardless of religion or marital status. The shipboard wedding is the first time Gaitree has ever experienced kindness from other Indian women: in her rural village, where she is *Chamar* (*Dalit* leather worker) and of lower caste than her husband, her typically ogreish mother-in-law is the chief agent of her misery, treating her as a slave, stealing Gaitree's sons' affections, and in the end attempting to poison Gaitree. At the depot, the loan of jewelry—wealth worn on the body—establishes the migrant women as Gaitree's replacement family, her *jahaji bahene* or "ship sisters." Matikor is supposed to be performed by older female relatives; Gaitree's *bahene* handily step in, and it matters to no one that she is not a virgin being initiated into Indian wifehood. Perhaps in awareness of their impending *kala pani* "loss" of caste to be triggered by the oceanic crossing, the women also do not comment on the radically interfaith nature of the marriage: Gaitree is a Hindu, Janki is a Muslim, and the ceremony is both: they circle the fire in a Hindu ritual to prayers by a Muslim *moulvi*, "married, Janki and Gaitree, in the eyes of both their gods, before Allah and before Bhagwan. No one questioned this. It was as if they had already taken up new ways as they sat at the water's edge and waited on their passage to a new world."[110] Their coupling afterward is idyllic: when Janki sees her stretch marks—bodily evidence of pregnancy—"he asked no questions, just kissed each one tenderly. When she made as if to talk, he put a finger to her lips and shushed her. All their whole married life together he never asked."[111] Interreligious marriage between Indian Hindus and Muslims was not uncommon in the colonial Caribbean, as previously noted; and when, as a result of a dearth of Muslim women, Muslim laborers married Hindu women, the Hindu women usually converted to Islam.[112] Janki, though, is a particularly forgiving man who asks no questions and makes no demands of Gaitree. In the New World, their personal histories and sins in the eyes of their natal communities do not matter, if they are not spoken aloud.

In 1930s British Guiana, Aleyah's grandmother Nani—Gaitree's granddaughter—is no domestic Sita. Though married, Nani is an outspoken young woman who acquires a reputation for helping poor Indian female and male sugar and rice workers by offering them the vision of organized labor. Nani acquires socialist principles from the mysterious Pandit Seecharan, a Hindu religious leader—even while fraternizing with Hindus is frowned upon for a Muslim woman. Nani is bright enough to understand workers' rights ideologies and fiery enough to electrify others when she repeats them. In her old age, she tells Aleyah that she wanted to help other women in more destitute positions and alludes to historical incidents in which "strikers were shot in the back," requiring revenge and restitution.[113] Nani's problem is that she literally upstages her husband Nazeer, a quiet man who is talented in the implied feminine pursuit of dancing. She speaks on stage at unionizing meetings and is far more articulate than he. Despite the presence of vocal women in Guianese labor movements, in Nani's village, labor organizing is "man's work. The managers dealt with men."[114] At her final workers' rally, Nani answers political questions her husband cannot; the crowd murmurs and laughs, and Nazeer walks away. He stays out, lying in a punt trench, until dawn, and his hair turns white overnight.[115] When he comes home, Nani—then called "Baby," a common feminine, affectionately infantilizing "call name" (nickname) for Indo-Guyanese women—is so panicked at the idea of losing her husband, her social net, and legitimacy as an Indian wife, that she apologizes repeatedly and cries, "Nazeer, Nazeer, I'm going to stop all this now. All the books and leaflets— look, I am tearing them up. They're dead. I'll burn them. I'll bury them. I'll be a wife to you and a mother to Shabhan, that's what I'll be from now on."[116] Burning books on colonialism burns history and burning the promises of socialist pamphlets burns the present of labor organizing and the future of postcolonial independence. Nazeer believes it is futile to disavow reality by destroying the words that signify it. Baby's invocations fail when Nazeer refuses her promises of change, saying: "If you ever stop-up your words they'll choke you. You aren't like the other women round here who just keep to their skirts and their kitchens. I like the fire in you, but I can't be who you want. You want to change the world. Me, I just want to enjoy it. You push me how you want to go and I try to speak your words and fight your fights. Now I'm 'Baby's boy.' That's what the men call me. That and worse. . . . Shame's gone deep to the roots."[117] Personal, gendered shame has gone literally to the roots of Nazeer's hair, which turns white with inadequacy;

but he also implies that all the ancestral roots of Indians in the Caribbean are besmirched by his wife's lack of submission to him. Her inability to be silent is a gendered flaw that prevents him from being a properly patriarchal jahaji bhai, defined as the head of household who speaks for all members of his family. Nazeer hangs up his dancing bells, takes to his room, and never emerges again. The social and marital damage has been done. Nani gives up her organizing work and goes as far as to remove Shabhan, Aleyah's mother, from school, declaring that books and learning cause unnecessary heartbreak for women. Nani's granddaughter Aleyah is in turn also bookish, causing two elderly female relatives to say to each other, "It's the books that worry me." "The words are heavy-heavy." "They carry the weight of the world." "And the weight can crush." "And kill."[118] That is what happened to Nani: her voice and learning, words spoken and written, crushed her husband and ultimately killed him. Women's nonadherence to traditional gender roles, and their mere *speaking up*, the novel suggests, actually causes men to die.

The violence of the Caribbean plantation was not confined to abuses of plantation managers against indentured workers and to men against women. One documented response to plantation working conditions was suicide, a theme that, as I will discuss, Shah takes up in her novel. Mohammed writes that the high male suicide rate was worrisome to colonial officials, who blamed it, again, on the immorality of women.[119] The indentureship legacy of suicide haunts Guyana to this day. The World Health Organization reported in 2012 that Guyana had the highest suicide rate in the world. In a nation of less than a million people, Guyana had an age-standardized suicide rate of 44.2 per 100,000 inhabitants.[120] This phenomenon has been poorly studied, but reports seem to indicate the population at highest risk is (still) rural Indo-Guyanese men.[121] Long before 2012, the alleged "coolie" people's tendency to kill themselves—usually over family rows or failed love—was a source of gallows humor in Guyana, where Indians were said to be always "drinking Malathion" (an insecticide), and in Trinidad, where they were always "drinking Gramazone" (Gramoxone, an herbicide). Both of these poisons are older agricultural pesticides to which estate laborers had access. The substances are capable of killing all Caribbean "pests"—taking any kind of life that was an impediment to sugar plantation economics, from weeds to weevils to workers. Today, domestic violence rates in the Caribbean, in the Indo-Caribbean and in Caribbean diasporas, remain abysmally high. The first recorded murders of both 2017 and 2018 in New York City occurred in the Indo-Caribbean enclave of Richmond Hill, Queens; in the 2018 incident, 26-year-old Indo-Guyanese immigrant mother Stacy Singh was brutally killed by her abusive 46-year-old Indo-Guyanese husband Vinny Loknath, who then committed suicide.[122] The gendered links between colonial plantation violence and high contemporary rates of domestic violence and suicide in Caribbean communities remain undertheorized.

The great reveal of *A Silent Life* is Nani's secret that she enabled her husband to kill himself by literally giving him the rope to hang himself. It is the inverse of the plantation "coolie-wife murders," when Indian men killed their wives and sexual partners. Nazeer first threatens to kill himself when his wife Baby/Nani offers to help a poor Indian woman receive compensation from the manager of the sugar estate on which her husband had died. Nazeer is terribly offended that Baby would have the temerity to speak up to a white man. He says, "I'm not going to stand by and watch. Not this time. . . . I'll kill myself, I tell you. I'll hang myself first."[123] The exasperated Nani, it seems, eventually hands him a rope, and he hangs himself in depression, and perhaps, spite. Aleyah's family and neighbors all know the story, but no one will repeat it until confronted by Aleyah, who experiences a dream-vision of the event the night before leaving her homeland for London. That night she hits Nani, who says nothing. In the morning after the dream, Aleyah at first feels as if nothing has happened, "But as I cross the floor, I tread on something soft. I reach down and pick up a small bundle of threads. They are pale gold and coarse. Directly overhead is the beam where my grandfather threw the rope. I take these strands of rope to my room and put them away carefully in a corner of my suitcase."[124] The rope represents the possibility of escape from the world via suicide, in a continuation of gendered plantation violence. Linear temporality is disrupted when women usurp their husbands' roles; the golden rope is always there, haunting women, waiting to be used by men. Indeed, in the 2018 Indo-Guyanese immigrant murder-suicide of Stacy Singh, her killer husband hung himself.

In the novel, Nani goes hysterically and temporarily blind after she finds Nazeer's body, and gives up all participation in the world. She "took to her rocking chair and turned herself into an old woman, killing herself with her memories," and seeing only "a long piece of rope."[125] The community was not without feeling: "People felt so sorry for us. A dead that got carried off with a rope round his neck is not supposed to get prayers said for him, but the moulvi came. He felt so sorry for us, and said the prayers asking Allah's pardon."[126] Suicide in Islam, as in many other religions, is usually deemed prohibited by both *hadīth* and a Qur'anic verse that implicitly forbids it through forbidding murder; the Muslim suicide bomber is a political phenomenon, not a religious one.[127] There is *hadīth* evidence that the Prophet Muhammad did not offer the funeral prayer (Salāt al-Janāzah, or for subcontinentals, Namāz-e-Janāzah) for a person who committed suicide, but permitted others to do so; it is therefore a matter of compassion and reasoning on the part of individual clerics. The moulvi of Shah's novel chooses to comfort the family with the prayer. Nonetheless, individual pity for the man who committed suicide and for his bereft family—which is left without a male protector and provider—does not preclude assigning the incident to its proper place of disgrace in the community narrative. The entire township considers Nani's lapse into silence "rightful penance for her sin" and indeed what she and her family should have righteously done in the first place.[128] Aleyah says people "look on my mother and father as good children who are taking care of their family worries with correct fortitude: they have not bruised the neighborhood with bitter talk, or thrown their mother out to suffer among strangers."[129] Nani and women like her are hitches in the group transformation into a spotless Indian-Caribbean community ripe for the national stage: one in which family and community take care of their own, but do not publicize their domestic woes.

Aleyah's family, the Hassans, are Muslim, not Hindu. Yet the Muslim Indo-Caribbean is culturally Indian and heavily influenced by their majority Hindu neighbors, as had been the case in India. Aleyah's parents hold a Qur'anic prayer to send her off to London, which she considers

> strange because we do not usually observe the rituals of our religion. . . . We keep up the holy days and holidays but they are little more than excuses to gather in the family for feasting and celebration. But now my parents seek comfort in the sing-song reading of the Koran and the chanting of age-old Arabic prayers. I lay a white lace orni on my head and place my palms side by side like an open book, and follow the moulvi's prayer as he asks Allah to grant me success, and protect me from the temptations of the world.[130]

Islam may not have much of a role in the family's everyday life, but it is always at the ready if needed. The Hindu Caribbean women's practice of "singing *Ramayana*," chanting the parts of the *Ramayana* that detail Sita's suffering at the hands of her husband Rama and her lascivious kidnapper the demon Ravana as a form of ritual feminine mourning and sustenance, becomes, in this novel, Nani's incessant humming of Arabic verses from the Qur'an and Islamic prayers. At Nani's husband's funeral, her daughter observes that "when you hear them singing in the old Arabic way it makes you remember that you belong to a long line of family that goes all the way back to the time when the world had just started spinning round."[131] In this way, the same "singing" that marks death sustains life, and it is both prayer and incantation for Nani. She rarely speaks, and the religious humming is her only real mode of verbal expression. That sustained humming, says Aleyah, "kept her safe, I believed, anchored her to this side of the world. . . . If the humming ever stopped, Nani would disappear."[132] Nani also hums to "guard her tongue from talking," a possibility even though, having seen the "unforgivable," her "spirit flew away one day but her body goes on breathing. That happens when the spirit gets frightened; it breaks away because its eyes look on a deep, dark hell."[133] Nani speaks her story at the end of the novel and dies shortly thereafter, having waited for her granddaughter to grow up, endure her own marital oppressions, and escape them with her mind intact. Singing *Ramayana*, or in this case singing Qur'anic *suras*, guards the tongue and inhibits the chaos that might result from women speaking the truth before the time is right. It can also, unfortunately, be a kind of complicity with patriarchy.

In *A Silent Life*, Aleyah's introduction to the domestic violence intended to subdue Indo-Caribbean women comes early, when she observes the family's reaction to a great-aunt being beaten by her husband: the women of the family reassure themselves that being beaten is proof of love, while paradoxically hating the great-aunt for refusing to leave. Nani desires for this to not be Aleyah's fate, and Aleyah leaves then-British Guiana for educational exile at university in England. As her grandmother Nani's first grandchild and "hope," she has been blessed and cursed by visions of the old lady's struggles and sins all her life, and even her parents say that "if we believed in reincarnation, you'd think she thought that you were herself reborn, that you're her karma."[134] The specter of marriage as living death causes the prescient Nani, upon hearing of her granddaughter's engagement, to fall into a sort of coma as though she herself were dying, after which she "[gets] up and start[s] to hum again, but all her songs are sad." The rest of the family, however, is typically happy upon the news of Aleyah's marriage, especially as the groom is eminently suitable young trainee accountant Dean (Mohammed Dean Yacoob), the son of Indo-Guyanese Muslims who had migrated to Britain in the 1950s.

As the "hope" and karmic descendant of Nani, Aleyah is predictably doomed to repeat the pattern of driving her husband and then herself to madness over an inability to be a traditional Indian and Muslim wife. Aleyah and Dean marry and have two sons, but all is not connubial bliss. Unlike successful economist Aleyah, Dean is not rising at work, and he has become obsessive about it, competitive with Aleyah, and uncommunicative. Aleyah irrationally blames herself for his disappointments when she tells him that she has been made financial director of World Aid, and she observes that "Even though he was full of congratulations, I saw how he sat before his books that night, his back rigid, unbending."[135] Dean's back and his Indian masculinity are rigid and unbending. Aleyah is later offered a promotion and transfer to Barbados to be Caribbean director of World Aid. She builds castles in the air where Dean can start over and the family can be happy, but his reaction to the news at the dinner table is to push his chair to the floor and leave the house, slamming the door and leaving his family behind.[136] He stays out overnight as decades ago Nazeer did. When Dean returns, they have a conversation over power that parallels that of Baby/Nani and Nazeer, except Dean is more strident and less passive in his manipulation than Nazeer. He asks, "What of my career? And since when do you make the decisions for the family? I'm the head of this house. You go where I go. It's never the other way around," and then Aleyah thinks, "I had stepped over his authority. I had overstepped mine. No, we were not partners. Whatever gave me that idea? My highfalutin theories of women's place in the world?"[137] Dean attempts to wheedle Aleyah by telling her she should not be selfish and throw away her family life because of her "highfalutin" feminist ideas about professional work. Instead, she withdraws and suffers a mental breakdown, where she is haunted by visions of Nani's "inviting" rope, appearing to her as golden "streaks of sunlight."[138] That the rope is the only brightness and possibility in her life after Dean rejects her and even decides to institutionalize her suggests that she may be doomed to suffer Nani's punishment of eternal karmic suffering for betraying her role as a wife. However, there is indication that the "cursed" female line will end with Aleyah, as she has only sons.

Aleyah's says "I did not set out to be a sinner," but she believes that she has nonetheless become a sinner.[139] The framing of Indo-Caribbean woman's agency as "sin" may be rooted in the idealization of the *Ramayana*'s Sita as the paragon of Hindu and Indian feminine virtue.[140] Sita is commonly referred to by Indo-Caribbean Hindus as "Ma Sita," in the sense that she is a mother to all of humanity, as she was also found as a baby lying in and produced by the Earth. The end of *A Silent Life* comes when Aleyah learns that her great-great grandmother Gaitree had left behind not only her husband but also her twin sons in India. Nani reports that Gaitree had said, "'I loved my sons, but I wanted to live, I wanted to live. God, forgive me.' She cried like this to my mother, my mother Lena, named for the ship that brought her mother to this new earth."[141] Gaitree's descendants seem doomed to repeat this pattern of child abandonment. Nani believes she has failed as a woman because she has had only one child—a daughter, at that—and also, paradoxically, because her daughter Shabhan, Aleyah's mother, did not break the domestic cycle. Aleyah repeats the pattern of maternal guilt when she ultimately decides to divorce her husband, leave her sons with him in London, and return to Guyana to salvage her own mental well-being. It being a woman's responsibility to ensure the health and viability of her offspring, Aleyah's in-laws the Yacoobs also deem her irresponsible for passing on an alleged genetic legacy of "madness" to her sons. A fed-up Aleyah decides to go home to Guyana, maybe to help rebuild her country, and finally finds the courage to stand up to her husband Dean and tell him what she has thought of him all along: that he is a failure as an accountant and that he should become a shopkeeper, a destiny to which, the novel implies, he was born. Shopkeeping is an ironically Naipaulian destiny, in that Naipaul's works suggest it is the kind of nonintellectual, money-grubbing work to which Indians are most suited and which they most enjoy. But while the novel implicitly mocks Dean and he takes offense at the suggestion, Aleyah herself does not mean to insult him; she genuinely believes he has the potential to be a successful shopkeeper, and that it is an honest occupation. Ultimately, Dean "is disappointed that I am not a simple girl from back home after all, someone comfortable with the old ways."[142] Aleyah is no Sita. Being Ma Sita is far too much pressure for Aleyah, for Nani, for Mona, or for any human woman.

On her deathbed, after Aleyah returns to independent Guyana, Nani whispers to Aleyah, "Now that you are home, daughter, the rope will never again throw itself over . . ." and Aleyah responds, "No, no! No, Nani, not that! Never! I could never have done . . ." Nani shushes her, and with her dying breath, says, "Safe. We are all safe, safe, safe."[143] It is unclear who or what is "safe" in this moment. Nani may be safe in death, and Aleyah is safe because she has just finally filed for divorce from her husband and returned to Guyana, exercising agency over her own life for the first time. Mere material safety is not enough for Aleyah. Neither is compromise.

She reflects, "How does one manage? Compromise. It is a mature word. It is used by happy people and unhappy people. . . . You whittle away at your youthful ideals so that they fit into the grown-up requirements of the world. Then you are rewarded. Then you are blessed. Then you know peace."[144] But she and all of her maternal ancestors have compromised, and it did not bring them peace. As the Indo-Guyanese jahaji bahin, inheritor of the courage of Nani and other female plantation workers who protested colonial labor conditions, Aleyah must now actively take part in the nation's destiny. Aleyah's private realization of her family history is perhaps the first step in giving postcolonial Indo-Guyanese women a voice in the public sphere. Her education, life experiences, and eloquence thrust her into a leadership role.

Upon her return home to Guyana, Aleyah finds a country that has been economically devastated by an Afro-Guyanese dictatorship, but which, supervised by ex-U.S. president Jimmy Carter and his international peacekeeping Carter Center, has for the first time elected an Indo-Guyanese president in "free and fair" elections. Like her grandmother, she becomes an advocate for Indo-Guyanese women, exposing sexual crimes formerly deemed unspeakable because they intersected with racial violence. At a multiethnic meeting of younger educated people, Aleyah says she heard "not just about the burning of buildings and the looting and beatings, but of Indian women being stripped in the streets while the opposition thugs—including women—stood about laughing."[145] The group falls silent and she becomes acutely conscious that she is the only woman and one of only a few Indians in the room. Finally, "one young black man says in a low voice, his head in his hands, 'It shames us all.'"[146] Conciliatorily, all assembled then agree that racism was "the tool of the colonizers" who "taught us well," thereby absolving themselves and postcolonial historical perpetrators of responsibility.[147] The gathered men also do not apologize for sexism.

Gender and every social issue in this postcolonial Guyanese context is problematically reduced to race and the political struggle between Indo- and Afro-Guyanese. Aleyah, however, may have the power to overcome racial differences by becoming Ma Sita again, this time by employing the trappings not of individual wifehood, but of abstract, public maternity. One young man urges Aleyah to run for office as a potential "Mother to a troubled nation," as "During the years you were away the position of women in this country really changed. They were the most energetic traders. They played a big part in the unofficial economy."[148] Women have gained some autonomous economic power, it seems, but not yet political power. Having rejected being a mother to her sons, Aleyah is encouraged to be a mother to her people and her nation. But at the close of the novel, she remains uncertain about reassuming the mantle of any kind of motherhood. The transition from the traditional female indentured migrant's occupation of plantation weeder to postcolonial contender for the presidency need not be framed in gendered terms or as a return to Sita's idealized domestic womanhood. If Aleyah is to be a politician and leader, it will be on her own terms, in the spirit of her revolutionary grand-mother and other women who raised their voices in colonial protest.

CONCLUSION: UN-SILENCING THE FULLAWOMAN

In both Shah's *A Silent Life* and Monar's short stories, the memory of a Muslim Indian past continually intrudes into the present, demanding to be heard and seen with such insistence that in Shah's novel it can become visible to women, allow-ing them to see time itself as a circle that is sometimes a looped rope of suicide. In Monar's stories, the Indo-Muslim past drives men to violence against other men who infringe on their control over their families, and against Muslim women who threaten community cohesion through relations with the majority others of the Guyanese nation-state—Afro-Guyanese and Hindu Guyanese. The narratives suggest that women's true ancestral stories cannot be erased if their descendants are to have a future in which they are free to live their lives as they wish, but that does not mean they must also give up their Indo-Caribbean Muslim particularity.

Aleyah moves toward national participation while renouncing her marriage but not her heritage; the two, the novel shows, are not synonymous. The voyaging jahaji bahin is the feminist model that her own daughters, born in the first and rigid generation of Caribbean community formation, could not be; but her post-colonial granddaughters have the freedom to continue the work of creating a woman who is Indo-Caribbean, rather than a mimic woman conservatively aping "Indian" female mores that are more than half-invented. Monar's "*kala pani* moder-nity" and the jahaji bahin of Shah's novel both posit Indo-Caribbean Muslim ful-lawomen subjects who are defined neither by rupture from India, nor by their estate or domestic labor, nor by cultural hybridity, but rather by a mode that is both continuity and invention, insisting on its particularity while accommodat-ing the outside. Most importantly, Monar's and Shah's fullawomen demonstrate that breaking the titular ethnofamilial *silence* of Shah's novel is key to the postco-lonial future of Indo-Caribbean women.

Indo-Caribbean Muslim women's fullawomen history cannot be divorced from that of their jahaji bahin Hindu women; they are one ethnic community in which there is much familial and neighborly interreligious exchange, and in which race has been privileged over religion since the community's inception. Here, then, I have allowed an inversion of what usually happens, when the Ramayanic Sita represents the idealization of domesticity for all Indo-Caribbean women. The silencing of Indo-Caribbean *Muslim* women has become the metonymic experi-ence of Indo-Caribbean women's lives. But this turn also allows Anesa Ahamad's khutbah, the sound of her voice in the mosque in Trinidad, to be an achievement for all Indo-Caribbean and all Muslim women in the Caribbean.

3 · THE MARVELOUS MUSLIM

Limbo, Logophagy, and Islamic Indigeneity
in Guyana's El Dorado

The storytelling of the Muslim Indo-Caribbean is not limited to the political and identitarian novels, short stories, and poetry noted in the previous chapter. The community has produced its own folkloric, magical figure: one Sheikh Sadiq, depicted as an old man with a beard and possessing the sometimes-good, sometimes-evil powers of the supernatural *jinn* of Arab and Islamic mythology. In his anthropological collection of Indo-Caribbean folkloric figures, Kumar Mahabir's elderly Indo-Trinidadian interviewees describe Sheikh Sadiq the *jinnī* as possessing people, residing in their genitalia, subject to Hindu mantras and Muslim prayers, being a once-handsome man who was now headless after being punished by God for adultery, flying on an eagle, and requiring containment in a bottle after prayerful exorcism.[1] Said one Ms. Sheriffa, 77 years old and hailing from San Juan, Trinidad: "Only women can see this jinn, and as a woman, I was lucky to see Sheik[h] Sadiq. A woman can only see this jinn if she has a beard, or a mole on her face with two grains of hair sticking out."[2] Sheikh Sadiq's appellation of "Sheikh" indicates that he is (or was, before losing his head) a Muslim man (or otherworldly jinnī) of some learning or community standing—which is at odds with his jinn impishness and implication in a possible sexual morality story: a cautionary tale for learned men. Sheikh Sadiq is not otherwise to be found in the written literature of the Muslim Caribbean, and he is not well known outside of older community members. The myth and magic of the Muslim Indo-Caribbean has manifested in significantly more indirect—and much stranger—marvelously real literary texts.

The Guyanese writers Wilson Harris and David Dabydeen are among those literary inheritors of the Latin American and Caribbean magical and marvelous real whose work suggests that the Caribbean will never be free of colonialism until it (re)invents its myths. As Aimé Césaire says, "[t]he true manifestation of civilization is myth. Social organization, religion, partnerships, philosophies, morals, architecture and sculpture are the representations and expressions of myth."[3] Dabydeen's poem "Coolie Odyssey" (1988), originally from a collection of the same name, is written in Guyanese Creolese and exemplifies the struggle of those subalterns who as a result of the depredations of slavery and indenture believe they "got no story to tell" and are "born stupid," but who persist, even as they face the open grave of cultural loss, in "seeking fables" of the self that will create a postcolonial future.[4] This search for lost and new myth is complicated by the looming shadow of the colonizer's foundational fable of El Dorado, empire of gold. There is no El Dorado, as Sir Walter Raleigh (never) realized, but the specter of the magical city of prosperity still haunts the inhabitants of the developing Eldoradian nations—Guyana, Suriname, French Guiana, Brazil, Venezuela, and Colombia—that overlay the majority of the Amazonian jungle.

This chapter reads Harris's novella *The Far Journey of Oudin* (1961) and Dabydeen's novel *Molly and the Muslim Stick* (2008) as marvelous realist texts that integrate Islam and Muslims into the complex landscape of the Caribbean marvelous real, particularly through the temporally nonlinear, mimetic functions of *limbo* and doubling, and also through curiously similar incidents of what I call "logophagy," the literal eating of words and the Word of God and creation. I argue that both texts interpellate the Muslim into the Caribbean through a magical negotiation with indigeneity and environmental space. Islam, they show, does not always require direct mediation through the Afro-Caribbean in order to be naturalized as Caribbean. The Afro-Caribbean presence is nonetheless implied, as all people who travel through and reconstitute themselves after the Middle Passage pass through what Dionne Brand notes is the African "Door of No Return."[5] Harris names limbo the liminal, contortionist "gateway between Africa and the Caribbean" that signifies "a profound art of compensation which seeks to re-play a dismemberment of tribes . . . and to invoke at the same time a curious psychic re-assembly of the parts of the dead gods or new gods."[6] "Limbo" carries all the connotations of the Caribbean dance and game, and of the Roman Catholic place of waiting for the unbaptized dead—both infants and those born before the time of Jesus.[7] The limbo game, wherein people dance under a pole that is lowered closer and closer to the ground until a flexible winner who can bend backward almost horizontally is the only one left "standing," is, as both Harris and the Barbadian poet Edward Kamau Brathwaite point out, related both metaphorically and materially to the Akan trickster-spider-god Anansi whose fables survived the ship journey to the New World: "there was so little space that the slaves contorted themselves into human spiders."[8] Those who adapt themselves and their cultures win in the most basic biopolitical way—they live. As Derek Walcott says in his defense of colonial and postcolonial cultural mimicry and imitation in the Caribbean, "What have we been offered here as an alternative but suicide?"[9]

Caribbean literature has been commonly associated in the genre of "world literature" with the magical real, the marvelous real, and the unreal at least since

Alejo Carpentier's novel *El reino de este mundo* (1949), a mythical novel of the Haitian Revolution. Carpentier is however preceded in his exploration of the Caribbean literary fantastic by Franco-Caribbean, pan-Africanist writers like the French
Guianese author René Maran, winner of the 1921 Prix Goncourt for his novel *Batouala*, and most famously by the Martinican poet Césaire, who adapted French
surrealism in the 1930s to define Afro-Caribbeanness through *Négritude*.[10] Négritude as a literary movement is associated with a poetics that exposed the global
colonial suffering of all black people and advocated for Marxist African diaspora
consciousness and a cultural turn to Africa as solutions to imperialism and European hegemony. Césaire, who was most well-known for his poetic *Cahier d'un
retour au pays natal* (1939) and critical *Discours sur le colonialisme* (1955), saw anticolonial revolutionary potential in surrealism's artistic automatism: the oppressed
black unconscious could be released through rejection of the barbarism of the real
and a subsequent semiotically rejuvenating "magical contact." As such, said Césaire, for the purpose of Afro-Caribbean liberation, "I'm calling upon the magician. . . . I'm calling upon the Enraged."[11]

Carpentier's *lo real maravilloso*, the "marvelous real" as described in *El reino de
este mundo*'s original prologue, precedes Latin America's and the Caribbean's literary tradition of "magical realism."[12] The prologue is not usually included or
translated in English versions of the text, but Carpentier describes the marvelous
real as "an unexpected alteration of reality (the miracle) . . . an extension of the
scales and categories of reality, perceived with particular intensity by virtue of an
exaltation of spirit that leads to a mode of 'limit state.' To begin with, the sense of
the marvelous presupposes a faith" (my translation).[13] The "magic" proceeds from
material reality under the conditions of preexisting belief in the potential for
change, the existence of forces that can cause change, and specially gifted agents
of change who perceive their world's liminality. The marvelous real produces
hyperreality, rather than a state of existence that is completely alien to or opposite from its antecedent. Shalini Puri specifies that magical (and marvelous) realism involve, in postmodernist narratives, "a *reformulation* rather than a refusal of
realism."[14] "Magical" and "marvelous" realism are often used interchangeably, but
Carpentier's marvelous realism is, strictly speaking, the aforementioned reformulation of the real, whereas magical realism has come to encompass almost any
nonlinear narrative in service of the postcolonial nation-state. It is literary convention that "realism" is characterized primarily by a linear narrative and Cartesian
subjectivity, causing magical realism to become its other. As Carpentier originally
defined *lo real maravilloso*, marvelous realism is indeed a reclamation of the truth
of the real. It is the lived real of the Other; and for the Other's real, the Other's
own myth of self, to show itself in the grand narrative of colonial reality, it
must be as magic. Marvelous realism, the literary paradigm I use in this chapter, adds to religious potential the possibility of metamorphosing material
form to reflect the fullness of the empowered spirit. It is thus the methodological

how and revolutionary *why* of Harris's limbo, previously defined as the sea-change dismemberment and reassembly of parts and persons on the voyage to the New World.

The Far Journey of Oudin is the second of four novellas in Harris's *The Guyana Quartet* (1960–1963). Each novella addresses the limbo intersections of multira-cial becomings in Guyana with mythic projections of indigenous land and sea. But *Oudin* is a work that deals strictly with the restructuring of the Indo-Guyanese Muslim family and the changing roles of Indo-Guyanese women in Guyana, rather than with Harris's usual subjects, his own Creole mixed-race and Afro-Guyanese communities.[15] Characters in *Oudin* die and are reborn in a limbo cycle of impre-cise "doubling" that privileges repetition with incremental change, rather than imitative mimicry, as the state of the Caribbean postcolonial. Sara Upstone calls this temporal mode in *Oudin* a "pattern of re-play, which leads to a disjunction opening up possibilities for resistance."[16] Hena Maes-Jelinek sees the novella as "shaped like a circle, a complete whole containing discontinuous time phases which correspond to different ways of apprehending life."[17] The characters believe their lives to be sequential: there is an ancestral Indian past and its representa-tive, the Hindu patriarch Ram; a gendered liberatory future represented by the woman Beti and her child; and a present represented by the oft-reincarnated "Mussalman" Oudin and his half-brothers. However, the written narrative of *Oudin* is not linear, and neither is the sum of the characters' preindependence Indo-Guianese existences. The circumstances of death that precede each reincarna-tion are often too mysterious to tell exactly what happened, and bodies shift appearances—in this story, no one is ever quite themselves.

Dabydeen's *Molly and the Muslim Stick* is set in working-class World War II England and follows the horrific childhood and young adulthood of a white woman named Molly who is sexually and emotionally abused by her father until two marvelous things happen: her personified walking stick comes alive and talks to her, and an indigenous native of the colony of British Guiana appears on her doorstep. She follows this native, whose name is Om, back to his Guianese Ama-zonian village, where she loses herself in the jungle and finds psychological relief in being in a place that feels timeless. In the novel, the crutch named Stick weirdly speaks of the many origins of his wooden ancestors, and is the anthropomorphic manifestation and prop of temporal, historical Islam *and* stereotypically atempo-ral Guyanese "Amerindian" indigeneity. Brathwaite says in his poem "Caliban":

stick is the whip
and the dark deck is slavery

limbo
limbo like me [refrain]

Drum stick knock
and the darkness is over me[18]

Dabydeen's Stick is Brathwaite's poetic limbo stick and whip of the Middle Passage, lowering itself closer to earth as it leads the physically and psychologically disabled and abused Englishwoman Molly to an awareness of interconnected world subalternity and the simultaneous peace of jungle oblivion. Molly is white, but she is an emotional and sexual slave to her father, and her life is a series of limbo shimmies and dodges in a war-torn Britain that threatens to knock her to the ground permanently. In this space Om the indigenous appears, and she follows him back to an Amazonian village that is less Conradian heart of darkness and more, for a victim of domestic violence, a soothing area of alienness. Ah: and in addition to the animate Stick in this madcap fantasy being Muslim, they also encounter a Muslim terrorist.

Neither *Molly* nor *Oudin* are Caribbean "island" novels—they are of the Guyanese continental landscape that haunted Abdur-Rahman Slade Hopkinson, and their environs are the jungles and savannas of British Guiana, the wild tropical, antipastoral landscapes of the British Empire that could never be molded into genteel English gardens. *Oudin* was written and set in the period of British Caribbean independence in the 1960s, whereas *Molly and the Muslim Stick* is a contemporary product of the intersection of Caribbean postcolonialism and the concerns of global Islam, as exemplified by Stick's personal civilizational clash between his Crusades origins in Muslim seed and Christian timber, and his even stranger penchant for understanding tribal languages of Demerara—all indigeneity apparently having a connection in deep time. Both Dabydeen's and Harris's works, however, leave the postcolonial future, or rather the decolonial future, where the concern is addressing the old empire's and neoliberalism's culture wars and environmental exploitation, wide open.

OUDIN THE DOUBLE: WILSON HARRIS'S
THE FAR JOURNEY OF OUDIN

The work of the knighted Sir Wilson Harris, prolific Guyanese novelist, poet, critic, and winner of the 1987 and 2002 Guyana Prize for Literature, has, since his first and most famous novella *Palace of the Peacock* in 1960, been characterized by engagement with the myth of El Dorado, the complexity of the Guyanese landscape and its relation to various ethnic groups, the inadequacy of linear time as a temporal structure for narratives of the enslaved and indentured, and an unusual attention to the indigenous peoples of Guyana, whose presence is often neglected by writers more focused on the politically dominant Afro- and Indo-Guyanese communities.[19] Jodi Byrd points out, however, that while Amerindians serve as a "catalyst" for Harris's work, "there is a sense that the Amerindian presence is not a fully realized one, that it . . . is a latency that the conquering cultures and descendants of enslaved cultures must learn to access, to channel, and to recognize in order to fully grapple with modernity."[20] For Harris, Amerindians, even when they are embodied, tend to exist as part of the mythic landscape of Guyana through which others must limbo in the process of creolization.

Césaire asserts that "the only avowed refuge of the mythic spirit is poetry. And poetry is an insurrection against society because it is a devotion to abandoned or exiled or obliterated myth."[21] Harris, like Césaire, argues that a preliminary (re) creation of founding myths is essential to historicizing the Caribbean, as "a cleavage exists in my opinion between the historical convention in the Caribbean and Guianas and the arts of the imagination. I believe a philosophy of history may well lie buried in the arts of the imagination."[22] Limbo is the second of two types of mythic imagination available to the Caribbean through Africa. But even the first, direct myths, have "suffered a 'sea-change' of some proportions" and are "in curious *rapport* with vestiges of Amerindian fable and legend."[23] Limbo is a state of transition and transmission, and of leaning backward to move forward. In moving toward the future, limbo, as previously noted, "is also intent on a curious reassembly of the god or gods."[24] In multicultural Guyana, these gods may be indigenous, polytheistic African, Christian, Hindu, or Muslim.

The Far Journey of Oudin illustrates the changing social mores of rural Indo-Guianese village life, including conflicts between the Hindu majority and Muslim minority, on the cusp of Guyanese independence from Britain in 1966.[25] The story begins in medias res with the death of one Oudin, laborer, who mysteriously appeared in a rural savanna settlement in 1951. But this is his second death: Oudin is the reincarnation of an unnamed man who was once murdered by his half-brothers Hassan, Kaiser, and Mohammed over land inheritance. This Indo-Guianese family is Muslim but significantly influenced in custom by the Hindu majority: they are quintessential fullamen. Over the course of the narrative, which swings wildly in time, the three half-brothers also die and reappear one by one—a familiar theme in *Palace of the Peacock*, the more well-known first novella of the *Quartet*. The second thread of the story concerns Oudin's employer Ram, a craven Hindu Indo-Guianese cattle rancher who is very much set in his traditional, patriarchal ways, though the reader understands that no traditional Hindu raises cows for beef. Oudin's and Ram's narratives are linked by Beti, "Daughter," an illiterate Indo-Guianese woman who is lusted after by Ram but who becomes Oudin's wife and births his child just as he dies. Beti and Ram are the only characters who do not have "doubles," reincarnated selves who appear in thinly disguised forms after the deaths of their predecessors. In the novella, Ram embodies the colonial past, and Beti, with her baby and her shedding of traditional Indian dress, is the avatar of the future. The paradoxical present is represented by Oudin and his brothers, all of whom constantly die, are born again, disappear, reappear, and demand to be taken to India even while killing each other in order to possess land in Guyana. This is Indo-Guiana on the eve of independence, when the question of "who we are," asked since the 1890s by the first native-born Indo-Guianese, is first answered by the term "postcolonial."[26]

Oudin and his Indo-Guianese relatives and associates likely live on the southern Rupununi savannas, where the majority of cattle ranching is done in Guyana. This locale immediately delinks them from the continuous history of Indian indentureship on sugar estates, placing them adjacent to the agricultural mercantile category of Indo-Guianese small farmers who eventually rose to become, through rice farming, the postindenture Indo-Guyanese middle class. The Muslim brothers represent the potential of Indo-Guyanese to diverge from the state of "bound coolie" on the plantation. Their inland savannas represent Guyana's third most important ecosystem after the arable farmland of the coast and what is locally referred to as "the interior," the Amazonian jungle.[27] Each ecosystem has its own natural resource economics: the sugar plantations are located on the coasts, which are below sea level and still continually drained by dikes and canals built by the Dutch in the seventeenth and eighteenth centuries; the grassland savannas are the site of cattle ranching; and the interior is where indigenous villages remain and where gold, bauxite, and other minerals are dredged from the rivers. Though Raleigh sought El Dorado in the interior, the majority of the contemporary Guyanese population lives on the coasts.[28]

The Guyanese landscape is crucial to the identity of its inhabitants in *Oudin*. Much of *The Far Journey of Oudin* describes Oudin's kidnapping of the sixteen-year-old Beti, daughter of Rajah and niece of Hassan and Kaiser, on behalf of his employer Ram, the old, corrupt Hindu cattle rancher who is only slightly less poverty-stricken than his neighbors. Ram's desires are one axis around which the novella revolves. His first desire is wealth; his second is for Beti and the promise of an heir: "It had all started in the beginning of time with the dream of an heir in the heart of an old man like Ram, and in the unconscious womb of a child and daughter like Beti."[29] Beti's father and then her uncle Mohammed prove reluctant to marry her to Ram, as a result of which Oudin is made to kidnap her; on the archetypal journey away from her home, Beti and Oudin enter a pact wherein he takes her as his wife. Oudin and Beti traverse the entirety of the Guianese natural landscape, from savannas in view of the mountains, through rivers, to swamp and jungle. Throughout the novella, the seemingly aware landscape watches, tests, and waits for them to become truly "real," permanent inhabitants of the Guianese landscape. The Mussalman Oudin has not yet fully manifested in Guiana. His Indo-Guianese farming community lives on the savanna grasslands of the interior, bordered by a fecund, overgrown coconut plantation. The environment has a kind of sentience: "There is a somber conspiracy in every line and twig, a power so droopingly conscious of itself. . . . The concert is too perfect to be other than *consciousness*. But a consciousness clothed with gloom and impending horror and despair."[30] The gloom, I argue, is for the memory of conquest and death of the indigenous; the impending horror is for the uncertainty over what the postcolonial nation will be.

Helen Tiffin describes "landscape" as "a form of interaction between people and their place, in large part a symbolic order expressed through representation."[31] This is a seemingly unproblematic relationship for the autochthonous, whose language and cognition are in harmony with their environment. But for the displaced, "for the exile or migrant, 'landscape' consists in the formation or (re)formation of connections with the adopted place. . . . And for colonized peoples who are also ancestrally migrant, any coming to terms with the 'new' landscape frequently involves a journey back through the depictions of that land by the imperium whose perceptions and representations of it exert a powerful hegemonic influence on the colonized."[32] The journey undertaken by Oudin and Beti is different. It occurs entirely in the new landscape and is self-determined and independent of the imperial gaze. For these Indo-Guianese, victims of labor exploitation, the landscape is not necessarily dangerous; even though it broods, it does not lash out—perhaps it even tries to help. In *Oudin*, doubles attempt to redeem the actions of earlier selves. They are not evil doppelgängers, particularly because they do not exist at the same time as their "original," but their motives and origins are so mysterious as to verge on the sinister. Marina Warner describes the figure of the double as epitomizing "a threat to personality on the one hand, of possession by another, and estrangement from the self. But . . . the doubling also solicits hopes and dreams for yourself, of a possible becoming different while remaining the same person, of escaping the bounds of self, of aspiring to the polymorphous perversity of infants."[33] The different forms of doubles like those in *Oudin* include, says Warner, "a second self, or a second existence, usually coexisting in time, but sometimes sequentially . . . a lookalike who is a false twin, or, more commonly, someone who does not resemble oneself outwardly but embodies some inner truth. In this sense, the double, while wholly dissimilar, unnervingly embodies a true self."[34] I use doubling here as a way of describing people who have sequential incarnations, look close to identical in each incarnation, and remember their past lives. They do, however, have different names, concerns, and roles to play in each incarnation. As they are sequential, they are not a product of splitting or fission. They are literal body doubles that, as Warner suggests, embody some kind of true self, or perhaps more properly, in Harris's work, a specific archetype. In the vein of hailing the multivalent future, I suggest that Oudin and his half-brothers are not allowed to rest in death and are reanimated by the savanna itself to try again because of their chronic inability to get being a truly Indo-Guyanese Muslim "right." This type of mystical, environmental, and spiritual postcolonial work is neither science fiction nor fantasy; it is the fundamental Latin American and Caribbean marvelous real. Who is to say that in the haunted Americas, the land has no agency?

Harris is not the only Guyanese writer who sees Guyana as producing its own mythical avatars, especially when people fail at being either stewards of the land or their human brothers' keepers. As I have elsewhere discussed, Cyril Dabydeen's novel *Dark Swirl* (1998) describes the intervention of the mythic reptilian beast the *massacouraman* in rural Indo-Guyanese postcolonial identity becomings.[35] Pauline Melville's short story "Erzulie" (1998) tells of the coming of the Afro-Caribbean goddess Erzulie (who as Ezili is in Haitian vodou the goddess of fearsome love) to wreak vengeance on the Canadian mining company and its Guyanese governmental coconspirators responsible for the very real 1995 Omai gold-mining disaster, in which 300 million gallons of cyanide and mining waste slurry were spilled into the Essequibo River, Guyana's largest river and one that empties into the Atlantic. The Indo-Guianese of *Oudin*, inheritors of the legacy of indenture, are too disenfranchised to have much direct role in the national sphere, and their local treatment of each other leaves much to be desired. They also lack the understanding that they are now Guyanese and not just displaced subcontinental Indians and Muslims. Their worldview is inharmonious and unsustainable: it is tied to a mythical India, rather than to the material environment in which they live. Limbo, however, requires a journey away from and through ancestral myth.

The opening scene of the novella describes Oudin in insubstantial, ghostly form watching his wife, the pregnant Beti, announce his death after he is murdered by his brothers. This noncorporeal form is closer to what Warner calls the "true self" than are any of the novella's other physical doubles. Oudin and his death are immediately linked to a temporal Caribbean geography, as it seems as though his death "had happened in the depth of time long before the vain echo of the announcement."[36] The being that is Oudin dies twice. This opening scene that harks back to an originary time reflects Walcott's call for a turn to a naturalized neo-Adamic state that does, however, make room for history. Jana Braziel writes that the temporal tendency of Caribbean writers is to return to genesis as if to the site of an originary crime, a place of an infraction against the natural world in order to unearth the idea of a beginning that is intrinsically tainted and marred. Their representations of Caribbean genesis refuse a static Eden, a fixed Paradise; rather, their Caribbean geneses are plural, becoming, autonomously flowing, and above all, dynamic.[37]

This dynamic genesis is metamorphic. Oudin's present, his now, is traced backward then forward through time, and he is repeatedly made anew. He is the walking, talking body double of the original Caribbean victim of fratricide, a veritable Abel to his three brothers' Cain(s). This original victim is not named; nonetheless, when his double returns to "haunt" his brothers, they recognize him immediately and somehow intuit that his true name is Oudin. They recognize their sin when shown it by a force greater than themselves, just as the biblical Cain does. Upon seeing him, Mohammed, one of the brother-murderers, thinks, "Certainly

this was *not* Oudin. Who was *Oudin*? Where had the name sprung from? The man
he beheld on the road—who looked like the spirit of Oudin—was his half-
brother."[38] In his 1984 prefatory note to the *Quartet* collection containing *The
Far Journey of Oudin*, Harris writes that "Oudin's struggle with Ram [his corrupt
employer or, rather, master] . . . mirrors a 'covenant' or reversal of truth. It is a
rehearsal in which 'doubles' appear to invoke the dead and the living who revisit
or re-play the deeds of the past in a new light of presences woven closely into the
tapestry of past actions."[39] Harris's commentary on his own work is sometimes
disingenuous and stylistically as existential as his fiction; his frequent notes are
additions to the works, rather than analyses. Precisely how the doubles are connected to each other in *Oudin*'s extremely convoluted narrative seems less important than the point Harris makes about the novella as rehearsal. Oudin and the
others are rehearsing their roles in the grand play of postcolonial nationhood.

With the single exception of Beti's child, who is the incarnation of a person
whose identity is left undetermined, all the doubles appear as full-grown adults
who seem to spring from the savanna itself. Oudin, for example, materializes "no
one knew from where and when. He may have come from the sand-hills a long
way off topside but this was unlikely since he was not of Amerindian stock, neither trace nor ghostly feature was his. . . . The truth was no one knew whom he
represented or where he had sprung from."[40] Harris's work always lends itself to
suggestions that Guyanese land has agency that is related to hauntings by the
indigenous. Though there are no indigenous characters in *Oudin*—unusually for
Harris's fiction—the reader is continually reminded of their "trace" presence and
link to the land. The unknown narrator of *Oudin* protests overmuch that the
brown-skinned Oudin could not be of any indigenous stock. "Whom he represented" and "where he sprung from" are unknown quantities to the villagers
because the answers are in the process of becoming and do not yet exist. The material, persistently recurring body of Oudin precedes the formation of a multicultural, multiracial postcolonial identity for himself and for Guyana. It already is,
but it is also what will be, if or when the state catches up to what people are
becoming.

The doubled self is another alternative to the doomed Naipaulian Indo-
Caribbean mimic man, who has lost his own ancestral culture and is doomed to
imitate and repeat the colonizer's mistakes. The murder of the half-brother who
will become Oudin, the event that sparks the doubling of individuals in the novella,
is the result of a property inheritance dispute, which sees the full brothers Hassan,
Kaiser, and Mohammed and their cousin Rajah disinherited by the dying pater-
familias in favor of the "imbecile" murder victim precisely because they have
become mimic men. As Hassan says, "He believe we all really gone soft, driving
car, and getting so Englishified in all our style. . . . Year after year you throw away
every tradition the old man prize."[41] The "old man" was brought from India by his
own father as a child. He despises these sons for being less than they ought to have

been: they are neither Indian nor yet Guyanese. When he is dying, Mohammed, the eldest, didactically tells his relatives the family story of emigration, exile, and loss, but concludes, "Why had he translated their little life into such grandiose terms? It baffled him."[42] The feeling of being bit players in a grand narrative of history is a Naipaulian one, exemplified by the titular character of *A House for Mr. Biswas* (1961), that suffuses the literature and politics of the Indo-Caribbean, manifesting in a tendency toward self-depiction as perpetual victims.[43]

Mohammed's story of exile is grand because it is both particular and representative of every Caribbean story except that of indigenous Amerindians. The death of the father represents a sundering with the Indian past that threatens to be final: when he dies and the brothers decide to kill their half-brother heir, they feel as though "[s]omething small and secure had been broken beyond repair. It was a unity of faith and family. . . . They had never dared to overthrow completely— until now—the secret participation and magic of ancient authority and kinship."[44] The brothers have rejected a continuous lineage and are in danger of losing themselves forever. Their neighbors fear them not simply because they are murderers, but because they have committed a fratricidal murder that threatens community identity and integrity. At the local rum shop, the brothers are shunned as "the acknowledged representatives of a dark deed in the region and the estate and the world."[45] Their punishment for fratricide is Cain's: to wander the earth forever. As the God of Genesis forbade every man to kill Cain and put him out of his misery, so too do Oudin's half-brothers die by no man's hand—only by acts of God or Nature—and they are continually reborn.

In death, however, the brothers Hassan and Kaiser regain their connection with the past and with India, which requires a literal and metaphorical ritual purification and sacrifice by fire. Felled by a stroke, "Hassan was the first of the brothers to die, at the zenith of life, after the plot and conspiracy that eliminated their imbecile half-brother. . . . [he intuited] that he would not rest in his grave, unless his corpse was fired on a pyre, in the ancient way of his ancestors, before they had dreamed to cross the ocean to Demerara."[46] So the family obtains governmental permission for his Hindu cremation on a pyre, rather than an Islamic burial, despite the fact that they are Muslim. India at this time (the 1950s), having passed through its parallel independence struggle from the British Empire, had just experienced the bloody 1947 postindependence events of Partition, which eventually relocated the majority of Muslim Indians to Pakistan and Bangladesh and Hindu Indians to India. Knowingly or not, Harris allays this religious divide in the New World, though unfortunately by aligning Hassan with an extreme but popular strain of the Hindu nationalist ideology *Hindutva*, which supposes that most peoples of the subcontinent are Hindu by ancestry and are therefore potential "reverts."[47]

After their deaths, the brothers' doubles appear to help and hinder Oudin, the double of the half-brother whom they killed. Hassan appears as a fisherman who helps Oudin and Beti escape the wrath of Ram and Mohammed, and he clearly identifies himself to Oudin as a double of the original Hassan.[48] In both incarnations, the roundness of Hassan's face is compared to that of a serene Brahmin priest, so it is him. Having been burnt on a pyre, his ashes buried near and cooled by a nameless Guyanese river that empties into the Atlantic and (in theory) eventually reaches the Ganges and India, he is still tied to the New World in a state of purgatory. As a result of his sins, he will continue to appear and reappear until a final fire of cleansing that may never happen. For now, he works his way up the karmic ladder by helping the one he had murdered.

The next brother to die is Kaiser, who dies when the aforementioned local rum shop and site of community gathering burns down; "his charcoal death was the duplicate of Hassan's."[49] Trapped in the burning building, "He collapsed. And yet it seemed to him that he had risen after all and was walking in blackening trousers and feet. He was light and floating in the sky of the mirror that had grown veined like a tree." As Kaiser transitions into ghostly existence, his dead brother Hassan appears to him: "Hassan had just got the obstinate idea in his burning head that he wanted to return to India to circulate his ashes on mother-soil. Kaiser protested. If he returned he would be looked upon as an outcast and an untouchable ghost. . . . The ceremonies and sacraments he fitfully observed were not a patch on the real thing."[50] Like Hassan, all real-life potential Hindu "reverts" must undergo purification. The usual prescription, a dip in the Ganges, is geographically unavailable to Hassan; relatedly, he is in even worse spiritual straits than the average Muslim Indian revert, since all Indo-Caribbean ancestors lost their Hindu caste rights and their very Indianness when they crossed the *kala pani* (black water) of the Atlantic.[51] Hassan's ghost, then, desires the "real thing" that not even his cremation ritual achieved: a return to India itself. But Kaiser's ghost rightly points out that his status in India would be that of an untouchable, even among ghosts. Their lot, therefore, is in the New World, which has already staked its claim on them, and it is there that they are reborn. Kaiser reappears as a "negro woodcutter" who temporarily imprisons Oudin and Beti during their flight. He looks like the first Kaiser and is even *named* Kaiser, but his face has literally been burnt black in the fire in which he died. Upon seeing him, Mohammed, his still-living eldest brother, thinks "[n]o one knew where this black, artificial beggar had got that relative name from. . . . Names were so funny and contrary to all expectations. There was nothing in a name, and there was everything, of all mankind, as well."[52] The similarity of the non-Muslim name "Kaiser" to "Caesar" and the German "Kaiser" is intentional, as Harris has the character extraneously discuss his name, and the narrator says that recent world events included the World War II development of the atomic bomb, which may or may not have affected this Caribbean world of dreams.[53] This Kaiser, though, is ironically far more follower (of his brother Mohammed) than leader. Perhaps he is rather more an embodiment of *kaise*, the usual transliteration of the Hindi word that asks the question "how?"

How, really, did rural Indian villagers find themselves in this strange land, and how are they to live there?

Brother Mohammed, in his turn, is killed too, but his death is not associated with fire. He is eventually gored to death by that embodiment of Hinduism, the sacred bull: "Mohammed turned to see where the collision had occurred that split his skull. He stumbled and fell over the hoof of a falling tree, as over his own body of necessity and self-gratification. He had turned into an animal with a horned bullet in a blind eye."[54] He is the bull that kills him, and has gored out his own eye. He is an embodiment of traditional Indian religion and patriarchy, of a dead and stubbornly nonlocal worldview, and has therefore killed himself. He is the only brother who has no double—but there is an unborn child, fathered by Oudin but destined to be heir to Ram, whose identity is yet to be determined. The potential exists for Mohammed to be reborn in this child.

The question is who Beti's child will be. Will the future be Oudin again, Mohammed the murderer, or a new being entirely? Mohammed does not appear destined to be reborn. Just before his death, "Mohammed recalled Ram telling him that a grown man should never lean on ghosts."[55] The unborn child has been fathered by Oudin, a different kind of ghost than Hassan or Kaiser, a ghost with a future. For Mohammed, "Oudin bring a curse . . . time itself change since he come. Is like if I starting to grow conscious after a long time, that time itself is a forerunner to something. But Ah learning me lesson so late, is like a curse."[56] Oudin is the one whose refusal of linear existence acknowledges an Indian past while preparing for a New World future, a double feat that could not be accomplished by his half-brothers, murderers who vacillate between "Englishified" mimicry and a static memory of India.[57] They are not metamorphic and cannot *become*, and so are destroyed by Oudin. The brothers are not unaware of the threat to themselves; Oudin's wife Beti recalls that before their marriage, the first time Oudin appeared at their settlement, "*He* was the man who had rapped on their door, in the savannahs, seeking employment, shortly before her father died. He had looked like a bundle of death then—as wild and terrible as he looked now—and her father had thrown him out, swearing he wanted none of him."[58] Beti herself believes that "she had never known him in any permanent sense, save only in the knowledge that he eluded her because of her abysmal ignorance."[59]

The cycle of birth and death in the novella arrives at no revelatory moment about Indo-Guyanese or Muslim diasporic ethnic and national identity: Harris's concern here is more about nature and less about nation. But the cycle does point to the ongoing struggle of the migrant to belong to the land, and suggests hope: the persistence of the cycle indicates a will to succeed, and perhaps even support of the indigenization of Indo-Caribbean people by the land itself, which incorporates the production of human life into its own natural cycles. It is as though an essential Oudin has taken root; and when one shoot dies, another takes its place. Harris clearly references the Hindu cycle of rebirth into higher forms in order to attain nirvana. At the beginning of the text, when Oudin reawakens in noncorporeal form after his second death, he "knew it was still a dream, the dream of the heavenly cycle of the planting and reaping year he now stood within—as within a circle—for the first time in his life. He felt his heart stop where it had danced. It was the end of his labor of death."[60] Oudin has the chance to be reborn and achieve more than the nihilistic existence (and end) of the history-less indentured laborer—but he does not yet fulfill his promise.

These Indo-Guianese people, barely one generation removed from indentured servitude, are either Hindu or Muslim, but the Muslims often reference Hinduism and believe in the Hindu doctrine of reincarnation. Ram and Beti are Hindu. The names of the brothers, Kaiser, Hassan, and Mohammed, indicate that their family is Muslim. "Oudin" is an ambiguous name closest in Guyana to "Odeen," a name usually associated with Muslims that is likely the colonial Anglicization of the Muslim name suffix "-uddin," or the Arabic "ad-Dīn," which carries the theological meaning "[of] the [Muslim] way of life" or "[of] the [Muslim] judgment." The resulting colloquial Muslim way of denoting the collection of beliefs that constitute the religion of Islam is "the deen." The argument that Oudin may be a Guyanese representative of the deen is borne out by Ram's peculiar religious sense of Oudin: when Oudin turns up without knowledge of his identity, "Ram adopted him and christened him a Mussulman, whatever that meant."[61] Oudin cannot say who he is, and it is unclear to what extent Ram knows him from his previous life, but his body and affect are perceived by the Hindu Ram as being inherently of the Mussalman of India—but it is as yet unclear, in this new landscape where Muslims can reincarnate, what a Muslim Guyanese is.

The early postindenture blurring of boundaries between Muslims and Hindus represented in *Far Journey of Oudin* is characteristic of what Raymond Chickrie, Aisha Khan, Brinsley Samaroo, and others have identified as the Indo-Iranian legacy of indentureship-era Islam in Guyana, as I will discuss in the final chapter. This Indian Islam is viewed by younger, Arabized Muslim Caribbean purists as necessitating "a continuous attempt . . . to purge 'cultural Islam' of 'un-Islamic' innovations (*bid'a*)."[62] Bid'a or "innovation" is a particularly fraught notion of impermissibility to Muslims, who are wont to apply it to any and all manifestations of modernity and perceived "Westernization." Bid'a includes what was not the case during the Prophet Muhammad's time, or intended by the Prophet and his Companions to be the case in the future, as judged by scholarly interpretations of the spirit of the Qur'an, the *sunnah* (contemporarily recorded verbal sayings, doings, and implied permissions of the Prophet), and *hadīth* (collected sayings and judgments of the Prophet with substantiated chains of transmission). There is no faster way, among observant Muslims, to foreclose discussion— or discipline one's wayward children—than to label a thing bid'a. In this worldview, any religious or cultural creolization of Islam is bid'a; but as should be evident, there is much room for interpretation.

Crucial to the perception of Oudin as Mussalman—and perhaps bid'a embodiment of the deen—is Ram's early observation that "Oudin was a dream, a fantasy and an obedient servant who had come to him at last across an incredible divide of time and reality."[63] On the other side of time and reality is the pre-Partition India from which Oudin's Muslim father emigrated. Oudin as servant echoes the Islamic idea of the Muslim as 'abd Allah (Abdullah), servant or slave of God, which is also the name of the Prophet's father and a frequently occurring term in the Qur'an. "Islam" and "Muslim" themselves are etymologically related Arabic words with a consonant root meaning clustered around submission (to the will of God) and peace (as the individual and community reward for submission). But Ram, who employs Oudin as a cowherd and sometime cow-thief—reminding us that the British employed very large numbers of Hindu ahir-caste cow-minders as colonial indentured laborers—is no god. Oudin is an obedient servant to someone or something else: Allah, perhaps, or Guyana, or both.

In the 1950s and 1960s, on the eve of Guyanese independence from Britain, the people of British Guiana are in the process of becoming, and the "true self" sought by doubling and repetition is an ideal as yet undefined. This is the characteristic migrant fragmentation of self in the New World begun with conquistadors and explorers, who, as Walcott says, "behold the images of themselves beholding. They are looking into the mirror of the sea, (the phrase is mimicked from Joseph Conrad), or the mirror of the plain, the desert, or the sky. We in the Americas are taught this as a succession of illuminations, lightning moments that must crystallize and irradiate memory if we are to believe in a chain of such illuminations known as history."[64] The migrant acquires another self at the moment of stepping foot on terra incognita, becoming a collection of selves that linear history does not acknowledge as continuous and continuously shifting. In Harris's work, the Caribbean mirror double is aware of itself as both discrete and continuous, and therefore as a narrative self, rather than as a single instance in the linear chain of momentary flashes that Walcott describes as known history.

What is dangerous in Oudin is not live nature, but the static, dead constructions of man: after dawn, Oudin's "hut emerged suddenly, ordinary and dead as day. The vague eternity and outline vanished. There was no mystery in the poverty of its naked appearance—a few planks nailed together and roofed by bald aluminum."[65] Even Mohammed's motives for killing his half-brother involve an unacceptable, colonialist attempt to tame the land by building a house with his ill-gotten inheritance: postindependence, he surmises, "[a] new building and rehabilitation programme would have been launched on the sugar plantations of Demerara, and a lot of old-fashioned overseers' frames would be going dirt-cheap then for anyone who saw himself becoming a new kind of ruler."[66] But even while he imagines himself in a big house like the former English overseers, he understands that "in his image of time the family lived in the same illusion of dark space they had always occupied and rented. They had the same room or rooms, as in the cottage where they were in the present, while the remainder of the dreaming mansion of the future was bare and unlived in, and unoccupied as ever, and altogether too big, he knew."[67] Ram's inability to metamorphose, to *become*, is the same as Mohammed's. Ten years after the marriage of Oudin and Beti, Ram recalls the promise of their wedding procession and thinks that "still he could not yet accept the evolution and change in appearance" of the world and its future.[68] Mohammed and Ram are Muslim and Hindu men whose fear of change, fear of the future, fear of the land, and fear of death have made them willing to live the colonial lie into the postcolonial future. The hope, as I will later discuss, lies not with Oudin, or even with his child, but with the Indo-Guyanese woman-to-be, Beti.

THE MUSLIM MARVELOUS REAL: DAVID DABYDEEN'S *MOLLY AND THE MUSLIM STICK*

The Far Journey of Oudin is an example of what Jutta Schamp calls Harris's Jungian literary will to "implement internal and external change" through "facing one's mortality and revisiting the traumas one might have experienced in life to finally transform, and, thus, transcend them."[69] The reader never learns whether Ram, Oudin, and Beti transcend their circumstances, but there is some suggestion that in repeating the cycle of life they will transcend it. In her discussion of Dabydeen's *Molly and the Muslim Stick*, Schamp argues that Harris's and Dabydeen's works share the postcolonial aesthetics of "trauma and transfiguration": "Like Harris, Dabydeen is interested in how to create beauty in the light of human suffering and catastrophe, caused by domestic violence, incest, the Holocaust or colonization."[70] Trauma and transfiguration combine to produce transcendence, though this last is less obviously a metaphysic of Dabydeen's work. *Molly*, says Erik Falk, is also "related to Wilson Harris's literary universe of metamorphoses and merging of dream and reality" as it "signals its dedication both to the recognizably concrete and the strangely fairy-tale-like from its opening sentence."[71] The novel's opening sentences, "Once upon a time—the night of Wednesday 26th October 1933, when I was fifteen—it happened. It. It. The dripping down my thighs. Sticky, then thickening to treacle. As bloody as flesh from Leviticus," are emblematic of its combining of religious, sexual, and colonial parables.[72] The reader is thrust into the incestuous, unwaveringly brutish colonial English world of teenage Molly, who is not, as may be surmised, experiencing menarche, but a first rape by her father.

The dreamlike and metaphorical qualities of much of Harris's work do not lend themselves to depiction of such visceral, sexualized bodily experience, and indeed Harris himself has said about Dabydeen's 1984 poetry collection *Slave Song* that it is "the pornography of empire."[73] *Slave Song*, a collection of poems that depicts the plantation experiences of both African slaves and indentured Indians in British Guiana, is arguably Dabydeen's most famous work, characteristic of his use of Guyanese Creolese (each poem has multiple versions in Creolese and cannily mistranslated "standard" English), foregrounding of female subjects and their bodies, demand for recognition of Indo-Caribbean history, and strict attention to the postcolonial literary task of addressing the depredations of Empire. *Molly* does not employ Guyanese Creolese; nor does it engage with what Anjali Nerlekar calls Dabydeen's ambivalent, "intriguing and conflicted relation with the idea of 'Indianness,'" whereby his poetry moves toward a "state of flux by its problematic refusal *and* acceptance of one's history."[74] The theme of "refusal and acceptance of one's history" is preeminent in *Molly*, a British-Caribbean novel that intriguingly employs the theme of Islam *without* mediation by the Indo-Caribbean, Dabydeen's customary literary demographic and the one usually implicated in the practice of Islam in the Caribbean. Colonial England and Islam are instead mediated by Guyanese indigeneity, a device often used by Harris and another Guyanese novelist and poet who is more often considered Harris's direct literary inheritor— Dabydeen's aforementioned cousin Cyril Dabydeen.

Molly is different from much of David Dabydeen's oeuvre: it is the type of late-career novel about which critics begin reviews with a bemused assessment of the author's apparent changed state of mind and the subsequent befuddlement (and resistance) of fans: an unsettling "[s]omething has definitely happened to David Dabydeen's novels," says Michael Mitchell, implicating *Our Lady of Demerara* (2004) and *Molly and the Muslim Stick* (2008).[75] The "something" is evidenced by the fact that "*Molly* appeared as part of Macmillan's Caribbean series, rather than with a mainstream British imprint," suggesting that between the graphic depictions of incest, gang rape, class warfare, Islamic terrorism, and wise natives in the timeless jungle, no big fiction publisher would touch the novel, and "regional" Caribbean literature was a lesser and safer home for such a text.[76] It is a short novel for such dizzying thematics—a mere 177 pages. Dabydeen's own description of the book to a *Guardian* reviewer is mundane, with the exception of the stick's description: "It's about a white woman who was abused by her father, goes a little mad and starts talking to a walking stick. . . . The stick talks back, claiming to have Muslim ancestry. I've set the story at the time of the Suez crisis, which enables me to look with some distance and perspective at issues that are still relevant today—religious fundamentalism, the suffering of the Palestinians and the fear of the Israelis for their own survival. It's a book that seeks to explore rather than condemn or criticise."[77] The novel is about all the things he mentions, and a few more. *Molly* is highly allusive, in keeping with "the intensely intertextual character" of Dabydeen's other work.[78]

Shakespearean references are especially frequent in the novel, and though Molly calls the talking stick her Puck, Schamp argues that "Stick is an amalgamation of several Shakespearean characters, such as the mischievous witch Sycorax, the mother of Caliban" as well as "rebellious Caliban" himself.[79] Nerlekar says that in Dabydeen's poetry, "the Guyanese culture becomes equal to the actual past of English and European culture by this alignment of the Creole with Shakespearean writing... 'primitive' Guyana thus becomes 'ancient' Guyana, the precursor of modern-day England, and part of its ancestral history."[80] This is an interesting proposal applied to *Molly*, which ends in "ancient" Guyana with an Englishwoman for whom the jungle functions as a womblike incubator of oblivion, and perhaps a chance to be born again. Shakespearean allusions, though, are almost casual in this novel; they are a natural part of the landscape of the British/Caribbean world. Stick could be a Caribbean Caliban, the "native" in the colonial encounter, but there is a human who might better fit that role in Dabydeen's novel: Om. Notably absent from Dabydeen's *Guardian* summation is the fact that *Molly* is thoroughly haunted by his Guyanese homeland, as embodied by that mysterious Guyanese indigenous man. Molly and Stick end their existences in Om's Guyanese jungle, El Dorado, which functions as a site of return to a somewhat unfortunate primevalness—not primitiveness—that dispels the horrors of postwar Britain.

Falk reads the novel and its landscapes through the lens of Graham Huggan's "postcolonial exotic," an unholy transactional exchange between postcolonial writer and expectant readers (those poor souls who may have been "unsettled" by *Molly*, as previously noted), whereby postcolonialism and postcoloniality "work in tandem; postcoloniality by valuing cultural difference, and postcolonialism by 'certifying' the goods that are sold as culturally different, through a particular politically inflected jargon and through the authority of its practitioners."[81] In baser terms, Dabydeen the native informant stands accused of pillaging his own culture for the exotic literary fodder of marginality and difference to feed the hungry monocultural white readers of the old colonial metropole.[82] His goal may be "aesthetic—and possibly commercial—gain."[83] This may well be true, but given the writer's literary talent and productivity, the creative mandate of "write what you know," the financial mandates of paying the rent and receiving just recompense for artistic labor, and the neocoloniality of the idea that an ex-South London foster child and son of a former indentured laborer who paid his way through an English law degree by working in a cake factory is improperly observing a literary standard, the man may deserve a pass.[84] Every postcolonial or nonwhite writer could be accused of packaging their work for prurient consumption by a metropolitan majority, should there be even a hint of the Other that is the Self in the commodity.

This is not to say that the "exotic" can never be a useful lens through which to read a postcolonial text, but applying market logic to literature and authors heralds a slippery slope of standards, value judgments, and imprecise and inept quantification of narratives. In *Molly*, says Falk, "Exoticism results not because the *already foreign* (to a Western metropolitan audience) is filtered through narrow representational codes; it happens rather when the *relatively familiar* (to a Western metropolitan audience) is transformed into something foreign and strange."[85] Presumably, Islam and the Caribbean are the "already foreign" and industrial war-

time and postwar Britain the "relatively familiar" made foreign by the sheer horror of Molly's hidden life. But there is now no such thing as a homogeneous "Western metropolitan audience" that is unfamiliar with Islam, and the Caribbean is
also "the West." The publishers and some readers, it seems, were taken aback by
the novel, but that is not because they are unfamiliar with any of the settings or
themes; they in fact believe it to be *too* familiar, as it is sexually explicit print literature in a world saturated by online pornography. At Dabydeen's stage in his
respected literary career, such anxious policing of high- and lowbrow literary standards matters less—the novel will still be published and read.

Mitchell reads the novel as an example of "realist magicalism rather than magical realism," where representation is "dependent on the perceptions of reader and
author as well as related events."[86] The "realist magical" is Carpentier's "marvelous real." Though the marvelous real is a far older literary framework than the postcolonial exotic in which to consider a Caribbean novel, it remains a useful one.
Magical thinking gives permission to people, literature, and criticism to become
anything or stay in flux, and the thematic of magical transformation as Césairean
resistance is inescapable and recurring in Caribbean and Latin American literature. Caribbean literature heeds Martinican Frantz Fanon's call for a literary
nationalist creativity—a "literature of combat"—to reframe the colonial narrative
of history from the perspective of the formerly enslaved and the oppressed indigenous.[87] In the contemporary academy, magical and marvelous realism are
deemed characteristic of Latin American and Caribbean literature because of the
extreme loss of ancestral histories and the surreally harsh conditions of slavery
and servitude in the Americas.[88] The descendants of slaves must perform the irony
of inventing ancestral histories in addition to constructing postcolonial futures.
Only the marvelous can adequately describe a state of fundamental violence
wherein a group of human beings is robbed of their myths of identity and reduced
for generations to an Agambenian *homo sacer* (sacred man), who is robbed of
rights appropriate to the human and determined by the sovereign power to be the
sacrificial, rather than sacred other to the citizen in the constitution of the body
politic.[89]

I read Dabydeen's combined use of Islam, magic, and Guyanese indigenous
spiritualism as a limbo becoming that exposes the colonial lie of English cultural
supremacy and its prescribed conditions of existence, showing that the marvelous is always ready to invade even England itself to spirit away an Englishwoman
for de- and reconstruction in the Americas. The marvelous hyperreal, the *real* real
that drives the impulse to postcolonialism as a way of thinking against hegemony,
is unconcerned with the boundaries of nation, geography, time, and body. *Molly*
is a postcolonial novel, and its confused reception is only further proof; for as
Harris and many other Caribbean, Latin American, and African American writers have pointed out, the result of slavery and colonization is a world rife with
tricksters.

Molly's first engagement with Judeo-Christian religion begins, as previously noted, in the novel's first lines, with Levitical Old Testament allusions to incest, sin, and punishment. Soon after, Molly's father Norman hits her while she is reading to her near-catatonic mother from the Bible; her reaction is to continue reading. He slaps the Bible to the floor, and it "open[s] up at a passage from John, which I read to Mum. It told of the risen Christ refusing Mary's embrace, denying her gratitude for His survival."[90] Molly is certainly a sacrificial lamb to her father's lusts for sex, power, and money; and her mother's choice to reject poverty and patriarchy by turning inward and leaving Molly to the cruel mercies of the father when Molly is 14 years old warrants rejection of both parents. They are no Mary and Joseph, and Molly survives in spite of them. The novel establishes its grounding in a Judeo-Christian ecumenism in this moment, and it engages widely with Islam, Christianity, and Judaism throughout. All past and present references of West and East, from Shakespeare to Muhammad to 9/11, the Holocaust, and the Israeli-Palestinian conflict, are available to Dabydeen in the postcolonial moment. The image of the Bible falling to the ground, Judeo-Christianity lying in wait and waiting to be picked up, heralds the first, rather blasphemous mention of Islam in the text: the moment Molly catches her father in a crouch, peering voyeuristically through the floorboards to see a woman washing herself in a bathtub below: "One day I wandered into his bedroom to find him crouching on the floor, his face touching it, like a Muslim at prayer. One hand steadied him, the other was sheathed in his trouser pocket. He bolted upright and shooed me away. When he left the house I entered his room and I discovered the hole he had made in a floorboard to peep at the women bathing."[91] The bathtub, a luxury commodity unavailable to many during World War II, belongs to the family, but the father rents it to the neighbors as a means of bringing in income. He is not drafted as a soldier in either World War because he is a coal miner whose body and mind spend most of their time underground and in darkness. Norman is a cynical, greedy man obsessed with renting everything other than himself: his bathtub, his wife's services as a fortuneteller to the gullible, and later, his daughter's body. Molly calls the voyeur on the floor, kneeling in an obscene parody of Islamic prayer, "a toad-like Moor aroused by vision, preparing to leap into pagan space."[92] These first comparisons to Islam are hardly flattering, but not atypical for a barely literate northern Englishwoman from a poor industrial town who knows nothing of the outside world save for a few stereotypes that trickle up from war-embroiled colonial headquarters in London. At this point in the novel, "Muslim," "Moor," and "pagan" are interchangeable markers of sexual degeneracy and otherness to Molly, even as her own English father and living conditions are the real perversions.

It is thus fortunate that the strange but mitigating advents of both the Muslim Stick and the indigenous Om precede Molly's encounter with Islamic fundamentalism. The latter event comes in the form of "a Middle Eastern tourist, one El Kada who turned out to be a terrorist bent on blowing up the Houses of Parliament."[93] El Kada's name and actions bear a striking but anachronistic resemblance to "Al Qaeda," the organization responsible for destroying the World Trade Center's Twin Towers in New York City on September 11, 2001. Molly leaves home at age 30 and eventually, after the deaths of her parents and a few understandable psychological crises, becomes a teacher. The encounter with El Kada happens when Molly, Stick, Om, Molly's student and protégé Carolyn, and Molly's one adult English friend, a fellow teacher named Eileen, visit the British Museum to see its vast collection of Egyptian religious and art objects. The contentiousness of these objects' acquisition during the colonial era is paralleled by the fact that the 1956–1957 Suez conflict between Britain and Egypt has just begun. In the "terrorist" episode at the museum, Molly sees a "man in Arab dress holding a dagger aloft" screaming "Allahu Akbar!" Eileen says that it must be an Egyptian come to take back their artifacts from the British Museum as a result of the Suez conflict; and Molly replies "Poor Arab," for Stick's benefit and because though she "had not the least interest in world affairs . . . it did intrigue me that some imperial war at the far side of the world should have direct impact on small folk like us." Eileen's rejoinder: "Times like these call for patriotism."[94] This cartoonish "terrorist" episode featuring an orientalized Arab villain complete with raised dagger and foreign dress seemingly fits right into what Mahmood Mamdani calls the "culture talk" that occurs in contemporary U.S. and European discussions of links between Islam and terrorism: "the predilection to define cultures according to their presumed 'essential' characteristics, especially as regards politics."[95]

But here, not everything is as culturally essentialist as it seems. In their colonialist labeling of ancient Egyptian and many other cultures' sacred and other art objects as the products of "antiquity" and therefore a legacy left to all humanity, and in their presumption that they alone can provide the security historical artifacts require, the British Museum and government, and other pilfering Europeans, continually justify their refusal to return the objects to the plundered countries. The objects are also implicated in the ideological argument that Egypt's ancient North African civilization distinguishes and divorces it from the rest of "underdeveloped" Africa—the old justification of the transatlantic slave trade in West and Central Africa. "Ancient Egypt" currently occupies an entirely different set of galleries in the British Museum than does the "Middle East," separating the ancient and modern Arab histories of the region as though they were entirely different places in the world.[96] Molly and her friends jump into this fray, easily exposing its hypocrisies by identifying the religious fundamentalist, the nationalist Egyptian angry over Suez, and the patriot who wants the return of his ancestral legacy (Muslim conquest of Egypt in the 600s A.C.E. aside)—in other words, the Muslim, the Arab, and the ancient Egyptian indigene—as one and the same. This is the decolonial refusal of imposed borders afforded by the marvelous real, with El Kada as Carpentier's agent who reaches an "exaltation of spirit." In the end, El Kada is found not guilty of all charges, but Eileen the English

schoolteacher is revealed to be his possible secret lover and recruit, having herself been previously sympathetic to communism and thus other subversive
-isms. She is shunned by all except Molly, and he is deported, according to the
magistrate, "for his own safety, given public sensitivities over the current conflict between our nations."[97] The British government and the British Museum are
not ready to give up the colonialist temporal and racial separation of ancient
Egypt from contemporary Egyptian political crises. Molly and her crew of "small
folk," though, already live on the margins where linear time and cultural boundaries fracture; and in this limit state, no one (thing) is a greater example of the
improbable manifesting as real than the animate Muslim walking stick.

Stick declares to Molly that his reason for existence is as object to her "true
subject, though I am your servant and pedicle."[98] It is unclear whether he (Dabydeen does not gender Stick, but Molly comes to call him "my peculiar husband")
means that Molly is the actor who acts upon him, or whether he is a literal object
to whom she is a subject.[99] He is also an imperious individual for one who declares
himself servant. Molly is injured in her twenties in 1941 during the second World
War, in a bomb blast that also kills her mother. It is yet another of her parents'
many betrayals, as she and her mother are only walking outside at the behest of
the mother, who has developed a sudden desire, after many years, to leave her bed.
No one is sympathetic: "The local newspaper, desensitised by war casualties,
poked fun at her: 'Accrington medium fails to foresee her death. Daughter Molly
blinded by blast.' (I was blinded but only for a day, my sight returning suddenly)."[100]
This confluence of wartime psychosomatic blindness, literal physical blindness,
mind-blindness, and Molly's metaphorical awakening to her mental abuse by her
mother (and not just sexual abuse by her father and his friends), is accompanied
by a leg injury from the blast that results in a permanent limp. Molly is so damaged at this juncture that she is completely numb; she reflects, "Mum had damaged me. I would limp all my life. She had gained cruel revenge over Dad and his
men, yielding me up to them as damaged, never to be quite as desirable as
before."[101] This seeming lack of emotion allows her to survive, though she does
not live. Still, she has experienced a literal dismemberment that is the beginning
of limbo becoming; and Stick marvelously appears to facilitate the reassembly.
As soon as Stick develops the ability to speak, he offers her a diagnosis and a prescription: "Yours is an inward malady and blight of soul. Serum, transfusions,
new medicines, deodorants, insect repellents, changes in hygiene, all these stay
or even cure diseases but only prayer can ease yours. Come, kneel beside me, open
your heart to Christ our Saviour and to Allah for They truly know the shame and
the pain of males."[102] Stick is both doctor and mystic—in effect, a shaman, and a
gender-sensitive one. He declares himself Muslim, but with ancestral ties to Christianity, and at the outset invokes the historical beginning of conflict between
Muslims and Christians—the Crusades. Stick is an unusually proud product of
the Crusades, casually noting that "One branch of the family tree beheld crusaders

engaging with Saladin at the Battle of Jerusalem," and "my sap is the splendour of merged continents, at once Muslim and Christian."[103]

Stick sometimes wavers between ancestral commitments, though his "Muslim side" usually—not always—wins out. After meeting the indigenous Om and being reminded of origin stories, he goes into extensive "family tree" detail. "The more I discourse with him, the more I feel Muslim," Stick says, claiming that his origin was as "a fresh seed gathered up from Muslim lands by the hand of a crusader [that] was sown in England, sprouted, flowered, and somehow mated with a native plant . . . so that the memory of Islam in the original seed faded with age, dunes echoing with the chants of the muezzin giving way to English forests and the song of nightingales."[104] Stick also names and is proud of Muslim mathematical and artistic accomplishments. But he too is ready for a rearticulation of self. Although "feeling Muslim" is equated with a return to origins that is facilitated by the indigene par excellence Om, Stick has a limited understanding of Islam, having been English for centuries. He celebrates the Golden Age of Islam by attempting to impose a piece of Islam on the newly arrived and as yet nameless indigene, demanding they name him Om partly after the zero symbol invented by medieval Muslim mathematicians, and partly because it was some of the Muslim name Omar.[105] Many religions are implicated in the naming: "zero" and "Omar" are Muslim; another O-related Greco-Christian concept to which Stick refers is God in the Book of Revelation declaring himself "the Alpha and the Omega," the beginning and end (of the Greek alphabet and existence); and "Om" "sounded Hindu," as Stick says, because it is the cosmic sound of the soul and the universe in Hinduism and Buddhism, repeated in many mantras.[106] Om is the everyman of religion.

Stick's limited Muslim religiosity, filtered through his Englishness, unfortunately includes a belief that being Muslim involves a certain inherent violence, as reflected in the way he insults Molly: "'You blasphemous daughter of a pig, you vile progeny and very symbol of barrenness,' Stick cursed, trying to sound Koranic. It raised itself as if to hit me."[107] Of Eileen, the possible El Kada schoolteacher recruit, he says "She's a brave soul, she stirs the memory of Islam in me, works me up to a rage. . . . She's probably deserving of whatever medals you Muslims hand out to martyrs, but at the end of the day she's a mere Englishwoman, not a bloody Moor."[108] Stick's fullaman "knowledge" of Islam is a collection of half-truths any layperson might have: medieval Muslim achievements in mathematics, astronomy, and architecture; Moors in the Iberian Peninsula; harems and slave markets; blasphemy, pigs, illegitimacy, and infertility as Islamically problematic; suspicions that Muslims might be brave but also filled with rage and desiring martyrdom; and a belief that the Qur'an employs the archaic, punitive language of the Old Testament, King James Version. The anti-Semitism, though, belongs mostly to Molly, who filters her own experience of sexual abuse through Shakespearean stereotypes of Shylock the moneylender and World War II images of concentration camps.[109] Harold, the main Jewish character, is a wealthy man who orchestrates her abuse with her father—he watches and collects money, but never touches her. That Molly equates herself with a concentration camp victim is not illogical, given the extent of her mental and physical childhood abuse and her confinement at home. But here Dabydeen deliberately plays with the idea of the sacrosanctness of the Jewish Holocaust in Nazi Germany and Europe, particularly in Molly's realization—near the end of the novel, when she is in the British Guiana jungle trying to make sense of her life—that "I loathe the Jew for she is myself, not even my shadow or twin."[110] It is still problematic, historically and for a European Christian who has lived through the Second World War, that "the Jew" is the internalized object of self-loathing.

Molly, the Englishwoman, is the real bringer and embodiment of violence. While Stick has pretensions to violence, it is she who tells him in the jungle that he should help Om's pacifist tribe arm themselves: "You have to use all the military knowledge of your Muslim forebears and show them how to make weaponry, powder that will explode, metal-tipped spears, whatever will repel the crusaders." Stick's retort is that "You want to bring your civilisation to them, at the heart of which is war."[111] The British colonizer, it seems, cannot help herself, even when she has herself been the victim of violence. She is in Demerara—once a Dutch then a British colony, now incorporated as an administrative region into independent Guyana—to find, through Stick and Om, a "new creed," but the environment of the New World stirs the ancestral impulses to conquer and kill the Other.[112]

Om is the antithesis of these impulses, though he is, as later discussed, a murderer himself. He appears on Molly's doorstep in England one day, unable to speak, and with "flesh so burnished . . . [it was] sable."[113] His "clothes were flimsy, pasted to his body so that he appeared naked, his crotch bulging against thin cotton trousers. He shivered, sneezed, and a sycamore leaf fell from his hair. I gazed at the traces of bark and twigs caught there, and struggled for words."[114] He looks like the incarnation of a jungle, and more importantly, he smells like it, to the point where "he is different in essence, he is another kind of person altogether, another species."[115] Om never quite attains personhood in the novel. He is a smell, a body produced by the Guianese landscape—as in *Oudin*—and a language only Stick is able to decipher, describing it first as "a mixture of Sanskrit and a Greek dialect, but all in pidgin," and then "More like Aramaic than anything else."[116] Aramaic is the Semitic language of Jesus's time and place, preceding both Hebrew and Arabic. Om is therefore linked to Old World religious origins in addition to his own Guianese indigeneity. He is a figure that refuses linear temporality and, according to Stick, even bodily fixity:

> He comes from a place where people don't have names or reckon their ages. Demerara, in the jungles of British Guiana. I'm not sure how he travelled here. If I under-

stand him properly he flew in. In Demerara people apparently are not merely human but also partly winged or four-footed or crawling. All the creatures of the jungle are of one body, none of them are male or female, but neither and both. It's probably all bullshit. By the looks of him he's stowed away in the hull of a ship bringing a load of timber and bananas to this country.[117]

Molly then tries to imagine Om as "a man-boy or boy-woman, ageless, sexless, an inhabitant of earth and river and air."[118] This story of Om's inhuman, shapeshifting origins echoes European naturalist accounts and drawings from the fifteenth- to seventeenth-century Age of Discovery that render the human, animal, and plant inhabitants of the Americas as creatures both wondrous and grotesque. Atemporality and a strong connection to nature are traits attributed to "natives" in the colonial schema, and the novel perpetuates this idea, as it similarly does not refute the generativeness of the womb-like Eldoradian jungle. Om also smells like "cathedral wood," specifically the wood of an English cathedral bombed by the Germans; it is later revealed that Om did in fact stow away on a timber boat bringing wood from the colony in Guiana to rebuild the cathedral in England.[119] Stick declares him a relative not only for linguistic connections and sparking Muslim memories, but because Om smells like wood: "He's my human relation though the Demerara jungle is a different species of trees from ours. His is green-heart and mahogany and mora and helisong. They're not yew"—and not "you," a pun directed at poor Molly, who so far has had no contact with nature.[120] Om's smell of nature is tainted when they name him "Om," for they "had given him a bad odour. We had besmirched his nature by our baptism ceremony," which involved an unceremonious christening with beer.[121] He is simply not meant to be in England, and is eventually deported when some "malicious person or persons" report Molly "for harbouring an illegal immigrant."[122] When the racist English police seize him, they tell Molly "Madam, this country will soon be overrun by coloureds. They'll threaten our way of life. They're an idle lot, scroungers, pickpockets, beggars"; whereupon she replies, "No different from folk around here then."[123] Here Molly and the author acidly insert themselves into contentious contemporary debates over immigration and refugees in Britain, which have added to mid-twentieth-century hand-wringing over Caribbean, Asian, and African immigrants from the former colonies, a new-old religious dimension: Islam and its "clash of civilizations" with English Christianity. The novel, though, emphasizes that Christianity imposed upon the colonies and people of color first.

Om's journey to England began with the advent of a nameless Christian missionary from Coventry Cathedral to his village in the Guianese jungle. The villagers leave the missionary in peace, even building him a hut and providing him with food, until his proselytizing becomes aggressive: "He held up his book— obviously the Bible, but they were not to know, never before having seen a book. He read from it. He waved it over them. His voice was stern and sugary in turns.

Their confusion turned to fright. Om stopped him."[124] "Stopping him" is the only thing the villagers understand Om, a village leader, to have done. Stick explains to Molly that "it was not murder. People here don't know how to murder. . . . It happened. They took the body to the riverside and lowered it in, hoping their ancestors would fathom the mystery of the event. . . . For the first time in their history they began to doubt whether the effects of what Om did—what they all did, since Om was all of them—could be withstood by their ancestors."[125] The villagers, or rather their individual bodies, are not immortal; they experience death by natural causes, but they do not murder. Christian Molly and Muslim Stick are by contrast well acquainted with killing in all individual, divine, and communal ways. The villagers' history is "not history in the ordinary sense for time seemed marked by natural cataclysms" from which they are repeatedly saved by phenomena they see as interventions by their ancestors.[126] Their time-lessness is related to their lack of distinction between self and other. Molly discovers near the end of the novel that Om's "true name" is "Apotu, which is the name of his village—apparently none of the inhabitants have names except that of the village . . . it was a word without meaning. It signified everywhere and nowhere, everything and nothing, so it had no meaning."[127] Om, again, is Guiana's landscape. That Stick does not complete the formulation "everywhere and nowhere, everything and nothing, so it had no meaning" with "and every meaning" is an ironic refusal of potential.

Throughout the novel, Om/Apotu is problematically invested with every meaning: all indigeneity, all ancient culture, all religion, all environmental landscapes, all time, and both life and death. He is a catalytic agent for both Molly and Stick, allowing the Christian woman leaning on her Muslim crutch to transcend their base Old World civilizational configuration. In England Molly calls Om "the boy-man whom I would adopt as mystery and legendary child," but in Guiana she is the child he teaches to observe and commune with nature in order "to stop time, to reach back and retrieve something from the past, to hold it up in my mind and marvel at it as Raleigh would have done when he dreamt of discovering his first nugget of gold."[128] Raleigh's myth of El Dorado is Molly's only referent for the jungle. What she wants from the experience, though, is not to conquer, but to contemplate—to change her temporal mode. Demerara, a "swamp or sanatorium I know not," shows her that she has been living without understanding, and that she needs to slow down in order "to glimpse some design."[129] "Slowing down" to examine discrete particles in one's cache of memories and experiences or decipher a grand divine plan is different from a desire to "stop time" completely; these two modes of resisting a linear temporality that is bound up in colonial narratives of civilizational progress are conflated in the novel. She desires to drift awhile in an inactive state in which she is nonetheless sole agent of her body and destiny. Most of her belongings are swept away by a flood in the village, so she is not bound by material possessions either.

Stick, who has traveled with Molly to Guiana, also stays behind, having literally and figuratively rooted. The novel concludes with Molly bidding her crutch and friend farewell and seeing "a tiny sprig issuing from a crevice in its body, auguring mongrel leaf and bud and flower. The Demerara jungle has embraced Stick in a new kinship and adventure into life. A thousand years after I've turned to dust it will bear witness, as a living tree, to the love, to the grief, which stops us now from speaking words which have become needless."[130] The wooden Stick is now Muslim, Christian, and Guianese, nature converging with its human counterpart Om. Molly disappears into the jungle as have many Europeans before her, but her quest is not for glory or public recognition—it is another stereotypic European quest in the colonies, the search for self. She is explorer without being colonizer, relatively unafraid of the jungle in contrast to colonial Europeans who found it to be, as Achille Mbembe says, "a space of fatigue, danger, and exhaustion for the colonizer," where he or she is beset by dysentery, death, and the ceaseless "vertigo" and "whirl" of obscene, excessive plants and animals, including such animals as gorillas, "hybrid animals par excellence—half-human, half-beast."[131] A superabundance of natural life does not frighten Molly, who has experienced so many iterations of the marvelous and unnatural. What is important in the end is the perseverance of life, and she speaks of her wish to witness that flowering in Stick and in the rest of the jungle: "I want to be eternal witness, or if not eternal I want to believe that my witnessing of them held some meaning."[132] Witnessing, as she says when describing Stick becoming a living tree, is to be present in and for life in a more fundamental way than allowed by mere words.

LOGOPHAGY: EATING THE WORD AND NEW WORLD RELIGIOUS REINVENTION

Witnessing and speaking words are different for Molly because words carry the power of signification, and can alter reality by altering its perception. Words can lie, or create, or both. *Molly and the Muslim Stick* and *The Far Journey of Oudin* share one peculiar additional instance of Caribbean trick(st)ery: in both texts, the primary female characters literally eat words (written on paper), a phenomenon I call logophagy and define as both the consumption of any written words, and the metaphysical and material eating of the Word of God. The theological idea of "the Word," as I will describe, plays an important role of Islam and Christianity, the religious contexts of Dabydeen's *Molly* and Harris's *The Far Journey of Oudin*. Beti, wife of Oudin, performs one main instance of logophagy in Harris's novella: she swallows the piece of paper on which Oudin contractually promised their unborn child—the future of the Indo-Guyanese people—to the landowner Ram. In Dabydeen's novel there are multiple instances of word-eating: the adult Molly eats a letter written to her by the banker and pimp Harold that accompanies a payoff, reminisces about her teenage degradation, and asserts that even in

death he will be watching her; and the indigenous Guianese villagers eat the
Christian missionary's Bible after Om kills him. Beti, Molly, and the villagers all
consume the signifiers that call into being realities they reject, but ingestion is
incorporation into the body, so they are not free of those realities.

Eating the Bible—the eating not just of words, but of the Word of God—is, in
Molly, a rejection of colonial Christianization, but it also echoes the multiple biblical instances in which either prophets or the laity are exhorted to consume the
Word. In Deuteronomy is the famous biblical verse in which mankind is told that
"one does not live by bread alone, but by every word that comes from the mouth
of the LORD"; Ezekiel eats a "written scroll" of prophetic knowledge extended
from God's hand that "had writing on the front and on the back, and written on it
were words of lamentation and mourning and woe"; and in the Book of Revelation (of the Apocalypse), which closes the New Testament and harks back to
Ezekiel, John takes from an angel and also eats the "little scroll" containing the
knowledge that will allow him to prophesy.[133] In Ezekiel's case, the scroll tastes "as
sweet as honey," and in John's case the scroll is also "sweet as honey in my mouth;
but when I had eaten it, my stomach was made bitter."[134] The consumption of the
Word by mankind in Deuteronomy similarly follows a description of the eating of
(presumably sweet) manna. All in all, the biblical Word, the beginning of Creation, may be described as both a sweet and bitter pill to swallow.

The Guianese villagers' ingestion of the Bible and the biblical word is reminis-
cent of Christian transubstantiation and the lapsarian fall from the Garden of
Eden: they eat the pages and gain knowledge of evil, and lose their connection to
the ancestors that they previously worshiped. After Om kills the missionary, the
villagers "decided to end all trace of him, burning his clothing and eating his Bible.
Eating it, for he had held the book aloft and spoken from it, words coming from
his belly and mouth. Burning the Bible would not do, it had to be returned into
the body, so each villager was fed pages."[135] The bodies of the missionary and the
villagers are analogous, in this reckoning, if they can chew the cud of him. The
jungle is a place that demands acknowledgment of the continuity of nature.

Though there is no logophagy mentioned in the Qur'an, there are multiple and
regionally diverse instances of "eating the Word" associated with Islam. Rudolph
Ware documents the long tradition of children in West African Qur'an schools
and adults licking the written *basmala* from their hands, or drinking or eating it,
in the quest to embody the Word through learning and deed.[136] This follows "a
number of medieval medical treatises in the well-known Ṭibb al-Nabawī (Medicine of the Prophet) genre. Many medieval scholars recommended physical assimilation of the Word of God (through ingestion and/or bathing) as a central
aspect of healing."[137] In twelfth- and thirteenth-century Egypt and Syria, and later
Iran and India, spiritual wellness and prophylactic medical traditions included ink-
ing or inscribing the words of the Qur'an in a bowl, and then drinking water from
that bowl in order to receive the blessings (*baraka*) of the words. *Al-Ṭibb al-Nabawī*,

the aforementioned Prophetic medicine, also involved the ingestion of amulets on which Qur'anic verses were written to guard against the "evil eye" and black magic. Muslim jurists of the period generally ruled that *intent* was crucial, and that permissible "ingestion is to be distinguished from destruction" of the Word.[138] In addition, as discussed in the first chapter, a type of simultaneously oral communication and written literacy plays an important part in the Qur'an: the first word of the Qur'an revealed to the Prophet Muhammad is generally taken to be *'IQRĀ*, an Arabic command meaning "Read!" but also "Recite!"[139] The command is given to the Prophet and humanity by the angel Jibrīl (Gabriel), who recites and reveals the Qur'an. The tradition of eating Qur'anic words therefore links the oral functions of speaking, eating, reading, and reciting, with literacy and the recorded codex in tantalizing ways revolving around the embodiment of the Word of God.

In *Molly and the Muslim Stick*, Molly's ingestion of Harold's letter is an attempted rejection of filthy lucre and her unmentionable past of being sold for money, but she cannot escape that easily. She attempts to vomit it up, but the letter, and symbolically his control of her body, "was lodged within me."[140] There is nonetheless a successful purging. The letter has been brought to her at a mental hospital by Harold's spectral and oppressed wife, who is his mouthpiece. When Molly defies Harold's wishes by ingesting the letter and rejecting the money he sends her, through his wife, Harold "spoke again, this time not in words but in a cornucopia of metal. A shower of sovereigns, half-crowns, crowns, erupted from his wife's mouth, fell upon my head. The shower became a hailstorm, soon the hospital floor was awash with coins."[141] Molly tells her fellow patients and hospital Matron who are scrambling for the money that "It's the product of an enema," but "they would not heed me, heaping up the turds of metal."[142] Here the processes of digestion cooperate to eject what ought not to have been ingested and incorporated; in the vomiting and excretion of money by Harold's wife, Molly's body is by proxy rejecting being sold. The consumption of words and the Word and the marvelous realist expulsion of money from the viscera are limbo dismemberment and refashioning.

Beti in *Oudin* is also a woman in the process of becoming Caribbean. She is a postindenture Indo-Guyanese woman whose grandfather came from India but who is nonetheless still "the representation of a slave despite her secret longing and notion to be free. . . . She had the refined emaciated face of an East Indian and Guyanese woman that looked older than it was, bearing the stamp of a well-known ornament."[143] The ornament is either a forehead *bindi* (dot) or *tilak* (a longer mark, *tika* in Guyana), the "third eye" Hindu mark on the forehead, or a *nakphul*, the classic Indian nose pin or ring discarded by Indo-Caribbean women in the generations after indenture. Beti "eats the contract between Oudin and Ram and saves the inheritance for her unborn child," seemingly acknowledging that "history is the body of the other that must be swallowed" and becoming "Kali, the Goddess of Death, [who] devours all, including time itself, thus renewing her promise of fulfillment and regeneration."[144] In essence, Beti ingests history, which becomes nutrition for her unborn child. As this is history in writing, however, it is also a speech act that Beti commits. She is the one through whom the omnipresent Caribbean issue of the loss of oral ancestral language, as well as a peasant illiteracy that transcends location, is addressed: "She had swallowed it the night and morning of Oudin's death—in a wave and spasm and panic—for any kind of mysterious paper and appearance was to be swallowed, she knew, and given a chance to be digested. It was the oldest crumb of fear and habit binding the illiterate world of reflection around her. . . . She extracted it from his [dead] fingers, ate it and swallowed it before Ram arrived as she knew he would. Whatever unholy bargain had been consummated she had shattered in her breast."[145]

There was a single piece of paper possessed by illiterate Indian indentured laborers to the Caribbean and their near descendants: the "blue paper," their indentureship papers, issued by British bureaucrats of Empire and containing the only written documentation of their past. This documentation included names of parents, village, and region in India from which they had come; the name of the ship on which they had come to the New World; dates and period of indentureship; and the name of the Guianese sugar plantation to which they were allocated as labor. The majority of these papers, which functioned as totems rather than records for people who could not read, have been lost to history (until the advent of immigration "papers" to the United Kingdom and North America in the twentieth century, official papers in Guyana tended to be referred to a singular item, "a" paper). Though illiterate, Beti understands that to change the world, one must consume that which attempts to fix it as history and memory: the written document. She eats the contract that gives her child to the representative of a traditional past, Ram, and also symbolically eats the paper of colonialization. Beti's child's destiny involves a new language too—English. Mohammed, Oudin's brother, blames his father for the loss of Hindi: "But is who fault if the only language we got is a breaking-up or a making-up language?"[146] But Beti's illiteracy in the old language also promises literacy in the new.

Unlike Beti, Oudin falls short of being the harbinger of the future. His promise to give his child to Ram is the cause of his mysterious second death. Abraham is not actually permitted to sacrifice Ishmael (in the Qur'an; Isaac, in the Bible). Oudin unfortunately does sign the child away, and that is the end of him. His second demise is foreshadowed when he initially kidnaps Beti and they are on the run. Beti thinks that Oudin looks as though he has come from "a grave that left its vision of dead empires in him. . . . What she had to do was to make her kind of secret mark on him—the obvious mark an illiterate person must make in lieu of a signature and a name. With her toes she drew in the sand an incomprehensible fertile figure within a hollow cage at Oudin's feet. It was a way of saying she was equal to him after all."[147] The future is with Beti, with the woman (Harris does not shy away from this old reproductive trope), and not with Oudin, or the rest of the male Mohammed clan, or with old Ram, who imagines himself arbiter of the Indo-Caribbean future. *Oudin* ends with Ram, the masculine threat, reflecting that "Beti was another name for 'daughter,' the daughter of a race that was being fashioned anew. He must do everything to repair the damage he had unwittingly set in motion that she was a free woman at last."[148]

This chapter is less about globalizing the Muslim Caribbean than it is about Muslims settler-colonizing the Caribbean; an accurate way of putting their taking up residence, at least in the Guyanese landscape, through marvelous real mediation by Amerindian indigeneity. The land, however, whether it is sentient or not, does not annihilate them or treat them as it might a European colonizer. In a sense, those who are oppressed by forced labor origins or personal abuse are given a New World pass from destruction. But they must reinvent themselves, blend in, and conform to the natural dictates of the savanna and jungle. This leaves the troubling, unresolved concern of the absent-present Amerindians of Caribbean literature, and their deployment to establish authenticity of national belonging. They are not literary foils; they are real, politically underrepresented, and generally impoverished rural people who continue to live in Guyana.

Beti, the Indo-Guyanese logophagic, preliterate woman, embodies the future, after the land has failed to reproduce men to suit itself, and her child is temporarily written off. Harris leaves the Muslim Indo-Caribbean with a number of possible futures. The only certainty is what at first seems to be cyclical repetition, but may perhaps be more aptly described as a spiraling outward of parallel concentric whorls that repeat ad infinitum until they encompass all lands. And, characteristic of most of Harris's work, the land itself evinces agency and participation in the future. Harris reflects that "[t]he very *fixed* stages—upon which we build our cities—are *sentient* and *alive*. . . . The life of the earth needs to be seen *in fiction* as sensitively woven into the characters that move upon it, whose history, may I say, reflects a profound relation to the earth."[149] People must reflect their earthly and local geographic origins and movements. Stick, in *Molly*, embodies the sentience of the living earth, as well as an unfixed Muslim mobility. Not only is his life intertwined in the lives of human beings, but like the mythic flying Sheikh Sadiq the jinnī, he travels with people from the Old World to the New, symbiotically propping them up in his role as, he says, an anchoring pedicle. The function of the descending Caribbean limbo stick is not, then, to cause the human being to fall, but to encourage the spine to bend (as a vertebral pedicle does), forcing flexibility and a different way of walking the Caribbean. The marvelous real literature of environment suggests that Muslims in the Caribbean must consume the old and shape it into the new in their bodies: fullaman Muslims adapting to the Caribbean landscape, rather than the landscape adapting to them.

4 · "MUSLIM TIME"

The Muslimeen Coup and Calypso in the Trinidad Imaginary

The new calypso songs written for Trinidad's Carnival in February 1991 were focused on one unprecedented theme: Muslim insurrection in the Caribbean. Vincentian Brother Ebony and Trinidadian calypsonians, including the Mighty Sparrow, David Rudder, Cro Cro, and Preacher, sang of the Muslim coup d'état that had occurred a scant seven months earlier in Trinidad in July 1990, and the resulting state of emergency that had been lifted shortly before Carnival. The insurrection was led by Imam Yasin Abu Bakr (b. 1942), who is still leader of the St. James, Port of Spain–based coup organization the Jamaat al Muslimeen. I argued in the previous chapter for the "becoming native" of Muslims through a magical realist interpellation into the natural landscape of the Caribbean and through negotiation with Amerindian indigeneity. Muslims may thus acquire the legitimacy of mere presence, but *acceptance* into the fold is contingent on creolization and a demonstrated willingness to accept cultural hybridization: that is the condition of being a Caribbean citizen and political subject. The Trinidadian attempted coup by the Jamaat al Muslimeen disrupted the subsuming of Muslims into postcolonial Creole citizenship.

Abu Bakr—a tall and physically imposing man who often dresses in an Islamic *kufi* hat and white thobe, and who was filmed on early Trinidadian national television during the 1990 coup bearing arms—personally occupies the symbolic places of Trinidad's own Muslim(een) bogeyman and the originary Caribbean "terrorist." He is still the leader of the Jamaat al Muslimeen and still lives in Trinidad. His international movement is limited by the fact that he is on the North American no-fly list. In May 2019, he agreed to an interview with me that became lengthy, informative about the shifting grounds and demographics of Caribbean Islam in the twentieth century, frank in some surprising ways, and pointedly non-incriminating in others. It did matter to him that I identified myself as a Muslim, and a local mutual contact helped establish trust. He has given quite a few interviews, but in a way, at this time, he was in his late seventies and ready to talk. A charismatic character used to being a leader and a person of repute, Abu Bakr framed his own Trinidadian positionality as "this is my book. I am the author of this revolution," but "you would have to ask the people how they perceive me. I have no perception of myself. I am who I am."[1] As borne out by this and similar statements, the Imam well knows and enjoys his notoriety as a political public figure in Trinidad, the Caribbean, and the Western Hemisphere, but nonetheless views himself as a man of the people. He liked the 1991 calypso sung about him by the famed Mighty Sparrow (Slinger Francisco), he said, as it was "very positive."[2] Indeed Sparrow's calypso "Abu Bakr" very thoroughly detailed the Muslimeen's pre- and postcoup conflicts with the Trinidadian government over corruption, land grabs, the cocaine trade, and "political mischief."[3] Of Abu Bakr himself Sparrow asked in the song if Abu Bakr was "liberator," "gladiator," "agitator," "patriotic," "fanatic," or "idiosyncratic."[4] All may be true, to varying degrees.

As I will take up in the next and final chapter, as a result of the 1990 coup, Abu Bakr and the Muslimeen are now linked consistently and inaccurately by the Trinidadian government and international media to transnational terrorism associated with the Syrian Islamic State. In this chapter I focus on the time and aftermath of the coup itself. I examine Trinidadian American writer Brenda Flanagan's historical novel about the coup, *Allah in the Islands* (2009), and Trinidadian calypso music about Muslims and the Muslimeen coup. Flanagan is Abu Bakr's younger sister, though she does not advertise this fact in her work. I show that the Muslimeen coup is a watershed chronotopic Caribbean Muslim event that suggests ways of rethinking the trope of Caribbean creolization through the particularity of Islam and in the present moment of the global connectivity of the worldwide Muslim *ummah* (community). In general, I argue that Islam, as an ancestral and contemporary religion of both Afro- and Indo-Trinidadians, pushes against the structure and processes of postcolonial Trinidadian creolization that fix Christians of African descent and Muslims and Hindus of Indian descent as permanent communities in racial, cultural, and economic conflict with each other. Following Rhoda Reddock, I examine Trinidadian "creolization" in Edward Kamau Brathwaite's terms of a hybridization of race and culture that is inherently hierarchical.[5] Theologically speaking, there should be no racial hierarchy between Indian and African Muslims, but intra- and interreligiously, negative, racialized perceptions remain in Trinidad. In addition, no Muslim group is interested in subordinating itself to what is perceived to be either a nonreligious or Christian "Creole"—predominantly Afro-Creole—culture. The larger Muslim community in Trinidad is in a state of becoming, and the way that local Muslims engage with the global Muslim community shapes all Trinidadians' perceptions of Islam and the specter of global terrorism.

I make five major points about the contemporary mediation of Trinidadian creolization by the Islam of the Muslimeen-influenced national imaginary. First, harking back to the previous chapter, I show that the Muslimeen's impetus is to perform a *grounding* to establish a postcolonial Muslim Caribbean place of Islamic immanence that is a belonging to the land, and thus a belonging to the nation that proposes a citizenship not dependent upon religious or racial creolization.[6] The Muslimeen have done so by extending the geographic sphere of their private compound into national space, becoming a metonym of Islam's growth in Trinidad. Second, I argue that the Muslimeen create a circular, Afro-Caribbean "Muslim time," as David Rudder's postcoup calypso "Hoosay" describes, by ideologically recalling Islam as an ancestral African religion hostile to European colonization.[7] Islam is then characterized as Afro-Caribbean in its resistance, without passing through a process of syncretism with Christianity or Europe. The Muslim insurrectionists in Trinidad in 1990 were, with very few exceptions, Afro-Trinidadian, motivated by, they argued, social ills rather than religious concerns. The Jamaat al Muslimeen was a predominantly black Muslim nationalist organization with ideological links to the Islamic Party of North America and other groups abroad, as I will discuss.[8] Third, I argue that the base structure of racial-religious creolization and "douglarization" (Afro- and Indo-Trinidadian race-mixing) which historically polarizes Trinidad into two majority groups—Afro-Trini-Christian and Indo-Trini-Hindu/Muslim—is disrupted by the advent of contemporary Afro-Trinidadian conversion to Islam. Postcoup, Islam is visibly no longer an "Indian" religion. Fourth, the dress of Muslim Trinidadian women and marriage practices are—as in many places where Islam is a minority religion—the marker of "Islam" in Trinidad. I argue that the young female Muslimeen practice of "dressing Indian" as a way of "dressing Muslim" implicitly critiques the polarities of Trini creolization. Fifth, I show that creolization is a force that pushes back: calypsos about the coup emphasize its carnivalesque Trini nature and integrate the event *and* Muslims into the national story through a specifically Trini political and musical form, thereby *resisting* Islamic particularity.

In the coup calypso "Abu Bakr Take Over," Brother Ebony (Fitzroy Joseph) imagines what life might be like for men and women in a Muslim Trinidadian state ruled by Abu Bakr. Ebony sings:

> Ah done start to contemplate
> Livin' in a Muslim state
> Fire Mistah Abu Bakr take ovah
>
> Thinkin' how Ah go survive
> When I have meh seven wives
> Fire Mistah Abu Bakr take ovah[9]

Ebony's joking concern is about how he can handle multiple wives (there are four possible, not seven) in a Muslim state, but he ends with the real question: the thrice-repeated refrain "Who's de leada?" followed by "Robinson or Bakr?"[10] Ebony asks who is really in charge of Trinidad, Abu Bakr or then prime minister and coup hostage A.N.R. Robinson (1926–2014). The calypsonian warns that music and feteing (Trini music-and-dance partying) is the real national religion that Trinis would rise up to defend if they were suppressed in a Muslim or a secular state: "Deh go be mo' bacchanal / If dey say no Carnival."[11] As shown in the "Fire Mistah Abu Bakr take ovah" chorus of Ebony's song, the idea of "fire," Kevin Birth says, was after the coup associated with "widespread arson" and "being hot" in literal and figurative ways, as "a good fete is a hot fete . . . such heat is not only metaphorical but is also linked to Trinidadian ideas of the body and its functions."[12] Fire—there is also wordplay in the song implying that the government or Abu Bakr should be "fired" from leadership—is not a typical metaphor of Caribbean becoming or creolization, as it consumes and spreads. In Ebony's calypso, however, fire illustrates the nation's discomfort and fascination with the specter of Islam in the Caribbean. A non-Muslim calypsonian is containing Muslim fire in the traditional regional entertainments of Carnival and calypso—the great Trini cultural equalizers—just as those music and dance celebrations contained first slavery, and then postcolonial socioeconomic ills, by providing an outlet to endure them while integrating them into nation-building narratives. In 1991, calypso fete music did partly succeed in redirecting and defusing fears of Islamic propagation, reminding Trinidadians that theirs is a multiethnic society that has already integrated Muslims and representatives of almost every race and creed, and has the tools to attempt creolization of any cultural manifestation.

AFRO-TRINIDADIAN ISLAM: FROM MANDINGO MUTUAL AID TO ABU BAKR AND LIBYA

Muslims constitute about 6 to 8 percent of the population of Trinidad and Tobago and are mostly Indo-Trinidadian and Sunni.[13] Indian indentureship in Trinidad began in 1845 and ended in 1917. The first ship to bring migrants from Calcutta to Trinidad in May 1845 was owned by an Indian Muslim merchant and named the *Fatel Razack*, or the *Fath al Razack* (Victory of the Provider [Allah]).[14] But Islam in Trinidad, as discussed in the first chapter, begins neither with a "Muslim" ship of indenture and its Indo-Muslim contract laborer passengers, nor with early Muslimeen converts. It begins, as in Guyana, Jamaica, Suriname, and elsewhere in the Anglophone New World, including the United States, with the legacy of enslaved Africans. Guyana retained the term "fullaman" from the Fulani; Trinidad has a word of similar origin and definition to represent Muslims, "Ma(n)dinga." "Mandinga," or "Madinga" in Trinidadian parlance, occupies the same linguistic place as "fullaman" in Guyana. "Madinga," from "Mandingo," is sometimes used in Trinidad by Hindus "in jest."[15] That non-Muslims use these terms in jest but not necessarily rancor may be attributable to the fact that

Muslims were a small and mysterious minority in Trinidad—at least until the Muslimeen coup.

Many of the enslaved Africans in the New World who were literate and could leave written records of themselves were Muslim Fula or Mandingo (Mandinka), as noted in the first chapter and evidenced by the Jamaican Arabic autobiographical fragments of Senegambian Mande Muhammad Kabā Saghanughu, and Abū Bakr al-Ṣiddīq of Timbuktu. Trinidad's colonial Afro-Muslim history centers on one early nineteenth-century, pre-Emancipation association of mostly Mandingo men who bought their own freedom.[16] In addition to building a community "to maintain their religious profession," with the Senegalese Samba Makumba serving as "priest," the men embarked on a mutual aid society project of liberating other Muslim Africans right off of slave ships. Makumba related that "association members would be the first on board when a slaver landed and would redeem the Muslims. In turn, the newly freed men had to work and pay their dues to the group in order for another coreligionist to be released from bondage."[17] The Mandingo mutual aid society of Muslims in Trinidad had more power than might be expected for freed slaves in their time and place—especially when African slavery in the Caribbean is viewed inaccurately through the lens of chattel slavery in the United States. The society redeemed 500 African Muslims and may have been responsible for 17 percent of the 2,956 manumissions in Trinidad between 1808 and 1834.[18] In no way did the Trinidadian Mandingo Muslims exercise any state power, but they were evidently left alone in the early nineteenth century—crucially, when the abolitionist movement was gaining traction in England—to associate with each other, earn money, buy and liberate their fellow Muslims, and petition the government. The image of association members being "the first on board when a slaver landed [to] redeem the Muslims" is a powerful and complicated one. The "Mandingo society" counted a Senegalese majority, but included men from a number of different West African tribal groups; there was, says Sylviane Diouf, "conflation of Muslim and Mandingo" in Trinidad.[19] The association chose to liberate only Muslims, a pragmatic choice for freedmen of few resources, and they sometimes had to choose religious affinity—fellow Muslims—over members of their own tribes or regional African groups. This choice foreshadows the post-Muslimeen coup fear of Trinidadians: that Muslims would always be loyal to coreligionists before other fellow citizens.

Enslaved Africans were emancipated in Trinidad in 1834. Members of the society of free Mandingo attempted to leave Trinidad and return to Africa several times. Their petitions for repatriation, including requests for armed protection in international waters, were repeatedly denied by the British colonial government. Upon their final departure attempt in 1838, their then imam and leader Yunus Mohammad Bath (sometimes rendered Jonas or John Mohammed Bath), who claimed to be a "sultan of Gambia" and remains "one of the most notable and revered names of African Muslims in Trinidad," was informed by the governor of

Trinidad that "the administration in London wanted the men and their families to know that they would face danger in going back to Africa, including the possibility of being enslaved again."[20] After this crushing disappointment the Mandingo Muslim society fades from the historical record, leaving no Muslim direct descendants.

There is other evidence of Muslims in Trinidad beyond the Mandingo and their society. Diouf writes that at times, "the attorney general accepted affidavits from Muslims who had sworn their oaths on the Holy Book. It was a recognized practice, and again, apparently, no question was raised as to their origin"—echoing Magistrate R. R. Madden's acceptance of the origins and education of the enslaved Muslims he met in Jamaica.[21] In addition, "Mohamed, Abouberika, Hammadi, Malick, Mohammado, Abdoulie, Salhim, Mohammed, Mohammedu, and Mohammedou were some of the Muslim names surviving in Trinidad."[22] Stories about African Muslims also come to us through the remembered surprise of the earliest Indian Muslim indentured laborers upon encountering fellow Muslims in Trinidad. Historian and former Trinidad government minster Brinsley Samaroo—who had contentious dealings in 1987 with the future Muslimeen, when, as Minister of Local Government and Community Development, he negotiated a land dispute with them, writes,[23] "Evidence of the African Muslim presence, and of their religious fervour, is acknowledged by East Indians who arrived in Trinidad from 1845. In 1946 for example, an elder in the Indian Muslim community recalled that in his early boyhood he had been shown a copy of the Qur'an in Arabic by someone whose father had received it as a gift from a Mandingo. At the present time there is a Mandingo Road in South Trinidad, and it is not unusual to hear rural people refer to Muslims as 'Mandingas.'"[24] Diouf argues that African Muslims in Trinidad did not leave descendants who identified as Muslim for a number of reasons: as elsewhere in the Americas, the women were not Muslim; conversion in lands where there was no supporting history and educational structure for Islam was rare; and Islam is ostensibly a strict monotheistic religion that was less receptive to syncretism than Catholicism in the New World.[25]

Still, Islam has many strains: like Talal Asad, as I discuss in the introduction, Aisha Khan argues that there is a "need to probe our speculations—any teleological predeterminations inhering in our historical narratives—as well as revisit our analytical categories."[26] Khan's anthropological findings on Indo-Muslim-Trinidadian perceptions of *simi-dimi*—cultural practices and ideas that are religiously influenced but outside the purview of religious doctrine—appear to corroborate that Caribbean Islam is subject to similar "high" (doctrinal) and "low" (cultural) parallel traditions that Paul Younger and Steven Vertovec argue is characteristic of Hinduism in the Caribbean (and India).[27] Simi-dimi is framed by some Muslims as, variously, "common knowledge [that] is undisciplined knowledge," the "ingression of heterodoxy . . . the consequence of comess," and, ultimately, "dilution and loss of identity—absorption into the cultural hegemony of Afro and Christian Trinidad."[28] In my own experience, in Trinidad and Guyana there is often crossover between what is quasi-religiously attributed to simi-dimi (or *semi-jemi*, depending on local accent) and what is attributed to *kala jadoo* (Hindi, black magic), or to the Afro-Caribbean syncretic spiritual practice of Obeah. Maintaining the religious "authenticity" of Islam is folded into discourses of racial mixing and creolization in Trinidad. Khan's fieldwork in Trinidad suggests, paradoxically but unsurprisingly when it comes to knowledge not believed to be doctrinal, that the efficacy of simi-dimi is publicly condemned by many Trinidadians but privately believed by most. In the twentieth and twenty-first centuries, such beliefs are frowned upon by Caribbean Islamic neo-traditionalists, including those who hail an ancestral religious legacy of African Islam to bolster their political aims.

The Muslimeen, who are mostly Afro-Trinidadian, counted as many as 2,000 members during 1960s and 1970s "uprisings" in Trinidad, but their numbers dwindled to about 500 in 2012.[29] Their earliest and much smaller protests were connected to the African American civil rights movement in the United States and to land disputes in Trinidad as the petro-economy grew, but they dissipated and the Muslimeen remained quiescent for two decades. The 1990 coup is what changed national perceptions of Muslims.

On July 27, 1990, led by Abu Bakr, 114 armed members of the Muslimeen seized control of the Trinidadian government and held Prime Minister Robinson and other government ministers hostage, in an attempted coup that lasted six days before the Muslimeen were promised amnesty and a cease-fire, and surrendered to the army and police. Perhaps the most vehement point Abu Bakr made to me was his disagreement with how the end of the coup is typically framed as a Muslimeen "surrender," arguing that "it was not a surrender, it was an agreement. . . . I refuse to submit to that, that there was a surrender . . . when you surrender the first thing you do is lay down your arms . . . there was no laying down arms, I was insistent that the international community—because there were journalists from all over the world by that time—did not have the false idea that there was a surrender. . . . You can see me coming out of TTT and my gun is in my hand. Now you don't surrender with a gun in your hand, you got to put it down."[30] Whether in surrender or agreement, Abu Bakr holding a gun, then Abu Bakr raising his empty hands above his head and at times smiling, are the first of many clear media images Trinidad and the world saw of the Muslimeen's leader (see fig. 4.1). Those images remain influential and linked to Muslims in the Trinidadian imaginary.

The wounded Robinson and other members of his cabinet were held by the Muslimeen at the seat of Parliament, the Red House. The Muslimeen also took control of the national television station Trinidad and Tobago Television (TTT), firebombed Police Service Headquarters, and attempted to burn down or capture the National Broadcasting Service and other public buildings.[31] Abu Bakr immediately began broadcasting over TTT a series of addresses to the nation, book-

FIGURE 4.1 Yasin Abu Bakr speaks with other freed members of the Jamaat al Muslimeen in Port of Spain, Trinidad, on July 1, 1992, two years after their attempted coup in 1990. (AP Photo/Willie Alleyne.)

ended by political calypso music. As journalist and eyewitness Selwyn Ryan reported, Trinidadian viewers at first believed the coup was a prank. When Abu Bakr and the head of TTT issued a television declaration of the coup, many "felt that the announcement was either a 'joke' or a promotion for some theatrical event."[32] Theatricality, "mas" (masking) play, Anansi trickery, and dissimulation were familiar elements of a Caribbean culture shaped by colonial African slavery. It was a few months too early for Carnival, but Trinidadians could be forgiven for assuming the singular TTT declaration of a coup was an elaborate and humorous pre-Carnival hoax. The medium of television was also relatively new to Trinidad, and TTT was the only television station. Raoul Pantin (d. 2015), a journalist who was taken hostage at the Red House, noted that at the time of the coup, the television medium and the revelations it had brought about the government when filming Parliament were so new to Trinidadians that they were still "shocked, mortified, and scandalized to see their elected representatives on television actually carrying on like seasoned fish-market vendors, hurling invective and vituperation across the floor, lolling back in their chairs, reading newspapers, or eating nuts during debates."[33] Trinidad was then treated to the spectacle of the coup unfolding on television and radio—perhaps its first sensational national media event.

Trinidadians did not consider late twentieth-century Trinidad (or the Caribbean) to be the kind of place where coups, much less Muslim religious coups, happened; such events were assumed to be limited to neighboring Latin America, the faraway Middle East, and the crumbling Soviet Bloc. But the television announcement was no joke: thirty-one people allegedly lost their lives as a direct or indirect result of the coup, while approximately 700 were wounded, and arson, looting, and property damage costs were estimated at anything from TT $50 million to $350 million.[34] As a condition of their surrender or agreement, the Muslimeen were promised amnesty. Abu Bakr alleged to me that attorney general and hostage Selwyn Richardson attempted to trick the Muslimeen about the promised amnesty, writing the wrong Constitutional amnesty provision number on pardon documents until he was stopped by Minister of Energy Kelvin Ramnath, and taking the Muslimeen's copies of the signed amnesty; a copy was smuggled out in Ramnath's jacket and discovered by Abu Bakr's wife when Ramnath, reportedly an asthmatic, was taken to the hospital.[35] Nonetheless, the Muslimeen were arrested and imprisoned without trial for two years. They were eventually given amnesty and released. From prison, says Abu Bakr, he was able to influence December 1991 Trinidadian elections against Robinson's National Alliance for Reconstruction (NAR) with two letters published in the newspaper, because the people were sympathetic to him and his cause: "People have told me many times, 'Boss, if we didn't, that you wasn't coming out of jail . . . we need to continue to get people who would stand up and speak for us against all of these great injustices that we have suffered as enslaved people.' . . . It's chattel slavery and that's the end of it . . . and indentured labor is also slavery, yes, same slavery."[36] Abu Bakr links Muslimeen advocacy to anticolonial struggles against both African slavery and Indian indentureship, making him strikingly inclusive in the racially polarized field of postindependence Trinidadian politics. The Jamaat al Muslimeen remains as a relatively quiet and smaller community in its Mucurapo Road compound in St. James, though government and police scrutiny has continued to fall upon its members, for reasons I will discuss further in the next chapter.

It had been 150 years since Trinidad encountered a black Muslim.[37] Nonetheless, "awareness of the two centuries of African Muslims' presence in the Caribbean, along with the far longer history of Islam in Africa, prompts Afro-Trinidadian Muslims to refer to themselves as 'returnees' rather than as 'converts.'"[38] New Muslims in the Caribbean and in the United States also, these days, refer to themselves as "reverts." Though it has special ancestral resonance to people of African descent in the Americas, especially for groups like the Muslimeen that conceive of Islam as antiracist, the idea of return and reversion to Islam has broad application. It derives from an Islamic jurisprudential belief drawn from a combination of *hadīth* Prophetic sayings and actions and Qur'anic verse that all babies are born Muslim and in a state of *fitra*, a state of primordial human innocence and Islamic submission to God that rejects the Christian doctrine of original sin.[39] *Fitra* is the doctrine of the always-already Muslim in a state of immanence. Abu Bakr and his followers were not, it could be said, Caribbean converts to Islam; they were African Muslims who had always followed Islam through both a continental and a human legacy.

The Muslimeen, though they invoked African roots, sought the ideal of a "pure" Islam devoid of cultural influences. In late twentieth-century Trinidad, faced with a newly visible Afro-Muslim group, Indo-Muslims were divided in their attitudes toward the Indian cultural overlay of their Islam.[40] They were also divided in their reactions to the coup. Some cited support for their "Muslim brothers," but most condemned the Muslimeen's violence and status as "converts" who "were not 'true' Muslims; nor, it was alleged, did the Muslimeen fully understand the teachings of Muhammed."[41] Daurius Figueira, in a witness account of the Muslimeen coup that problematically ascribes *shirk* religious practices and *kuffar* unbeliever status to non-Muslimeen and non-Sunni Muslim and state actors, nonetheless reaches some truth about race in Trinidad when he alleges that "it is the racism, basic and primordial of Indian Islam that drove the urban, Afro-Trinbagonian Muslim to form Jamaats on their own, divorced from the Muslims who are Indo-Trinbagonians."[42] It is also the case that some Afro-Trinidadian converts felt "uncomfortable" with perceived Indian and Hindu influences at Indo-Trinidadian mosques.[43] Nonetheless, many Indian Muslims wanted to distance themselves from the event not only because it was militant but because they felt little racial allegiance to Abu Bakr's predominantly black Muslim group. Ryan asserts that since the advent of the Muslimeen in the 1980s, "Given its ignorance of Africa and the Middle East and its antipathy to anything Indian, creole society assumed that Islam was an Indian religion." In regard to the Muslimeen, the Christian Afro-Trinidadians were hostile and uninformed, the "Hindus were also curious," and the "Muslim Indians were also not very enthusiastic."[44] For his part, Abu Bakr "denied that he was anti-Indian. He was simply aware of who he was as a black man," he said around the time of the coup, and more educated than Indian Muslims on how "no race had special claims to Islam since among the followers of the Prophet were to be found Africans, including Bilaal, the first Muezzin of the faith."[45] Islam as an African *and* universal practice was one of Abu Bakr's central talking points. He insisted that "Islam began in Africa," but that "A Muslim is a Muslim no matter what race or colour. Allah does not give any race or tribe rights over anybody else. A Muslim is not an Arab or anything else. A Muslim is any person who believes in God."[46]

There is one way in which the Muslimeen inadvertently acknowledged Trinidad's history of Islamic racial and religious unity: in the form of the Muslim colonial festival of Hosay, in which, as discussed in the introduction, both Indo- and Afro-Trinidadians participated. The Trini former calypsonian Daisann McClane is one of very few commentators to have realized that "Mr. Abu Bakr's coup occurred on Hosay, an Islamic holiday usually marked by a parade with small flags."[47] The first day of the coup, which lasted six days, was July 27, 1990, in the Gregorian calendar and Muharram 5, 1411, in the Islamic one, squarely in the traditional annual period of Hosay celebration. Abu Bakr, though, seemed surprised at being asked if there was a link, and related to me that the coup timing had nothing to do with Hosay, which "had no importance in our plan. It is just that our planning was expedited because we found out that they were coming."[48] That is, the Muslimeen believed there was an impending government raid of their compound. But the Muslimeen could not control reception of the coup, a spectacular media event. Other citizens, like the calypsonian David Rudder, took the coincidence of the most well-known Muslim events in Trinidad to be symbolic.

Rudder, who is known for the political nature of his songs, and whose songs were played on TTT by Abu Bakr during the coup, penned a postcoup calypso called "Hoosay" that directly invokes the Hosay festival as an Islamic precursor to the Muslimeen coup:

> Because under the crescent moon
> And above the bloody asphalt
> Strange dogs were barking, deep in the night . . .
>
> The night that they say
> That the martyrs died . . .
>
> So the roll of the tassa
> Began to sound like the rhythm of bullets
> And the thundering boom bass
> Well that was a bomb, was a bomb
> In this Muslim time
> When the Hosay is number one.[49]

In her analysis of the song, Tejaswini Niranjana points out that the crescent moon is a symbol associated with Islam, *tassas* are "Indian" drums used during festivals like Hosay, and the song illustrates how the coup "forever changed the perception of Trinidad as a Carnivalesque paradise where no serious violence ever took place."[50] Rudder calls life in Trinidad a "lovely lie, lovely life," that is, "Until a man opened a door" and "all our Mecca'd illusions / Walked right on by."[51] The man letting Mecca through Trinidad's door was Abu Bakr, who pointedly dismissed Hosay to me as "that culture thing that David Rudder sang about in 1994."[52] For Abu Bakr, Hosay, with its Shi'a origins and festive expression, has nothing to do with doctrinal (Sunni) Islam. But it is not that he is against all "culture thing[s]," as he knows the calypso scene quite well and played calypsos during the coup. For calypsonians and their Trini audiences, including Abu Bakr, time and culture are marked by calypsos. In "Hoosay," Hussein is the obvious historical festival martyr, though Rudder cannily leaves open the possibility that there were other martyrs at coup time—but were they Muslimeen, government hostages, or average Trinidadian citizens? "Strange dogs" are presumably Abu Bakr and the Muslimeen, who ushered through the door a "Muslim time" in Trinidad. "Muslim time" is the temporal marker of a new stage in Trinidadian modernity, where Islam has entered public discourse as a revolutionary threat to the postcolonial nation. In this way state actors in Trinidad, the United States, Europe, and the Middle East may define themselves as being in "Muslim time." But "Muslim time" is not, I argue, inherently antistate in this calypso. Ethnic and cultural creolization is a project of the Trinidadian postcolonial state. Perhaps for the first time in the history of the Trinidadian calypso form, Rudder mentioned Hosay, the Indo-Muslim festival, as the cultural framework and religious antecedent of the Afro-Trinidadian Muslimeen coup. The Hosay-coup connection illustrates that though some Trinidadian Muslims resist secularization, *intra-Muslim creolization* is proceeding apace, both in the actions of Muslims and in the perception of non-Muslims.

The Afro-Trinidadian majority government of the time was unsympathetic to the Muslimeen's political and religious challenges to the state, and did not think the Muslimeen were on the side of ecumenism or racial unity—particularly as Abu Bakr declared to the nation during the coup that it was not "military might," but God who had defeated the government, as "He [Abu Bakr] himself had no power . . . he did not 'recognize man's law, only the law of the Almighty Allah.'"[53] The Muslimeen's main original conflict with the government was over their compound at No. 1 Mucurapo Road, which was located on a plot of swampland that had been offered in 1969 to a precursor Muslim organization, the Islamic Missionary Guild, "to build an Islamic Center for the propagation of Islam."[54] The area was later developed by their offshoot the Muslimeen, but legal wrangling over titles and permissions lasted from 1979 to 1990 and embittered Abu Bakr, who was imprisoned for twenty-one days in 1985 for resisting a court order to stop building a mosque on the land.[55] Said Abu Bakr, "they unleash[ed] the state machinery on us . . . every Friday at our prayer they would invade the mosque, they would arrest people. We had no rest."[56] The attempted government coup occurred a mere two days after a final judgment against the Muslimeen, whereupon Abu Bakr had declared he was going to "break up the place."[57] While the Muslimeen were in prison after the coup, Abu Bakr said to me, "they did exactly what they were planning to do. They destroyed everything on the compound, everything, everything, everything they destroyed. They came with the army explosives and they blow up everything except the mosque. When they tried to break the mosque the tractor overturn. . . . So the mosque was left standing and everything else was destroyed."[58] Muslimeen member Wazir Bilaal Abdullah in 1985 cited a Qur'anic provision that forbids the demolishing of mosques, writing that the organization would "choose confrontation [with the Court] rather than with Allah," and "the Imam was the shield of the Jamaat, and *war would be fought for his defense*" (emphasis in original).[59] This wrangling over land is an important detail because the Muslimeen's greatest ire was roused not by Trinidad's social ills, but by the government's attempt to demolish mosque buildings—in other words, by the threat to Islam, and by the resistance to the visible manifestation of immanent Islam on

Trinidadian soil. The Muslimeen were, in their fashion, nationalists, concerned with Trinidadian social problems; but they wanted to define their citizenship as a *Muslim* Trinidadian citizenship. Abu Bakr himself, though he picked up his "religious fervor, the new tough fundamentalist posturing, the camaraderie among brothers, the international contacts with the wider Muslim world" as a young man in Canada, was and is a Trinidadian through and through: Pantin, the hostage, called Abu Bakr "[a] Trinidadian Black Muslim. A fundamentalist. One of the new in-fashion 'Allahu Ackbar' men around town. From the newspaper files I knew of Yasin Abu Bakr as the full Muslim name assumed by Lennox Phillip, a boy who'd grown up poor in Carenage," who had once been a mounted policeman himself.[60]

In their early days, the Muslimeen were alleged to have had direct political and religious connections with Muammar Qaddafi's Libya, with Abu Bakr rumored to have lived in Libya.[61] Ryan notes that "the Jamaat al Muslimeen was in fact represented by Bakr at a World Islamic Popular Conference held in Tripoli between March 17 and 21, 1990."[62] Abu Bakr was quite frank with me about his Libyan connection: "I worked with the World Islamic Call Society in Libya for 28 years. And Libya did quite a bit of work in Guyana and I was the representative for South America and the Caribbean. So I used to organize conferences and things like that."[63] As I will discuss in the next chapter, the Libyan World Islamic Call Society was a *da'wah* (proselytization) organization that had a branch in Port of Spain, and was also active in Guyana between the 1970s and 1990s. In that context involving Libya, Abu Bakr said, he came to know Hamilton Green, a Muslim convert who eventually became prime minister of Guyana and then mayor of Georgetown; Forbes Burnham, who was prime minister and then president of Guyana between 1964 and 1985 on a socialist, race-based Afro-Guyanese platform; and Cheddi Jagan, Indo-Guyanese leader of the opposition from independence in the 1966 to the early 1990s, after which he became president from 1992 to 1997.[64] The tantalizing Trinidad/Guyana connections facilitated by Libyan, Muslim, and pan-African international influences are a subject requiring further, separate investigation.

One of Abu Bakr's most well-known precoup conflicts with the Trinidadian government was linked to Libya. In January 1990, the same year as the attempted coup, the Trinidadian government first approved and then refused his offer to donate (allegedly) $800,000 worth of childhood leukemia and other cancer drugs and medical supplies that were imported through UNICEF with the financial assistance of the Libyan World Islamic Call Society. The Trinidadian prime minister decided that Abu Bakr was "a serious threat to National Security who had to be denied the legitimacy which accepting the offer of drugs would have afforded him."[65] Abu Bakr—who was known to say "he was going to overthrow the government" before he tried—was beginning to "appear in public as a spokesman for and defender of poor people, as a scourge-in-the-flesh of all that Carnivalesque looseness and slackness of Trinidad, but he also took his own militant action to clean up the society," with armed Muslimeen seizing illegal drugs, among other vigilante actions.[66] The cancer drug scuffle was really over sovereignty: the Muslimeen stepped into an extragovernmental leadership role after coming to believe that the Trinidadian government was failing in its health care obligation to citizens, failing to stem the cocaine trade, and failing in one specific instance to prevent the murder of policewoman Bernadette James, whom Abu Bakr says witnessed corrupt government and police airport cocaine trafficking and came to him, a former police officer himself, for protection.[67] The government was initially open but then rejected the Muslimeen cancer drug donation offer, as it would have given the Muslimeen local legitimacy and painted the government to its powerful Trinidadian oil-importing neighbor to the North as in bed with the Libyans. Figueira disputes the influence of Libyan funding on the Muslimeen, and also points to them being branded "a Muslim extremist, terrorist organization" since August 1983, when they were widely blamed for a bombing of the Ahmadiyya convention in Chaguanas in which fourteen people were injured.[68] They have also been linked to a 1986 fatal shooting of a Pakistani British Ahmadi missionary, Muhammad Anwar, in Guyana.[69] I note here as full disclosure that I was present as a child at the 1983 Trinidad bombing, and that Anwar's 1986 murder in Guyana occurred on the doorstep of my grandfather's home in Georgetown where he was being hosted. Nonetheless, I am proceeding on the fact that no charges were filed in either case.

Ahmadi Indians were the earliest organized group of Muslim missionaries to the Caribbean, with, most notably, the advent of the Punjabi British Fazal Karim Khan Durrani to Trinidad in 1920.[70] They produced an early complete English translation of the Qur'an by Maulana Muhammad Ali, and were also, beginning in 1920, Muslim proselytizers to African Americans in the United States. Their first missionary, Mohammed Sadiq, was detained for seven weeks under the U.S. Immigration Act of 1891 on the grounds of being a Muslim and therefore an inadmissible "polygamist."[71] Ahmadis found racial common cause with African Americans. Richard Brent Turner calls Ahmadiyyat "one of the most significant movements in the history of Islam in the twentieth century, providing as it did the *first multi-racial* model for American Islam."[72] The Chicago Ahmadi mission has been in continuous operation since 1922.[73] Sylvia Chan-Malik writes that early African American Ahmadi women attended meetings where "Sadiq or another teacher would emphasize the equal status of women in Islam," and their reading materials illustrated "both the focus on race pride and Islam as a solution to the race problem."[74] Gender parity for Muslim women is a universal Ahmadi concern, as Anesa Ahamad's previously discussed 1995 *khutbah* in Trinidad at an Ahmadi mosque illustrates.

As a result of successful missionizing to Indo-Caribbean Muslims who were generally ignored by the Indian motherland and the global Muslim world during the colonial period, Ahmadis, not Shi'a Muslims, are the minority "other" to the Sunni majority in the Caribbean. The Muslimeen are linked to anti-Ahmadi activity in the Caribbean in the context of the Lahori and Qadiani Ahmadiyya revivalist sects being constitutionally declared non-Muslim in 1974 in their originating Pakistan, where they are heavily persecuted.[75] They are globally vilified by the Sunnis from whom they stemmed for doctrinal reasons (the Qadiani believe Mirza Ghulam Ahmad, 1835–1908, was the Mahdi [Reformer] and eschatological Messenger; the Lahori believe he has no prophetic status). In Trinidad, suspicion over any anti-Ahmadi and antigovernmental activity still regularly falls on the Muslimeen, though their global connections have diminished considerably. Moreover, after the coup, many Jamaat members left to form the Islamic Resource Society, which "has very cordial relations with the Indian Muslim community and belongs to the United Islamic Organizations, a coordinating body of Muslim groups in Trinidad."[76]

Jeanne Baptiste proposes a theory of "Muslimeenism" as the postcolonial identity that defines the organization as a local Muslim community in a non-Muslim nation-state, arguing that "the very presence of the Muslimeen designates the nation-state a unique Muslim space, both a part of and apart from the global *ummah*," and the Muslimeen "continue to shape actively the history of Trinidad and Tobago as they persist in the preservation and hypervisibility of their Muslimeenism."[77] Muslimeenism is a useful way to model the influence of the coup in Trinidad, the Muslimeen relation to land and space, and the Muslimeen's connections to global Islam. I also emphasize the need to clarify Muslimeen interaction with other Trinidadian Muslims, and the cultural role of music and literature in mitigating the specter of "political" Islam by attempting to creolize it. The Muslimeen are political citizen-subjects whose place in the nation is in perpetual flux because they challenge creolization through various means. While others frame the Muslimeen as a discrete, globalized element in Trinidadian society, the Muslimeen perceive themselves as that *and* as local, not new, and linked to a long history of Islam in Trinidad and in the Caribbean.

In 1990, the nation learned that the Muslimeen were prepared to propagate and defend their ideals and vision of the Trinidadian state—a cause to which much of the rest of Trinidadian Creole society simply did not respond. As demonstrated in Brother Ebony's coup calypso "Abu Bakr Take Over," the greatest visible symbol of the Muslimeen's difference, and the one upon which Trinidadians hung all their doubts about Islam, was the way that women dressed and were incorporated into the community.

"PIOUS SEXUALITY": POLYGAMY AND WOMEN'S ISLAMIC DRESS

Brother Ebony sings in his postcoup calypso that if Abu Bakr were to "take over" and Trinidad became a "Muslim state," he, Ebony, would benefit by obtaining "seven wives" (as noted, Islam allows four). At the same time, Ebony tells a woman she would have to "Throw 'way she bikini," a statement that he follows with "Deh go be mo' bacchanal / If dey say no Carnival."[78] "Bacchanal" in Caribbean parlance means the Greco-Anglophone "drunken party," following the god Bacchus, but it can also mean any kind of dramatic, anarchic public scene. Ebony threatens rioting if Muslim puritanism prevents Trinidad's biggest party, Carnival, of which women in bikinis are fixtures. As a calypsonian political voice of Trinidad and St. Vincent, he is not altogether pleased by what he perceives to be the Muslim attitude toward sexuality and women: the benefit for men would be more than one wife, but the downside is that women would have to cover up their bodies. This type of modesty is too excessive, he implies, for the Caribbean.

Abu Bakr fired up the Trinidadian libidinal imagination by himself having more than one wife; it is through him and the Muslimeen that Islamic polygamy and related concerns over Muslim women's dress entered Trinidadian national discourse. By 1990, Abu Bakr appeared to have three wives, the third of whom, Fatima Juman, was a Muslim Indian woman whose family opposed her marriage.[79] Trinidad is not, as a majority Christian former British colony, a legally polygamous society. Nonetheless, Abu Bakr was not prosecuted—Anglophone Caribbean governments in general being loath to interfere in people's romantic lives, except in the case of homosexuality—and Trinidadian society was conflicted over the issue. Indo-Trini Muslims were divided over polygamy, Afro-Trini Muslims were more tolerant of it, and a few people claimed that "even though Trinidad was officially a monogamous society, it was de facto a polygamous society in which the tradition of the 'deputy' was well established. . . . Trinidad law made no distinction between children of different relationships and . . . the term illegitimate was no longer used."[80] "Deputy" is Trinidadian Creole slang for "mistress." Though wives may tolerate men keeping mistresses, they understand that greater social power resides in the title of "wife." While Trinidadian law now gives the same inheritance rights to children of wives or mistresses, the woman herself is treated differently under the law depending on her legal status, and the one place where the law has always legally differentiated between people of different religions is in (heterosexual) marriage rights, as noted in the second chapter.

Muslim and Hindu marriages were not recognized as legal until 1946 in British Trinidad. The Muslim Marriage and Divorce Act of 1961 clarified two issues specific to Muslims.[81] First, the Trinidadian civil procedure to legally dissolve a marriage supersedes any Islamic divorce law.[82] Second, the Muslim Marriage Act stipulated that Muslim boys could be married at the age of 16, and Muslim girls could be married at the age of 12—the youngest permissible age for anyone to marry in Trinidad.[83] Hindu girls were allowed to marry at 14, girls of other faiths at 16, and all non-Muslim boys at 18.[84] Muslim boys or girls under 18, however, were required to obtain consent from a father, guardian, mother, or national president–appointed person—in that patriarchal order, a guardian's permission being privileged over a mother's. A January 2017 Parliamentary Act aimed at curbing child marriages amended the marital age to 18 for males and females of all religions. The former rationale for the young permissible marital age of Muslim girls was that it was a nod to Muslim community practice and the fact that *shariʿa*, in its most conservative iteration, allows girls to marry at the age of 9. That Islamic ruling is based on the age at which the Prophet is said to have consummated a marriage with his wife Aisha—the Qur'an does not specify a numerical age for marriage for anyone.[85] In Trinidad, marriage laws enshrined preexisting practice and the separation of religions.

The colonial milieu is the backdrop upon which contemporary Trinidadian attitudes toward Muslim women are situated. Indian women and Muslim women have always been presumed different from other women in Trinidad: capable of marrying earlier, tolerating greater family interference and restrictions on their lives, and submitting to patriarchal practices without complaint. The fact that in 1990 Abu Bakr's wives "all claimed to be quite happy with their marriage arrangements" served only to reinforce the Trinidadian view that Muslim women were a breed apart.[86] His Indian third wife Fatima, who had been previously divorced, publicly opined—with the agreement of Anisa Bakr, Abu Bakr's first wife (m. 1975)—that she, Fatima, was independent, not oppressed, and not jealous, as "none of the wives are considered superior to the other, regardless of marriage seniority, age or academic status."[87] The Trinidadian public found it difficult to believe in 1990 that polygamous women could be satisfied with their marital arrangements. Nowadays, most Muslimeen men and women are in monogamous marriages, with the exception of Abu Bakr and his closest (and eldest) advisers.[88] After spending time doing field research in the Muslimeen compound, Baptiste praised the Muslimeen men's general attitude of respect toward women.[89] Muslimeen women, who currently number about 150, affect what Baptiste calls a "pious sexuality, where piety and sexuality are not diametrically opposed but coterminous and extend beyond the borders of the bedroom."[90] That is, the Muslimeen women perform their piety and sexuality through what they wear and through the way they interact with or perform for each other.

In Baptiste's account, contemporary Trinidadian Muslimeen women divide themselves by dress and politics into older and younger factions. It is the older, mostly Afro-Trinidadian women who "embody a black consciousness" by dressing conservatively in "monotone, plain, heavy cotton fabric" sewed into burqas, chadors, niqabs, gloves, and stockings.[91] These women witnessed or participated in the 1990 coup. Their political "black consciousness" is signified by ultraconservative Muslim dress: racialized political difference combined with gendered religious difference as a challenge to Trinidadian postcolonial Creole society. But creolization is a strong force in the multiethnic Caribbean, and pushes back.

Younger Muslimeen women, whether converts or born into Islam, have found a different way to "dress Muslim" without covering up fully. In the process, they have signified a particular Muslim avenue of creolization, rather than separatism from the Trinidadian nation-state. In the search for a way to dress differently from the general Trinidadian public—as a marker of both religious adherence and pride—young Muslimeen women have chosen to dress *Indian*. Such women came of age in 1990s and 2000s Trinidad, where postcolonial "creole" society is more fully realized, and racial divisions are less insurmountable. In the Muslimeen compound mosque, the younger women, who are majority Afro-Trinidadian, "dress in what was traditionally considered Indian fashions: elaborate and lightly textured sari material with brightly colored, beaded, sequined *shalwar* chemises and ostentatious yet color-coordinated headscarves. . . . A group of young women ranging from late teens to early twenties, two already married and one of them a mother, attend juma very ornately adorned, including wearing a noticeable amount of gold jewelry, sporting several piercings in each ear and multiple rings on each finger, so many that some fingers are invisible for all the jewelry adorning them."[92] The precoup, late-1980s Muslimeen were divided over Muslim practices that came from the subcontinent, like the celebration of the Prophet's birthday, the offering of optional prayers during Ramadan, and whether to follow the majority Sunni Hanafi *madhab*, but also over "differences related to whether to wear the topee, the Shalwar and other forms of Indian dress" (see fig. 4.2).[93] The mainly Afro-Trinidadian Muslimeen wanted to differentiate themselves from Indo-Trinidadian Muslims, who were also none too happy about the emergence of the group. Young black Muslimeen women wearing the traditionally Indo-Muslim mosque dress of *salwar kameez*—"Indian fashions"—is a significant shift and a discretely Muslim take on ethnic creolization conflicts in Trinidad and the Caribbean. Contra other trends in Muslim dress in the Caribbean, where it is also now common to see black and Indian Muslim men attending mosques in Gulf Arab thobes, the young Muslimeen women's clothing is the one instance in which the trend is *away* from Arab dress, and toward a different, local understanding of what "Caribbean Islam" means. The Muslimeen young women's dress shows that there are ways to achieve what is the *ideal* of postcolonial Caribbean politics, the unity of African and Indian descendants of colonial labor, without flattening out religious difference.

The young Muslimeen women's sartorial inclusiveness and gesture toward incorporating Islam into a type of creolization through dress has not extended to the rest of the population. As Lila Abu-Lughod, Leila Ahmed, Franz Fanon, Saba Mahmood, Fatima Mernissi, and many others have written, paternalistic Western antipathy toward the hijab and veil on behalf of Muslim women is a foundational part of discourse on Islam that serves to conceal neocolonial agendas.[94] Ahmed writes that from the nineteenth century on, calls for unveiling "came already marked with notions of who was civilized and who was not, and already replete with the markings of colonizer/colonized, European/non-European."[95] Unlike in Austria, Belgium, Cameroon, Chinese Xinjiang, Denmark, France, Morocco, the Netherlands, Sri Lanka, Tunisia, Turkey, and Quebec, to name a

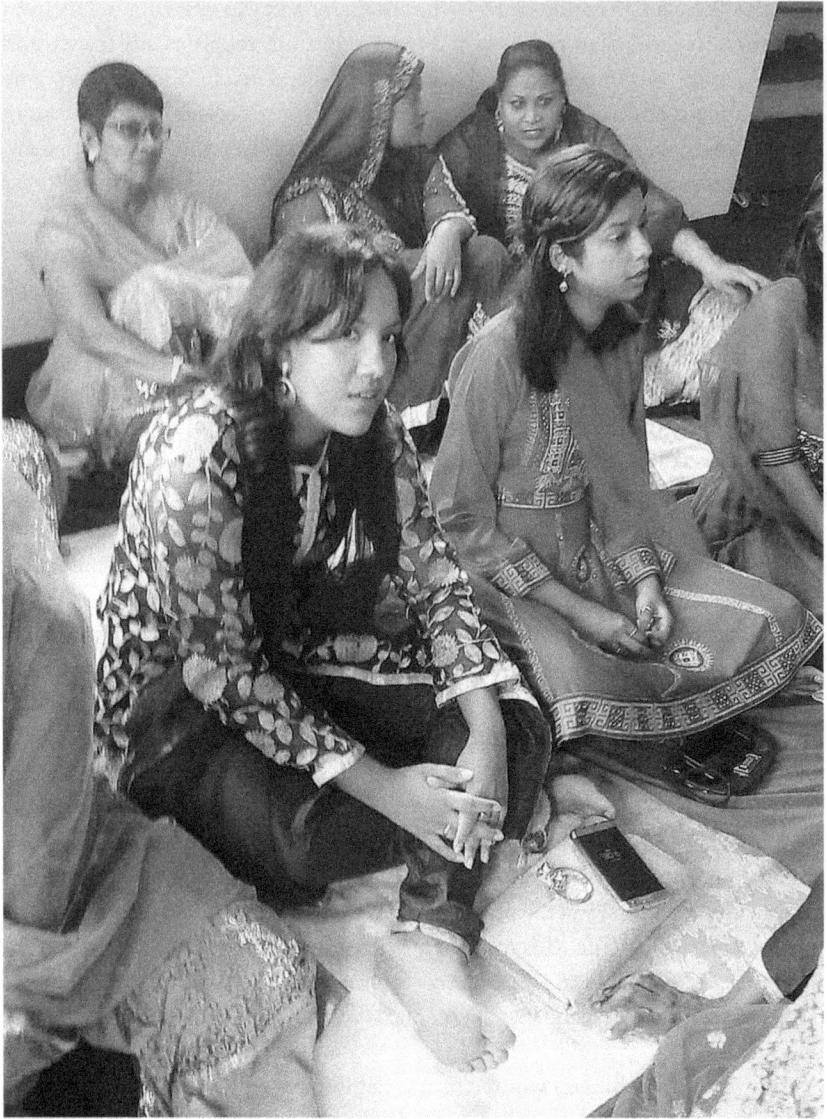

FIGURE 4.2 Muslim women in "Indian dress" celebrating Eid al-Fitr at the end of Ramadan. New Grant Mosque, Trinidad, 2018. (Courtesy of Fazil Rasheed.)

few locales, there is no legal ban on any kind of Muslim hijab, burqa, or *niqab* face veil anywhere in the Caribbean. But two postcoup cases illustrate the Trinidadian antipathy to conservative Muslim women's clothing. In 1994, an 11-year-old Muslim girl named Summayah Mohammed was refused admission to a Catholic high school because she wore a hijab, and "the Catholic, Anglican, Presbyterian, Baptist and Hindu boards of education released a joint statement prohibiting the wearing of the *hijab* to class in their state-supported schools."⁹⁶ The girl's parents sued, claiming constitutional freedom of religion and pointing to the fact that the school accommodated Catholic nuns in full veil. After a year of legal wrangling, the judge ruled in favor of the child, but limited the ruling to that single instance: Summayah was able to attend a Catholic school wearing her hijab, but Christian- and Hindu-run schools that received government money were still permitted to discriminate against other girls who wore the hijab.⁹⁷

The second incident is more recent. In 2007, an unnamed woman—who was also not racially identified—wearing a full face-concealing niqab and burqa appeared to serve as a juror at a criminal court in Port of Spain. The *Trinidad and Tobago Guardian*, T&T's oldest national newspaper, reported in disbelief: "On the first day, the court's attention was directed to the form of her attire. The woman was covered from head to toe in a voluminous black robe. Her head and face were covered, save for a slit in the area of her eyes."⁹⁸ The woman, who was not chosen as a juror, was nonetheless detained after the selection process. She refused to remove her face covering in front of male court officers for the purposes of iden- tification. The resulting recriminations among the "Attorney General, the Law Association, the Criminal Bar Association and the United Islamic League" (i.e., the government, two law associations, and a powerful mainstream Muslim organ- ization) led to a 2010 High Court ruling that under the Trinidad Jury Act, "the court had no jurisdiction or authority of its own motion, or upon any other basis, to disqualify a person from serving as a juror on the sole basis that the individual was wearing a burka."⁹⁹ Such limitations of Muslim dress is Islamophobia, which Louise Cainkar and Sunaina Maira define as "a persistent strain of essentialist ide- ologies that criminalize Arabs, South Asians, and Muslims by claiming that these groups deviate from normative cultural citizenship and pose a threat to the nation."¹⁰⁰ The hijab and burqa cases showed that nonlegislative actors in Trini- dad were ready and willing to block Muslim women's and girls' full participation in the nation-state if they dressed "too" Muslim. Head and face coverings, in par- ticular, were viewed as antithetical to Trinidadian and Caribbean citizenship, and as an infringement of the social contract in an ostensibly "Western" society.

"MUSLIM TIME": ALLAH IN THE ISLANDS

Trinidadians processed the sociopolitical impact of the coup through art: calypso and literature. The 2009 novel *Allah in the Islands* is a historical novelization of the Muslimeen coup, and a not-quite sequel to Trinidadian writer and Davidson College professor Brenda Flanagan's first novel *You Alone Are Dancing* (1996). Fla- nagan, a childhood singer of calypsos who emigrated from Trinidad to the United States in 1967, is, as previously noted, the younger sister of Yasin Abu Bakr. In addition to her novels, she is the author of the short story collection *In Praise of Island Women & Other Crimes* (2005). The plot of *Allah in the Islands* closely follows the events of the real attempted coup. Abu Bakr himself is represented by the novelistic coup leader and imam "Haji," a charismatic religious and nationalist figure with several wives. When asked about *Allah in the Islands* and his fictional alter ego Haji, Abu Bakr evinced pride in the writing and teaching accomplishments of Flanagan, whom he consistently and affectionately refers to as "my baby sister," but of *Allah in the Islands*, he admitted "I have not read it in detail."[101]

The novel takes place on the imaginary Anglophone Caribbean island of Santabella, described as the sister island to Tobago, Trinidad's smaller neighbor.[102] Santabella overlooks the real Trinidadian Gulf of Paria; was colonized in turn by the Spanish, French, and British; and is home to a majority Afro-Caribbean population living on the sites of former cocoa plantations.[103] The major issues of the Muslimeen and the coup, including disputes with the government over land, the Islamic dress of Muslimeen woman, and the Afro-Trinidadian Muslim conflict with Indo-Trinidadian Muslims, are all faithfully replicated in the novel. The end of the novel, as I will discuss in the next section, uses calypso music in a way that both reflects and is different from Brother Ebony and postcoup Trinidadian calypsonians: through musical performance, the novel holds out unambiguous hope for the promise of Muslim creolization into, rather than alienation from, the nation-state.

I read *Allah in the Islands* as a historical novel that temporally explores the Trinidadian religious, political, and national possibilities of time during and after the coup: the island in the grip of "Muslim time." The novel in the Caribbean, says the Jamaican theorist Sylvia Wynter, is always historical, and though it is a form produced by capitalism and colonialism to reflect themselves, it does not remain a creature of the market economy.[104] Wynter argues that the novel inherently critiques the historical process and drive toward individualism that created the form itself, and that "history, then, these things that happen, is, in the plantation context, itself, fiction; a fiction written, dominated, controlled by forces external to itself. It is clear then, that it is only when the society, or elements of the society rise up in rebellion against its external authors and manipulators that our prolonged fiction becomes temporary fact."[105] In the dystopic colonial plantation context, a chronotopic space-time outside of time in which the reason and agency of human beings are stripped from them, history is the same as fiction. The Trinidad of the Muslimeen is still processing the legacy of colonialism, and struggling with the multiplicity of elements, culture, and people that must be incorporated into a single creolized, postcolonial state. Flanagan's fiction produces and interprets the coup in this context. Wynter suggests that the correlation between the *plots* on which enslaved Africans grew their own food, and the *plots* of literary novels, is that both are plot systems of "resistance to the market system and market values."[106] Rather than plot, per se, it is fictional *narrative* and the agglomeration of individual stories that, as I argue elsewhere, produce Caribbean history in the absence of the voices of the oppressed within the written archive.[107] Édouard

Glissant similarly proposes that a "'literary' implication ... orients the thrust of historical thought," and that, in the context of the Caribbean, "history as a consciousness at work and history as lived experience are therefore not the business of historians exclusively. Literature for us will not be divided into genres."[108] It is not that in the Caribbean, literature is fact or history. But given conditions in which most subaltern people could not speak for or record themselves, literature represents the possibilities of their consciousness and thought, lived experience, and worldview. As Wynter notes, "Prolonged fiction becomes temporary fact" when the powerless rebel against "external authors and manipulators."[109] The rebellious Muslimeen speak for themselves, but their ongoing story has been sensationalized by news coverage and spun by the Trinidadian government. They are, in the Trinidadian national consciousness, objects of mystery and fear, capable of producing "Muslim time" antithetical to the state. Flanagan's novel *Allah in the Islands* explores the Muslimeen point of view and aspirations for Muslim *and* black nationalist state participation through fiction, suggesting a "Muslim time" that could incorporate the Muslim Caribbean without sacrificing its particularity.

Allah in the Islands is a sequel to the Michigan Hopwood Award–winning novel *You Alone Are Dancing*. Thirteen years separate the publication of the novels, and they have different concerns. *You Alone Are Dancing* is about Afro-Santabellan heroine Beatrice Salandy's postcolonial feminist struggle to liberate herself and her fellow islanders from sexism, classism, and government corruption. The semirural village from which Beatrice hails is subject to both hurricanes and the whims of an uncaring, corrupt government in league with U.S. oil companies—very much a Trinidadian and Tobagonian story, as T&T's economy is dependent on its oil resources and trade relationship with the United States and other countries. Book-smart Beatrice has the chance to immigrate to North America, but she chooses to stay in Santabella and stand up to the men who oppress her and to the island government that allows an American company to divert the village's water supply and drill for oil on village land. She lands in jail under suspicion of embezzling money from the government to help the villagers. At the end of the novel, she is exonerated with the villagers' support.

Allah in the Islands is divided into three chronological parts. The novel picks up where *You Alone Are Dancing* leaves off, beginning with Beatrice's second exoneration, this time for killing a wealthy Chinese Caribbean man who had raped her and was in league with the Americans (she had committed the murder in the first novel). Beatrice's personal story is interwoven through the novel's descriptions of the actions of Haji and his Muslims, and the Santabellan islanders' shifting perceptions of the Muslims. Early in the novel, after Beatrice is released from prison, she takes a nighttime walk in the local botanical gardens, where she is accosted by another attacker and rescued by men dressed in camouflage who patrol the area at night in an attempt to stop an epidemic of attacks on women. They identify themselves to Beatrice as "belong[ing] to the Masjid Compound."[110]

The men immediately frame their world as Muslim and gendered differently from the typical Afro-Santabellan one when they call a nearby woman who is also Muslim to take charge of Beatrice after they have rescued her.[111] The novel's point of view shifts back and forth among third-person omniscient, third-person limited, and first-person perspectives of Beatrice, a Miss Ann, and Haji's follower Abdul. The narrative alternates temporally between a linear account of the events leading up to the coup, and Abdul's retrospective telling. Abdul moves the plot along by relaying the doings of the Muslims and tying their story together with Beatrice's (he falls for her and contemplates marrying her); Miss Ann is the voice of the Santabellans who do not trust the Muslims; and Beatrice remains the postcolonial woman who must choose between deteriorating sociopolitical conditions in the Caribbean homeland and exile and nebulous promises of a "better future" in North America. In the end, she makes the opposite decision from the one she made in *You Alone Are Dancing*: she decides to leave even before the climax of the novel, the failed coup by the Muslims.

Allah in the Islands is introduced by first-person narrator Abdul describing his daily errands for a man he and his friends call Haji (a title of respect given to a man who has made the obligatory Muslim hajj pilgrimage to Mecca), who had just been detained and questioned at the airport by Customs after an international flight.[112] Thus the novel establishes immediately the conflict between Haji and his people and the Santabellan government as represented by the airport authorities, framing Haji as both local and foreign; a legitimate and observant Muslim who has been to hajj, but an automatic suspect implicated in frightening discourses of airport security and international terrorism. That Haji is Muslim supersedes his citizenship as a Santabellan, and *that* is the major conflict of the novel: which identity will Haji's followers pick? Neither they nor the other Santabellans are sure. As one Santabellan woman tells Beatrice of Haji's right-hand man Abdul, "I don't want no Muslim trouble in my yard, cause with this one, religion thicker than blood."[113] The idea that new religious loyalties might be antithetical to the postcolonial state's definition of a "good" citizen because they are more loyal to religion and also represent change is enough to make cantankerous old village woman Miss Ann don her Saint Christopher medal and declare, "When I look round Rosehill, everything changing, and it start when the Muslims come and take over the school. What I wanted to know was how they could do that. How the government could just let them waltz in and take over like that. Is a lot of *simidimi* and *ratchefee* going on in this country."[114] The only explanation for how Muslims could "waltz in" and take over government functions like schooling—which they did as charity because the government would not provide village children with school supplies—was *simi-dimi* and *ratchefee*, religious-supernatural magic that is both effective and a racket meant to scam good people.[115] Muslims, then, appear to possess otherworldly "powers" that others do not have and cannot understand. The fearful contemporary rhetoric of the Muslim Other and terrorism would suggest this idea is not limited to Trinidad. These powers are perceived as corrupt and meant to trick others. Simi-dimi and ratchefee represent the Santabellan attitude toward Muslims even when the Muslims are performing social services like helping small children buy schoolbooks.

In *Allah in the Islands*, the postcolonial Santabellan public is thoroughly uninformed about the existence of Muslims in Africa and the history of African Muslims in the Caribbean. In Trinidad and Santabella, the emphasis on the Libyan connection—Abdul specifically references a madrassa in "Banghazi" (Benghazi) where Haji sent several Trinidadian men and a few women to receive Islamic schooling—is cited as proof of Islam's historical foreignness and newness to the Caribbean.[116] Miss Ann, the quintessential Caribbean matriarch and busybody, also firmly believes Islam is an Indian religion. Ann tells Melda, Abdul's aunt: "Muslim is Indian. What Muslim have to do with Africa? You talking chupidness. . . . In Santabella, all my life, is only Indian people practice Muslim religion. In America, yes, they have some people calling theirself Black Muslims, but I never hear about them mixing Shango and Islam." "Ah," replies Melda, "but Haji say all over Africa, people practice their own African religion and Islam at the same time. So why not here?"[117] Miss Ann is talking about a young man named Sammy, who, in his search for precolonial, non-Christian African roots, is in the process of switching from practicing Shango, a Yoruba-Caribbean syncretic religion, to practicing Islam. Midconversion, he and others in the community appear to be practicing both religions without contradiction—because Haji has told them that Islam is an ancestral African religion. Sammy tells Beatrice that she had the strength to challenge governmental corruption because "the ancestors put that in you because you carry their spirit. . . . The old ones pick you."[118] He gives Haji the same ancestral credit, saying that he has joined up with Haji not because of the "Muslim business," but because "In him I see the spirit of the ancestors, and that mean more to me than religion.[119]

While Sammy is content to associate Islam with syncretic African animist spirituality, believing they both encompass a mandate from African ancestors to help their descendants, that is not the perspective of Haji and his most loyal followers like Abdul. Shango is a first postcolonial step away from a history of enslavement and forcible conversion to Christianity, but it is a creolized religion and therefore not African enough for their liking. Islam, Haji says, is more authentically African (that Islam was brought to Africa by Arab traders is not an issue). Though he knows "the history of the Islamic Africans who had been brought to the islands, including Santabella, and forced into slavery by the British and the French, and prohibited from practising their religion," he does not argue that they are his group's direct ancestral community.[120] For Haji and his followers, "real" African Islam terminated on the slave ship. Authenticity must flow directly from Africa. Haji agrees with Miss Ann: his Muslims are not the "Black Muslims" of the United States. Like Abu Bakr, he says to Santabellan newspapers that though he had studied and learned about Islam in the United States, "he was not a *Black* Muslim; he had nothing to do with Elijah Mohammed and the Black Muslims in America except that they shared the same faith. He had come home to help his people; to get them to see that their lives had been stifled by the powers in Santabella who kept them ignorant."[121] Despite the disavowal, the Santabellan Muslims are also black nationalists who fight against local racism, poverty, and social inequity. Their opponent is the Santabellan government that is in league with the Catholic Church to control access to education. But Haji's righteousness of belief and authority does not and cannot come from the United States, which is shown in *You Alone Are Dancing* to have oil interests in his island and no regard for dispossessed Santabellan villagers. His authority and sovereign rights come in the form of Islam, directly from ancestral Africa.

Like Abu Bakr's Muslimeen, Haji's Santabellan Muslims, who are mostly Afro-Caribbean, are highly critical of Indian Muslims, whom they perceive as having "lost" their religion during and after indentureship. Abdul criticizes the Indian Muslims for their lack of Islamic orthodoxy, characterized by their not broadcasting the *adhān*, the Islamic call to prayer, and their listening to "dirty" calypsos (calypsos about sex, as opposed to political calypsos) along with non-Muslims.[122] "Old-time" Indian Muslims who "lost they self" and "forgot how to conform to religion" are not themselves wholly to blame: they are also victims of colonialism.[123] The implication is that "cultural" Indo-Trinidadian Islam is a poor imitation of a more "authentic" subcontinental or Arab Islam.

During the period of transatlantic slavery, the flourishing of African Islam in the islands would have required the kind of sustained influence from abroad not possible until the present era of transportation and communication, when the real Abu Bakr and the novel's Haji could go abroad to study then return home to proselytize while maintaining close ties with the global *ummah*. Haji tells his followers he "had been to Mecca" for the hajj and "had connections way beyond Santabella's borders with powerful people who wanted to help their fellow Muslims."[124] He "travelled three or four times a year. To the Middle East, rumour said. And he always came back with money. What did the poor people of Santabella care where he got the money? So the Libyans wanted to help Santabellans? Let them. Santabella's government surely wasn't."[125] Unlike the Santabellan government, Libya is willing to help not just Muslim Santabellans but all Santabellans. The Muslim global *ummah* connection, the novel suggests, is not necessarily a danger to Caribbean governments; it may be a source of help, alliance against U.S. economic imperialism, and moral betterment.

The only Qur'anic passage directly referenced in *Allah in the Islands* is a brief enjoinment on Haji's mosque's notice board that declares "Say No to Alcohol and Gambling, The Qur'an 2–219."[126] The Qur'anic verse to which the notice refers is one of many that gives detailed guidelines on how to live a Muslim life—in this case, proscribing addictive alcohol and gambling, and reminding Muslims to give to charity. On the Santabellan mosque's notice board, the seemingly simple alcohol and gambling reminder is followed by a somewhat ominous declaration of the social and perhaps political aims of the Muslims:

WE the willing
led by the unknowing
are doing the impossible
for the ungrateful.
We have done so much
for so long
With so little, we are
now qualified to do
anything with nothing.[127]

The "willing" are the new Muslim reverts to Islam, and the "unknowing" is God; the "impossible" is helping the poor residents of Santabella, who have been, for "so long," thoroughly "ungrateful." As a result of the ungratefulness and lack of recognition and reward, the Muslims "are now qualified to do anything with nothing." "Anything" is a word that implies the totally unprecedented (e.g., staging a coup d'état to take over the government). The declaration that the Muslims have "nothing" is ironic; they have received no material thanks for their charitable efforts, notably their efforts to construct a school for poor children, but they believe themselves to have the backing of God. The juxtaposition of the Qur'anic verse reference with the Muslims' Santabellan agenda shows that they are not bereft of aid. As Haji says to Abdul right before the coup, "I wish I had made some better decisions in who we have as friends, but, at the time, I didn't have any other choice. You play with the hand you get. I just have to believe that Allah will see us through to a good end."[128] Playing "the hand you get" is a subtly ironic choice of gambling metaphor, especially as these Muslims seek to change the game.

In the novel, Muslim women are foils for the propagation of the Santabellan Muslim political agenda. Beatrice, a non-Muslim, is a feminist agent of change. Anisa Bakr, Abu Bakr's first wife, is the model for Sister Farouka, Haji's first wife in Flanagan's novel. Haji too has three wives: Farouka, Amena, and a mysterious "Chinese lady"—number three is racially different and not Afro-Caribbean, paralleling Abu Bakr's real-life marital arrangement.[129] Farouka visits Beatrice the morning after the latter was rescued from her park attacker by the Muslims, informing Beatrice that Haji has been watching her, as he watches all political persons and events in Santabella. Farouka invites Beatrice to Friday Juma (*Jumu'ah*) prayers, telling her "You would make a good Muslim woman, Sister. The Haji knows about your case with the government and he was really proud of how you handled yourself. He knows how this government could get nasty. We've been fighting them for years, as you know, so we rejoice in your victory,

Ahamdullillah."[130] Farouka is dressed in a "yellow veil," and "Only her brown eyes were visible, and these hardly so, for from head to toe, her tall straight figure was draped in the all-covering costume adopted by local black Muslim women."[131] Here the novel acknowledges that, as elsewhere in the world, in Santabella the visible signifier of Islam and culture war flashpoint is the female Muslim body.

The characters in *Allah in the Island* struggle like Brother Ebony and many Caribbean others with the way some observant Muslim women dress. Abdul says that some parents of Muslim convert daughters threw the girls out of their homes—ironically, as "those girls could dress up in all kind of shorty-short clothes, walk half-naked in the street with their belly pomp out, and the parents ent saying nothing. Let them join the Muslims, put on a long dress or cover their heads, and is as if they commit a felony. Is that kind of backwardness we having to deal with in Santabella."[132] Abdul sees a Caribbean double standard: Santabellans do not mind if women—their own daughters—dress in revealing clothing, but they do mind if women cover their bodies for religious reasons, which "is as if they commit a felony." The crime is not the modesty of the clothes, but changing ideology and visibly differentiating oneself from one's fellow female citizens. Abdul and Beatrice have an enlightening dialogue with his Tante (Aunt) Melda, who is skeptical of his conversion:

[MELDA:] Why the women and them have to dress up as if they playing Midnight Robber, covered in black from head to foot? . . . I thought all you Muslims don't believe in Carnival?

[ABDUL:] Women should present theirselves modestly in public. The Bible says that too. . . . If you are a good woman, you do not present your body in public to encourage men to look at you, to be tempted by you. You save yourself, the way you look, for your husband. . . . When you become so wrapped up in how you look, you spend your money on clothes and shoes. . . . Who is the real you? In Islam, women concern theirselves with their soul, not only their bodies.

[BEATRICE:] I saw women with lipstick and powder. . . . Even black eye-shadow. But you know very well it's not about make-up or sexy clothes. Is about carrying yourself decent in the world, and if you want to do that, then you dress decent.[133]

This is a rare and surprising moment in which young, rebellious Beatrice agrees with one of her society's conservative strictures on women, in this case that women should dress "decent." She makes the point that the Muslim women have not eschewed cosmetics and therefore still embrace conventional femininity, despite Melda's grouchy but humorous allegations that the women wear "shapeless long-long dress" and no makeup, swooping around like the sexless robed Carnival figure Midnight Robber, a thief in the night. The dialogue is really between the younger and older woman about women's dress and its implications for sexual and social agency; Abdul occupies the role of pompous male overseer of the rules of propriety. His pronouncements on women's obligation to not tempt men with their dress and to eschew vanity are indeed, as he says, neither Christian nor Muslim—they are sexist. "Decent," as Beatrice uses it, is not synonymous with Abdul's use of "modest." "Decent" is about the self: "carrying yourself decent in the world" is demanding through your dress that you be treated respectfully. "Modest," however, is about other people, namely men: it means that you are "a good woman" and "You save yourself, the way you look, for your husband." "Modest" can be an absolute moral value, whereas "decent" is a situationally dependent value; Beatrice is in the home of someone she knows well, so there is no issue with her wearing, as Melda says, "tight pants."

Allah in the Islands also picks up on the issue of the "deputy," polygamy, and adultery, with Abdul relating the controversy as "Some women say they would never do that, share their husband with a next woman, even when they know the man have a deputy in the Toco, and a next one in San Juan."[134] Abdul says that "Miss Farouka and Miss Amena, they know where their husband is when he's not with them. I think it's better that way, but you have to have big money for that kind of arrangement," implying what Baptiste notes of the Muslimeen, that only older male leaders really engage in polygamy.[135] The novel, however, suggests impious sexual deviance in Haji's polygamy: he is shown to have more than just a political interest in Beatrice and her conflicts with the Santabellan government. In a meeting with her that is ostensibly about him hiring her to be a teacher, he tells her "I admire you a lot, Beatrice," and puts his fingers on her lips and inside her mouth.[136] The reader only learns his full name near the end of the novel, when he writes her a letter about how he will pray for her future and how "there are people in this country who have a special love for you," and signs it "Imam Haji Ben Yedder."[137] Beatrice does not object to his advances; in fact, in light of his desire to improve life for Santabellan citizens, she develops feelings for him. Poor Abdul, the perennial sidekick who wants to marry her but is afraid to make advances, is left in the dark. Haji is shown to be not entirely selfless, and polygamy not entirely pious.

Abdul is the character in the novel whose first-person narrative (repeatedly) foreshadows the coup and its fatal results, and these hints are dropped whenever he thinks or speaks of Sister Farouka. Early in the novel, he describes her as a civil servant when she met Haji, with a daughter named Yassi at university in Canada. That daughter "would be dead too, and the poor girl didn't have one thing to do with what Haji or any of us do."[138] Shortly before the climactic moment of the coup, he says that he could not accept the innocent girl's death, and "Maybe that was to teach us a lesson. Teach us that we hadn't really reached the point where we should have acted. We was too hasty."[139] Unlike other Santabellans, Abdul also believes that Haji's wives were unaware of the coup plans. Farouka has given up her life as an educated woman to be Haji's wife, suggesting that there is something about the Muslims that is attractive to women that they cannot obtain in the "modern" world. The reader learns in the references to Farouka and her to-be-deceased daughter that Abdul is relaying the story after it has happened, and that the coup will fail. The accidentally shot Yassi has no role in the novel other than to foreshadow the failure of the Muslims to seize the government and to be her saintly mother's daughter. Unlike for the Muslimeen, in the novel, the role of women in a future "Muslim time" of creolization and national unity is undetermined and fairly passive.

CARNIVAL, CALYPSO, AND CREOLIZATION

Music is a primary way through which people work out for themselves the meaning of "creolization" in Trinidad. Even in song, the subject of Afro/Indo race- and culture-mixing is controversial, and references to (heterosexual) black and Indian "douglarization"—race-mixing—particularly when the woman is Indian and the man black, are even more hotly debated. "Dougla" in the Caribbean is a word derived from the Bhojpuri-Hindi word *dogla*, literally meaning "two necks" and figuratively meaning "bastard," with the connotation of the illegitimate child of a prostitute.[140]

The desire of many Indo-Caribbean people—not just Indo-Muslims—to resist all forms of creolization and remain culturally and racially apart is a source of regional suspicion. In postcolonial Trinidad and Guyana, the perceived greatest threat to Indo-Caribbean cultural retention is the specter of douglarization or miscegenation between Indo- and Afro-Caribbean people. Douglarization becomes the representational fear over the postcolonial survival of Indians as a discrete national group. "Dougla" has long been a pejorative term for a person of mixed African and Indian descent in Trinidad and Guyana, but Shalini Puri calls for ethnic solidarity on the basis of a "dougla poetics" in an attempt to rehabilitate the word.[141] Racial "purists" and members of the Trinidadian general public nonetheless continue to use "douglarization" to mean assimilation and "racial dilution," rather than an integration that allows for cultural difference.[142] Puri also argues against the reductive, interchangeable ways in which the terms "douglarization" and "creolization" tend to be used by noting that it is a distinction "both the African and the Indian orthodoxies have an interest in erasing, in fears over 'dilution' and 'self-contempt.'"[143] Reddock is careful to point out that neither "mixed" nor "dougla" means "multiracial" in the Caribbean, nor does identifying as mixed— as opposed to *being* mixed—necessarily convey social benefit, as "the term 'dougla' does not preserve a record of 'mixing' over time" because dougla people after the first generation tend to pass into Africannness or Indianness.[144] Puri sees douglarization and creolization as two distinct types of racialized hybridity. Douglarization, I suggest, is in fact a racial subset of creolization, as it is a more specific term that always includes Indian-black miscegenation, while creolization broadly encompasses any type of cultural and ethnic hybridization and generally privileges Afro-Caribbean ways of being Caribbean. Being a postcolonial "Creole" in

Trinidad means to identify as predominantly Afro-Caribbean and likely Christian, while having pride in ancestral admixture and influence from other peoples and cultures.

The political Afro-Trinidadian calypsos that dealt with social ills instead of love and sex until the 1990s did not mention Indian women at all—only Indian men. It is as though in the public realm of politics and society, only the Indian man could appear as a rival to the Afro-Creole man, a rival who won by deceit, cunning, or sheer numbers. By contrast, the Indian woman was integrated into the Creole musical imaginary through cohabitation, marriage, and her supposed desire to leave behind the patriarchal structures of the close-knit Indian community.[145] Calypsos in general presumed that Indian women should *want* to leave their fathers and husbands' domination, and should want to creolize as a better alternative to the strictures of being Indian. Drupatee Ramgoonai, the most well-known female Indo-Trinidadian singer of chutney-soca—a popular form of dance music that uses some Bhojpuri-Hindi lyrics and instrumentation—embodies the possibility of being both an Indian and a Caribbean woman in music. When she rose to national prominence in 1987–88, male Indian commentators stated flatly that "no Indian woman has any right to sing calypso" and that, ironically, "Indian women have been a disgrace to Hinduism."[146] Brinda Mehta points out that Indo-Caribbean female writers are similarly subject to "cultural constraints" and "the fear of social ostracism that still threaten[s] Indo-Caribbean women writers, who are forced to confront Hindu sexual prudishness and sexual censorship in their writings on a regular basis."[147] Drupatee's oeuvre was negatively contrasted with classical Indian religious dance and music forms, though she began her career as a respectable singer of popular Indian film songs and Hindu religious songs, or *bhajans*. She is rooted in Indian tradition but is of Trinidad.[148] Indian women publicly performing and dancing chutney is an extraordinary literal display of freedom of movement that is both Indian and Trinidadian. The vast majority of Indo-Caribbean female music performers are from a Hindu background. Muslim women may perhaps have faced even greater community censure at the prospect of dancing in public, on stage, and participating in the people's festival of Carnival, as previously suggested in Ryhaan Shah's novel *A Silent Life*.

Reddock and Niranjana cite the 1996 controversy over the (in)famous calypso "Jahaji Bhai" by calypsonian Brother Marvin (Selwyn Demming), a self-identified dougla with an Indian wife, as a flashpoint in the representation of Indo-/Afro-Trinidadian political relations through music. The song, which Marvin wrote for the Calypso Monarch Carnival competition, extols common labor migration origins and shipboard kin groups; uses English and Hindi lyrics, Indian tassa drums, and Shango invocations; and criticizes ignorance of shared roots. Marvin reasonably pointed out that "jahaji bhai" (ship brothers)—family relationships created on the ships of colonial labor migration—ought to have been an appellation used between Indian and African Trinidadians, not just among Indians. He sang that his heritage was "Fifty percent Africa, fifty percent India," thus making him a descendant of the "Brotherhood of the boat."[149] Marvin performed the song at Carnival with his young daughter, who was dressed in an Indian *dupatta* and *lehenga* (shawl and long skirt), while he wore a West African caftan and hat—the family embodied their song and the Trinidadian future they wanted to create. "Jahaji Bhai" was a commemoration of the 150th anniversary of Indian arrival in Trinidad, and Indians "responded to the song in a way that they had never before responded to a calypso."[150] As Reddock points out, the calypso was unrelated to but nonetheless immediately followed the first victory of the Indian-majority United National Congress/National Alliance for Reconstruction (UNC/NAR) coalition over the Afro-majority Peoples National Movement (PNM), giving the song weight in the public sphere.[151]

"Jahaji Bhai" is one of the most popularly well-known and academically studied calypsos Trinidad has ever produced. Because Marvin uses Bhojpuri-Hindi lyrics and invokes the image of the *jhandi* flag erected by Caribbean Hindus after a *puja* prayer ritual, Indianness is usually assumed to be represented in his song by Hinduism. What I wish to point out, however, is that in the song Marvin names all three main religions in Trinidad—Christianity, Hinduism, Islam—as part of "this land," and explicitly says "I would be a disgrace to Allah / If I choose race, creed or colour."[152] Thus Marvin names himself inheritor of Hinduism and Islam in equal measure, and does not specify whether Islam comes from his Indian or African heritage.

The general public's original enthusiasm for the song was followed by push-back from Afro-Trinidadians "who felt that the calypso privileged the Indian part of Marvin's heritage over the African part. . . . Marvin might be a dougla, some said, but that did not mean that every Afro-Trinidadian would find in his or her ancestry a man praying in front of a [Hindu] jhandi [flag]."[153] "Jahaji Bhai" spawned rebuttal calypsos like 1997's "Jahaji Blues," in which Afro-Trinidadian calypsonian G. B. (Gregory Ballantyne), dressed in his own West African agbada, riffed on the title and lyrics of Marvin's song to give Marvin a thorough dressing down in history and race pride. "Ungrateful Negro / Boy you make me sing Jahaji Blues," he sang to Marvin in the chorus, and

I feel you mistake a shokoto and call it a dhoti . . .

No problem if your roots are in India
But distorting black history, that's a different matter . . .

Jahaji bhai was a term used by Indians only
When they broke with caste, religion and language on their long journey . . .

Brotherhood of the boat is about boats like *Fatel Razack* . . . [154]

A shokoto is the pant of the Yoruba agbada, and a dhoti a long loincloth associated with the Indian subcontinent, notably with Hindu priests and with M. K. Gandhi in his campaign for Indian independence from Britain. Marvin has his traditional menswear and his roots confused, says G. B. *Fatel Razack* (Victory of the Provider [Allah]), as previously mentioned, was the first ship to bring Indian indentured migrants to Trinidad in 1845. G. B. suggests that "jahaji bhai," the "brotherhood of the boat," is a linguistic and familial formulation specific to Caribbean Indians and cannot be extended to every person transported on every boat to the Caribbean as plantation labor, especially not to the descendants of enslaved Africans. Brother Marvin's inclusivity does not achieve national unity, says G. B., because it "projects the poor black man like if he Indian crazy" (i.e., obsessed with Indianness).[155]

Race and race pride do not operate as simple binaries in Trinidad, however. Niranjana notes that G. B. has had a long career as songwriter for noted Indo-Caribbean chutney singers Drupatee Ramgoonai and Rikki Jai, among others.[156] When I reached him by phone at his home in Trinidad, G. B. was both a jokester and serious about his song "Jahaji Blues." Laughing, the first thing he asked me was whether I was sure I had the right song and the right man: "Jahaji Blues" and him rather than "Jahaji Bhai" and Marvin, because ironically, people still mix up the songs and the men, and "I just want to get that out of the way."[157] In "Jahaji Bhai," Marvin suggests that racism, forcing people to choose a particular racial identity, and discrimination against particular creeds are all sins in Islam, a "disgrace to Allah." G. B.'s "Jahaji Blues" is about respecting the historic specificity of African origins. The two calypsonians' perspectives converge in the Muslimeen framework of reversion to an ancestral African Islam that was antiracist, as the oppression of Africans and Afro-Trinidadians was a product of colonialism. Marvin does not identify himself as a Muslim, but he still cares what Allah thinks, because Islam is part of his Trinidadian heritage. Islam is part of both the Trinidadian past and future, he says: the indentured and enslaved past, and the ecumenical postcolonial future. In this most famous calypso gesture at Trinidadian racial unity, Muslims, despite their smaller numbers and after the Muslimeen coup, are still firmly embedded in the nation and its futurity. They have not renounced their right to Trinidadian citizenship by rebelling against the state, because for the Muslimeen, Santabellans, and indeed the Trinidadian public at large, the state is an untrustworthy entity in which corrupt government officials look after their own interests. The state and the people are not one.

The real representation of the people, Trinidad's biggest event, is the annual February Carnival, a multiday subversion of sovereign power there as elsewhere—as Mikhail Bakhtin describes—but a temporary reversal of power that does not involve force of arms.[158] The power of Carnival in the Trinidadian imaginary is so great that, as explored in Earl Lovelace's classic novel of Trinidadian postindependence national development *The Dragon Can't Dance* (1979), many citizens live their lives from Carnival to Carnival and spend the entire year planning their costumes and band performances. Bakhtin describes the European medieval carnival as a space that allows "the suspension of all hierarchical precedence," embraces the grotesque, dons the mask of change and reincarnation that is related to "transition, metamorphoses, the violation of natural boundaries, to mockery and familiar nicknames," and exposes laughter and humor as "not a subjective, individual and biological consciousness of all people," but "the social consciousness of all the people."[159] These descriptors also apply to the pre-Lenten French- and African-influenced colonial history of Carnival in Latin America and the Caribbean, as the period of time before the Christian season of meatless fasting and atonement when social norms were (not quite) inverted, but when enslaved Africans could dress up as their masters, dance and sing publicly, and roam the streets more freely than usual. Like its medieval European counterpart, Caribbean Carnival is on its surface deeply Christian, in countries that are as a result of colonialism majority Catholic and Anglican Church of England. The pre-Lenten significance of colonial Carnival, however, has long been partly subsumed into a culture of tourism-influenced feteing in Trinidad; into related climate and island tourism expediency, as in Grenada's 1981 moving of its Spice Mas celebration to August to suit temperate-zone tourist schedules; and into nationalism, as in Guyana's absorbing of the phenomenon into the ostensibly indigenous but nationalist harvest festival celebration of Mashramani. In Trinidad, Guyana, and Suriname, integrating large populations of Hindus and Muslims that arrived in the nineteenth century into already-established traditions of Afro-Caribbean carnival and music has been an issue, as described by Niranjana and Puri. Bakhtin calls Carnival a time when a person caught in the irony of laughter becomes aware of the self as "a member of a continually growing and renewed people," capable of "the defeat of power, of earthly kings, of the earthly upper classes, of all that oppresses and restricts."[160] Expanding Trinidadians' concept of their Creole body and dispossessing earthly kings are precisely what the perpetrators of the 1990 coup sought, and the event unfolded as a carnival spectacle and performance. Speaking on television during the coup, Abu Bakr called for calm, but also for "the revolutionary forces to control the streets."[161] For Trinidadians, perhaps the biggest indictment of the coup was not that Abu Bakr and the Muslimeen failed to effect any substantial political change and were arrested, but that the event resulted not in the "revolutionary forces," but the mob taking to the streets, in a grand finale Trinidadians bleakly and jokingly called "de Lootout."[162]

The public did not respond to Abu Bakr's call to join the revolution. Instead, many took the distraction of the police and army as an opportunity to commit days of mass robbery of businesses in Port of Spain. After the coup, blame for the Lootout was leveled against many parties: Syrian and Indian businessmen for being, historically, "the quintessential [capitalist] looters"; "young black males who existed on the margins of Trinidad society"; "newly arrived and poorly integrated black immigrants from the smaller Caribbean islands"; the International Monetary Fund, as per Jesse Jackson who weighed in from afar and "described the looting as 'IMF Riots'"; the general "failure of the authorities over the years to enforce the laws of the land"; and of course, the Muslimeen and perceived inherent Islamic militancy.[163] Prime Minister Robinson observed after the coup that the Muslimeen "gravely miscalculated the mood of the people of Trinidad and Tobago," as citizens saw the Muslimeen as a strange, foreign-influenced sect with some righteous social causes.[164] In typical Caribbean, carnivalesque fashion, Trinidadian anxiety over the Lootout and the specter of descent into anarchy was in short order mediated by calypsos, laughter, and jokery.[165] From robbers who did not recognize modern technology but nonetheless stole it, to thieved luxury goods that were too small for poor homes, to the proliferating drug trade, to the failed pilferer of only one shoe, and the entrepreneur selling body fresheners to sweating looters, Ryan's description of the Lootout would not be out of place in one of Gabriel García Márquez's novels of magical realism in a failed banana republic.[166] In the postcolonial kleptocracy, the government, everyone understood, was the biggest looter of all.

The coup jokes were dark; and Pantin said that in his observations of a Muslimeen teenager holding him hostage, his feeling was "we had failed him . . . we hadn't harnessed their idealism, all that youthful energy and enthusiasm and capacity to believe in something large and grander than themselves. But Bakr had."[167] But what "Trinidadians, I would soon discover, didn't want to hear" was that the Muslimeen "were soft-spoken, polite, never mind they always had their guns in their hands. . . . People felt better if you told them that the Jamaat gunmen had all been just a bunch of cold-blooded murderers and thugs. They felt more comfortable with that stereotype."[168] Interpellation into song, recourse to jokery, and framing the Muslimeen as exceptional but also conventionally "evil," rather than a new social phenomenon, were how Trinidad made sense of the societal threat posed by the coup and the political emergence of a religious group about which most knew next to nothing: Muslims.

PM Robinson, leader of the NAR, had been given a mandate for change after years of rule by the PNM but was viewed as ineffective. Robinson, who had been held hostage and refused to resign after the coup, was a joker too.[169] During his captivity, when he was shot (not life-threateningly), he told his fellow captives that he wanted his epitaph to read "Here lies A.N.R. Robinson, a man with a good heart and a good soul. He was not too bright, but loved his country."[170] There is no record of why Robinson believed he was "not too bright," but presumably he meant the statement as irony, as he believed himself a near-martyr for Trinidad. In a rousing postcoup convention speech to his NAR party in December 1990, Robinson assured attendees he had heroically told Abu Bakr's followers to "kill me and save the rest."[171] He said that Abu Bakr "had proclaimed a new government without a single intelligent clue as to what to do thereafter. The new breed of fanatics claimed divine inspiration, but acted in satanic fashion."[172] The Muslimeen and any future politicized Muslims were thus identified as "a new breed of fanatics" whose religion was "satanic," at odds with majority Christianity, and had no links to the historical, African Muslim "Mandingo." Before the coup, Abu Bakr had referred to NAR's and Robinson's proposed expensive erection of a monument to the deceased Gene (Jean) Miles, a woman persecuted by the PNM for being an oil industry anticorruption campaigner—the character of Beatrice Salandy resembles her—as an "act of Satan," in contrast to his own regular acts of God.[173] No one in Trinidad, it seemed, had a monopoly on Satan, God, or martyrdom.

Widespread looting is also a result of the coup in *Allah in the Islands*, and Santabellans are just as ungrateful to the Muslims. Abdul asks bleakly, "That is what we sacrifice for? For bandits to run up Belmont with a microwave on their heads? For women to ramsack the stores for a few panty? . . . that is the mentality of a lot of people in Santabella. Let me see what I could get without paying for it. But somebody have to pay. Somebody always have to pay."[174] From the alliterative bandits running up Belmont, to the women ransacking stores for one or two pairs of panties, this is the same "funny side" to the Trinidadian Lootout that Ryan describes. It is just as ironic too, since the Muslims intent on saving Santabella are the ones who "pay" for the looted goods when the army starts shooting. Birth argues that the Trinidadian coup was cemented as comedy by Carnival calypsos, though Carnival "does not transcend social boundaries but tends to recognize and to play with them. The play is one of subversive relationships, not of opposition."[175] Carnival and calypsos cannot alone provide resolution of social issues, but they illustrate relationality and play, and influence opinion.

As noted, former Trini calypsonian McClane took to the *New York Times* in March 1991 to explain to U.S. readers the strange goings-on in their neighbor to the south, and to elaborate the nature of the coup's relationship to music. As she said, Abu Bakr played "politically aware" calypsonians, including David Rudder and Cro Cro, and the imam's "stint as revolutionary video host demonstrated what Trinidadians have long known: calypso (and soca, the modern multitrack studio version of this traditional music) is as important as politics in this lively, noisy, multi-ethnic Caribbean democracy."[176] Calypso *is* politics, in its Trinidadian historical incarnation as a genre of music that first explicitly critiqued colonialism, and then postcolonial governments and social ills. McClane wrote to her American audience that Abu Bakr turned TTT into "calypso MTV" and, aided by an adviser who was an ex-calypso promoter, turned himself into a practitioner of "calypso diplomacy."[177] Calypsonians were the people in Trinidad who "speak the unspeakable—and politicians put up with it, perhaps because this ritual serves to diffuse discontent that might otherwise find more turbulent channels."[178] McClane cited Superblue's "Get Something and Wave" as a 1991 calypso that was particularly ingenious in defusing religious and racial tensions following the coup. The calypso urged the nation to wave flags, "a key element in the rituals of three important local religions: Shango, Hindu and Muslims," which McClane interpreted as "an affirmation of Trinidad's multi-ethnic culture and a determination to bind the wounds of the coup."[179]

Rather than a simple suturing of the "wounds" of the coup through a show of religious unity, Birth argues that the major societal function of the coup calypsos was to integrate the coup "into a teleological cultural image of Trinidadian history," which smoothed over the disruptive violence of the coup with the calypso "resolution in favor of youth and freedom. . . . Following a device important to all counterpoint, the dissonance between coup and Carnival was transformed into harmony."[180] Though the Muslimeen failed to take over the government, the counterpoint *at the moment of the coup* may be said to have been resolved "in favor of youth and freedom" because it illustrated to young people that political change was possible, and because Abu Bakr appears to have rehabilitated young people involved in crime and drugs.[181] However, I do not believe that calypso harmony was achieved, or that the militant coup was "calypso diplomacy." The Muslimeen raised fears of global terrorism reaching Trinidad that have only been heightened in recent years with, as I will discuss in the next chapter, a few young Trinidadian and other Caribbean men seeking to travel to Syria to fight for the Islamic State. The Muslimeen never quite attained (regained) the moral status of Trinidadian citizens: they continue to be viewed with suspicion, as always-already religious traitors to the state. But through music, the coup was incorporated into the national imaginary as a Trinidadian event with links to slave and indentured rebellions past.

CONCLUSION: SING A PRAYER FOR ABU BAKR

As McClane illustrates with Superblue's calypso, the coup's musical integration into Trinidadian history necessarily included nods to racial unity and the ideal of a multiracial Creole society, the themes that Brother Marvin took up five years later. The musical integration of Muslims is also an important aspect of the novel *Allah in the Islands*, though that integration happens before and not after Haji's coup. As the Muslims of the novel become more politically active and ordinary Santabellans poorer, the situation becomes, in Caribbean parlance, so "dread" that calypsonians craft a song begging their former colonizers,

> Massa leh me go to your country
> Help me escape this misery.[182]

Like their Trinidadian counterparts, the Santabellans alleviate national suffering by turning it into a pleasurable carnival performance. Despite the melancholic, escapist tone of the misery and migration calypso, "Santabellans, and people all up and down the islands, had made the calypso a road march hit, dancing to it on Carnival day as if the dance itself was a cleansing ritual for the dread they lived

every day."[183] Carnival and calypso are repetitive "cleansing rituals" when Santabellans (and all Caribbean islanders) understand that the colonial and corrupt
causes of daily suffering remain. Song and dance make the quotidian bearable.

In Santabella, calypso is the part of Caribbean culture that Haji's Muslims won't
give up. Abdul says, "My faith doesn't mean that I can't enjoy our culture. . . . the
calypsonians are the major singers, and a lot of them were friends with the Haji.
They are the ones, aside from men like us, who really represent the people, and
every year, they try to put to music the troubles Santabellans seeing."[184] There is
a seamless connection between the Muslims' and calypsonians' desires to address
economic and political ills and the legacy of colonialism in Santabella. Abdul
invokes another group with similar concerns: Rastafarians, and their and the
Caribbean's number one folk hero, Robert Nesta Marley. Abdul names Marley's
"Redemption Song" as the song that made him think about Afro-Caribbean history. Notably, Marley concludes by quoting Marcus Garvey. It is Garvey who first
said "Emancipate yourselves from mental slavery / None but ourselves can free
our minds."[185] For Abdul, the Muslimeen coup is a latter-day revolutionary act
against transatlantic slavery—it is a move toward what Rastamen also use spirituality to attain: emancipation from white, colonial, capitalist Babylon.[186]

The Santabellan Muslims stage their own musical performances for national
unity, in defiance of some conservative Islamic norms that frown on instrumental music. As discussed in the introduction, there is much debate among Muslims
about the permissibility of music in various forms. Some Muslims disapprove of
music for the exact reason that calypsonians sing: because music can influence
opinion and behavior. The difference between some religiously sanctioned musical forms like a capella *nasheed* chanting and the calypsos embraced by Santabellan and Trinidadian Muslims is not that the calypso is *popular*—so is Islamic
religious chanting, and it has celebrity performers too—but that traditional
calypso has the secular, subversive function of uniting the people by criticizing
their rulers in "jest." When the Caribbean Muslims want to participate in national
culture, they choose not only their potentially alienating religion as a vehicle, but
also the music common to all the people.

Like Rudder, the Afro-Santabellan Muslims invoke Hosay and religious unity
with Indo-Santabellans through music. After Haji gives a stirring speech about
poverty and education at a Muslim-organized rally, he wisely brings in the band—
both drummers and calypsonians. There are Afro- and Indo-Caribbean drummers playing Indian *tassa* drums and African drums, and it does not matter who
is playing what. Beatrice asks her friend Jestina, "If Indian boys can beat steel pan,
and Indian women could sing calypso, what's so wrong with Creole men beating
tassa drums?"[187] Similarly, Abdul muses, "Them guys—two Indian and two
Creole—could drum too bad, and they never take any pay. They realize that what
Haji doing is for people like them, poor people in this country catching their *nenen*
day in and day out under this government."[188] The drummers "seemed mesmer-

ized, tranced by the rhythmic creation that drew from the souls of unsettled waters flowing in the Ganges and the Niger."[189] It is not far-fetched for the Santabellans to imagine both *races* playing drums together, but Muslims are still an *Indian* breed apart. After the drumming, the Muslims bring on Santabellan calypsonian The Mighty Shadow to sing his calypso "Poverty Is Hell." Shadow (Winston Bailey, 1941–2018) was a real Trini calypsonian and "Poverty Is Hell" was one of his hit calypsos in 1994. Less irruption than seepage, this subtle breakthrough of the real into the fictitious at the conclusion of the novel cements Wynter's assertion that in the Caribbean, history is a narrative journey of fiction into fact, with the change precipitated by a climactic people's revolution. Beatrice's reaction to Shadow, despite her earlier realization that any Santabellan can play any ancestral Caribbean musical instrument, is to be "stunned. Calypso? Kaiso? At a Muslim rally? And drums? African drums? What kind of Muslim was this?"[190] Shadow's calypso is expressly political and secular, and the musical form is intrinsically Caribbean— and Islam, to Beatrice, is still a prohibitive foreign religion. Haji's Muslims show Santabellans that racial differences do not matter when both black and Indian citizens—who have a common culture, as demonstrated by their complementary Old World drumming in the New World—are suffering at the hands of the post-colonial government.

After the Muslimeen coup, the Trinidadian calypsonian Cro Cro (Weston Rawlins) sang a 1991 calypso in which he condemned the coup for being rash: "In we democratic society the coup was wrong without a doubt."[191] But then, he says, "Bakr did it for all of us. . . . So get conscious brother and sister / Say a prayer for Abu Bakr."[192] The song is called "Say a Prayer for Abu Bakr," and in the complexity of calypsonians' and other Trinidadians' feelings about the Muslimeen coup, that is the sentiment that wins out: that Abu Bakr and his Muslim followers were doing something related to a revolutionary's "getting conscious," something righteous for postcolonial Trinidad. Abu Bakr himself is appreciative of Cro Cro's spiritually supportive sentiment, declaring firmly to me that of the coup calypsos, "the best of them was done by Cro Cro."[193] In the end, Abu Bakr and Haji— Muslims, polygamists, coup leaders—are anticolonial Trinidadian heroes. Cro Cro and the nation therefore sing calypso prayers to and for them. Calypso, in Trinidad, is the vehicle of history, including Muslim history. "Calypso diplomat" Abu Bakr summed up the importance of the music and himself for me by saying that "in Trinidad calypso is the culture and in calypso stories are told," adding that even in 2019 people were still singing new calypsos with "my name . . . in it."[194] Trinidadians, he said, joke with him that "they [still] can't leave you out of the calypso at all. And this is thirty-something years. . . . It's part of the cultural history and . . . the history of Trinidad and Tobago, the events of 1990."[195] In Trinidad and Santabella, not-so-secular calypso and Islamic coup are both invocations for a "Muslim time" that hail the full breadth of the Caribbean past and ancestral roots in search of a truly decolonial future.

5 · MIMIC MAN AND ETHNORIENTALIST

Global Caribbean Islam and the Specter of Terror

"If she had taken off the hijab so that her face could be seen, that would have been alright.... I don't dislike Muslims, some of my best friends are Muslims and I usually get along well with them," Hukumchand added.

Parts of the [terrorist] conspiracy, as conceived by Mr. Defreitas, had bizarre aspects. He declared that he wanted the attack to be "high-tech" and "ninja-style" in execution, according to the tapes. At one point, he suggested that the plotters could create a diversion by flooding the airport's main terminal with a horde of rats.[1]

Twenty-first-century news reports on Caribbean Muslims can be virtually Naipaulian in their absurdist attempts to comprehend the incongruity of people who hail from the islands of sun, sand, and sea tourism but are also Muslim and entangled in some of the darkest, most violent affairs of the Americas and the world. The hijab and the beach bikini are metonymically incompatible to the uninformed. As described in the previous chapter, the Muslimeen's attempted coup and very existence were viewed as shocking by some Trinidadians because the Muslimeen were their countrymen, and Muslims seemed to belong to some other faraway place. Even apparently sympathetic media stereotypes Muslims and legitimizes racism, in what Evelyn Alsultany identifies as "simplified complex representations [that] are the representational mode of the so-called post-race era."[1] One factor is that mere *inclusion* does not really challenge bias and stereotype. As Edward Said brought into early focus in his *Orientalism* trilogy, Muslims demographically and visually epitomize the geographics of "East" and "Orient."[2] As discussed in the introduction, Mustafa Bayoumi, Sylvester Johnson, Junaid Rana, and others continue the work of deconstructing the othering of Muslims though their racialized embodiment in the post-9/11 world. Simply put: in the public discourse of the Americas (and Europe), Muslims, regardless of color, are conceived of and treated as a minority race that is incompatible with the white racial majority's cultural norms, coded as "Christian" and "Western" values. The damning "evidence" of Muslims' incompatibility is dress. That racialization of religiosity is how the Muslimeen were framed as cultural outsiders to Trinidad, even though their members were mostly Afro-Trinidadians—the racial majority. As Johnson says in the context of the continuous FBI surveillance of Muslims that begins with antagonism toward the African American Nation of Islam as nonwhite enemies of the state, "Racialization is achieved through the colonial form of political order when this dominated population is marked as perpetually, ineluctably alien. They are treated as incapable of truly belonging to the state. In the eyes of the state, neither the passage of time nor the adoption of new cultural form alters this alien status . . . they are people of a fundamentally different type (this is 'differential essence'). They are *in* the society bur not *of* it, even if they have been born in that society."[3] In countries in which they are not a religious majority, Muslims may thus occupy the status of a static, racialized internal colony. They are people who may not even be or are incapable of becoming people—defined both as morally human and as citizen-subjects—as they are of a "fundamentally different type."

The rightful demands of African diaspora and migrant Muslims to be treated as equal citizens of the nation-states of the "West" in the twentieth and twenty-first centuries have thus been met with responses ranging from wonder, pluralist embrace, and tolerance, to antipathy, disgust, and an overweening sense of the unwanted intrusion of the Old World Other into the historical projects of hemispheric American colonization and Manifest Destiny. Women are particularly implicated in what is framed as a culture clash. The first epigraph of this chapter is from a June 2013 report by Guyana's major national newspaper *Stabroek News* on the controversy surrounding a court case in which defense attorney Hukumchand refused to cross-examine a Muslim female witness wearing a *niqab*, a full face veil, unless she first removed it.[4] The major representative body of local Muslims, the Sunni Central Islamic Organisation of Guyana (CIOG), entered the fray, condemning the attorney for his bias and "insult to the Muslim community," whereupon Hukumchand asserted that while wearing a hijab did not legally violate "the court's mode of dress," "a hijab covering your face so that only your eyes are seen would be in violation as it conflicts with the principle of observing the witness's demeanour."[5] In this episode "the court" implied the Georgetown Magistrates' Court and its judicial apparatus, including judges, attorneys, and witnesses, all of whom were expected to abide by trial procedures that drew heavily from colonial British Common Law in the service of postcolonial Guyanese Western democracy. The appearance of the witness was so orientalized, so foreign and alien to the court and the State, that her *niqab* was incorrectly named a hijab, the headscarf-only Islamic female covering, by both the attorney and the newspaper. Though she was a Guyanese woman, she did not have the proper "demeanour" of one: not sartorially, not in (missing) facial expression, not in gendered affect—she refused to comply and remove the *niqab*—and ostensibly not in legal standing, though Hukumchand the lawyer could not specify what law was being broken. Her appearance *felt* wrong to him in a moral and legal way that violated the social contract of the Guyanese public sphere. Certainly, she was not one of his Muslim friends.

As discussed throughout this book, race is typically concomitant with religion in the Caribbean, including in Guyana. Because her race could not be determined, the Muslim woman disrupted national identity constructs that demanded all Muslims be Indian. From his name, Hukumchand was likely Hindu Indo-Guyanese, of the majority faith of the majority population in Guyana, and the court was associated with the political trappings of colonialism, as well as Christian Afro-Guyanese and their 1960s–1990s dominance of government. The covered Muslim woman's Guyanese positionality was, at first, entirely uncertain. The interference of the CIOG, the traditional representative of Indo-Guyanese Muslims, normalized the fray into the traditional Guyanese dialectical constructs of black/Indian and Muslim/Hindu, providing relief to all concerned about the Muslim woman's locus of enunciation. Hukumchand could be friends with any Muslim again because in the Guyanese context, Indian racial solidarity has traditionally been more important than religious differences. In the new millennium and in the context of post-9/11 discourses on Muslims and terrorism in the Western Hemisphere, however, the alliances of race and religion in the Caribbean have begun to shift.

The second epigraph of this chapter is from a report of the proceedings of a case that escapes the boundaries of the Guyanese local into the global "war on terror": the 2007 "JFK terror plot" in which three Guyanese and one Trinidadian were accused by U.S. federal prosecutors of plotting to explode fuel tanks and pipelines at John F. Kennedy airport in New York City. The three Guyanese—including the ninja Pied Piper and the former cargo handler Russell Defreitas—were each sentenced to life in prison, and the Trinidadian to fifteen years for his supporting role. All of the men convicted of involvement in the plot were Afro-Caribbean converts to Islam. Abdul Kadir, who was alleged to have ties to Iran, was a former Guyanese parliamentarian from the People's National Congress—Reform (PNC-R), the political party traditionally associated with Afro-Guyanese, and the four were also linked to the Jamaat al Muslimeen, which denied the connection.[6] The *New York Times* and other U.S. newspapers reporting on the case had nothing to say about the men's ethnicity, focusing instead on their religion; but it is immediately obvious that the men were *black* Muslims and converts, disrupting the racialized Caribbean association of Islam with Indians. What was also clear to the Guyanese reading between the lines was that the men were perhaps framed as more dangerous by U.S. prosecutors than they really were. They seemed to be classic postcolonial, incompetent, absurd bumblers with inflated senses of their own religiosity and importance, as "while a prosecutor said during her opening statement that the men were aspiring terrorists, defense lawyers described one man as an empty boaster and the other as little more than a bystander," and Defreitas, the rat whisperer and alleged mastermind, was described by his own lawyer as being incapable of turning on a video camera.[7]

Transnational focus on the JFK case was renewed in 2019. Abdul Kadir, the Guyanese alleged plotter, died in prison in the United States in June 2018. On April 26, 2019, the ruling Guyanese A Partnership for National Unity + Alliance for Change (APNU+AFC) coalition party, including its majority PNC-R arm, passed a "sympathy motion" in the Guyana National Assembly honoring Kadir for his parliamentary service. The motion was passed during the traditionally majority Indian People's Progressive Party/Civic (PPP/C) opposition boycott of the House. An editorial in the Guyanese *Stabroek News* alleged that the motion was a racialized ploy to appeal to the APNU+AFC party base in Kadir's majority Afro-Guyanese hometown of Linden.[8] Regardless of local political impetus, the sympathy motion received stinging condemnation from the U.S. Embassy in Guyana, on behalf of the U.S. government. The Embassy questioned Guyana's reputation as a "a model to the world on religious tolerance and understanding," accused the National Assembly of "plac[ing] this resolution in direct contradiction to the efforts of security cooperation between our two countries," and declared that Guyanese lawmakers had "left a stain on their legacy as representatives of the Guyanese people and on their commitment to the rule of law."[9] The European Union and Canada followed suit in condemning the sympathy motion, with the Canadian High Commission in Guyana declaring that it was "disappointed" with the Guyana National Assembly.[10] The Guyanese government responded with a statement asserting that "it had no intention of conveying the impression" of honoring terrorism and was simply recognizing Kadir's parliamentary service, as "The Government of Guyana continues to condemn terrorism in the strongest possible way" and "reaffirms its commitment to continue and intensify the fight against terrorism in any form and is proud of its record to date in this regard."[11] The U.S. Embassy's outrage over transnational security concerns and implied religious tolerance insult to Guyana was met with a combination of both defiance and backpedaling; but the National Assembly neither apologized for nor withdrew the motion, suggesting an ongoing Guyanese government resistance to U.S., Canadian, and European influence in the hemisphere, including in dictating responses to terrorism.

In this chapter I show that in Guyana and the Anglophone Caribbean, Islam is no longer figured as solely a regional, religious legacy of Indian indentureship, but rather, as a transnational religion characterized by local multiethnic adherents' participation in a twenty-first-century "global Islam" that is popularly figured as undergoing a modern process of conservative Islamization. The Guyanese "Islamic Revival," as it is called by some Muslims around the world, exists within the context of 1970s-onward revivalist *tajdīd* and reformist *islah* projects in many places in the Muslim world, from Egypt to Saudi Arabia to Afghanistan to Malaysia to Turkey.[12] In media and in some academic depictions, the Caribbean has become embroiled in stereotypic Americas discourse on terrorism without attention to the particularities of its historical relationship to Islam. The literature of Islam in the Caribbean, however, resists essentializing Muslims by insisting on the very real simultaneity of local and global Islam, and demanding engagement of ethnoreligious identifications with the dominant Caribbean postcolonial trope of creolization.

I begin by identifying the genesis of the postcolonial Muslim Caribbean "mimic man" in the work of V. S. Naipaul. In Anglophone Caribbean discourse, the mimic man of literature is the postcolonial who hybridizes the scant remnants of his African, Indian, indigenous, or other originary ethnic heritage with an inaccurate aping of the British colonizer's culture and behavior. Naipaul's fiction pioneers both the mimic man trope and its Muslim iteration. I then identify the contemporary Caribbean Muslim mimic man as a fullaman in Jan Lowe Shinebourne's 2010 novel *Chinese Women*, which addresses, in the Guyanese context, the burning global obsession with finding reasons for the Islamic radicalization of societally disenfranchised Muslim men. "Why do they hate us?" as President George W. Bush famously asked a Joint Session of the U.S. Congress on September 20, 2001, and how do they get that way?[13] His rhetorical answer and the continuing U.S. governmental answer was because "they hate our freedoms, our freedom of religion, our freedom of speech, our freedom to vote and assemble and disagree with each other."[14] And certainly it can be said of Shinebourne's Indo-Guyanese Muslim protagonist Albert "Sonny" Aziz that he hates everyone's freedoms, because he himself is not free. Bush's articulation of "freedoms," however, is a generalization of the U.S. Constitution and its amendments. Aziz's captivity is postcolonial and Caribbean, a function of the very particular interplay of race, religion, and class in Guyana. The disciplining social narratives of both Bush and Aziz improbably produce the same figure: an antisocial, fundamentalist adherent to Islam whose goal appears to be to destroy "Western" civilization, and in his refusal to be saved by it, himself. The novel *Chinese Women* demonstrates that the answer to the orientalist query posed by Bush is almost entirely local and individual, so there will never be a single answer to the question of the motives of the terrorist. In addition, the subject and object of the inquiry itself are unstable, as "they" are often "us."

Stuart Hall uses the example of the Caribbean to argue that even in diaspora, "their" and "our" ethnicity and cultural identities are embedded in place: ethnicity "is located in a place, in a specific history."[15] At the same time, "ethnicity is the necessary place or space from which people speak, and identity is always consti-

tuted in opposition to the Other."[16] Ethnicity is not merely race or color; it is actu-
ated by geography, history, culture (including religion), and a determination of
where, what, and who constitute "home" and "abroad." Ethnicity is here differentiated from race; its use as a sometime-euphemism for race disguises racist attention to phenotype, thus illustrating that ethnicity can encompass more, including
language and region, than does race. Race, as Johnson says, is not phenotype,
biological code, "mere discourse," feelings, or antipathy, and is in fact "a state practice of ruling people within a political order that perpetually places some within
and others outside of the political community through which the constitution of
the state is conceived."[17] Muslims are racialized in the United States and thus
placed outside of its body politic. The same has been true in the Caribbean, at least
in the case of the Muslimeen. Race is particularly useful in examining intranational
treatment of Muslims.

I shift here, however, to working with the transnational, geographic implications of ethnicity. Cultural identity, I suggest, is constituted in large part of ethnicity, together with a collective local understanding of the familial, behavioral,
and economic components of citizenship and an individual's history of personal,
affective encounters with the State's apparatus and with its other subjects. Rather
than being functionally superstructural in the Marxist sense, cultural identity is a
temporal through line rendering basal relations of production and superstructure
porous to each other. Both cultural identity and its ethnicity component masquerade as ineradicable markers of being, but they are fixed only in the moment, and
are, Hall says, positionings rather than essences.[18] Cultural identity is a matter of
both similarity and difference, and in its difference it "is a matter of 'becoming'
as well as 'being.' It belongs to the future as much as to the past . . . identities are
the names we give to the different ways we are positioned by, and position ourselves within, the narratives of the past."[19] Of particular concern here is that the
U.S. construction of the race/ethnicity/religion identity paradigm cannot be
neatly overlaid onto the Caribbean, and that Caribbean Muslims' relation to global
Islam has only been (partially) mediated through the United States and Canada
since the 1970s, with 9/11 as a watershed moment.

I argue that beginning in the Caribbean independence period of the 1960s, the
historical alignments of various ethnicities with Islam in the production of cultural identity in Guyana have temporally and geographically shifted in two ways.
First, for the Caribbean Muslim "mimic man" subject of postcoloniality, the metropolitan center has shifted from the colonizer's white, Christian England, to the
Arab "Middle East" with Wahhabi Saudi Arabia at its own center. This is an iteration of the center/periphery national, postcolonial model variously described in
the work of Benedict Anderson, Étienne Balibar, Homi Bhabha, Said, Immanuel
Wallerstein, and many others. The model is not universally applicable, but it cannot be discounted that Islam has a geographic, historic, and metaphoric center:
it is Mecca and its Ka'ba, toward which all Muslims must turn to pray five times

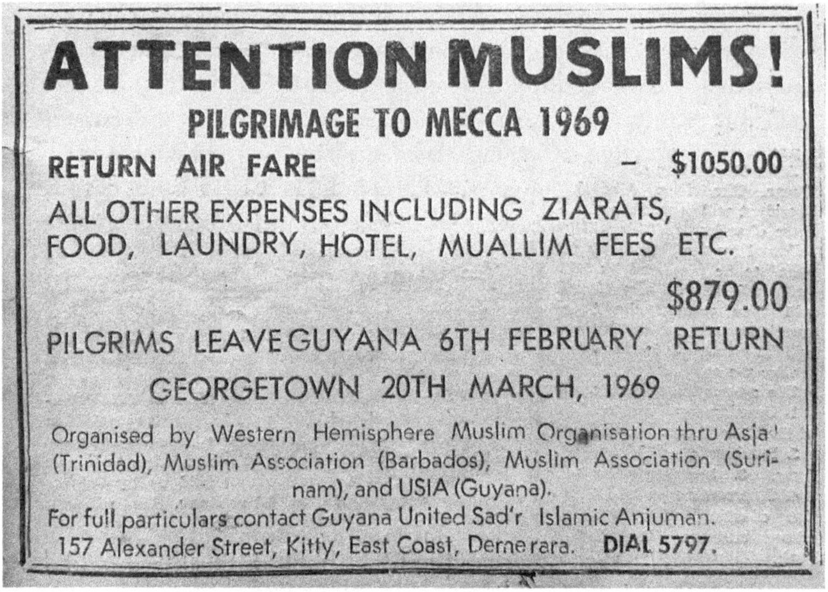

FIGURE 5.1 A 1969 hajj travel advertisement in the October 1968 issue of the *Voice of Islam*, the official newspaper of the Guyana United Sad'r Islamic Anjuman of Guyana. Pilgrims from Guyana, Trinidad, Suriname, Barbados, and other Caribbean nations typically traveled together. (National Archives of Guyana, Aliyah Khan.)

a day, and to which they go on the hajj pilgrimage—two of the five pillars of Islam. Caribbean Muslim pilgrims began traveling to hajj by air after World War II, on a British Overseas Airways Corporation route from British Guiana to London to Mecca (see fig. 5.1). Previously, the major hajj route was by ship from Trinidad.

Shinebourne's novel *Chinese Women* shows that the contemporary fullaman Indo-Caribbean Muslim looks neither to England nor to India, but to the Arab world to articulate religious and cultural identity. In so doing he or she becomes entangled in global conflicts over Islamic identity. In *Chinese Women*, Aziz's cultural and racial ideal shifts from the British plantation owner to the conservative Arab Salafist. At the beginning of the novel, the "dark brown Indian teenager" Aziz wishes he were white, or in a distinctively Guyanese historical alternative, Chinese, so as to escape the legacies of enslavement and indenture offered by blackness and Indianness.[20] The adult Aziz, however, comes to believe he is visibly Arab, saying of himself when passing through airports, "They know I am a Muslim because of my Semitic face with my hawk nose and pointed beard and it makes them afraid."[21] In Muslim postcolonial mimicry, not only religious identity but ethnicity itself is malleable. A beard may be symbolically grown or removed or reshaped, but not so, usually, a nose. This application to oneself of the ethnicized cultural stereotypes of Islamic orientalism—physical features, dress, treatment of women, all the trappings of various Arab cultures that may or may not have any-thing to do with the religion of Islam itself—is what I call here *ethnorientalism*.

Second, I argue that *Chinese Women* disrupts the 1960s independence-era and after association of black Caribbean Muslims (like Defreitas) with "political" Islam, and Indo-Caribbeans with a "cultural" Indo-Iranian Islam that is friendlier to the postcolonial national-building project: not fully assimilable, but relatively quiescent. The history of Muslims in Guyana follows the same trajectory as in Trinidad and Jamaica: as a result of British colonialism, there was a first wave of enslaved Mandingo and Fulani African Muslims whose Islam was poorly docu-mented and did not survive the horrors of the plantation; and, beginning in 1838, a second wave of indentured South Asian Muslims arrived, and their Islam sur-vives through direct descendants into the present day.[22]

Brinsley Samaroo defines three phases of "Islamic reconstruction" for Indo-Guianese migrants: in the late nineteenth and early twentieth centuries, the rapid establishment of mosques and pan-Indian mutual-aid organizations; in the 1914–1945 interwar period, the establishment of separate Islamic organizations addressing Muslim social and political concerns; and after 1947, the year of the Partition of Indian, and 1952, the year of the Egyptian Revolution, a period defined by looking outward for "international support for the creation of a political space for colonial Muslims."[23] Clem Seecharan notes, however, that during and after Partition, on the grounds of racial solidarity, "Hindu-Muslim unity in British Gui-ana was more robust than anywhere in the Indian diaspora, including neighbour-ing Trinidad."[24] The metropolitan focus of the third transnational period of "Islamic reconstruction" shifted permanently in the 1970s from the migrants' ancestral India and Pakistan to the Arab world, with the advent of Arab mission-aries and the curious Cold War intersection of Non-Aligned, socialist Guyana with Muammar Qaddafi's Libya.

The Libyan World Islamic Call Society, which still exists in Libya, was founded by the international Muslim Brotherhood. After the 1969 Libyan army coup, it was funded by Qaddafi to promote the Arabic language, the strengthening and Ara-bizing of local Islams, and the tenets of his Green Book, through the exporting of Muslim preachers and Qur'ans around the world.[25] The remaking of Non-Aligned Libya into the Socialist People's Libyan Arab Jamahiriya (state of the masses) in the 1970s included Libya's forging of diplomatic and social ties with Cuba, Guy-ana, and other leftist Latin American and Caribbean states. Such ties in socialist Guyana included everything from cooperative Libyan ownership of fishing and shrimping trawlers in Caribbean waters, to, once the Libyan government realized there were Muslims in Guyana, funding and shaping local Islam through the Islamic Call Society.[26] The Libyan political presence and subsequent Arabization of Indo-Iranian Islam in Guyana are in large part due to the efforts of one man: Ahmad Ehwass, Libya's ambassador to Guyana from 1977 to 1981, who was eventu-ally killed in 1984 in Libya in an attempted coup against Qaddafi. Ehwass established the Guyana Islamic Trust (GIT) organization as a means of propagating "pure" Islam in the Caribbean, leading to the "Islamic Revival" in Guyana.[27] Ehwass is still remembered fondly by many Muslims in Guyana. A pseudonymous February 27, 2011, *Stabroek News* letter to the editor from someone jokingly calling himself "Abu Bakr" begins by expressing sadness over Libya's twenty-first-century political and economic turmoil, saying, "For many of us Muslims in Guyana and the Caribbean, the revolt in Libya is lived as an event that touches us personally. The former Libyan chargé d'affaires in Guyana, Ahmed Ehwas [*sic*], was almost single-handedly responsible for the renewal of Islam here at the end of the seventies. All of the brothers in the Guyana Islamic Trust and the CIOG will remember the work he did in extending the foundations laid by the Indian Muslim immigrants in the century and a half preceding."[28]

As previously noted, the CIOG, the Central Islamic Organization of Guyana, is the main Sunni Indo-Muslim organization in Guyana; the GIT was founded by Ehwass. The contemporary GIT is viewed by Guyanese as the local revivalist Salafi (roughly, those who seek a return to the traditions of the first three generations of Arabian Islam) or Saudi-like Wahhabi Muslim organization, generally appearing in the news when there is some national or international event or person deserving moral condemnation. The organization has, for instance, publicly condemned the "dreadful" actions of IS in Iraq and Syria and Boko Haram in Nigeria, issuing a public statement in August 2014 saying that the groups' "origin, existence and operation are for the most part shrouded in mystery, in no way represents the pristine and beautiful teachings of Islam. . . . The GIT called on all Muslims to decry this 'deliberate perversion of our Faith and to dissociate themselves totally from such dangerous groups who intentionally use the name of Islam in their ongoing campaign of distortion and destruction.'"[29] This statement reveals that the GIT sees itself as being involved in the international affairs of the Muslim *ummah* while being wedded to the vision of a peaceful but conservative vision of Islam in Guyana. The latter position is exemplified by the organization's September 2013 fatwa against the British Muslim singer Sami Yusuf, otherwise known internationally as "the King of Islamic Pop," who proposed a tour of Guyana wherein he would sing his contemporary popular religious songs for Guyanese of all backgrounds. The GIT referred to Yusuf as a "person of low moral standing," employing the refrain that "professional singing and most musical instruments [are] not permissible."[30] As implied in the previous chapter's discussion of the Muslimeen and their fictional counterparts, this is an unpopular position on music in the Caribbean, including among Guyanese Muslims, for whom the Urdu *qasida* (or Islamic praise song), is a favorite cultural tradition brought from India.[31] Yusuf's tour went ahead to great acclaim—in no small part because it was cosponsored by the GIT's rival organization, the Sunni CIOG. The CIOG, though mainstream, is not however a liberal group. Johannes de Kruijf ascribes to them a desire for a "cleansing of local Islam. Despite their approval of certain contested customs, they advocate a religion cleansed of the alien elements that have stained it ever since its arrival in Guyana. They also share the vision of a purified Islam as being not only disengaged from traces of Hinduism and Christianity/Westernization, but also as being solely Sunni and free of all non-Sunni interpretations."[32] The "certain contested customs" include *qasidas* and other features of Indian Islam like the celebration of the Prophet Muhammad's birthday, which is the Guyanese national holiday Youman Nabi or Mawlid al-Nabi.[33] The commemoration is contested by religious purists as *bid'a* innovation and possible *shirk* (the sin of ascribing partners to God, polytheism) because it celebrates the Prophet rather than God. However, the holiday is supported by the Guyanese state, wherein the Sunni CIOG has long acted as the major mouthpiece for Muslims.[34] There being very few Shi'a in Guyana, much of the CIOG's ire has been directed toward Ahmadis, Caribbean and global antipathy toward whom is described in the previous chapter. The 1980s globalization of sectarian vitriol against Ahmadis from South Asia to the Americas foreshadows the contemporary conflict between the forces of local, traditionally assimilative moderation and simultaneously local and global conservatism in the Muslim Caribbean.

De Kruijf identifies "purification" and "neotraditionalism" as the two main forces in Indo-Guyanese Islam today, arguing that "the distinct past and present of the faith and its adherents cause religious globalization to materialize in Guyana in the form of a battle over culture, a clash between advocates of a deculturalized Islam, and those who stress the importance of Indian traditions and ethnoreligious brotherhood."[35] Raymond Chickrie similarly sees the divide as a generational culture clash between older people who are wedded to their ancestral Indo-Iranian Islam, and younger people who disparage this tradition as being influenced by Hinduism and look instead to the Arab world for "authentic" Islam.[36] Afro-Guyanese Muslims tend to be excluded from these movements and narratives because they are generally converts, rather than "hereditary" Muslims, and because there is a long history of racial conflict in Guyana and Trinidad that has nothing to do with religion. The shifting racialization of Caribbean Islamic discourse and the fundamental association of Islam with terrorism in the Caribbean is signposted in the late twentieth century not by the anti-Ahmadi bombing and murder discussed in the previous chapter, but by the 1990 Muslimeen coup—though, as in the United States, Afro-Caribbean Muslims have described themselves as tied to projects of civil rights and anticolonial liberation since the 1960s. The novel *Chinese Women*, however, poses a protagonist whose struggles with his Indo-Guyanese Muslim heritage are what lead him to a global vision of Islam that is apocalyptic. He disengages entirely with the postcolonial Caribbean strategy of employing racially and culturally creolizing mottoes like "One People, One Nation, One Destiny" (Guyana) and "Out of Many, One People" (Jamaica)— variants of the U.S. "E pluribus unum"—to construct and maintain the democratic Americas nation-state. His focus is global; he claims to be a citizen only of the *ummah*, a transnational identity that I show is catalyzed by the events of September 11, 2001.

NAIPAUL'S CARIBBEAN MIMIC MUSLIM

Media characterizations of alleged JFK airport plot leader Defreitas, leading his army of literal and figurative Muslim migrant rats through the porous borders of South America and north to the United States, were not unreminiscent of the way in which V. S. Naipaul depicts overly religious Caribbean men, the Trinidadian Hindu "Mystic Masseur" of his eponymously titled novel preeminent among them. They are feckless, corrupt, and too stupid to be proper villains; the reader laughs in mockery of their antics and aspirations while harboring a great and dark sense of foreboding about a national future exemplified by their poor memory of "Eastern" Indian or African pasts and their postcolonial mimicry of ostensibly superior "Western" culture. Defreitas and his coconspirators were failed mimic men par excellence.

Naipaul's literary vision of the Indo-Caribbean is inextricably linked to the trope of the postcolonial "mimic man." The mimic man, a colonial subject who apes and later perpetuates the culture of the colonizer, is usually depicted in post-colonial literature as the embodiment of craven survival and a barrier to nationalist postcolonial identity and achievement. In the Naipaulian view of postcoloniality, a true *post*colonial state is not possible, and *de*colonial thinking, such as the "epistemic de-linking" promulgated by Walter Mignolo, Aníbal Quijano, and other Latin American scholars, is outside of the capabilities of the colonized.[37] Postcoloniality lacks the authentic productive relationships necessary to create a society, and instead attempts to create a social base from a flawed reiteration of the power hierarchy of the colonial state: robotized former colonials following their slowly degrading, archaic programming into perpetuity. Two of the quintessential mimic men of Caribbean fiction are Naipaul's Indo-Trinidadian creations: the title character of his most well-known novel *A House for Mr. Biswas* (1961), and protagonist Ganesh Ramsumair of the aforementioned *Mystic Masseur* (1957). Biswas is henpecked, terminally unhappy, and builds a house of cards of both his life and his actual dwelling. As mentioned in chapter 2, in England, Ganesh Ramsumair renames himself G. Ramsay Muir, colonial Parliamentarian and knight of the realm, cut off from his Indian roots, his Caribbean inheritance, and any hope of an identity that is more than an Anglo-Indian shadow of an idealized British "native" subject.[38] For this type of mimic man, there is no hope for the future, and nothing productive to be gained from even the strategic essentialism of a British colonial identity that does not exist, except as it is produced in the fantasies of colonial subjects. In Naipaul's view, "although its politicians have taken to calling it a country, Trinidad is a small island."[39] Mimic men are incapable of governing either the microcosm of their homes or the macrocosm of their countries. The corrupt, corpulent, postcolonial native dictator, attended by apish sycophants and living in a palace of costly European furnishings while his people starve, the Trujillos and Mugabes of the Third World, is the most common literary—and real world—symbol of the inability of the formerly colonized to govern themselves democratically. Naipaul is often accused by his literary critics of being out of touch with the common people and of constructing the postcolonial Caribbean as a no-win scenario. This is partly true. But sometimes, Naipaul in his cantankerousness is right: right about vicious postcolonial racial dynamics that his more politically correct literary contemporaries would rather idealize; right about governmental, religious, and economic corruption that they would rather ignore; right about the intertwined fear and intolerance that, being once colonized, the people of the Caribbean would rather not expose to outsiders, preferring instead to maintain a clear separation between public and private domains while victimizing each other behind closed doors.

The theoretical scope of postcolonial mimicry as an affective state is vast. Walter Benjamin in 1933 defines mimicry as a type of similarity created by play, which does not require defined parameters or a defined goal.[40] For Benjamin, mimicry is a positive learning behavior; for his contemporary Roger Caillois, it is pathological. Caillois begins his theorizing of mimicry with observations of the natural world and behaviors ascribed to "Nature," calling insect mimicry of plants and each other suicidal "legendary psychasthenia" wherein insects succumb to the "lure of space" and "depersonalization by assimilation into the environment."[41] Caillois sees one creature's mimicry of another in terms of the death drive. Naipaul's mimic man employs the type of mimicry suggested by Caillois, where imitative behavior is pathological, and the results are diminishment of the subject and the production of hybridized cultural phenomena that are neither one thing nor the other. Homi Bhabha, drawing on the work of Benjamin, Michel Foucault, and Frantz Fanon, links mimicry to postcoloniality by arguing that "mimicry does not merely destroy narcissistic authority through the repetitious slippage of difference and desire. It is the process of the fixation of the colonial as a form of cross-classificatory, discriminatory knowledge within an interdictory discourse."[42] Mimicry is, paradoxically, an ongoing process of producing difference that fixes the positionality of the colonial subject. Mimicry is harmful to the colonizer's distinction between self and Other, but its transformative political power is not total: its ambivalence "does not merely 'rupture' the discourse, but becomes transformed into an uncertainty which fixes the colonial subject as a 'partial' presence."[43] In essence, mimicry functions as an ontological disruptor in the production of the colonial subject through a process of othering that exposes the tension between desire for/of the colonial subject, and difference. That othering requires constant (re)production through every means available, and is as such doomed to failure. There is, however, nothing inevitable about the fixity of the colonial as partial presence, particularly as mimicry continually produces the subject. The partial presence of the colonial may be fixed only in moments. The mimic man, I suggest, represents a limit state beyond which mimicry is indeed unproductive.

Naipaul's rendering of the Caribbean subject as culturally inauthentic is predicated on the notion that authenticity lies with Old World cultures, whether European, Asian, or African. Though there is a Naipaulian hierarchical distinction between the "Eastern" and "Western" cultures of the Old World, it is not a question of "authenticity": all Old World cultures are inherently authentic because they are older and seemingly autochthonous, if one chooses to ignore histories of mass migration and conquest. The New World is too visibly new, a hodgepodge pidgin region in a world of fully fledged languages and civilizations (indigenous Americans have never been Naipaul's concern). What plagues Naipaul is a conviction that the sum of cultural parts does not add up to a whole. There is no vigorous hybrid striding forth into the postcolonial future, only a bastard beholding himself in the mirror of culture, feebly waving amputated limbs in imitation of some lost *ancien régime*. Mimicry is to Naipaul an inevitable but unproductive, dead-end cultural strategy; the situation for the Caribbean postcolonial, bereft of memory and native ethnic landscape, thus seems hopeless.

In Naipaul's mimic man I emphasize the affective quality of *shame*. Naipaul's Indo-Caribbean mimic men are shameful and shamed, and are people to be ashamed of, because they represent the inability to resist material and spiritual conquest. This shame is most evident in physical descriptions of mimic men whose seemingly quotidian features are rendered grotesque, engendering revulsion in the reader. Naipaul's depictions of mimic men afflicted with religious propensities are particularly unflattering. Though most of his male Indo-Trinidadian mimic men are nominally Hindu, a few are Muslim. In *A Way in the World* (1994), a sequential collection of fictional, nonfictional, and autobiographical episodes, vignettes, and musings linked through the very Naipaulian and Caribbean general themes of colonialism and exile, a schoolteacher tells the narrator, who is perhaps Naipaul himself, about an encounter with lapsed Muslim undertaker and cake decorator Leonard Side:

> He knew he was a Mohammedan, in spite of the picture of Christ in his bedroom. But he would have had almost no idea of where he or his ancestors had come from. He wouldn't have guessed that the name Side might have been a version of Sayed, and that his grandfather or great-grandfather might have come from a Shia Muslim group in India. From Lucknow, perhaps; there was even a street in St. James called Lucknow Street. All Leonard Side would have known of himself and his ancestors would have been what he had awakened to in his mother's house in St. James. In that he was like the rest of us.[44]

Naipaul's use of the archaic and inaccurate colonial term "Mohammedan" emphasizes that the narrator, "everyone" in Trinidadian society, and Side himself are distanced from and ignorant of Islam and practicing Muslims. In the Caribbean colonies, far from India, indentured Muslims and their descendants might have called themselves by the Urdu term "Mussalman," if they did not use "Muslim"; they never called themselves "Mohammedan." The assertion that Side, his ancestors, and by extension all "the rest of us" Caribbean colonials retained only vestiges of their ancestral religions and cultures is a rampant generalization. Some mimic men, but not every mimic man, are as deracinated as Side. Though they gave the region the Muslim Muharram festival of Hosay, Shi'a Muslims were mostly absorbed by the Sunni majority in Trinidad and Guyana, making Side's lack of knowledge of that aspect of his origin plausible. But Hosay was also conserved in Side's natal St. James despite successful British attempts to stamp it out elsewhere, making him and his Shi'a ancestors deeply linked to Muslim history in Trinidad (Naipaul is contrarian enough to ironically imply this). There is also no reason why a contemporary Indo-Caribbean person might not know his or her surname has been anglicized in spelling, pronunciation, or both. The Indo-Caribbean is filled with, for instance, Muslim Bacchuses (in the earliest colonial indenture records, "Bux") who know they are likely Bakshes, and Hindu Persauds who know they are probably Prashads. But the Naipaulian mimic man is incapable of introspection about his identity, being well into the Cailloisian death process of assimilating into nonspecific space. Side is "very much a man of his job," and neither he nor the people he serves think about the fact that he is a Muslim preparing Christian bodies for burial. Moreover, he owns a picture of the radiant Jesus Christ, which is positioned so that "the blessing of the finger would have seemed aimed at the man on the bed."[45] The belief that one can receive blessings from many gods while claiming adherence to only one religion is not an uncommon one in the religiously syncretic Caribbean: Haitians may be Roman Catholics who identify the Virgin Mary with the vodou *lwa*/goddess of love Ezili, Cubans may be Catholics who practice Santería, and Guyanese may be Hindus who utilize Ashanti-derived Obeah.[46]

Islam has not syncretized in the Caribbean into a new religion, though in practice people may hold spiritual beliefs derived from a variety of sources. There is some scholarly theorization about the simultaneous involvement of enslaved Africans—in particular, the priest and revolutionary leader Boukman—in both Islam and the vodou rituals accompanying the start of the Haitian Revolution in 1791. Aisha Khan notes, however, that the existing information about Boukman is apocryphal and "constitutes a historical footnote in terms of the dearth of agreed upon information about his identity currently available."[47] Islam is a monotheistic religion in which the cardinal sin is *shirk*: the polytheistic establishment and worship of any partner or rival alongside the one God.[48] The fundamental precept of the religion is *tawhīd*, the unity of God, which discourages the type of inclusivity and potential for absorption of other beliefs offered by polytheistic Hinduism; by the Ashanti, Yoruba, and Congo *orisha* belief systems brought through the

Middle Passage; and by Catholicism, which historically offered the trinity, the Virgin Mary, and folk hagiographies of the saints as corollaries to African *orisha* deities in the Caribbean.[49] It is therefore all the more striking that the ostensibly Muslim Leonard Side entertains Christ. In his mimic man ignorance and uncaringness, his mixing of religions also incorporates a Hindu taboo mingling, that of food, sickness, and death. When the teacher enters Side's home, "There I found Leonard Side, very sick and trembling, but dressed for a meeting with the doctor. He was in a shiny brass fourposter bed with a flowered canopy, and he was in green silk pyjamas. His little hairy fingers were resting on the satin or silk spread he was using as a coverlet. He had laid himself out with great care, and the coverlet was folded back neatly."[50] The material decorating the room is borrowed from coffins, and there is a textual focus on Side's fingers, which are later described as appendages used to lay out bodies, knead dough, "and then squeeze out the terrible little blobs of icing."[51] As Imraan Coovadia points out, the juxtaposition of the handling of food with the handling of dead bodies, life with death, shows that Side's body is a site of polluting mingling, especially as his occupation implies that "the handling of dead bodies, a lower-caste occupation in traditional Hinduism, has been farmed out to Muslims."[52]

Corpse-handling is a traditionally lower-caste Hindu occupation because it is viewed as polluting to the soul and living body, and pollution with death has implications for food handling in Trinidadian (and all South Asian) Hinduism. Khan describes *juthaa* as "food and drink that have become polluted by being partially consumed by others, and a significant manifestation among East Indians in Trinidad of the concept of pollution that derives originally from caste-based social stratification in India."[53] *Juthaa* is not "regurgitated food, that which already has been consumed . . . it signifies the remaining food that has been symbolically tainted by association with another person (really, another person's essence, concretized as bodily substance, e.g., saliva, sweat, etc.)."[54] Cake prepared by Side is *juthaa* to observant Hindus for many reasons: he is, though lapsed, Muslim; he has been in physical contact with dead human bodies and their effluences; he is ill; he is described as dark-skinned, placing him lower down on the Indo-Trinidadian color and class hierarchy among Hindus *and* Muslims; and he is possibly homosexual. Though he does not eat the cake, it has been in contact with his "little hairy fingers," a simultaneously emasculating ("little") and masculinizing ("hairy") description that does not suggest proficiency at cake decorating, typically "women's work" in Trinidad. Coovadia and Allison Donnell read in the frailty of Side's body, his strange occupations, and his description as nonetheless good-looking, a suggestion of homosexuality.[55] Donnell calls Side a queer figure through whom "Naipaul finds a way to make a nascent ethical gesture towards his Caribbean belonging via the shared loss of inheritance and of deterministic signatures of being—his name Side, a synonym for 'athwart,' being a corruption of Sayed (like, of course, Edward Said's)."[56] Whether Side is really homosexual is not the issue; what is important is the suggestion that the mimic man, among his other cultural issues, is lacking in masculine virility or vigor. Donnell's argument that Side "brings pressure to bear on assumed normativities" rings true, but rather than viewing the character's portrayal as Naipaul's acknowledgment of his and others' differences, losses, and Bhabhian "partial presences," I suggest that Side's characterization simply reifies the mimic man's positioning as culturally and biologically deficient and emphasizes an association of homosexuality with death. There is no discernible evidence in Naipaul's work for sympathy toward or understanding of queerness. The very acknowledgment of the existence of queers in the Anglophone Caribbean is a new and fraught sociopolitical issue, and not one with which Naipaul or most of the older generation of male, exilic Caribbean writers engage. The character of Side reads as a reminder of Naipaul's shame in loss.

Donnell's observation that the last name "Side" is "a synonym for 'athwart'" and "a corruption of Sayed (like of course, Edward Said's)" is an interesting one in light of the fact that Said was a harsh critic of Naipaul's depictions of Islam, and Naipaul has never been above a bit of literary revenge.[57] Naipaul's first work that focuses on Islam is *Among the Believers: An Islamic Journey* (1981), an account of his journeys through and evaluations of Muslims in Iran, Pakistan, Malaysia, and Indonesia. The general tenor of the book is exemplified by the title of its Malaysia section, "Conversations in Malaysia: The Primitive Faith." The believers and their faith are portrayed as retrograde in thought and as quite literally uncivilized, lacking in civilization. This book was followed by *Beyond Belief: Islamic Excursions among the Converted Peoples* (1998), a sequel travelogue documenting Naipaul's experiences in the same four countries from (more or less) the points of view of the "believers." The titular expressions "beyond belief" and "converted peoples" are, again, emblematic of that book's contentious attitude toward its subject: Islam, or more specifically, *political* Islam. As Morris Mottale says, "In Naipaul, political Islam is rage, anarchy, destruction, mayhem."[58] In these books, Naipaul has sympathy for average Muslims, whose lives and struggles are shown to be complex. The trouble is that they are victims of the uncompromising faith of Islam and its purported tendencies toward jihadist conquest.

It is striking that Naipaul chose to explore Islam through the cultures of the "converted peoples" (i.e., non-Arabs). Islam is an ancestral religion of Arabs, he emphasizes; to everyone else it is a foreign imposition, brought mostly by conquest. The insistence on the status of Persians, South Asians, and Southeast Asians as multigenerational Islamic converts questions the legitimacy of their Muslimness. They are Muslim mimic men for whom the metropole is the Arab world, but as non-Arabs, most of whom do not speak Arabic, they are not "authentically" and ancestrally Muslim. Said describes Naipaul as having a "particularly intense antipathy" for "the whole postwar wave of Islamic anti-imperialism in the Third World."[59] This antipathy is at its height in Naipaul's inclusion of Persians—who are not Arabs, a fact that many non-Muslims forget—in the roster of "converted peoples," though Persians became Muslim by caliphate conquest almost at the beginning of the global advent of Islam, between 630 and 650 C.E. (the Prophet Muhammad himself died in 632). Naipaul insists at a very particular moment in time that the world remember that Iran was once Zoroastrian Persia: in the immediate aftermath of the 1979 Iranian Islamic Revolution, the international visual symbol of which is the image of urbane Iranian women dressed "Western"- style in short skirts donning voluntary and then state-mandated black chadors. That Persians have been Muslim almost as long as Arabians (who only became Saudis in 1932) is immaterial. They are still non-Arab converts, and thus "Islamic anti-imperialism," which was part and parcel of the originally leftist Iranian Revolution against the U.S.-backed regime of the Mohamed Reza Shah Pahlavi and the Pahlavi dynasty, is not for Naipaul a liberatory ideology. In all his works Naipaul is deeply suspicious of religiosity, and for him Islam promotes retrogression, not civilized progress. Nor is he a believer in communism, socialism, communalism, anarchism, Marxism, or any of the secular ideologies of postcolonialism. That, in essence, leaves capitalist democracy as the postcolonial nation-state's main ideological alternative, but as the historical tenets of that socioeconomic governance model are European, the production of the mimic man is inevitable. As a novelist, Naipaul is not in the business of offering political solutions. But his positioning of Muslims in Asia and Iran as imitating converts foreshadows his and Shinebourne's development of the contemporary literary Muslim mimic man in the Caribbean. Naipaul has never focused any of his works on Muslims in the Caribbean; Muslims appear as incidental characters, or more tellingly, their religious identities are subordinate to their (Indian) ethnic ones. The Caribbean remains the New World for him, a site of struggle and loss where race determines cultural identity and its manifestations.

THE ETHNORIENTAL FULLAMAN

Albert "Sonny" Aziz of Shinebourne's Chinese Women is a Muslim, Indo-Guyanese mimic man in the Naipaulian tradition of mimic men. Like Leonard Side, he has an anglicized first name; he is physically weak; he is oppressed by British whites and his fellow colonial Guyanese of every race; he hates his own Indianness, and as a child, his Muslimness, about which he had little historical and religious knowledge; he craves power but never really obtains it; he may in fact be mad; and no one, least of all women, loves him. The novel is a short and linear bildungsroman: the reader meets Aziz as a child born in 1947 and leaves him as an older, middle-aged man in the first ten years of the twenty-first century. Chinese Women is told from Aziz's first-person perspective and is divided into three sections. The first is the story of Aziz's British Guianese origins as the spoiled only son of the Indian field overseer of a debased, racist, class-stratified, and sexually licentious rural Berbice plantation, with a focus on his life between the formative ages of 10 and 14 (1957–1961). The second section is set in 2006, mostly in London, and contains the strange story of Aziz's failed pursuit of his childhood crush, a Chinese Guyanese British woman named Alice Wong, after he has become a staunch Muslim and a successful immigrant engineer in Canada. The short third section of the novel is a conclusion of sorts, a few pages describing Aziz's engagement with the destruction of the World Trade Center Twin Towers in New York City on September 11, 2001, and the related aftermath of his attempt to pursue Alice. There are two major narrative threads running through the novel and Aziz's life: his strange and historically related obsession with and fetishization of Chinese women, and his ethnoreligious identity as a Guyanese Muslim fullaman.

The Guyanese writer Jan Lowe Shinebourne is one of few literary writers of Chinese descent from the Caribbean, though she has lived in England since 1970.[60] Trinidadian arts icon Willi Chen and the Guyanese British Meiling Jin are two other major fiction writers who identify as authors of Chinese Caribbean descent. Shinebourne's oeuvre includes the novels *Timepiece* (1984), *The Last English Plantation* (1988), *Chinese Women* (2010), and *The Last Ship* (2015), and the short story collection *The Godmother and Other Stories* (2004). Her novels before *Chinese Women* have been of interest to critics not because they represent the experience of Chinese migrants in Guyana but because they seem to *resist* particularizing that experience, engaging instead in the type of documentation of and speculation about the future of the multiethnic postcolonial state that is usually deemed the province of the grandfather of Guyanese fiction Wilson Harris. Shinebourne's characters are often mixed-race people of Indian and Chinese descent, and she does not always connect a "Chinese" physiognomic appearance to specific cultural practices. Her fiction focuses less on racialized community experiences than it does on rural experiences common to people of all races in places like the one where she was born in 1947, Plantation Rose Hall in Berbice.[61] Shinebourne's most recent work, the novel *The Last Ship* (2015), is the story of three generations of a Chinese family in Guyana. As in her previous novels, there is a strong focus on racial conflict in 1950s and 1960s Guyana, but *The Last Ship* represents a departure in Shinebourne's work, as it privileges and explores the Chinese Caribbean migratory experience in a way that her previous works do not. Her seeming refusal in her earlier novels to focus on the Chinese diasporic experience have caused frustrated academics to assess her as a writer who "is skeptical about her identity as a 'real Chinese,' with a strong question of what exactly it is."[62] Anne-Marie Lee-Loy rightly speaks of postcolonial critics' "desire to label Shinebourne and her writing as 'Chinese,' a wish that forces us to acknowledge how difficult a task it is to resist the strong emotional pull of cultural essentialization that remains at the heart of many articulations of diasporic identities in general, particularly in situations when physical features can be easily read as the boundary of diasporic community."[63] Shinebourne is, like Naipaul, a Caribbean fiction writer who does not give postcolonial critics the empowering ethnonation-alist identity politics they may expect or want. These writers remind us that litera-ture is representative of life: messy, impolitic, and resistant to essentializing. And whether they emphasize it at every literary moment or not, both writers are deeply haunted by the specters of their own ethnic Caribbean communities, which always inform or appear in their work.

The title of *Chinese Women* and, as Judith Misrahi-Barak points out, a Peepal Tree Press cover featuring an "oriental" image of two Chinese women in nineteenth-century Chinese dress playing traditional musical instruments, sug-gest a focus on the Chinese Caribbean migrant experience.[64] But the novel's pro-tagonist is an Indo-Guyanese Muslim man. Chinese women are his fetish objects. As chronicled by Lee-Loy and Walton Look Lai, though 200 Chinese indentured laborers arrived in Trinidad in 1806 as potential replacements for African slaves, the majority of about 18,000 Chinese arrived in the West Indies between 1853 and 1866, overlapping with the 1838–1917 Indian indentureship period.[65] Most Chinese were initially bound for the plantations of British Guiana, but a great number of those subsequently departed for better economic opportunities in Trinidad, Jamaica, and Suriname.[66] Misrahi-Barak notes that for both Indian and Chinese migrants, "push factors were stronger than pull factors" (i.e., migrants left home more because their nineteenth-century living conditions in Asia were oppressive than because the New World drew them with promises of riches). Unlike Indians, however, a majority of Chinese migrants came not as laborers who indentured themselves at the depots of departure, but as passengers who paid their own fares or as modified "sponsored" contract laborers who promised to reimburse their sponsors for the passage fare.[67] The Chinese also came to occupy a place as entre-preneurial "middlemen" between the upper class of whites and the lower classes of blacks and Indians in the nineteenth-century Caribbean, a "buffer zone" of people characterized in colonial reports as "tractable, orderly, and not easily discontented . . . mild and easily managed" that preserved white domination of colonial society.[68]

Chinese economic prowess is for Aziz and his society represented by, as he says, the "one thing that gave me relief from my fear and terror of East Indian poverty—the Yhips' shop, or as people called it, the 'Chinee shop,'" where the Yhip family sold food, helped the indigent of all races with free meals and other care, and pro-vided, whether they wanted or not, a place for the fractured community of Enmore sugar estate to meet.[69] The historical situating of the Chinese as middlemen is a crucial one in the novel *Chinese Women*, as a major part of Aziz's fascination with Chinese women and Chinese people in general is their perceived *neutrality* in the race and class wars of British Guiana. Aziz describes the 1960s indepen-dence period as a time when "Blacks and Indians began to kill each other in a political struggle," resulting in children racially segregating themselves in school. The situation is more complicated for him as a Muslim child: as he says, "The East Indians stuck together but I avoided them because they were mainly Hindus and I knew they hated Muslims. The Chinese were not implicated in the racial politics of the country and this gave Alice a neutrality that made her popular. To be her friend was to be politically innocent."[70] This is the political moment during which he is first drawn to his schoolmate Alice Wong. Though she later loses her neutrality and aligns herself (he thinks) with an Afro-Guyanese teacher, she represents a haven of sorts and an innocence he believes no one else in British Guiana has, particularly on the Rose Hall, Berbice sugar estate to which he moves as a child after Enmore. Aziz describes Rose Hall—Shinebourne's birthplace—as a place where "very little divided beast and man. Both laboured, copulated, procreated and died exposed to the elements: in the mud, rain and canals, at the mercy of alligators, snakes, rats, vultures, mosquitoes and flies that sucked their blood and ate their flesh. The worst possible living conditions existed on the estate. I don't know how we did not all die of disease."[71] But for Aziz, all Chinese—not just Alice—rise above this morass. He paints Chinese migrants and their Caribbean history in glowing terms:

> They did not suffer the degradation of being enslaved and subjugated to regimes of brute labour. Their women were not raped and forced into relations of sexual miscegenation with Europeans. In any Caribbean country, you could travel to the most remote and inhospitable parts and find a solitary, isolated shop with a Chinese family working to supply food for several villages, and even though they were treated like outsiders and subjected to racial taunts and torments, they did not complain or give up. They kept aloof from the degradation around them, behaving as if it were some accident or bad luck that had brought them to those inhospitable places. I saw them like this in Guiana, Trinidad and Jamaica. Their dignity was like a miracle to me, a child from a Muslim family destroyed by the brutality the Chinese endured and overcame with stoicism."[72]

This characterization of Chinese dignity gives Afro- and Indo-Guyanese and their powers of survival little credit. Indians and Muslims, as epitomized by Aziz's father who beats his wife and children and whose workers disrespect him, are depicted by Aziz as being unable to endure the physical and psychic brutality of plantation society with dignity intact. What is interesting about Aziz's evaluation of the tenacity, economic persistence, and moral superiority of Chinese migrants is that it closely mirrors the white British planter narrative of the Chinese that reinforced their position as the buffering middlemen of plantation society. Lee-Loy points out that the paternalistic colonial descriptions of Chinese migrants in the Anglophone Caribbean stand in striking contrast to their stereotyping as threatening, permanent outsiders in the United States, Canada, Australia, and other majority white settler colonies.[73]

In the Caribbean, the Chinese were posed as a model minority in contrast to Indian indentured migrants and black ex-slaves: more hardworking and industrious, more assimilable to European cultural mores that included Christianity, speaking English, and wearing pants and dresses, and, intriguingly and in great contrast to the U.S. and European orientalist stereotype of the Chinese heathen, more "moral."[74] The British Caribbean belief in the superiority of Chinese morality—which was sometimes mitigated by accusations of opium dens and gambling—was directly connected to the economic perception that Chinese were hardworking but not money hoarders like Indians, and to the religious perception that they were "more willing to accept Christian instruction," with British Guiana magistrate Henry Kirke observing that in contrast to the Chinese, "the attempt to convert the Hindoo and Mohammedan immigrants to Christianity has been an utter failure."[75] Though like Indians the Chinese migrant community suffered from an extreme gender imbalance, Chinese women were framed as "more chaste" than Indian and other nonwhite women, which allegedly encouraged less domestic violence in their communities.[76] Aziz's statement that Chinese women "were not raped and forced into relations of sexual miscegenation with Europeans" is a commensurate feat of gendered victim-blaming, implying that nonwhite, non-Chinese colonial women carried a stigma from "allowing" sexual violence to be committed on their bodies.

The contrasting "purity" of Chinese women may be one reason why Aziz becomes obsessed as a child with not only the young Alice Wong, but an adult woman named Anne Carrera, the apparently mixed-race Chinese and Portuguese wife of a Portuguese overseer (the Portuguese being the other small group of "middlemen" indentured migrants to Guyana). He loses his infatuation with Anne when he observes her dancing "with abandon, winding her hips," with his visiting Indo-British cousin.[77] The scandal of her interracial dancing results in the Carrera family leaving the sugar estate in disgrace, and young Aziz's reaction is racially vicious and bitter: "Did I feel sorry for Anne Carrera? No. She deserved her punishment for dancing like a Black, without shame or modesty."[78] This moment does not end his fascination with Chinese women, because he wants them not only as romantic partners, but as personal redeemers with desirable cultural values. When the child Alice tells him to leave her alone and stop following her to her family's shop, "for the next forty years or more, I behaved like a rejected lover. . . . I think I felt I had a better chance of one day winning Alice over if the rejection came from her, but if it came from her race, it was insurmountable, because in British Guiana race was insurmountable.[79] Aziz wants to surmount what he views as the brutality of his own racial origins, even though he believes it an impossible task. The Chinese in the Caribbean were never *equal* to whites: they were considered a subject child race, but a tractable one, and when they "threatened colonial order, favourable depictions were quickly transformed into the more commonly held negative stereotypes of the period."[80] In the novel, the Chinese never really threaten the colonial order; they are foils against whom the crudeness of whites, blacks, and Indians is exposed. Naipaul might have called them relatively successful mimic men, but that is not who they are in the novel: they are depicted as people who retain a seemingly innate Chinese racial instinct for survival with dignity, served by strategic, superficial cultural adaptions that do not change who they really are. They become a model for Aziz, once he comes to accept his heritage as a Muslim: he biologizes Islam, ethnorientalizing himself into the fullaman he once despised.

Fullaman, spelled "fulaman" in the novel, is the crucial signifier of Aziz's identity, one that he spends his entire life trying to shed. Fullamen are colonized Muslims who know nothing about Islam. As an adult, Aziz tells Alice, "My family are not real Muslims. We are like those Christians who only go to church at Christmas. Going to a mosque to pray does not make you Muslim."[81] When she asks if he was nonetheless brought up with an understanding that he was Muslim, he answers, "You mean a Fulaman? Of course not. I did not like being a Muslim in the Caribbean. They hate us. I wanted to be Chinese like you. I idealised you."[82] As an adult he realizes that becoming something else, Chinese, is not the only alternative to being a deracinated fullaman. One could instead choose the route of religious and cultural purification, recovering the lost Islam of the fullaman. The first use of the word "fullaman" in the novel is when Aziz in his guise as first-person narrator defines it in societal and personal terms:

> In the nineteenth century, my ancestors were taken from India to British Guiana in ships, like the African slaves they were sent to replace on the sugar estates. Indians, both Hindus and Muslims, were the new slaves, but the Hindus did not want to be identified with us, the Muslims, so they called us *Fulamen*, after the African Muslim Fulani tribe who were among the original slaves in the Caribbean. I grew up at Enmore used to being called *Fulaman*. It was always an insult, a way of telling me not to get too big for my boots, and remember I was just a slave.[83]

In the novel, Aziz is prejudiced against Afro-Guyanese, as they are prejudiced against him. But his greatest ire is reserved for Hindu Indo-Guyanese, whom he believes exclude Muslims from Indianness because the Muslims have ancestral ties to Afro-Guyanese by dint of their religion. On Rose Hall sugar estate, the Hindu laborers his father oversees disrespects the father when "instead of addressing him respectfully as 'Mr,' they called him by his surname, Aziz, or called him names—*Fulaman* or *Bowfoot*," mocking his "facial tic and bandy legs."[84]

In the beginning of the novel, then, the fullaman Muslim is embodied as nonwhite, enslaved, and even physically misshapen. Aziz's childhood is marked by the racialized physical limitations of his body. In 1960, when he is 10, he sustains a fall that breaks all of his "major joints."[85] Even after being cared for by a white British doctor, his bones do not set properly, and he "accepted I would always be a cripple and a spectator. . . . The worst fate of the Black slave or the East Indian coolie was to be a spectator of the white man's lifestyle, knowing it was unattainable, knowing that he was forever orphaned from the white man's high standard of living, his wealth, property, luxuries, and his women."[86] The colonial inheritance of the fullaman is to be physically and psychically excluded from power. Aziz says that his fall left him with "a half-dead body and that afterwards I moved among the living like a ghost."[87] He is, though, less incorporeal than incarnated as a human automaton. He describes himself as a mechanism with "disjointed arms and legs, who moved like a robot, a clockwork creature that was once broken and had to be pieced together again by a white doctor who set his springs and screws again, who wound me up with a key and let me out so I could wind my way round his world."[88] Here the truth of the existence of the fullaman spectator to life is made visible in the body: Aziz is a mimic man, a creature created by whites who is not really human, who is only mimicking life. He is the Cartesian clockwork animal without human consciousness.[89] But he does not remain a singular automaton. He embraces his machine nature when he becomes fascinated with the estate overseers' motorized vehicles, and discovers a natural mechanic and engineering talent: "With engines and wheels, I forgot that my body was permanently damaged. Cars and machines became an extension of me."[90] The machines become both his limbs and his salvation: they allow him to escape his fullaman life and destiny in the Caribbean. He becomes an engineer who makes his fortune "designing the instrumentation for centrifuges" around the world, beginning "in the Caribbean with sugar ones," then gas and oil centrifuges in Asia and Canada.[91]

The first hint that Aziz's engineering business might not be entirely innocent is a reference to his subsequent travels to Saudi Arabia and his bald hint that after the sugar, gas, and oil centrifuges, "I had moved on to more modern kinds of centrifuges."[92] What he means is that he has transitioned from making technology in the service of colonial exploitation of natural resources to making technology in the service of politics and nations. "Modern" thus means "ideological," suggesting that it is possible for the fullaman to cease being a mere colonized mimic man automaton and recoup human consciousness. Consciousness, though, is linked to the development of a cultural identity distinct from anything offered by the British: the fullaman must become a "real" Muslim.

The metropolitan center for the fullaman shifts from England to what Aziz nebulously refers to as the "Middle East." He mentions that he has dealings in or has traveled to Saudi Arabia, Pakistan, and Iran, though he does not detail his experiences in any of these countries. He lies to the adult Alice, whom he meets in London, that he has been working as an "international oil engineer," but the climax of the novel is his revelation that he has instead been using his engineering abilities for a particular type of cause: building nuclear weapons.[93] He tells

Alice that he "had worked with A.Q. Khan at Urenco," "hoped to work in Iran," was part of "the Pakistan nuclear procurement network," "helped develop the centrifuge technology in Almelo in Holland," developed "a complete plant of nuclear centrifuges" for the Iran-Iraq war for which he was "paid five million dollars," and finally, that "I was planning to live in the Middle East to be part of the Middle East nuclear procurement network because I believe Israel must be destroyed and Muslims must be free from the tyranny under which they have been placed. As an Arab Muslim, which I am now, I would never be called a *Fulaman*, never again."[94] Not only has Aziz been involved in the 1980–1988 Iran-Iraq war, in Pakistan's ongoing nuclear cold war with India, and in work at the (real) Dutch Urenco plant that produces uranium for nuclear reactors, but he has apparently become a full-blown Islamic fundamentalist in the most stereotypic way, complete with conspiracy theories and hatred for Israel.

Aziz defines being "Arab Muslim" as being involved in major armed conflicts in the Arab and Asian Muslim world. "Arab" is a complex identity that involves multiple ethnicities, dialects of Arabic, religions, cultural practices, and national citizenships that accrue to the Arabian Gulf, the Levant, North Africa, and other parts of West Asia and Africa. The geographic and linguistic "Arab world" also includes a host of minority groups who do not identify as Arab. One of the ethnocultural identities "Arab" could not be said to encompass is Aziz's natal Indo-Caribbean. But he has ethnorientalized himself, applying the language, religion, culture, and political beliefs of parts of the Arab world to himself. He says that it is his decision to "choose my destiny and calling as a true Muslim and return to the Middle East, to live as a Muslim and do the work of a Muslim, helping to build the nuclear programme that would lead to the destruction of Israel. Sometimes, in my Calgary apartment, I dressed in my thobe, tagiyah, ghutra and agal and admired how noble I looked, like a Muslim prince."[95] Dressing as an Arab, living in the Middle East, practicing Islam, imagining himself as royalty, and plotting against Israel are all conflated into a single redemptive persona and cultural identity that Aziz labels "true Muslim."

Lee-Loy writes that in Shinebourne's fiction, "blood is largely irrelevant in defining communal and cultural identities."[96] Aziz manages to push the boundaries of belonging further, by imagining his "blood" changing. His ethnicity shifts, as "ethnic identification is as much a product of socio-political and economic standing and history as of shared cultural practices and bloodlines. The radical result of such an understanding is that in Shinebourne's fiction, ethnic identity can become a matter of choice rather than an inevitability."[97] Aziz truly believes he has become ethnically Arab, complete with Semitic features, because that is synonymous with being authentically Muslim, which one achieves by becoming involved in the orientalist clash of civilizations on the side of Islam. Aziz is an orientalist, as his world is starkly divided into all things "West" and all things Islam. Said argued in 1981 that the oppositional "labels" of "Islam" and "the West" must

be taken seriously because they are persistent and meaningful to people of all religious, political, cultural persuasions who use them. Such labels that attempt to
encompass "very large and complex realities are notoriously vague and at the same
time unavoidable."[98] The binary opposition of Islam and the West is "ideological
and shot through with powerful emotions," but the labels have "survived many
experiences and have been capable of adapting to new events, information, and
realities."[99] As evidenced by President Bush's post-9/11 speech and the ongoing
and vitriolic positioning of Muslims as "Other" in U.S. political and media discourses, the orientalist opposition of "Islam versus the West" is very much alive
and well.

Aziz says that his new identity as an Arab Muslim is the opposite of being a
fullaman Caribbean Muslim. "Arab Muslim" signifies an empowered, authentic
Muslim; fullaman is a degraded, mimic man Muslim. One physical feature that
does not appear to change in his transformation is his brown skin color. He mentions repeatedly that when he was a child and teenager, his skin was brown or dark
brown; in his "Arab" adulthood, he no longer speaks of color. He has no more deal-
ing with whites, Chinese remain a people unto themselves, and "brown" becomes
naturalized as the color of the Muslim; he was born to fit in with the majority of
Pakistanis and Arabs. In *Chinese Women*, black people are excluded from being
either Caribbean fullamen or Arab Muslims. The novel thus shifts the Caribbean
narrative of the politically radical Muslim from one that emphasizes the historical
role of Afro-Caribbean converts to one that includes Indo-Caribbean Muslims.

THE FULLAMAN AS TERRORIST

As in Trinidad, "political" Islam has early associations with people of African
descent in Guyana. This correlation was apparent at the time of independence
from Britain. In February 1966, inspired by Malcolm X—who had been assassi-
nated the year before—and Elijah Muhammad's Nation of Islam in the United
States, the Muslim Brotherhood of Guyana, also known as "Muslaman: Ujamaa
Wa Guyana," convened formally as the country's first Black Muslim organization.[100] The group had been active as the Black Muslim Movement of Guyana
during the previous year, but cohered politically as Guyana was preparing for its
May 26, 1966, independence date. Writing in the organization's newspaper *The
Clarion*, leader Malik Shabazz declared: "The reason we chose Islam as our religion is, one, it is the religion of our forefathers who were brought here as chattel
slaves and it is also the religion of our brethren in Africa today and the true Religion
of God and all mankind; and two, because the other great religion, Christianity
is in the hands of our foe; it has led us into Slavery, Imperialism, Colonialism."[101]
The Muslim Brotherhood considered itself dedicated to the causes of Guyanese independence and fighting white imperialism. Shabazz specified that the
organization, though a black nationalist one, was not interested in separatism:

"The Black Muslim Movement of Guyana, like the Black Muslim Movement of the U.S., is a radical movement. Unlike America's Black Muslims however the local Black Muslims are not working toward the goal of separation or partition."[102] Instead, he wrote, they were working "for the complete integration of the Guyanese society with each section recognising the rights, habits and customs of the other but loyally adhering to the principle of 'One people, One Destiny.'"[103] This goal is markedly different from that of the later Afro-Trinidadian Jamaat al Muslimeen, which attempted a government takeover. In this Guyanese period, a "radical" and "political" Muslim was an "anti-imperialist" Muslim, loyal to the cause of an independent Guyana, with Islam, contra Naipaul, providing theologically based anticolonial inspiration and an ancestral alternative to postcolonial mimicry. The Muslim Brotherhood of Guyana faded into the background of racial conflict in Guyana after independence.

The "new" radical Muslims of the Caribbean who involve themselves, as Aziz does, in global conflict, are of both African and Indian descent. In the last decade, there have been a number of local media-sensationalized stories of Muslim Guyanese, Trinidadians, and Jamaicans traveling to the Middle East to join and fight for Al-Qaeda or the Islamic State.[104] Per capita, Trinidad is the country in the Western Hemisphere from which the most citizens have traveled to Syria to fight for the Islamic State (approximately 100–130 out of a population of 1.3 million).[105] Simon Cottee notes that the demographics of Trinidadians who join IS differ from the worldwide norms: Trinidadians are older (average age 34), much more middle class (90%), more female (40%), include more converts (about 42.5%), take more children with them (40% minors), and most of the women are already married.[106] It seems obvious from these statistics that many family units, rather than lone young men or women, have traveled from Trinidad to Syria. Cottee cites the cost to make the 6,000-mile journey as one factor explaining the demographic differences, but hesitates to speculate further.[107] Grandiose ideological idealism and feelings of minority religious and cultural disenfranchisement in Trinidad, I suggest, also have roles to play.

The representative Trinidadian IS fighter was Shane Crawford, nom de guerre Abu Sa'd at-Trinidadi, an Afro-Trinidadian convert who was previously imprisoned for vigilante activity and antigovernment attack planning in Trinidad, whose new occupation as sniper in Syria was dramatically revealed in an interview and photographs in August 2016 in the now defunct, professionally produced IS magazine *Dabiq*, issue 15.[108] Former U.S. ambassador to Trinidad and Tobago John L. Estrada contextualized the Crawford case by claiming that "Trinidadians do very well with ISIL. . . . They are high up in the ranks, they are very respected and they are English-speaking. ISIL have used them for propaganda to spread their message through the Caribbean."[109] In February 2017, U.S. secretary of state Rex Tillerson issued a State Department public notice under Executive Order 13224 of September 23, 2001, naming Crawford a "Specially Designated Global Terrorist."[110]

In that same month in 2017, Crawford died "as a result of wounds sustained in a U.S. drone strike."[111] Crawford's biographical conversion story and incendiary rhetoric were fairly typical of *Dabiq*'s genre of foreign fighter interviews.[112] It is what he said about the Jamaat al Muslimeen, perpetrators of the 1990 coup in Trinidad, that was most interesting: "There was a faction of Muslims in Trinidad that was known for 'militancy'. Its members attempted to overthrow the disbelieving government but quickly surrendered, apostatized, and participated in the religion of democracy, demonstrating that they weren't upon the correct methodology of West."[113] As Cottee points out, "In T&T the JAM is widely regarded (and still feared) as a militant group, yet Crawford condemned it for not being militant enough, and for not practising the right kind of Islam."[114]

The Jamaat al Muslimeen remains the symbol of Muslim antistate action in the Caribbean, and is linked in the Trinidadian popular imagination to current IS membership and activity of Caribbean nationals. After September 11, 2001, the Muslimeen compound was searched by police, and in July 2015, Trinidadian newspapers breathlessly followed a war of memos between the Police Service Special Branch and Abu Bakr in which the Muslimeen were accused of "planning activities inimical to the state," "moving arms and ammunition," and planning to attack the prime minister's home and government buildings to free some of their members who had been arrested on suspicion of murder.[115] Abu Bakr denied the allegations.[116] Most Trinidadian IS recruits came not from Abu Bakr's Jamaat al Muslimeen in Port of Spain but from a radicalized Salafi postcoup Muslimeen splinter community founded by Imam Nazim Mohammed and centered around his Umar Ibn Khattab mosque in Boos Village, Rio Claro.[117] Crawford, who explicitly stated he considered the Muslimeen apostates, was an attendee at the Rio Claro mosque.[118] The Rio Claro group and its affiliates may have begun with the Muslimeen but split from them soon after the coup precisely because the Muslimeen do not share the transnational aims of "purifying" the faith.[119] There is no current evidence that the organization still led by Yasin Abu Bakr has developed new ties to radical groups abroad. The Muslimeen's concerns remain domestic Trinidadian ones. According to Abu Bakr, nowadays the Muslimeen still "provide services to the community, the poor and the oppressed. We feed the people, we look after their needs, we're trying to rebuild the hospital, the clinic that we had ... we're trying to rebuild the grocery ... after 1990 when we were in jail they destroyed everything."[120] His daily life as an imam would appear to corroborate these local community priorities: on days when I spoke to him, he was conducting a funeral, leading *iftar* meal and prayer services to break the Ramadan fast, and traveling to speak with mosque members in various locations. None of these actions exclude other political interests, but my argument is that focus on the Muslimeen and on Abu Bakr distracts from clarity around why and how some Muslims in Trinidad and the Caribbean have joined the IS and are attracted to fundamentalist theology. As Abu Bakr (rather proudly) said to me, the issue with the coup is that "certain events like that cannot be erased . . . they live on in the memory of people. It's part of the history of Trinidad and Tobago."[121]

The majority of Trinidadians who traveled to Syria did so between 2013 and 2016.[122] But before then, eyeing the Muslimeen post-9/11, Trinidad passed its 2005 Anti-Terrorism Act, which defined a "terrorist act" as an "act whether committed in or outside of Trinidad and Tobago" that could be perpetrated with a number of intentions, including "for the purpose of advancing a political, ideological or a religious cause."[123] A single offence carried a sentence of twenty-five years for a perpetrator, and twenty to twenty-five years for anyone deemed to be aiding or abetting. That the Trinidadian Parliament saw fit to clarify terrorism as possible both at home and abroad, and include "religious" causes when "ideological" alone might have sufficed, suggests perceptions that political events in Trinidad involving Muslims were linked to political events involving Muslims abroad, and that Muslims represented a singular cultural group that could be expected to act against the state.

The phenomenon of Caribbean nationals joining the IS received wide hemispheric attention when the United States Southern Command general John F. Kelly—later secretary of Homeland Security and White House chief of staff in the Donald Trump administration—declared during a March 2015 Pentagon press briefing that "about 100 Caribbean natives have traveled into Syria to join ISIS."[124] Trinidad, Jamaica, Suriname, and Venezuela were deemed "vulnerable" nations, as they and other "little countries" lacked "legal infrastructure and tracking capabilities to keep tabs on returning fighters."[125] According to the general, "While in Syria, they get good at killing and pick up some real job skills in terms of explosives and beheadings, things like that. . . . Everyone is concerned, of course, if they come home. If they went over radicalized, one would expect they will come back at least that radicalized but . . . with really good job skills that they picked up in the fight."[126] General Kelly's folksy alarmist statement included many of the buzzwords used in 2015 U.S. public discourse to implicate IS terrorism: "Syria," "killing," "explosives," "beheadings," and "radicalized." Associating Caribbean and South American coastal countries with such activities was new for the Pentagon, so Kelly linked the story to a familiar south-of-the-border regional narrative, that of undocumented migration and narco-trafficking: "To get into the United States from the Caribbean and South America, Kelly said, the fighters could take paths currently used by drug smugglers and human traffickers. The fighters would aim to 'walk across borders,' he explained. The amount of movement . . . and sophistication of the network overwhelms our ability to stop everything."[127] In this amazingly speculative narrative of hemispheric migration that poses walking across the borders of every country between the Caribbean coast of South America and the United States as an easy task, the heretofore unfamiliar phenomenon of the Caribbean Muslim is masterfully positioned in the categories of "illegal immigrant," "drug trafficker," and "terrorist": altogether, an "overwhelm[ing]" existential and material threat to the United States and "our ability to stop everything." Aziz of *Chinese Women* might concur, as he believes "The war on terror freed me from my invisibility as a Muslim."[128] One could imagine a character like Aziz, with his chameleonic aptitude for transformation and easy ability to move between places, taking such a continental stroll—appearing in Guyana one day and at the Mexican border with Texas the next. But Aziz is a fictional character, a colonially damaged braggart who may not be a terrorist after all.

9/11 AND FLIGHT

Aziz wants to fly. When as a child he falls from the tree, he says "I knew I was falling from my throne to something I deserved for my arrogance and conceit, and I allowed myself to fall willingly. I opened my arms and legs like wings to make me fly. Though so young, I was willing to embrace death."[129] Flying is the mode of all his transformations. He does not die, but this flight causes him to become the clockwork person. Later on, after he discovers his aptitude for working with machinery, "The motorcycle and car my father owned gave me wings to fly round the estate and helped me grow out of my fixation with Anne Carrera."[130] On these estate flights he begins his transformation into more than just a spectator, gaining a mobility that will later be international. His final engagement with flying comes on 9/11, in all the ways in which that day in New York engaged with flight: airplanes, fleeing people, and, as in the beginning of the novel, the human body itself flying through the air: the "jumpers," as they were morbidly called by newscasters on that day. Aziz sees the events of September 11, 2001, unfold on television in his apartment in Canada. His reaction, related at the end of the novel, shocks the reader:

> I jumped with excitement and anticipation because I knew there were many people in the building and they would begin jumping from the windows. Like the whole world I watched and waited to see it and sure enough, soon they began to fall from a great height, just like I did in 1957 in British Guiana, when I fell from a tree. When people began to fall from those windows, I saw them spread open their arms and legs just like I did when I fell. Watching them fall, I relived my fall in 1957. I was aware millions of people were watching them fall and it made me feel that the whole world was finally seeing me fall too. It brought a strange relief, as if a lifelong, weighty burden of loneliness fell from me. You see, we all need to be seen for who we are.[131]

This denouement most trenchantly emphasizes the striking similarity between *Chinese Women* and the earliest and most well-known post-9/11 fictional narrative that sought to answer the question of "why they hate us": Mohsin Hamid's *The Reluctant Fundamentalist* (2007).

As Anantha Sudhakar says in her review of Shinebourne's novel that compares it to Hamid's, "Both books are structured as the first-person monologue of an unrequited lover-turned-radical, and position 9/11 as a catalyst for their narrators' latent politicization."[132] The day is a catalyst of sorts, in that it finally prompts Aziz to think about his life, but 9/11 is not the reason for his politicization. Given his traumatic childhood, the options for his trajectory seem limited: an empty existence as a colonized mimic man, death, or becoming a radical of some sort. It is his strange *pleasure*, perhaps even his jouissance, in anticipating the jumpers that gives pause. This sentiment is echoed in Hamid's novel, when the Pakistani American protagonist, scorned by a white woman, reduced in means, and sensing an underlying American disgust for his brownness and Muslimness, reflects on his own reaction to 9/11:

> I stared as one—and then the other—of the twin towers of New York's World Trade Center collapsed. And then I *smiled*. Yes, despicable as it may sound, my initial reaction was to be remarkably pleased . . . when I tell you I was pleased at the slaughter of thousands of innocents, I do so with a profound sense of perplexity.
>
> But at that moment, my thoughts were not with the *victims* of the attack— death on television moves me most when it is fictitious and happens to characters with whom I have built up relationships over multiple episodes—no, I was caught up in the *symbolism* of it all, the fact that someone had so visibly brought America to her knees.[133]

Is this character so truly amoral that he delights in mass slaughter? Is Aziz? Is the average young male IS fighter who has traveled from elsewhere in the world to wage war in Syria and Iraq? What are their motivations? Why do they hate us— and we them? There are many particular life circumstances that lead individuals who, for instance, feel themselves to be victims of North American and European imperialism, down the path of becoming a religious fundamentalist to whom violence, as Frantz Fanon argued, is an acceptable means of enacting anticolonial social change.[134] Hamid's character is an immigrant who is not professionally unsuccessful but whose childhood is marked by a loss of class status in Pakistan, and in adulthood by racial discrimination. Aziz has his many Guyanese racial and colonial traumas. Changez, the "Reluctant Fundamentalist," offers the only answer that may be generalizable: "I do not now recall my precise motivations. I know only that I did not wish to blend in with the army of clean-shaven youngsters who were my coworkers, and that inside me, for multiple reasons, I was deeply angry."[135] That is, both Aziz and Changez are angry young men, very angry, because they live in places that seem not to want them, around people who perceive them either as perennial racial and religious Others or as acceptably assimilated immigrants whose individuality does not matter. As Aziz says, the crux is "we all need to be seen for who we are."[136] Both men want someone who represents power in the society in which they feel unrecognized to suffer for their perceived humiliations; as the Reluctant Fundamentalist says, the symbolism of America being punished carries a stronger emotional pull for him than does the suffering of others. Empathy is impossible for the men because they feel that life has wronged them.

Before both Aziz and Changez turn to religion as an avenue to express their disaffection, they blame women for withholding love from them. Women are convenient scapegoats for their lack of social power and inability to challenge power structures dominated by white men, whether Berbice sugar estate overseers or New York financial analysts. Aziz says of Alice, "I've never known what [love] is, I still don't and I never will. She was my only reason for looking for love. I hoped we would find it together but it was not to be."[137] He associates love with his desire to fly. As he watches people jumping from the Twin Towers to their deaths, he recalls his childhood fall and wonders, "Why, when I fell, did I open my arms and legs like wings. Did I hope that I might fly? I think I did. I don't know what it was in me that made me think I might fly, maybe the same thing that made me fall in love with Alice Wong. Something in me needs to defy my limitations. It made me think I might be able to fly and save my life."[138] Love, death, or religious radicalization is the option for releasing himself from his life circumstances; flying is the mode of transportation to his next stage of existence. On 9/11, the flights of planes and people take him to the Middle East and a newfound interest in Islam.

At the end of the novel, after Alice finally rejects him, Aziz unexpectedly retreats from his religious fundamentalism. He lives alone in a state of paralysis for several years, attempting to suppress the memory of her and imagining his return to the Middle East. Eventually, though, after somehow teaching himself how to take care of his body and mind without his Alice obsession, "One day, it dawned on me that I was perfectly happy and contented and I loved myself and I made the decision not to go to the Middle East but to continue to live by myself and enjoy my money and the rest of my life alone. I did not need a mission to justify my existence. I guess I have to thank Alice for this. If I had not gone to London to find her and she had not rejected me and sent me back to Calgary to live with myself, I might have blown up the world."[139] These are the final words of the novel. Understanding of and love for himself is apparently the key to mitigating Aziz's lifelong psychological distress; it seems too easy a solution for a man so afflicted that he has reinvented his cultural and ethnic identity and entertained ideas of ending the world in a nuclear holocaust.

Aziz's unreliability as a narrator does not come into focus until the end of the novel, with his rapid shift in motive and desire and the revelation that he is a conspiracy theorist. In his attempts to persuade Alice to love him, he makes her watch "documentaries about 9/11 on my laptop, showing her that the twin towers and Pentagon were never actually blown up and that there were no Muslim terrorists who ever flew planes into them. I told her Muslim terrorism did not exist. I also showed her my research on the Illuminati to try and show her that the Jews are a mafia and they blew up the World Trade Center."[140] Aziz believes three conflicting but linked Internet-popular conspiracy theories: that 9/11 never happened or was a staged production of the U.S. government; that an eighteenth-century German secret society known as the Illuminati still exist and influence world events; and that Jews, who are sometimes believed to be agents of the Illuminati, are united in a worldwide cabal that plotted 9/11. Aaron Winter writes that after 9/11, "al-Qaeda, 'Islamist' Extremists, the Middle East, and the wider Muslim and Arab world began to feature more prominently in extreme-right conspiracy theories and literature. While the mainstream right feared the threat posed by this region and people, the extreme-right saw them as potential allies in their war against the American government and Zionism."[141] Aziz's conspiracy narrative fits this model of alliance between "Western" and "Islamic" far right ideologies. Though such alliances "have been generally unidirectional and unsuccessful," they nonetheless represent a profane counterpoint to orientalism, suggesting that all extremists have more in common with each other than with anyone else.[142] But the extent to which Aziz believes conspiracy theories, coupled with his forty-year obsession with Alice Wong and his unstable childhood, leads the reader to suspect that he, like the real Defreitas, is an unreliable narrator with delusions of grandeur so extreme he believes that he alone could end the world.

Sudhakar argues that *Chinese Women* connects British colonialism, Islamic fundamentalism, and U.S. neoliberal imperialism through racialized "practices of surveillance and division" that "rupture intimate bonds within colonial and postcolonial private spheres."[143] In British Guiana, everyone on the sugar estate spies on and polices each other's intimate and family lives. In the contemporary moment, Islamic fundamentalists and the U.S. government continually monitor and plot against each other. Aziz, reading his global conspiracy theories online and traveling around the world, flies above it all, tracking and watching everyone in a bid to remake himself into a person worthy of life. *Chinese Women* suggests that for the Caribbean Muslim fullaman, colonial trauma cannot be overcome solely by reinventing an ancestral ethnic or religious past, creolizing it into something new, or seeking transnational connection in which Muslimness supersedes race and place. The fullaman has passed through his African or Indian Door of No Return, but if he still yearns for the agency provided by knowing his imagined ancestors, neither creolization nor seeking Mecca is a comprehensive solution to his loss. Perhaps unsatisfyingly, the novel *Chinese Women* and the figure of Aziz suggest a politics that begins simply with self-care and reflection, as the choice of "Islam or the West" has no meaning for a person who is both Muslim and native to the Caribbean.

CONCLUSION
"Gods, I Suppose"

Yasin Abu Bakr, the man occupying the place of the Caribbean's arche-
typal Muslim terrorist after leading the 1990 Jamaat al Muslimeen attempted
coup against the Trinidadian government, baldly declared to me in an interview,
"If Islam was this fanatical religion then we would have killed everybody in the
Parliament because they would have done the same thing to us . . . if Islam was
this terrorist religion and this terrorist people, how come we didn't do that? . . .
It's more political than it is religious because Islam has one point six billion people.
How come the rest of us are not blowing up ourselves?"[1] He makes a simple demographic and ideological point about Islam and (the now 1.8 billion) Muslims that
is willfully obscured in the Caribbean and around the world by fear, ignorance,
and xenophobia: regardless of their transnational connections through the *ummah*,
the global Muslim community, all Muslims, even antigovernment ones, even ones
who have perpetuated violent acts, are not the same, historically, culturally, theologically, or politically. Inevitably, most people's concerns are deeply local, even
when their local concern is global intrusion. In Abu Bakr's view, contemporary
worldwide antistate violence associated with Muslims, including the development
of the Islamic State in Syria, is the ongoing fallout of the U.S. invasion of Iraq in
August 1990, which he noted occurred one month after the Muslimeen coup in
Trinidad. Since 1990, he says, "there has been no stopping the world as it is," and
"all these things seem to be interwoven and intertwined in some way. Some of it
is class exploitation, some of it is Islam on the rise," but much of it is "people who
claim that people are occupying their land, and they want them out of their land
because they are there to take their raw material, which is oil. You think if Iraq
was growing cabbages anybody would be in Iraq? You think if Iran was producing
potatoes anybody would be in Iran?"[2]

It is a complicated thing to interview a person such as Abu Bakr, a thirty-year-
long figure of Muslim menace in the Trinidadian and Caribbean imaginary, allegedly associated with violent acts that personally impacted my family and me (as
I note in chapter 4), and find him to be completely up to date on world events,

loquacious but far too savvy to say anything that would incriminate himself, but also a consummate old Caribbean joker, in the same vein of regional jokery, word-play, and social satire that suffuses Anglophone Caribbean Creole language itself, and thus Trinidadian calypso music and Caribbean literature. If anyone could frame decidedly unfunny war and terrorist violence as possibly humorous, it is my fellow Caribbean natives. Shane Crawford, also known as Abu Sa'd at-Trinidadi, the now-deceased representative Trinidadian national who departed the Carib-bean to fight for the Islamic State, even managed to crack a Caribbean joke in *Dabiq*, the Islamic State magazine, amidst his psychopathic eschatological proph-esying about a religious clash of civilizations: "Some of my disbelieving Christian relatives have used the fact that I am a soldier of the Islamic State in their quarrels with others. They've said, for example, 'My relative is an ISIS terrorist, so you better watch out!'"[3] The implication here is that even though Crawford's rela-tives might have been mostly horrified by his life choices, he and they were proud enough of his notoriety to joke about it. Humor neither solves nor truly softens fearsome and deadly crisis, but it is a way to understand others and allevi-ate fear in service of workable and humane solutions. I am not suggesting that what Caribbean Muslims offer to an understanding of the complexity of con-temporary and historical Islam is dark humor, or, uncharitably, a fool's unserious approach to serious issues. Political joking, in fact, may require the joker to feel a certain amount of security in his citizenship; the key is that Abu Bakr and Craw-ford (at-*Trinidadi*, named in the Islamic State for his citizenship), despite being Muslim, despite being accused terrorists, are thoroughly confident in their Trinidadianness.

Thus I am suggesting broadly that the New World context of Caribbean Islam, with its geographic and historical distance from Mecca, Islamabad, Istanbul, Teh-ran, Jakarta, Jerusalem, and other representative sites and cities of Islam, offer a unique window into Muslim migration to majority non-Muslim countries in colo-nial and postcolonial modernity, refuting the ahistorical supposition that Mus-lim migration and displacement are new to the world in the late twentieth and early twenty-first centuries. In the Anglophone Caribbean we see Muslim migrants who have become settled people in heterogeneous societies unrelated to the ones from which they came: Muslims "*of* the West and not simply *in* the West," as Aisha Khan says.[4] In addition, those descendants of enslaved and indentured people who convert or revert to Islam perceive themselves as fully within the Caribbean mode of reestablishing and reaffirming religious and ethnic roots in Africa and India. Their Islam is inherently transnational and diasporic.

There are two main areas in which this book intervenes in the study of the Caribbean, and in the study of Islam and Muslims. First, I emphasize that Anglo-phone Caribbean Muslims are of Indian and African descent, and their position-alities and presence shift over time: in the early colonial period, most Muslims in the Americas were enslaved Africans, some of whom were literate and educated in Islam, and left autobiographical and religious writings but no direct Muslim descendants; in the later colonial period, the majority were Indian indentured plantation laborers, who sought to differentiate themselves from the majority of Indian Hindus; and now, the Muslim population consists of both Indian descendants and growing numbers of Afro-Caribbean converts, troubling traditional race/religion divisions. Second, I argue that the Muslim in the Caribbean, the fullaman, resists the framework of the essentialized pious, purist Muslim by entering the postcolonial Caribbean processes of creolization and postcolonial mimicry, as exemplified by the metonymic Muslim Caribbean festival of Hosay. But the fullaman never truly becomes a Caribbean Creole hybrid. His or her ethnoriental metropolitan reference shifts from Britain to the Middle East, in a practice of Islam that is simultaneously culturally local and global: as David Rudder's postcoup calypso "Hoosay" goes, that is the nature of "Muslim time" in the Caribbean. Fullaman belonging is performative, especially through scrutiny of the bodies and actions of Muslim women.

A few other points are noteworthy: Islam has since European medievality been conceived of as a racial category in the non-Muslim-majority world, particularly when it is linked to antistate violence; literature and music can unearth silences in the archival record, though they ought not to be conceived of as either inherently secular art forms or representative of lived experience; and religiosity is nonlinear, discursive, performative, and relational. Derek Walcott's first, weary reaction to a Trinidadian Hindu performance of the *Ramleela* was "Gods, I suppose," suggesting that the Caribbean was oversaturated with religion and religious ghosts: indigenous gods, African gods, Hindu gods, and every Abrahamic iteration of a monotheistic god.[5] This is true, but Walcott came to realize that not only was the combination new, creative, and particularly Caribbean, but the many gods were not hollow; they presupposed real and specific faith, as Alejandro Carpentier said of the faith required for the marvelous and magical to manifest the real.[6] The gods of the Caribbean are not an undifferentiated, syncretic Creole mass; their particularities and histories are important, partly for teleological reasons: they produce and are created by their worshipers' faith in remaining among the living despite the horrors of enslavement and indentureship.

This book focuses on Islam and Muslim literature and music in Anglophone Guyana, Trinidad, and Jamaica. What remains to be seen in Guyana is the effect that recent ExxonMobil discoveries of oil in that country's offshore waters will have on its domestic economy and its local and global relationships, including on its future positionality in the great web encompassing the United States and Muslim-majority oil-producing nations. Oil production in Guyana begins in early 2020, to the tune of 120,000 barrels a day.[7] In September 2019, the Guyana Civil Aviation Authority signed an Air Services Agreement with its state counterpart in Qatar to begin Qatar Airways flights between Qatar and Guyana; the very broad agreement allowed for the operation of "any number of services between both countries as well as beyond to any third country, with no restrictions on capacity, frequency, aircraft type and routing."[8] Qatar—which at the present time has major diplomatic disputes with Saudi Arabia, Bahrain, the United Arab Emirates, and Egypt, causing it to strike out on its own internationally—has also, through Qatar Petroleum, acquired a stake in two French-held oil blocks off Guyana's shores.[9] According to the Guyanese Ministry of the Presidency, the U.A.E. has also entered the fray, as it will "be lending assistance to Guyana in customs and taxation related matters."[10] As the major oil and gas players of the world trade interest in oil blocks and jockey for position before oil drilling has even begun, local Guyanese commentators have continually "raise[d] the question of whether Georgetown is aware of the scale of the financial transactions taking place and whether it had extracted the best terms possible."[11] In addition, one can only hope that Guyana and its Muslims do not enter conflicts in the Middle East by oil proxy.

As I have indicated in the introduction, further regional inquiry into the unique history of Indian and Javanese Islam in Suriname is also needed. Comparative study of Islam in the Anglophone, Hispanophone, and Francophone Caribbean is also a field ripe for more inquiry, as there are growing numbers of both Muslim converts and Middle Eastern migrants in Puerto Rico, the Dominican Republic, Cuba, Haiti, and other countries in the Caribbean—and continental Latin America, especially Lusophone Brazil. The global migration of Islam and Muslims, and worldwide images and perceptions of both, are so ongoing and complex that they cannot be appropriately and nonstereotypically quantified without attending to specificity of place.

I have engaged throughout the book and ended here with complicating the figure of the "Muslim terrorist," while resenting my motivation of humanizing my own Muslim community. No person should feel defensively compelled to prove him or herself ontologically a complex human. The terrorist is, however, the dominant image many non-Muslims have of Muslims in the twenty-first century, whether the figure appears as a fearsome, irredeemable, fanatical man who deserves only expulsion, extrajudicial imprisonment, or death, or his inscrutable female victim counterpart, saturated with pathos but never agency. And so, an inquiry into global Islam in the local Caribbean cannot simply be a literary, historical, or cultural academic study that does not acknowledge the politics of Islam in the world, or argue for a just representation of the diversity of Muslim life and experience.

ACKNOWLEDGMENTS

Writing is deeply solitary, but impossible without the many people who contribute materially and psychically to the creative thinking and well-being of the writer.

This monograph is a first book that is a new project and not a dissertation revision. It is the intellectual contribution I truly wished to make in this historical moment. However, I would have been unable to imagine and complete it in a timely manner without significant institutional and professional organization support. The book received the support of the 2018–2019 American Comparative Literature Association Helen Tartar First Book Subvention Award, the 2017–2018 American Association of University Women American Postdoctoral Leave Fellowship, and the University of Michigan Publication Subvention Award. I also received summer writing support from the University of Michigan's Center for the Education of Women, and the ADVANCE Program.

My editor at Rutgers University Press, Kimberly Guinta, had from our earliest discussions practical advice and unswerving confidence in the necessity of this book. Sincere thanks are also due to Rutgers Critical Caribbean Series editors Yolanda Martínez-San Miguel, Carter Mathes, and Kathleen López for their support, and the anonymous reviewers of my book for their thorough reading and indispensable revision advice.

An early version of the book was read and workshopped by my field colleagues Shona Jackson, Supriya Nair, Shalini Puri, and Magda Zaborowska. Their thoughtful and detailed comments were invaluable in refining my ideas and writing. Esra Mirze Santesso provided generous help with award applications and panel presentation feedback.

I thank my mentors Carla Freccero and Anjali Arondekar at the University of California, Santa Cruz, for their early belief in and ongoing support of my work. Vilashini Cooppan, Kirsten Silva Gruesz, and Wlad Godzich encouraged my thinking in their courses and supported me throughout graduate school. My first writing group readers Erik Bachman and Christine Montgomery provided feedback and friendship at a crucial time in my academic development.

The chairs of my two University of Michigan, Ann Arbor, departments, the Department of English Language and Literature, and the Department of Afroamerican and African Studies, have given me unstinting help and reassurance: David Porter and Matthew Countryman now, and Frieda Ekotto, Tiya Miles, and Michael Schoenfeldt in previous years.

Camaraderie, conversations, and friendship with Charlotte Karem Albrecht, Evelyn Alsultany, André Brock, Elizabeth Currans, Jocelyn Fenton-Stitt, Stephanie Heit, Shazia Iftkhar, ElizaBeth James, SE Kile, Petra Kuppers, Madhumita Lahiri, and V Jane Rosser kept me warm during each successive year of the Michigan polar vortex.

My current and former Michigan colleagues Su'ad Abdul Khabeer, Omolade Adunbi, Kwasi Ampene, Fernando Arenas, Michael Awkward, Hadji Bakara, Sara Blair, Bénédicte Boisseron, William Calvo-Quirós, Anne Curzan, Gaurav Desai, Angela Dillard, Sarah Ensor, Amal Fadlalla, Anita Gonzalez, June Howard, Tung-Hui Hu, Sandra Gunning, Lucy Hartley, Paul Johnson, Lydia Kelow-Bennett, Nancy Khalil, Meena Krishnamurthy, Larry La Fountain-Stokes, Aida Levy-Hussen, Karla Mallette, Khaled Mattawa, Peggy McCracken, Victor Mendoza, Joshua Miller, Farina Mir, Yasmin Moll, Supriya Nair, Lisa Nakamura, Scotti Parrish, Catherine Sanok, Xiomara Santamarina, Janum Sethi, SaraEllen Strongman, Ruby Tapia, Tessa Tinkle, Antoine Traisnel, Valerie Traub, Stephen Ward, Gillian White, Tyler Whitney, Damon Young, and Andrea Zemgulys proffered invitations, advice, listening ears, or camaraderie. Michigan graduate students Sarah Hughes, Mika Kennedy, and Aurelis Troncoso provided research and teaching assistance. All of my colleagues in English and DAAS have contributed to the career support I feel at the University of Michigan.

I have found inspiration and Guyanese jahaji bhai and bahin fellowship in the persons, writing, and activism of Gaiutra Bahadur, Anita Baksh, Nesha Haniff, Rajiv Mohabir, and Lisa Outar.

Journalist Sharmain Baboolal and the Copyright Music Organisation of Trinidad and Tobago (COTT) kindly facilitated my contact with sources in Trinidad. My Trini cousin Fazil Rasheed was always ready to lend a hand on the ground.

Many thanks to calypsonians Fitzroy Joseph (Brother Ebony), Weston Rawlins (Cro Cro), and David Rudder, and to Khāled Siddīq, for graciously allowing me to quote their music. I appreciate the input of Keith Carter, Eusi Kwayana, and Nigel Westmaas in verifying biographical details about Abdur-Rahman Slade Hopkinson and Martin Carter.

Maria Frangos and Heidi Morse read my work and gave me deep personal support over many years. Other longtime and dear friends have given me succor, strength, snacks, and professional and personal advice: Simina Calin, Melinda Faylor, Sabrina Hom, Jennifer Nelson, Irini Neofotistos, Sara Orning, Ivonne Rayo, Liz Roberts, and my inimitable Caribbean sister Penelope Williams. This book and I owe immeasurably much to daily exchanges with my fellow South American and beloved comrade Nilo Couret, who shares knowledge, opinions, affection, and puns without compunction.

Three teachers showed me from early in life an Islam that was generous, merciful, and intellectual: my mother Salima Khan, who taught me the kalimas; my madrassa and Qur'an recitation teacher and qaseeda singer Ustadh Nazim Bacchus, who saw no distinction of gender; and my grandfather Imam Mohamed Rasheed, son and brother of imams, for whom delivering a khutbah sermon, encouraging book learning and athletics, and feeding the hungry and poor are all the same thing. More recently, Imam Kamau Ayubbi introduced me to the beneficence of the Sufi Way. And my brother Javed Khan is always ready to joke and speculate about our Caribbean and Muslim community foibles.

Finally but foremost, I thank my father and mother, Jan and Salima Khan, for a lifetime of loving support and for the gift of an Indo-Guyanese and Muslim upbringing and familial history without which this book would not have been conceived.

NOTES

INTRODUCTION

1. Minor portions of this introduction appeared in another form as "Voyages across Indenture: From Ship Sister to Mannish Woman" in *GLQ* 22, no. 2 (2016): 249–280.

2. Siddīq, "My Grandfather was a Muslim." Lyrics from Khāled Siddīq's "My Grandfather Was a Muslim" are quoted by permission of KS Management. For more of Siddīq's Caribbean Muslim concerns and references, see also "On Deen (Part II)" and "Road to Palestine," the latter of which is set to the tune of Rastafarian (and Bob's son) Damian Marley's "Road to Zion."

3. Tijani, "Fulani Woman."

4. Tijani, "Baye Niasse (Boom Baye)." For more on the political and religious legacy of Baay Niasse, see Ware, Wright, and Sayed, *Jihad of the Pen*, and Hill, "Sovereign Islam in a Secular State."

5. Walcott, "The Antilles."

6. Ibid.

7. Kettani, "History and Prospect of Muslims in South America," 851–852; Kettani, "Muslim Population in the Americas," 128.

8. Kettani, "History and Prospect of Muslims in South America," 855; Kettani, "Muslim Population in the Americas," 133–134.

9. Samaroo, "Seeking a Space in the Politics," 202.

10. Mahmood, *Politics of Piety*, 3.

11. Kurzman, *Liberal Islam*, 5–6.

12. Fadda-Conrey, "The Passage from West to South," 23.

13. Ibid.," 22.

14. Khan, "Muharram Moves West," 492.

15. Retamar, *Calibán y otros ensayos*. For links between *The Tempest* and hurricanes, see Hulme, "Hurricanes in the Caribbees."

16. Byrd, *The Transit of Empire*, 59. "Arrivants" is the Barbadian poet Brathwaite's term for enslaved Africans brought to the Americas, as quoted by an unnamed Kumina Queen of Jamaica in the epigraph of *The Arrivants* trilogy. Brathwaite, *The Arrivants*, n.p.

17. Byrd, *The Transit of Empire*, 62, 67.

18. Mahmood, "Rehearsed Spontaneity and the Conventionality of Ritual."

19. Asad, "The Idea of an Anthropology of Islam," 8.

20. Ibid., 10.

21. Munasinghe, *Callaloo or Tossed Salad?*, 129, 16.

22. *Zami* or *zanmi* is Lorde's Grenadian and Carriacou term for "lesbian," or woman-loving-woman. That women *make*, rather than *are*, zami is a main concern. See Lorde, *Zami*.

23. Rana, *Terrifying Muslims*, 29.

24. Khan, *Autobiography of an Indian Indentured Labourer*.

25. Warner-Lewis, "Jamaica's Muslim Past," 294.

26. Spivak, ""Can the Subaltern Speak?," 87.

27. Naipaul, "Two Worlds."

28. Ibid.

29. For discussions of music in Muslim communities, see, among many others: Frishkopf and Spinetti, *Music, Sound, and Architecture in Islam* (2018); Rasmussen, *Women, the Recited Qur'an,*

and Islamic Music in Indonesia (2010); Shiloah, *Music in the World of Islam* (2001); Palmer Keen's ethnomusicological Indonesia recordings project *Aural Archipelago* at http://www.auralarchipelago.com/; and my niche favorites LeVine's *Heavy Metal Islam* (2008), Capper and Sifre's documentary *Heavy Metal in Baghdad: The Story of Acrassicauda* (2009), and Michael Muhammad Knight's punk rock Islam novel that spawned a musical movement, *The Taqwacores* (2009). At minimum, one should also listen to Ali Farka Touré's Mali blues and Nusrat Fateh Ali Khan's Pakistani-Sufi *qawwali* songs.

30. "But there is the sort of person who pays for distracting tales, intending, without any knowledge, to lead others from God's way, and to hold it up to ridicule. There will be humiliating torment for him! When Our verses are recited to him, he turns away disdainfully as if he had not heard them, as if there were heaviness in his ears. Tell him that there will be a painful torment!" Qur'an 31:6–7, 261.

31. "Vocal Recording in Trinidad and Tobago," 3–4, 6; *Discography of American Historical Recordings*, s.v. "Victor matrix G-133. Moulood-Sharief [No. I] / S. M. Akberali."

32. British Guiana became the Co-operative Republic of Guyana upon independence on May 26, 1966, and I will use the variant country spellings accordingly.

33. See Bahadur's outlining of the problematics of recovering the word "coolie" in the preface to her book *Coolie Woman*.

34. Adebayo, "Of Man and Cattle," 1.

35. Qur'an 25:28, 106–107.

36. Diouf, *Servants of Allah*, 24–25.

37. Ware, *The Walking Qur'an*, 35, 8–9.

38. Wright, "Introduction," 2.

39. Ibid., and Ware and Shareef, "Shaykh 'Uthman bin Fudi," 27.

40. Wright, "Introduction," 8.

41. Gomez, *Black Crescent*, 52.

42. Ibid.

43. Diouf, *Servants of Allah*, 136.

44. Henry, *Caliban's Reason*, 11–12.

45. Benjamin, "On the Concept of History," 392.

46. Khanam and Chickrie, "170th Anniversary of the Arrival," 205–206. Experiments with Chinese indentured labor began earlier, in 1806 in Trinidad. Lee-Loy, "Saying No to Chineseness," 296.

47. Khanam and Chickrie, "170th Anniversary of the Arrival," 205.

48. *Madrassa* and *maktab* are often used interchangeably in the Caribbean, though *madrassa* is preferred in Guyana as *maktab* is in Trinidad. Mustapha, "Islam in the Caribbean," 1133–1134.

49. For a history of Islamic organizations in Guyana and their politics, see Chickrie, "Islamic Organizations in Guyana."

50. At home, multilingual Indo-Surinamese usually speak Sarnami Hindustani or Hindoestani, which in the Caribbean denotes a language that is mostly the nineteenth-century Bhojpuri Hindi of Uttar Pradesh and Bihar.

51. Khan, "Muharram Moves West," 492.

52. Rocklin, *The Regulation of Religion*, 3, 8.

53. van der Veer and Vertovec, "Brahmanism Abroad," 157–158. Brahmins are the priestly, highest *varna* (class/caste) in Hinduism.

54. Henry, *Caliban's Reason*, 15.

55. Singh, *The Ramayana Tradition*.

56. Jackson, *Creole Indigeneity*, 4–5.

57. Munasinghe, "Nationalism in Hybrid Spaces," 665.

58. "Nuestra América" is a term coined by Cuban nationalist José Martí in his essay of the same name in *Revista Ilustrada* (New York) on January 1, 1891, and in *El Partido Liberal* (Mexico) on March 5, 1892, representing his pan-Latin American vision of revolution and decolonization.

59. Retamar, *Calibán y otros ensayos*, 11–12.

60. Quijano and Wallerstein describe British colonials as being loath to fraternize with their subjects in the Caribbean: the British created, in the "big houses," "European-societies-outside-of-Europe." "Americanity as a Concept," 552.

61. Puri, *The Caribbean Postcolonial*, 3.

62. Fernández Olmos and Paravisini-Gebert, *Creole Religions of the Caribbean*, 5.

63. Puri, *The Caribbean Postcolonial*, 4.

64. Rana, *Terrifying Muslims*, 5.

65. Johnson, *African American Religions*, 395.

66. Bayoumi, "Racing Religion," 269; In re *Ahmed Hassan* 48 F. Supp. 843 (E.D. Mich. 1942), 845.

67. Cainkar and Maira, "Targeting Arab/Muslim/South Asian Americans," 18; Alsultany, *Arabs and Muslims in the Media*, 21.

68. Puar, *Terrorist Assemblages*, 13.

69. Korom, Hosay Trinidad, 259.

70. Mohammed, "Island Currents, Global Aesthetics," 311.

71. Goring, "The Story of Hosay."

72. Ibid., 313.

73. Puri, *The Caribbean Postcolonial*, 177.

74. Rocklin, *The Regulation of Religion*, 7.

75. Brereton, *Race Relations in Colonial Trinidad*, 183.

76. Wood, *Trinidad in Transition*, 153.

77. Rocklin, *The Regulation of Religion*, 82.

78. Jenkins, *Lutchmee and Dilloo*, 256–257, 308.

79. Ibid., 278.

80. Korom, Hosay Trinidad, 6.

81. Ibid., 7.

82. Wood, *Trinidad in Transition*, 152.

83. Korom, Hosay Trinidad, 101.

84. Wood, *Trinidad in Transition*, 153.

85. Korom, Hosay Trinidad, 6.

86. Khan, "Muharram Moves West," 489.

87. Korom, Hosay Trinidad, 111.

88. Ibid.

89. Ibid., 116.

90. Ibid., 17; Rocklin, *The Regulation of Religion*, 88.

91. Korom, Hosay Trinidad, 98.

92. Khan, "Muharram Moves West," 498.

93. Goring, "The Story of Hosay."

94. Khan, "Muharram Moves West," 498.

95. See M. Jacqui Alexander's essay collection *Pedagogies of Crossing* for the multiple ways citizenship is constructed in Trinidad and the Caribbean through the criminalization of queerness, prescribed gender roles, and other social constructs.

96. See Johnson, *African American Religions*, 394, for a description of how Muslims can be racialized into "people of a fundamentally different type."

97. F. M. Denny, "Umma," in *Encyclopaedia of Islam, Second Edition*, edited by P. Bearman et al., 2012, doi:http://dx.doi.org/10.1163/1573-3912_islam_COM_1291.

98. Ibid.
99. Khan, "Contours," 28.
100. Cainkar and Maira, "Targeting Arab/Muslim/South Asian Americans," 18.
101. Hall, "The Local and the Global," 28–29.
102. Ibid., 33.
103. Castor, *Spiritual Citizenship*, 6, 12.
104. Ibid., 12.
105. Khan, "Contours," 26.
106. Young, "Postcolonial Remains," 25, 30.
107. Ibid., 30.
108. Abbas, *At Freedom's Limit*, 73.
109. Majid, *Unveiling Traditions*, 2.
110. Alexander, *Pedagogies of Crossing*, 295, 328.
111. Mignolo, "Delinking," 488.
112. Hartman, *Lose Your Mother*, 18.
113. Mackey, "An Interview with Kamau Brathwaite," 44; Glissant, *Caribbean Discourse*, 67; Harris, "History, Fable and Myth in the Caribbean and Guianas," 157; Carter and Torabully, *Coolitude*.
114. Khan, "Muharram Moves West," 491.
115. Glissant, *Caribbean Discourse*, 65.
116. Walcott, "The Antilles."
117. Wynter, "The Ceremony Must Be Found," 22.
118. Walcott, "The Antilles."

CHAPTER 1   BLACK LITERARY ISLAM

1. Madden, *A Twelvemonth's Residence in the West Indies*, 109.
2. Ibid., 121.
3. Poems from the collection *Snowscape with Signature* by Abdur-Rahman Slade Hopkinson are quoted by permission of Peepal Tree Press.
4. Addoun and Lovejoy, "The Arabic Manuscript of Muhammad Kabā Saghanughu of Jamaica, c.1820," 313. The manuscript is in the James Coultart Papers, Baptist Missionary Society Collection, Angus Library, Regent's Park College, Oxford University. Ibid., 333.
5. See ad-Darqawi, *The Darqawi Way*.
6. GhaneaBassiri, "Islam in America," 110.
7. Aidi, *Rebel Music*, 20–21.
8. Fadda-Conrey, "The Passage from West to South," 22.
9. Diouf, *Servants of Allah*, 27.
10. Curtis, "Why Muslims Matter to American Religious History, 1730–1945," 395.
11. Levtzion, "Islam in the Bilad al-Sudan to 1800," 6, 63.
12. Ibid., 68, 72.
13. Ibid., 72.
14. Ware, *The Walking Qur'an*, 8–9.
15. Levtzion and Powels, *The History of Islam in Africa*, 52. See Paul Lovejoy's *Jihād in West Africa during the Age of Revolutions* (2016) for contextualization of West African ideas of jihād in the eighteenth and nineteenth centuries.
16. Addoun and Lovejoy, "Muhammad Kabā Saghanughu and the Muslim Community of Jamaica," 207; Gomez, *Black Crescent*, 53–54; Madden, *A Twelvemonth's Residence in the West Indies*, 133–134.

17. See Fernández Olmos and Paravisini-Gebert, *Creole Religions of the Caribbean* for the local histories of each syncretic region.

18. Dayan, "Paul Gilroy's Slaves, Ships, and Routes," 7.

19. Khan, "Islam, Vodou, and the Making of the Afro-Atlantic," 29, 31.

20. Ibid., 44.

21. Curtis, "Why Muslims Matter to American Religious History, 1730–1945," 397, 399.

22. Shaheen, "Literary Form and Islamic Identity in *The Life of Omar Ibn Said*," 188.

23. See the Library of Congress's Omar Ibn Said digital collection at https://www.loc.gov/collections/omar-ibn-said-collection/.

24. Lovejoy, "'Freedom Narratives of Transatlantic Slavery," 100. Curtis, "Why Muslims Matter to American Religious History, 1730–1945," 395, 399–400. GhaneaBassiri, "Islam in America," 111.

25. Turner, *Islam in the African-American Experience*, 33.

26. Ibid., 32–33.

27. Curtis, "Why Muslims Matter to American Religious History, 1730–1945," 395.

28. Marr, "'Out of This World,'" 533–534.

29. See Susan Nance's *How the Arabian Nights Inspired the American Dream, 1790–1935* (2009) for the impact of the tales of *One Thousand and One Nights* on U.S. consumer and popular culture up to the Great Depression.

30. Marr, "'Out of This World,'" 524.

31. Reis, *Slave Rebellion in Brazil*, 99, 103.

32. Ibid., 500.

33. Ibid., 106.

34. Diouf, "African Muslims in the Caribbean," 85–86.

35. Dobronravin, "Literacy among Muslims in Nineteenth-Century Trinidad and Brazil," 219–220. The manuscript is held at Trinity College, Dublin.

36. Ibid., 222.

37. Ibid.

38. Trotman and Lovejoy, "Community of Believers," 222.

39. Ibid.

40. Diouf, "African Muslims in the Caribbean," 84–88.

41. Prorok and Hemmasi, "East Indian Muslims and Their Mosques in Trinidad," 34.

42. Dobronravin, "Literacy among Muslims in Nineteenth-Century Trinidad and Brazil," 221.

43. Ibid.

44. Ibid.

45. Addoun and Lovejoy, "Muhammad Kabā Saghanughu and the Muslim Community of Jamaica," 204.

46. Ibid.

47. Addoun and Lovejoy, "The Arabic Manuscript of Muhammad Kabā Saghanughu of Jamaica, *c.*1820," 318.

48. Addoun and Lovejoy, "Muhammad Kabā Saghanughu and the Muslim Community of Jamaica," 206.

49. Ibid., 205.

50. Addoun and Lovejoy, "The Arabic Manuscript of Muhammad Kabā Saghanughu of Jamaica, *c.*1820," 313–316, 320–322.

51. Addoun and Lovejoy, "Muhammad Kabā Saghanughu and the Muslim Community of Jamaica," 199–200.

52. Wilks, *Wa and Wala*, 99.

53. Ibid., 202.

54. Austen, *Trans-Saharan Africa in World History*, 96.

55. Ibid., 96–97.

56. Addoun and Lovejoy, "Muhammad Kabā Saghanughu and the Muslim Community of Jamaica," 201–202.

57. Ibid., 201.

58. Addoun and Lovejoy, "The Arabic Manuscript of Muhammad Kabā Saghanughu of Jamaica, c.1820," 314.

59. Warner-Lewis. "Religious Constancy and Compromise among Nineteenth Century Caribbean-based African Muslims," 250.

60. Addoun and Lovejoy, "The Arabic Manuscript of Muhammad Kabā Saghanughu of Jamaica, c.1820," 314.

61. Ibid., 315.

62. Kabā Saghanughu, "The Kitāb al-Salāt of Muhammad Kabā Saghanughu of Jamaica c. 1823," 330.

63. Ibid., 340.

64. Ibid., 327.

65. Addoun and Lovejoy, "Muhammad Kabā Saghanughu and the Muslim Community of Jamaica," 212.

66. Madden, *A Twelvemonth's Residence in the West Indies*, 133.

67. Ibid.

68. Ibid., 136.

69. Ibid., 136.

70. Ibid., 137.

71. Ibid., 133–134.

72. Ibid., 134.

73. Ibid., 146.

74. Wilks, "Abū Bakr al-Ṣiddīq of Timbuktu," 156.

75. Ibid.

76. Madden, *A Twelvemonth's Residence in the West Indies*, 121–122.

77. Ibid., 129–130.

78. Ibid., 129.

79. Diptee, *From Africa to Jamaica*, 101–102.

80. The Qur'an 2:284 and 2:286, 33.

81. Robinson, *Muslim Societies in African History*, 64.

82. Ibid., 63–64.

83. Ibid., 64.

84. Ibid., 68.

85. Ibid., 55.

86. Ibid., 71.

87. Ware, *The Walking Qur'an*, 8.

88. Levtzion, "Islam in the Bilad al-Sudan to 1800," 86.

89. Ibid., 85.

90. Ware and Shareef, "Shaykh 'Uthman bin Fudi," 27.

91. Ibid.; Levtzion, "Islam in the Bilad al-Sudan to 1800," 86. *'Ajamiyyah* indicates that the verse was in a local language that was frequently written in Arabic script, an *'ajami*. *Qādiriyya* denotes a West African Sufi brotherhood affiliation, and *qasīda* the major classical form of Arabic-Persian poetry. Meisami, *Structure and Meaning in Medieval Arabic and Persian Poetry*, 144.

92. Hopkinson, *Snowscape with Signature*, 15.

93. "Abdhur Rahman Slade Hopkinson—The Forgotten Poet"; Hopkinson, *Snowscape with Signature*, 10.

94. Hopkinson, *Snowscape with Signature*, 10.

95. Ibid.

96. Peepal Tree Press advertising blurb: see https://www.peepaltreepress.com/books/snow scape-signature.

97. Baugh, "A History of Poetry," 263.

98. Hopkinson, *Snowscape with Signature*, 10.

99. Ibid., 76.

100. Thifault, ""The Rhyming Irons of Abdur-Rahman Slade Hopkinson," 2, 9.

101. Bowen and Hopkinson, ""Slade Hopkinson on Slade Hopkinson," 74.

102. Ibid., 73.

103. Ibid., 66; Oakland, "In Search of a Better Life Toronto's 200,000 West Indians Didn't Come for the Climate," F3.

104. Hopkinson, "'Dream on Monkey Mountain' and the Popular Response (A Few Questions)," 77; "Abdhur Rahman Slade Hopkinson—The Forgotten Poet."

105. Bowen and Hopkinson, ""Slade Hopkinson on Slade Hopkinson," 67.

106. Ibid., 69.

107. Ibid.

108. de Bruijn, *Persian Sufi Poetry*, 9, 11.

109. Ibid., 11.

110. Ibid.

111. Bowen and Hopkinson, ""Slade Hopkinson on Slade Hopkinson," 68.

112. Ibid.

113. de Bruijn, *Persian Sufi Poetry*, 12.

114. Ibid., 58.

115. Hopkinson, *Snowscape with Signature*, 16.

116. Brathwaite, "Nation Language," 311.

117. Hopkinson, *Snowscape with Signature*, 77.

118. Meisami, *Structure and Meaning in Medieval Arabic and Persian Poetry*, 2–3, 7. Meisami writes in response that "what sets Arabo-Persian poetry apart from modern critical conceptions is not its 'Oriental' character, but its remoteness in time (its medievalness) and its lyric nature." Ibid., 5.

119. Thifault, ""The Rhyming Irons of Abdur-Rahman Slade Hopkinson," 1, 9.

120. de Bruijn, *Persian Sufi Poetry*, 48.

121. Ibid., 3.

122. Ibid., 4, 55.

123. Ibid., 51–52.

124. Ibid., 3, 31, 52.

125. Hopkinson, *Snowscape with Signature*, 63.

126. Meisami, *Structure and Meaning in Medieval Arabic and Persian Poetry*, 76, 108.

127. Hopkinson, *Snowscape with Signature*, 91.

128. Ibid., 118.

129. Ibid., 87.

130. Meisami, *Structure and Meaning in Medieval Arabic and Persian Poetry*, 108, 76.

131. de Bruijn, *Persian Sufi Poetry*, 54.

132. Ibid., 58.

133. Meisami, *Structure and Meaning in Medieval Arabic and Persian Poetry*, 109.

134. Hopkinson, *Snowscape with Signature*, 87.

135. de Bruijn, *Persian Sufi Poetry*, 52, 54.

136. Hopkinson, *Snowscape with Signature*, 85.

137. Ibid.

138. Ibid.

139. Ibid., 93.

140. Ibid.

141. Ibid., 89.

142. Ibid., 90.

143. Brown, *A Literary History of Persia*, 361.

144. Ibid.

145. Ibid.

146. Hopkinson, *Snowscape with Signature*, 88.

147. Ibid.

148. ad-Darqawi, *The Darqawi Way*, 77.

149. Ibid.

150. Ibid., 78.

151. Meisami, *Structure and Meaning in Medieval Arabic and Persian Poetry*, 125.

152. Ibid., 120.

153. Ibid., 105.

154. Ibid., 60.

155. Ibid.

156. Ibid., 75–76.

157. Hopkinson, *Snowscape with Signature*, 75.

158. Ibid.

159. Ibid.

160. Ibid.

161. Ibid.; de Bruijn, *Persian Sufi Poetry*, 7.

162. Hopkinson, *Snowscape with Signature*, 76.

163. de Bruijn, *Persian Sufi Poetry*, 7.

164. Meisami, *Structure and Meaning in Medieval Arabic and Persian Poetry*, 125.

165. Ibid., 76.

166. Ibid., 105, 107.

167. Hopkinson, *Snowscape with Signature*, 75.

168. Meisami, *Structure and Meaning in Medieval Arabic and Persian Poetry*, 393.

169. Hopkinson, "'Dream on Monkey Mountain' and the Popular Response (A Few Questions)," 78–79.

170. Hopkinson, "Be Careful with Details about Islam, Reader Urges," 7.

171. Bowen and Hopkinson, "Slade Hopkinson on Slade Hopkinson," 74, 76.

CHAPTER 2   SILENCE AND SUICIDE

1. Portions of this chapter appeared in another form as "Protest and Punishment: Indo-Guyanese Women and Organized Labor," in the *Caribbean Review of Gender Studies* 12 (2018): 269–298. Used by permission.

2. Graham, *Beyond the Written Word*, 5.

3. Ahamad, "Transcript of B.B.C.'s Interview with Dr. Anesa Ahamad-Khan (1995)," 2.

4. Ibid.; Kassim, "Identity and Acculturation of Trinidad Muslims," 170–171.

5. Ahamad, "Transcript of B.B.C.'s Interview with Dr. Anesa Ahamad-Khan (1995)," 2. See Rampersad, "Becoming a Pandita."

6. Anesa Ahamad, interview by author, Miami, October 6, 2018.

7. Ibid.

8. Ibid.

9. Ibid.

10. Ibid.

11. Mustapha, "Islam in the Caribbean," 1133.

12. Ibid. See the fourth and fifth chapters for discussion of Libya's Caribbean involvement.

13. Kassim, "Identity and Acculturation of Trinidad Muslims," 169.

14. Reddock, "'Up Against a Wall.'"

15. Kassim, "Identity and Acculturation of Trinidad Muslims," 169, 172.

16. Hosein, "Democracy, Gender, and Indian Muslim Modernity in Trinidad," 258.

17. Ibid.

18. Chickrie, "The Afghan Muslims," 387.

19. Chickrie and Khanam, "Hindustani Muslims," 114.

20. Chickrie, "The Afghan Muslims," 386, 389; Chickrie and Khanam, "Hindustani Muslims," 116.

21. Chickrie and Khanam, "Hindustani Muslims," 116.

22. Ibid., 117; Chickrie, "The Afghan Muslims," 389.

23. Chickrie and Khanam, "Hindustani Muslims," 119.

24. Winer, *Dictionary of the English/Creole of Trinidad & Tobago*, 926.

25. Spivak, "Can the Subaltern Speak?," 82–83.

26. Ibid., 82.

27. See Khan, "Protest and Punishment," a version of this chapter that examines Indo-Guyanese women's involvement in trade unionism and plantation strikes in the late nineteenth century through the interwar period.

28. Espinet, *The Swinging Bridge*, 15.

29. Spivak, "Can the Subaltern Speak?," 82.

30. Chickrie and Khanam, "Hindustani Muslims," 129–130.

31. Khan, "Voyages across Indenture," 261.

32. See Gaiutra Bahadur's archival family history *Coolie Woman* and Ramabai Espinet's novel *The Swinging Bridge*, for example.

33. Hock and Joseph, *Language History, Language Change, and Language Relationship*, 231.

34. Espinet, *The Swinging Bridge*, 275.

35. Mehta, *Diasporic (Dis)locations*, 5.

36. Kempadoo, *Sexing the Caribbean*, 38–39.

37. Singh, *The Ramayana Tradition*, 95.

38. Ibid., 135.

39. Ibid., 96.

40. Mohammed, "Changing Symbols," 13.

41. Mehta, *Diasporic (Dis)locations*, 65.

42. Shepherd, *Maharani's Misery*, xviii.

43. Mehta, *Diasporic (Dis)locations*, 64.

44. Niranjana, *Mobilizing India*, 82.

45. Mehta, *Diasporic (Dis)locations*, 72.

46. Ibid.

47. Ibid.

48. Mehta, "Engendering History," 21.

49. Lokaisingh-Meighoo, "Jahaji Bhai."

50. Poynting, "'You Want to Be a Coolie Woman?,'" 103. Rajkumari Singh produced mostly unpublished plays, poems, and short stories and is perhaps most well-known for her poem "Per Ajie" (1971), dedicated to the ancestral Indo-Caribbean indentured *aji*, or grandmother.

51. Mehta, *Diasporic (Dis)locations*, 8.

52. The poetry collection *I Want to Be a Poetess of My People* (1976) by Das (1954–2003) deals with the same themes of postcolonial Indo-Caribbean becomings as does the work of male authors like Naipaul and Selvon. The collection *Bones* (1988) is where Das finds her voice on issues specific to Indo-Caribbean women. *Bones* was published by Peepal Tree Press, which was founded in 1985 and is based in the United Kingdom. The press is dedicated to the reissuing, preservation, and growth of Caribbean and Black British literature, with a specific and unique interest in Indo-Caribbean literature. Most—not all, as Shani Mootoo and other Canadian Caribbean authors have other avenues open to them—Indo-Caribbean fiction and poetry that gains an international audience outside of the Caribbean does so through the efforts of this press.

53. "Creolese" is the colloquial Guyanese way of referring to any and all variants of the local Anglophone Creole dialect, as I will later discuss.

54. Jackson, "The Baptism of Soil," 16.

55. Ibid., 9, 19.

56. Ibid., 18–19.

57. Birbalsingh, "The Indo-Caribbean Short Story," 129.

58. Ibid., 118.

59. Ibid.

60. Ibid., 121.

61. Ibid.

62. Ibid., 127.

63. Monar, *Backdam People*, 58.

64. Rickford, *Dimensions of a Creole Continuum*, 65, 63.

65. Ibid., 63.

66. Monar, *Backdam People*, 59.

67. Ibid.

68. Ibid.

69. Ibid., 59.

70. Ibid., 61.

71. Ibid., 67.

72. Ibid., 68.

73. Birbalsingh, "The Indo-Caribbean Short Story," 125.

74. Ibid., 120.

75. Ibid.

76. Ibid., 123.

77. Ibid., 129.

78. Ibid.

79. Jackson, "The Baptism of Soil," 9.

80. Brathwaite, "Nation Language," 311.

81. Ibid.

82. Rickford, *Dimensions of a Creole Continuum*, 18.

83. Ibid., 22.

84. Monar, *High House and Radio*, 79.

85. Ibid., 74.

86. Rickford, *Dimensions of a Creole Continuum*, 258.

87. Ibid., 264.

88. Abrahams, "Joking," 117.

89. Monar, *High House and Radio*, 79.

90. Ibid., 78. A cutlass was traditionally the British sailor's short sword, but on Anglophone Caribbean plantations, it refers to the machete used for cane-cutting.

91. Chickrie and Khanam, "Hindustani Muslims," 131.

92. Monar, *High House and Radio*, 67.

93. Ibid., 60.

94. In the Qur'an: (1) "Husbands should take good care of their wives, with [the bounties] God has given to some more than others and with what they spend out of their own money. Righteous wives are devout and guard what God would have them guard in their husbands' absence. If you fear high-handedness from your wives, remind them [of the teachings of God], then ignore them when you go to bed, then hit them. If they obey you, you have no right to act against them: God is most high and great." The Qur'an 4:34, 54.

(2) In reference to the biblical and Qur'anic Job's wife, who advised Job to turn away from God to relieve his suffering: "Take a small bunch of grass in your hand, and strike [her] with that so as not to break your oath." The Qur'an 4:34, 292.

95. Monar, "Pork Eater," 49.

96. Ibid., 53.

97. Ibid.

98. Monar, "Pork Eater," 44. "Putagee" is Creolese slang for "Portuguese"; small numbers of Portuguese and Chinese were also indentured in Guyana. "Christian bottom-house" refers to the small homegrown churches established by white missionaries and later Afro-Guyanese.

99. Ibid., 47–48.

100. Ibid.

101. Naipaul, *The Mystic Masseur*, 208.

102. The term *jahaji bahin* (ship sister), with variant spellings, is newer to popular usage than *jahaji bhai* (ship brother). See Khan, "Voyages across Indenture," for further discussion of contemporary uses of the term.

103. Misrahi-Barak, "Ryhaan Shah's Silent Screams," 251, 257.

104. Khan, "Protest and Punishment," 1.

105. Shah, *A Silent Life*, 72.

106. Ibid., 40–41.

107. Ibid., 180.

108. Ibid., 178.

109. Mohammed, "Changing Symbols," 11.

110. Shah, *A Silent Life*, 178.

111. Ibid.

112. Chickrie and Khanam, "Hindustani Muslims," 117.

113. Shah, *A Silent Life*, 182.

114. Ibid., 24.

115. A punt trench is an open channel filled with shallow water through which oxen and/or tractors pull "punts," flat vessels loaded with cut sugar cane stalks. They generally run on streets between the roadway and homes, and during the colonial era, stretched all the way from plantations to coastal ports. Nowadays the trenches remain but are filled with garbage and wastewater.

116. Shah, *A Silent Life*, 27.

117. Ibid., 28.

118. Ibid., 52.

119. Mohammed, "Unmasking Masculinity," 60.

120. "Desperate Measures; Suicide," 44.

121. "The 'Werther Effect' in Juvenile Suicide in Guyana."

122. Tracy et al., "Woman Fatally Stabbed."

123. Shah, *A Silent Life*, 184.

124. Ibid., 57–58.

125. Ibid., 35.

126. Ibid., 30.

127. "Do not kill each other, for God is merciful to you." In common, nonacademic Sunni translations used for worship, this is often translated as variants of "And do not kill yourselves [or one another]" (Sahih International), and "nor kill [or destroy] yourselves" (Yusuf Ali)—that is, the reflexivity of the command is unclear. The Qur'an 4:29, 106–107.

128. Shah, *A Silent Life*, 45.

129. Ibid.

130. Ibid., 54.

131. Ibid., 30.

132. Ibid., 7.

133. Ibid., 8, 12.

134. Ibid., 46.

135. Ibid., 103.

136. Ibid., 118.

137. Ibid., 123–124.

138. Ibid., 184.

139. Ibid., 119.

140. Mehta argues that "patriarchal domination received its validation through mythical inscriptions in daily life that guaranteed the permanence and 'respectability' of varying levels of control. This model eliminated the notion of male accountability or responsibility while configuring itself 'as contingent on women's acceptance and collusion with the control of female sexuality.'" *Diasporic (Dis)locations*, 95. The Rama/Sita model is then an aspirational one for both men and women, if they are to be faithful Hindus.

141. Shah, *A Silent Life*, 175.

142. Ibid., 138.

143. Ibid., 185.

144. Ibid., 129.

145. Ibid., 164.

146. Ibid.

147. Ibid., 165.

148. Ibid., 166.

CHAPTER 3   THE MARVELOUS MUSLIM

1. Mahabir, *Indian Caribbean Folklore Spirits*, 25.

2. Ibid.

3. Césaire, "Calling the Magician," 120.

4. Dabydeen, "Coolie Odyssey," 267.

5. Brand, *A Map to the Door of No Return*.

6. Harris, "History, Fable and Myth," 157, 159.

7. Limbo is a medieval doctrine that was officially removed from Catholic theology by Pope Benedict XVI in 2007 on the grounds of God's mercy for unborn and born infants. However, the afterlife of adults who died before the advent of Christ and Christian baptism remains in question, and the related doctrine of Purgatory as an intermediate state of purification for sinners still stands. See Nick Pisa, "The Pope Ends State of Limbo After 800 Years," *The Telegraph*,

April 23, 2007, https://www.telegraph.co.uk/news/worldnews/1549439/The-Pope-ends-state-of-limbo-after-800-years.html.

8. Harris, "History, Fable and Myth," 159.

9. Walcott, "The Caribbean," 11.

10. Maran's *Batouala* is an ostensibly realist novel that describes the resistance of Bantu-speaking villagers to white imperialist materialism; but the rendering of the white *boundjous* as witches with a perverse view of the reasons for and rewards of work places the novel at the beginning of the tradition of postcolonial texts that account for colonial exploitation and brutality by magically reordering the world, so that the colonizer falls outside of the bounds of humanity. Césaire's invocation of magic in service of revolution is made explicit in his narrative poem "Calling the Magician: A Few Words for a Caribbean Civilization," originally published in *Haiti-Journal*, May 20, 1944.

11. Césaire, "Calling the Magician," 122.

12. Carpentier, *El reino de este mundo*, 10–11.

13. Ibid. for the original Spanish.

14. Puri, *Caribbean Postcolonial*, 143, 140.

15. The Indo-Caribbean is a transnational, triangular space the geographic apices of which are India, the Caribbean, and the secondary diaspora cities of London, Toronto, and New York. Wilson Harris is of a mixed-race background. In my view of academic identity politics and the demands of "authentic" world literature production, it is sufficient that the milieu of the story is the Indo-Caribbean, that the characters are Indo-Caribbean, that their concerns are those of the Indo-Caribbean community.

16. Upstone, *Spatial Politics*, 74.

17. Maes-Jelinek, *Labyrinth of Universality*, 92.

18. Brathwaite, *The Arrivants*, 194.

19. *Palace of the Peacock* precedes *Oudin* in the four books of *The Guyana Quartet*. Both are set in rural British Guiana and explore the themes of multiracial, multireligious postcolonial identities in the process of "becoming" through negotiation with land-based elemental forces.

20. Byrd, *The Transit of Empire*, 112, 88.

21. Césaire, "Calling the Magician," 120.

22. Harris, "History, Fable and Myth," 156.

23. Ibid.

24. Harris, "History, Fable and Myth," 162.

25. Upon independence in 1966, British Guiana was renamed (and respelled) "The Cooperative Republic of Guyana." Of the two other Guianas, colonial Dutch Guiana became postcolonial Suriname in 1975; French Guiana retains its colonial name and is still an overseas *département* of France.

26. One of the first recorded public speeches on the subject of Indo-Guyanese history and identity and their place in the nation is Joseph Ruhomon's "India—The Progress of Her People at Home and Abroad and How Those in British Guiana May Improve Themselves," a postcolonialist lecture delivered early, in October 1894 at St. Leonard's School in Georgetown, British Guiana. Ruhomon, "India."

27. There is yet a fourth unique ecosystem in the Guyanese imagination: the segment of the ancient Precambrian Pakaraima *tepui* plateau mountain range that includes its highest point, the 9,000-foot-tall Mount Roraima.

28. This division of ecosystems is not the way in which the geography of Guyana is usually cartographically represented. Scientifically speaking, there are five ecosystems: coast, rainforest, a belt of river and sand, desert savanna, and interior savanna, including mountains. But I have categorized the ecosystems according to the way in which they live in the Guyanese national

and creative imagination. What the land can *produce* or *embody,* its use-value, is still preeminent in this division.

29. Harris, *Far Journey of Oudin,* 234.

30. Ibid., 212.

31. Tiffin, "Man Fitting the Landscape," 199.

32. Ibid.

33. Warner, *Fantastic Metamorphoses,* 164–165.

34. Ibid., 153.

35. Khan, "Indigeneity and the Indo-Caribbean."

36. Ibid., 124.

37. Braziel, "Caribbean Genesis," 123.

38. Harris, *Far Journey of Oudin,* 148, 164.

39. Harris, "A Note on the Genesis of *The Guyana Quartet,*" 10–11.

40. Harris, *Far Journey of Oudin,* 140.

41. Ibid., 158.

42. Ibid., 161.

43. Viranjini Munasinghe provides a thorough argument for an Indo-Caribbean political shift in Trinidad from Indians in a subordinate role in European colonizer/Afro-Caribbean hierarchies of power to a wholly Indo-Caribbean community capable of self-determination in her "Redefining the Nation."

44. Harris, *Far Journey of Oudin,* 161.

45. Ibid., 171.

46. Ibid., 166.

47. *Hindutva* is the present-day term for the anti-Muslim Hindu nationalism promoted by, primarily, the ruling Bharatiya Janata Party (BJP) in modern India. But this movement has its origins in and derives rhetoric from a Hindu-centric narrative of Partition and its aftermath.

48. Harris, *Far Journey of Oudin,* 209.

49. Ibid., 180.

50. Ibid., 181.

51. As noted in the previous chapter, it was a common belief among nineteenth-century Hindu Indian emigrants to the Caribbean that they would lose their caste identities if they crossed the ocean, the *kala pani* "black water." The sea was the realm of the immortals—the goddess Lakshmi, for example, rose from the "Milky Ocean" after it was churned for 1,000 years by the gods—and was also a nebulous kind of underworld, though antipathy to seafaring was more traditional taboo than religious doctrine. The belief that caste would be broken upon crossing the sea is also partially a matter of religious defilement and ritual pollution (*juthaa,* when associated with others' food) that resulted from interacting with strangers of unknown origin and caste aboard ship and in foreign lands. The majority of Indian migrants to the New World were poor rural villagers of lower castes; the opportunity to earn money, coupled with the fantasy of returning to India wealthy, was enough of a reason to take the religious risk. See Khan, *Callaloo Nation,* and Younger, *New Homelands,* for in-depth anthropological analyses of Hindu Indo-Caribbean religiosity.

52. Harris, *Far Journey of Oudin,* 231.

53. Ibid., 182.

54. Ibid., 234.

55. Ibid.

56. Ibid., 198.

57. In this way the brothers experience what W.E.B. Du Bois (1903) describes as "double consciousness," being two people in the same body and having the ability to see themselves through the eyes of the oppressor or colonizer. But overall, doubling in Harris's novel is not the same as double consciousness, as the characters in the novel repeat their existences sequentially, and do not particularly reflect on the actions of their previous selves.

58. Harris, *Far Journey of Oudin*, 146.
59. Ibid., 165.
60. Ibid., 123.
61. Ibid., 140.
62. Chickrie, "Muslims in Guyana," 184. See also Samaroo, "Seeking a Space in the Politics," and Khan, *Callaloo Nation*.
63. Harris, *Far Journey of Oudin*, 141.
64. Walcott, "The Caribbean," 8.
65. Ibid., 124.
66. Ibid., 150.
67. Ibid.
68. Ibid.
69. Schamp, "'Everything Is Illuminated,'" 117.
70. Ibid.
71. Falk, "'To Say Profitably,'" 93.
72. Dabydeen, *Molly and the Muslim Stick*, 1.
73. Darroch, *Memory and Myth*, 172.
74. Nerlekar, "Living Beadless," 15.
75. Mitchell, "The Magic of Your Making," 136.
76. Ibid.
77. Arnot, "The Loose-Tongued Ambassador," 11.
78. Falk, "'To Say Profitably,'" 91.
79. Dabydeen, *Molly and the Muslim Stick*, 71; Schamp, "Everything Is Illuminated," 122.
80. Nerlekar, "Living Beadless," 24.
81. Falk, "'To Say Profitably,'" 87.
82. Ibid., 90–91.
83. Ibid., 92.
84. Arnot, "The Loose-Tongued Ambassador," 11.
85. Falk, "'To Say Profitably,'" 95.
86. Mitchell, "The Magic of Your Making," 147.
87. Fanon, *Wretched of the Earth*, 173.
88. The problem with conventional genre articulations of magical realism is "the global market's hyper-canonization of marvelous and magic realism as ideal forms of postcolonial writing . . . [which] has generated several postcolonial and/or Marxist rejections of the forms, on grounds that magic and marvelous realist texts *lend* themselves to co-optive, assimilationist, or dehistoricizing projects, whether within postmodernism or official postcolonial nationalisms" (emphasis in original). Puri, *Caribbean Postcolonial*, 139. Postcolonial literature is particularly subject to political historicization, depending on the critic's mode of reading.
89. Agamben, *Homo Sacer*.
90. Dabydeen, *Molly and the Muslim Stick*, 2–3.
91. Ibid., 26.
92. Ibid., 27.
93. Ibid., 137.
94. Ibid., 112–113.
95. Mamdani, "Good Muslim, Bad Muslim," 766.
96. The current British Museum gallery divisions and floor plans may be viewed at http://www.britishmuseum.org/visiting/galleries.aspx.

97. Dabydeen, *Molly and the Muslim Stick*, 138.
98. Ibid., 72–73.
99. Ibid., 94.
100. Ibid., 6.
101. Ibid., 38.
102. Ibid., 73.
103. Ibid., 72.
104. Ibid., 100.
105. Ibid., 101.
106. Ibid., 101. "'I am the Alpha and the Omega,' says the Lord God, who is and who was and who is to come, the Almighty." Revelation 1:8, Coogan, 2156.
107. Dabydeen, *Molly and the Muslim Stick*, 101.
108. Ibid., 128.
109. Ibid., 155–156.
110. Ibid., 156.
111. Ibid., 172.
112. Ibid., 133.
113. Ibid., 91.
114. Ibid., 90.
115. Ibid., 96.
116. Ibid., 92.
117. Ibid.
118. Ibid.
119. Ibid., 90, 145.
120. Ibid., 101.
121. Ibid., 128.
122. Ibid., 145.
123. Ibid.
124. Ibid., 166–167.
125. Ibid., 167–168.
126. Ibid., 161.
127. Ibid., 150.
128. Ibid., 94, 154–155.
129. Ibid., 157, 154.
130. Ibid., 177.
131. Mbembe, *On the Postcolony*, 184.
132. Dabydeen, *Molly and the Muslim Stick*, 154.
133. Deuteronomy 8:3, Coogan, 265; Ezekiel 2:10, Coogan, 1164; Revelation 10:8–11, Coogan, 2166. In the last, the Book of Revelation, John says: "Then the voice that I had heard from heaven, spoke to me again, saying, 'Go, take the scroll that is open in the hand of the angel who is standing on the sea and on the land.' So I went to the angel and told him to give me the little scroll; and he said to me, 'Take it, and eat; it will be bitter to your stomach, but sweet as honey in your mouth.' So I took the little scroll from the hand of the angel and ate it; it was as sweet as honey in my mouth; but when I had eaten it, my stomach was made bitter. Then they said to me, 'You must prophesy again about many peoples and nations and languages and kings.'" Exegetically, "The *little scroll* is distinct from the seven-sealed scroll in the right hand of God. . . . This scroll is in the angel's left hand." Coogan, 2166.
134. Ezekiel 3:3, Coogan, 1164; Revelation 10:10, Coogan, 2166. Exegetically, "*Sweet*, because it contains God's words; *bitter* because it involves God's terrible judgments." Coogan, 2166.

135. Dabydeen, *Molly and the Muslim Stick*, 168.

136. Ware, *The Walking Qur'an*, 61.

137. Ibid., 62; Flood, "Bodies and Becoming," 475.

138. Ibid., 477.

139. The Qur'an 96:1, 428.

140. Dabydeen, *Molly and the Muslim Stick*, 69.

141. Ibid., 82.

142. Ibid.

143. Harris, *Far Journey of Oudin*, 125.

144. Stephanides and Singh, *Translating Kali's Feast*, 39.

145. Harris, *Far Journey of Oudin*, 135–136.

146. Ibid., 165.

147. Ibid., 217, 218.

148. Ibid., 238.

149. Harris, "Epilogue," 263.

CHAPTER 4   "MUSLIM TIME"

1. Yasin Abu Bakr, phone interview by author, Ann Arbor, Michigan/Port of Spain, Trinidad, May 11, 2019.

2. Ibid.

3. Francisco, "Abu Bakr."

4. Ibid.

5. Reddock, "Jahaji Bhai," 572.

6. In Jamaican Rastafarian terminology, "grounding" is the process whereby Rastas use the sacrament of ganja-smoking in a "grounation" event to perform a critical "reasoning" and reflect on current and historical events affecting African and Afro-Caribbean liberation from political and psychological colonialism and contemporary government oppression.

7. Rudder, "Hoosay." Lyrics from "Hoosay" are quoted by permission of David Rudder.

8. Mustapha, "Islam in the Caribbean," 1132.

9. Joseph, "Abu Bakr Take Over." Lyrics from "Abu Bakr Take Over" are quoted by permission of Fitzroy Joseph (Brother Ebony).

10. Ibid.

11. Ibid. "Rise up" or "raise up" is an invocation to get up and dance in calypso, reggae, dancehall, and affiliated genres of Caribbean music, but it also carries the connotation of rising up against governments or injustice.

12. Birth, *Bacchanalian Sentiments*, 172–173.

13. Baptiste, "More Than Dawud and Jalut," 277; Samaroo, "Early African and East Indian Muslims," 208; Korom, *Hosay Trinidad*, 99.

14. See Samaroo, "The First Ship," for an account of the voyage.

15. Khan, *Callaloo Nation*, 192, 191.

16. I use "Mandingo" rather than "Mandinka" because "Mandingo" is what the group were called in their time, and what, as a result, Muslims are called in Trinidad now.

17. Diouf, *Servants of Allah*, 139.

18. Ibid., 139.

19. Ibid., 276.

20. Baptiste, "More Than Dawud and Jalut," 276; Diouf, *Servants of Allah*, 243.

21. Diouf, *Servants of Allah*, 168–169.

22. Ibid., 112–113.

23. Ryan, *Muslimeen Grab for Power*, 73.

24. Samaroo, "Early African and East Indian Muslims," 205.

25. Diouf, *Servants of Allah*, 256.

26. Khan, "Islam, Vodou, and the Making of the Afro-Atlantic," 39–40.

27. Younger, *New Homelands*; Vertovec, "'Official' and 'Popular' Hinduism."

28. Khan, *Callaloo Nation*, 228, 214. "Comess" is Trinidadian and Caribbean slang for "confusion," and is often used in the construction "nuff comess"—plenty of mixed-up confusion.

29. Baptiste, "More Than Dawud and Jalut," 277–278.

30. Yasin Abu Bakr, phone interview by author, Ann Arbor, Michigan/Port of Spain, Trinidad, May 11, 2019.

31. Ryan, *Muslimeen Grab for Power*, 52.

32. Ibid., 51.

33. Pantin, *Days of Wrath*, 2.

34. Ryan, *Muslimeen Grab for Power*, 55.

35. Yasin Abu Bakr, phone interview by author, Ann Arbor, Michigan/Port of Spain, Trinidad, May 11, 2019.

36. Ibid.

37. Baptiste, "More Than Dawud and Jalut," 276.

38. Khan, *Callaloo Nation*, 191.

39. Though the concept of *fitra* and its applicability to conversion is explained more thoroughly in the recorded sayings of the Prophet Muhammad than in the Qur'an itself, those sayings are his interpretations of a part of the seventh Qur'anic chapter *Sura Al-A'raf* ("The Heights"), which is addressed directly to him. This section of the Qur'an, recorded in the first period of prophetic revelation in Mecca, is a critical one, as it is aimed at reassuring the earliest converts from Arabian polytheism of the righteousness of their new monotheistic beliefs and the permissibility of conversion—certainly a concern of the early Muslimeen. See The Qur'an 7:172–174, 106–107.

40. Ryan, *Muslimeen Grab for Power*, 112.

41. Ibid., 104–105.

42. Figueira, *Jihad in Trinidad and Tobago, July 27, 1990*, xx.

43. Mustapha, "Islam in the Caribbean," 1132.

44. Ryan, *Muslimeen Grab for Power*, 87.

45. Ibid., 286.

46. Ibid., 67.

47. McClane, "Pop Music."

48. Yasin Abu Bakr, phone interview by author, Ann Arbor, Michigan/Port of Spain, Trinidad, May 11, 2019.

49. Rudder, "Hoosay."

50. Niranjana, *Mobilizing India*, 153.

51. Rudder, "Hoosay."

52. Yasin Abu Bakr, phone interview by author, Ann Arbor, Michigan/Port of Spain, Trinidad, May 11, 2019.

53. Ryan, *Muslimeen Grab for Power*, 52.

54. Ibid., 54.

55. Ibid., 75–76, 58.

56. Yasin Abu Bakr, phone interview by author, Ann Arbor, Michigan/Port of Spain, Trinidad, May 11, 2019.

57. Ryan, *Muslimeen Grab for Power*, 75.

58. Yasin Abu Bakr, phone interview by author, Ann Arbor, Michigan/Port of Spain, Trinidad, May 11, 2019.

59. Ryan, *Muslimeen Grab for Power*, 65.

60. Pantin, *Days of Wrath*, 10, 9.

61. Ryan, *Muslimeen Grab for Power*, 282; Figueira, *Jihad in Trinidad and Tobago, July 27, 1990*, xxxiv.

62. Ryan, *Muslimeen Grab for Power*, 282.

63. Yasin Abu Bakr, phone interview by author, Ann Arbor, Michigan/Port of Spain, Trinidad, May 11, 2019.

64. Ibid.

65. Ryan, *Muslimeen Grab for Power*, 53–54.

66. Pantin, *Days of Wrath*, 14.

67. Yasin Abu Bakr, phone interview by author, Ann Arbor, Michigan/Port of Spain, Trinidad, May 11, 2019.

68. Figueira, *Jihad in Trinidad and Tobago, July 27*, xxxiv, xxi; "Bomb Stopped Children's Song."

69. Hydal, "Ahmadi Murdered in Guyana," 5–6.

70. Ali, "Islam in Trinidad," 73; Kassim, "Education and Socialization among the Indo-Muslims of Trinidad, 1917–1969," 106.

71. Turner, *Islam in the African-American Experience*, 115.

72. Ibid., 109–110.

73. Turner, *Islam in the African-American Experience*, 406, 232.

74. Chan-Malik, *Being Muslim: A Cultural History of Women of Color in Islam*, 73.

75. Ibid., 231.

76. Mustapha, "Islam in the Caribbean," 1132.

77. Baptiste, "More Than Dawud and Jalut," 269, 273.

78. Joseph, "Abu Bakr Take Over."

79. Ryan, *Muslimeen Grab for Power*, 101.

80. Ibid., 101–103.

81. Muslim Marriage and Divorce Act.

82. For a discussion of the three types of divorces—*talaq, khul', *and *faskh*—permissible under *sharī'a* family law, related *mahr* (gift from a groom to a bride) contract issues, and their hypothetical compatibility with non-Islamic (in this case, U.S.) jurisprudence, see Asifa Quraishi-Landes, "Rumors of the Sharia Threat Are Greatly Exaggerated."

83. Muslim Marriage and Divorce Act, 7.

84. Hindu Marriage Act, 7; Orissa Marriage and Divorce Act, 7.

85. Rather than prescribing a specific age at which marriage is permitted, the Qur'an contains a number of enjoinments for boys to marry "upon reaching full strength," and for girls to marry "when they have reached the age of marriage"; the difference is between children who have reached puberty and children who have not, as elaborated in The Qur'an 24:58–59, 225.

86. Ryan, *Muslimeen Grab for Power*, 104.

87. Ibid., 104.

88. Baptiste, "More Than Dawud and Jalut," 284.

89. Ibid., 283.

90. Ibid., 281.

91. Ibid., 287.

92. Ibid., 288.

93. Ryan, *Muslimeen Grab for Power*, 112.

94. Mahmood, *Politics of Piety*; Abu-Lughod, *Do Muslim Women Need Saving?*; Ahmed, "The Veil Debate—Again"; and Mernissi, *Beyond the Veil*.
95. Ahmed, "The Veil Debate—Again," 152.
96. Mahabir, "Adjudicating Pluralism," 436.
97. Ibid., 449.
98. Joseph, "Burka-Clad Women."
99. Ibid.
100. Cainkar and Maira, "Targeting Arab/Muslim/South Asian Americans," 12.
101. Yasin Abu Bakr, phone interview by author, Ann Arbor, Michigan/Port of Spain, Trinidad, May 11, 2019.
102. Flanagan, *Allah in the Islands*, 16.
103. Flanagan, *You Alone Are Dancing*, 8–9.
104. Wynter, "Novel and History," 95.
105. Ibid., 95, 97.
106. Ibid., 99.
107. Khan, "Voyages across Indenture," 252.
108. Glissant, *Caribbean Discourse*, 65.
109. Wynter, "Novel and History," 95.
110. Flanagan, *Allah in the Islands*, 34.
111. Ibid.
112. Ibid., 7–8.
113. Ibid., 122.
114. Ibid., 180.
115. See previous discussion of *simi-dimi*. *Ratchefee* in Trinidadian parlance is a scheme or something that seems too good to be true.
116. Flanagan, *Allah in the Islands*, 73.
117. Ibid., 101.
118. Ibid., 192.
119. Ibid., 192.
120. Ibid., 44.
121. Ibid., 41.
122. Ibid., 58–59.
123. Ibid.
124. Ibid., 43.
125. Ibid., 44.
126. Ibid., 131. From *Sura Al-Baqarah* ("The Cow"): "They ask you [Prophet] about intoxicants and gambling: say, 'There is great sin in both, and some benefit for people: the sin is greater than the benefit.' They ask you what they should give: say, 'Give what you can spare.' In this way, God makes His messages clear to you, so that you may reflect." The Qur'an 2:219, 24.
127. Flanagan, *Allah in the Islands*, 131.
128. Ibid., 200.
129. Ibid., 12.
130. Ibid., 40.
131. Ibid., 39.
132. Ibid., 12.
133. Ibid., 153.
134. Ibid., 12.
135. Ibid.
136. Ibid., 144.

137. Ibid., 194.

138. Ibid.

139. Ibid., 188–189.

140. Reddock, "Jahaji Bhai," 574; Puri, *Caribbean Postcolonial*, 221.

141. Despite a desire to rehabilitate the term, "it is however, undeniable that 'dougla' carries many sedimented meanings, not all of which are politically suggestive or progressive. The figure of the dougla often functions in both African and Indian purist discourses, as well as in some pro-PNM discourses, as a code-word for assimilation and racial 'dilution.'" Puri, *Caribbean Postcolonial*, 197.

142. Ibid.

143. Ibid., 193.

144. Reddock, "Jahaji Bhai," 590, 593.

145. Niranjana, *Mobilizing India*, 136.

146. Ibid., 113.

147. Mehta, *Diasporic (Dis)locations*, 220.

148. Chutney lyrics generally deal with the quotidian of rural and working-class Indian experiences; it is folk music, the people's music. Mehta compares the movements when performed by Indian women on stage and in dancing to birthing, orgasm, and general female sensuality, and reads sexually suggestive "wining" as an expression of female agency. Ibid., 98.

149. Demming, "Jahaji Bhai."

150. Reddock, "Jahaji Bhai," 581.

151. Ibid., 577.

152. Demming, "Jahaji Bhai."

153. Niranjana, *Mobilizing India*, 163.

154. Ballantyne, "Jahaji Blues." Lyrics from "Jahaji Blues" are quoted by permission of Gregory Ballantyne (G. B.).

155. Ibid.

156. Niranjana, *Mobilizing India*, 163.

157. Gregory Ballantyne, phone conversation with author, Ann Arbor, Michigan/Curepe, Trinidad, May 11, 2019.

158. Bakhtin says, "Carnival is not a spectacle seen by the people; they live in it, and everyone participates because its very idea embraces all the people. While carnival lasts, there is no other life outside it. During carnival time life is subject only to its laws, that is, the laws of its own freedom." *Rabelais and His World*, 7–8.

159. Ibid., 10, 92.

160. Ibid.

161. Ryan, *Muslimeen Grab for Power*, 52.

162. Ibid., 208.

163. Ibid., 201.

164. Ibid., 171.

165. See Vásquez, *Humor in the Caribbean Literary Canon*, on how humor and jokery challenge colonial legacies in the Caribbean.

166. Ryan, *Muslimeen Grab for Power*, 208.

167. Pantin, *Days of Wrath*, 48.

168. Ibid., 50.

169. Ibid., 134.

170. Ibid., 148–149.

171. Ibid., 148.

172. Ibid., 171.

173. Ibid., 53.
174. Flanagan, *Allah in the Islands*, 215.
175. Birth, *Bacchanalian Sentiments*, 156, 151.
176. McClane, "Pop Music."
177. Ibid.
178. Ibid.
179. Ibid.
180. Birth, *Bacchanalian Sentiments*, 178.
181. Ibid., 165.
182. Flanagan, *Allah in the Islands*, 127. "Dread" means "terrible" with much suffering; but "a Dread" is a Rastafarian with dreadlocks.
183. Ibid.
184. Ibid., 73.
185. From an October 1937 Garvey speech given in Nova Scotia, Canada: "We are going to emancipate ourselves from mental slavery because whilst others might free the body, none but ourselves can free the mind. Mind is your only ruler, sovereign. The man who is not able to develop and use his mind is bound to be the slave of the other man who uses his mind, because man is related to man under all circumstances for good or for ill. If man is not able to protect himself from the other man he should use his mind to good advantage." Garvey, "Speech," 791; Bob Marley and the Wailers, "Redemption Song."
186. Rastafarians, referencing together the Old Testament stories of prideful, polyglot Babylon and Jewish exile in Egypt, use "Babylon" to mean oppressive human government and its material manifestations like the law and police.
187. Flanagan, *Allah in the Islands*, 98.
188. Ibid., 108. "Nenen" technically means "godmother," from Trinidad's mostly defunct Afro-French Creole dialect, but "to catch your nenen" now means to catch hell or to suffer a hard time.
189. Ibid., 97.
190. Ibid., 101.
191. Rawlins, "Say a Prayer for Abu Bakr." Lyrics from "Say a Prayer for Abu Bakr" are quoted by permission of Weston Rawlins (Cro Cro).
192. Ibid.
193. Yasin Abu Bakr, phone interview by author, Ann Arbor, Michigan/Port of Spain, Trinidad, May 11, 2019.
194. Ibid.
195. Ibid.

CHAPTER 5   MIMIC MAN AND ETHNORIENTALIST

Epigraph: "CIOG Slams Lawyer," 8.
Epigraph: Moynihan, "Life Sentence for Leader of Terror Plot," A24.
1. Alsultany, *Arabs and Muslims in the Media*, 21.
2. Said, *Orientalism; Covering Islam;* and *Culture and Imperialism*.
3. Johnson, *African American Religions, 1500–2000*, 394.
4. "CIOG Slams Lawyer," 8.
5. Ibid.
6. "Kadir Had Links to Iran," 9. The Jamaat al Muslimeen denied ties to the four men, with the *New York Times* reporting that twenty years after their attempted coup, the Muslimeen were

"both Islamists and islanders, devoted to God but also part of the multicultural mix that defines the Caribbean nation of Trinidad and Tobago." Lacey, "Trinidad Group Denies Link," A3.

7. Sulzberger, "Lawyers Dispute Suspects' Intent in J.F.K. Bomb Plot Trial," A29.

8. "Sympathy Motion for Abdul Kadir," 6.

9. "US Condemns Kadir Motion," 3.

10. "Canada Criticises Kadir Motion," 10.

11. Ibid., 21.

12. Hamid and Baksh, "Islam in Guyana," 393.

13. "A Nation Challenged," B4.

14. Ibid.

15. Hall, "The Local and the Global," 21–22.

16. Ibid., 36, 21.

17. Johnson, *African American Religions, 1500–2000*, 395.

18. Hall, "Cultural Identity and Diaspora," 234.

19. Ibid., 236.

20. Shinebourne, *Chinese Women*, 31.

21. Ibid., 89.

22. Chickrie, "Muslims in Guyana," 182.

23. Samaroo notes that by 1890, there were twenty-nine mosques in Guyana, and by 1920, fifty. Samaroo, "Seeking a Space in the Politics," 203, 202.

24. Seecharan, *India and the Shaping of the Indo-Guyanese Imagination*, 41.

25. Khaled Mattawa, e-mail message to author, January 28, 2018.

26. "Libya Joins Guyana," 2.

27. de Kruijf, "Muslim Transnationalism in Indo-Guyana," 110.

28. Bakr, "The Former Foreign 'Friends' of Gaddafi," 9.

29. "GIT Condemns Actions of Islamic State of Iraq," 9.

30. "'My Concert Is for All'"; "Sami Yusuf Concert Stirs Controversy in Guyana."

31. de Kruijf, "Muslim Transnationalism in Indo-Guyana," 114.

32. Ibid., 113.

33. Ibid., 114. Each of Guyana's three major religions—Christianity, Hinduism, and Islam—was apportioned two national public holidays upon the establishment of the independent post-colonial state. The other Muslim public holiday is *Eid-al-Adha*, commemorating the Abrahamic sacrifice.

34. Ibid., 113.

35. de Kruijf, "Muslim Transnationalism in Indo-Guyana," 106, 107.

36. Chickrie, "Muslims in Guyana," 183.

37. Mignolo, "Delinking," 450.

38. Naipaul, *The Mystic Masseur*, 208.

39. Ibid., viii.

40. Benjamin, "Doctrine of the Similar," 65.

41. Caillois, "Mimicry and Legendary Psychaesthenia," 99–100.

42. Bhabha, *The Location of Culture*, 129.

43. Ibid., 122–123.

44. Naipaul, *A Way in the World*, 8, 10.

45. Ibid., 8.

46. Dayan, *Haiti, History, and the Gods*, 59; Fernández Olmos & Paravisini-Gebert, *Creole Religions of the Caribbean*, 168, 171.

47. Khan, "Islam, Vodou, and the Making of the Afro-Atlantic," 32.

48. The Qur'anic justification for this belief is in *Sura Al-Baqarah* ("The Cow"): "Do not . . . set up rivals to God. If you have doubts about the revelation We have sent down to Our servant, then produce a single sura like it—enlist whatever supporters you have other than God— if you truly [think you can]. If you cannot do this—and you never will—then beware of the Fire prepared for the disbelievers, whose fuel is men and stones." The Qur'an 2:21–24, 6.

49. Fernández Olmos & Paravisini-Gebert, *Creole Religions of the Caribbean*, 43.

50. Naipaul, *A Way in the World*, 8.

51. Ibid.

52. Coovadia, *Authority and Authorship in V.S. Naipaul*, 120.

53. Khan, "*Juthaa* in Trinidad," 245–246.

54. Ibid., 246.

55. Coovadia, *Authority and Authorship in V.S. Naipaul*, 119; Donnell, "V.S. Naipaul, a Queer Trinidadian," 59.

56. Ibid., 60.

57. Said, *Covering Islam*, 8.

58. Mottale, "V.S. Naipaul and Islam," 71.

59. Ibid., 8.

60. Yamamoto, "Swaying in Time and Space," 175.

61. Lee-Loy, "Saying No to Chineseness," 298, 299.

62. Yamamoto, "Swaying in Time and Space," 175.

63. Lee-Loy, "Saying No to Chineseness," 308.

64. Misrahi-Barak, "Looking In, Looking Out," 10.

65. Lee-Loy, "Saying No to Chineseness," 296. See also Walton Look Lai's *The Chinese in the West Indies, 1806–1995: A Documentary History* (2000) and *Indentured Labor, Caribbean Sugar: Chinese and Indian Migrants to the British West Indies, 1838–1918* (2004).

66. Lee-Loy, "Saying No to Chineseness," 297.

67. Misrahi-Barak, "Looking In, Looking Out," 2.

68. Lee-Loy, "'. . . The Chinese Are Preferred to All Others,'" 220, 219.

69. Shinebourne, *Chinese Women*, 38.

70. Ibid., 53.

71. Ibid., 34–35.

72. Ibid., 51–52.

73. Ibid., 205–206.

74. Ibid., 216–218.

75. Ibid., 218; Henry Kirke, "Twenty-five Years in British Guiana" (London: Sampson Low, Marston & Company, 1898). Qtd. in Lee-Loy, "'. . . The Chinese Are Preferred to All Others,'" 217.

76. Lee-Loy, "'. . . The Chinese Are Preferred to All Others,'" 215.

77. Shinebourne, *Chinese Women*, 47.

78. Ibid., 47.

79. Ibid., 53.

80. Lee-Loy, "'. . . The Chinese Are Preferred to All Others,'" 222.

81. Shinebourne, *Chinese Women*, 79.

82. Ibid.

83. Ibid., 10.

84. Ibid., 33.

85. Ibid., 8.

86. Ibid., 30–31.

87. Ibid., 52.

88. Ibid., 31.
89. Descartes compares animals to "automata" and "moving machines." Even if they could speak or control their own bodies, they would still not be like humans because "they did not act consciously, but only because their organs were disposed in a certain way." Descartes, *Discourse on the Method*, 46–47. After his fall, Aziz, winding his way around the colonial world, could be said to be such a moving machine.
90. Shinebourne, *Chinese Women*, 32.
91. Ibid., 82–84.
92. Ibid., 82.
93. Ibid., 89.
94. Ibid., 89–90.
95. Ibid., 93.
96. Lee-Loy, "Saying No to Chineseness," 299.
97. Ibid., 302.
98. Said, *Covering Islam*, 9.
99. Ibid., 10.
100. "Muslim Brotherhood of Guyana," 5.
101. Shabazz, "Black Muslims Speak: The Role of Guyana's Black Muslims," 7–8.
102. Shabazz, "Black Muslims Speak: The 12 Principles of Guyana's Black Muslims," 7.
103. Ibid.
104. Coghlan, "Sun, Sea, and Jihad"; "El-Shukrijumah New Al-Qaeda Operations Chief—FBI"; Fraser, "Another Trini Discovered Fighting in Syria for ISIS"; Mosendz, "Jamaican Teenager Accused of Trying to Join ISIS"; and Powers, "Caribbean Nationals Join Forces with ISIS."
105. Robles, "In Caribbean, Racing to Foil Flow of Jihad," A1.
106. Cottee, "The Calypso Caliphate," 306–308.
107. Ibid., 306.
108. Ibid., 297; "Full Interview: *Dabiq* with Abu Sa'd at-Trinidadi."
109. Robles, "In Caribbean, Racing to Foil Flow of Jihad," A1.
110. Tillerson, "Department of State Public Notice 9944," 16466–16467.
111. Cottee, "The Calypso Caliphate," 298.
112. Ibid., 297.
113. "Full Interview: *Dabiq* with Abu Sa'd at-Trinidadi."
114. Cottee, "The Calypso Caliphate," 313.
115. "AgCoP: The Jamaat Al Muslimeen Threat Memo is True"; and "Jamaat Al Muslimeen: We Are No Threat."
116. "Jamaat Al Muslimeen: We Are No Threat."
117. Cottee, "The Calypso Caliphate," 312, 298.
118. Ibid., 313.
119. Ibid.
120. Yasin Abu Bakr, phone interview by author, Michigan/Port of Spain, Trinidad, May 11, 2019.
121. Ibid.
122. Cottee, "The Calypso Caliphate," 298.
123. Anti-Terrorism Act, 10.
124. Powers, "Caribbean Nationals Join Forces with ISIS"; and Mosendz, "General Warns of ISIS Fighters, Entering U.S. through Caribbean."
125. Mosendz, "General Warns of ISIS Fighters, Entering U.S. through Caribbean."
126. Ibid.

127. Ibid.

128. Shinebourne, *Chinese Women*, 89.

129. Ibid., 8.

130. Ibid., 32.

131. Ibid., 89–90.

132. Sudhakar, "Muslim, Interrupted."

133. Hamid, *The Reluctant Fundamentalist*, 72–73.

134. Fanon, *The Wretched of the Earth*.

135. Hamid, *The Reluctant Fundamentalist*, 130.

136. Shinebourne, *Chinese Women*, 90.

137. Ibid.

138. Ibid.

139. Ibid., 93–94.

140. Ibid., 79.

141. Winter, "My Enemies Must Be Friends," 35–36.

142. Ibid., 36.

143. Sudhakar, "Muslim, Interrupted."

CONCLUSION

1. Yasin Abu Bakr, phone interview by author, Ann Arbor, Michigan/Port of Spain, Trinidad, May 11, 2019.

2. Ibid.

3. "Full Interview: *Dabiq* with Abu Sa'd at-Trinidadi."

4. Khan, "Contours," 26.

5. Walcott, "The Antilles."

6. Ibid.; and Carpentier, *El reino de este mundo*, 10–11.

7. See https://corporate.exxonmobil.com/en/locations/guyana for an overview of Exxon Mobil activities and plans in Guyana.

8. "Guyana Signs Air Services Agreement with the State of Qatar."

9. "Qatar Petroleum Takes Stake in Total's Guyana Assets."

10. Ibid.

11. Ibid.

BIBLIOGRAPHY

I. LITERATURE AND SACRED TEXTS

ad-Darqawi, Mawlay al-'Arabi. *The Darqawi Way: Letters from the Shaykh to the Fuqara*. Translated by Aisha Bewley. Norwich, UK: Diwan Press, 1981.

Benjamin, Joel, Lakhsmi Kallicharan, Ian McDonald, and Lloyd Searwar, eds. *They Came in Ships: An Anthology of Indo-Guyanese Prose and Poetry*. Leeds: Peepal Tree Press, 1998.

Brand, Dionne. *A Map to the Door of No Return: Notes to Belonging*. Toronto: Vintage Canada, 2001.

Brathwaite, Edward Kamau. *The Arrivants: A New World Trilogy*. 1973. Reprint, Oxford: Oxford University Press, 1996.

Carpentier, Alejo. *El reino de este mundo (Relato)*. Mexico, D.F.: Edición y Distribución Iberoamericana de Publicaciones, S.A., 1949.

Coogan, Michael D., ed. *The New Oxford Annotated Bible: New Revised Standard Version with the Apocrypha*. 4th ed. New York: Oxford University Press, 2010.

Dabydeen, David. "Coolie Odyssey." In *They Came in Ships: An Anthology of Indo-Guyanese Prose and Poetry*, edited by Joel Benjamin, Lakhsmi Kallicharan, Ian McDonald, and Lloyd Searwar, 263–267. Leeds: Peepal Tree Press, 1998.

———. *Coolie Odyssey*. 1988. Reprint, Hertford, Hertfordshire, UK: Hansib, 2006.

———. *Molly and the Muslim Stick*. Oxford: Macmillan Caribbean, 2008.

———. *Our Lady of Demerara*. 2004. Reprint, Leeds: Peepal Tree Press, 2009.

———. *Slave Song*. 1984. Reprint, Leeds: Peepal Tree Press, 2005.

Das, Mahadai. *Bones*. Leeds: Peepal Tree Press, 1988.

———. *I Want to Be a Poetess of My People*. Georgetown, Guyana: National History and Arts Council, 1976, 1977.

———. *A Leaf in His Ear: Selected Poems*. Leeds: Peepal Tree Press, 2010.

Espinet, Ramabai. *The Swinging Bridge*. 2003. Reprint, Toronto: HarperPerennialCanada, 2004.

Flanagan, Brenda. *Allah in the Islands*. Leeds: Peepal Tree Press, 2009.

———. *You Alone Are Dancing*. Ann Arbor: University of Michigan Press, 1996.

Hamid, Mohsen. *The Reluctant Fundamentalist*. 2007. Reprint, Orlando: Harcourt Books, 2008.

Harris, Wilson. *The Far Journey of Oudin*. 1961. Reprinted in *The Guyana Quartet*, 2, 119–238. London: Faber and Faber, 1985.

Hopkinson, Abdur-Rahman Slade. *Snowscape with Signature: Poems, 1952–1992*. Leeds: Peepal Tree Books, 1993.

Jenkins, Edward. *Lutchmee and Dilloo: A Study of West Indian Life*. 1877. Reprint, Oxford: Macmillan, 2003.

Kabā Saghanughu, Muhammad. "The Kitāb al-Salāt of Muhammad Kabā Saghanughu of Jamaica c. 1823." Appendix, "The Arabic Manuscript of Muhammad Kabā Saghanughu of Jamaica, c.1820," edited and translated by Yacine Daddi Adoun and Paul E. Lovejoy. In *Caribbean Culture: Soundings on Kamau Brathwaite*, edited by Annie Paul, 326–332. Kingston, Jamaica: University of the West Indies Press, 2007.

Khan, Ismith. *The Jumbie Bird*. 1961. Reprint, New York: Longman, 1994.

Khan, Munshi Rahman. *Autobiography of an Indian Indentured Labourer: Munshi Rahman Khan (1874–1972): Jeevan Prakash*. Translated by Kathinka Sinha-Kerkhoff, Ellen Bal, and Alok Deo Singh. Delhi: Shipra Publications, 2005.

Lovelace, Earl. *The Dragon Can't Dance: A Novel*. 1979. Reprint, New York: Persea Books, 2003.

Madden, R. R. *A Twelvemonth's Residence in the West Indies, during the Transition from Slavery to Apprenticeship*. Vol. 2. Philadelphia: Carey, Lea and Blanchard, 1835.

Mahabir, Kumar. *Indian Caribbean Folklore Spirits*. San Juan, Trinidad and Tobago: Chakra Publishing House, 2010.

Melville, Pauline. "Erzulie." In *The Migration of Ghosts*, 135–167. London: Bloomsbury, 1998.

Mohan, Peggy. *Jahajin*. Noida, Uttar Pradesh: HarperCollins India, 2007.

Monar, Rooplall. *Backdam People*. Leeds: Peepal Tree Press, 1987.

———. *Estate People: A Collection of Short Stories*. Georgetown, Guyana: Roraima Publishers, 1994.

———. *High House and Radio*. Leeds: Peepal Tree Press, 1991.

———. *Janjhat*. Leeds: Peepal Tree Press, 1989.

———. *Koker*. Leeds: Peepal Tree Press, 1987.

———. "Pork Eater." *Bim* 19, no. 73 and *Kyk-Over-Al* 41 Joint Issue (June 1990): 44–54.

Mootoo, Shani. *Cereus Blooms at Night*. New York: Grove Press, 1996.

———. *Valmiki's Daughter*. 2008. Reprint, Toronto: House of Anansi Press, 2010.

Naipaul, V. S. *Among the Believers: An Islamic Journey*. 1981. Reprint, New York: Vintage, 1982.

———. *Beyond Belief: Islamic Excursions among the Converted Peoples*. 1998. Reprint, New York: Vintage, 1999.

———. *A House for Mr. Biswas*. 1961. Reprint, New York: Vintage International, 2001.

———. *The Middle Passage: The Caribbean Revisited*. New York: Vintage, 2002.

———. *Miguel Street*. 1959. Reprint, New York: Vintage International, 2002.

———. *The Mystic Masseur*. 1957. Reprint, New York: Vintage International, 2002.

———. *A Way in the World: A Novel*. 1994. Reprint, New York: Vintage, 1995.

Persaud, Lakshmi. *Raise the Lanterns High*. London: BlackAmber Books, 2004.

The Qur'an. Translated by M.A. S. Abdel Haleem. Oxford: Oxford University Press, 2010.

Shah, Ryhaan. *A Death in the Family*. London: Cutting Edge Press, 2014.

———. *A Silent Life*. Leeds: Peepal Tree Press, 2005.

———. *Weaving Water*. London: Cutting Edge Press, 2013.

Shinebourne, Jan Lowe. *Chinese Women: A Novel*. Leeds: Peepal Tree Press, 2010.

———. *The Godmother and Other Stories*. Leeds: Peepal Tree Press, 2004.

———. *The Last English Plantation*. 2nd ed. Leeds: Peepal Tree Press, 2002.

———. *The Last Ship*. Leeds: Peepal Tree Press, 2015.

———. *Timepiece*. Rev. ed. Leeds: Peepal Tree Press, 2012.

II. DISCOGRAPHY

Bailey, Winston (Mighty Shadow). "Poverty Is Hell." In *Dingolay*. Barbados: Kisskidee Records KR 1037, 1994.

Ballantyne, Gregory (G. B.). "Jahaji Blues." 1997. YouTube, March 13, 2013. https://youtu.be /ESIbaVBVWSM.

Bob Marley and the Wailers. "Redemption Song." In *Uprising*. Kingston, Jamaica: Tuff Gong/ Island Records 422-846 211-1, 1980, LP.

Demming, Selwyn (Brother Marvin). "Jahaji Bhai." 1996. In *Power of a Song*. Trinidad: Klub Karnival Productions RTR 737, 1997, LP.

Discography of American Historical Recordings, s.v. "Victor matrix G-133. Moulood-Sharief [No. I] / S. M. Akberali." 1914. Accessed October 16, 2015. http://adp.library.ucsb.edu /index.php/matrix/detail/600000582/G-133-Moulood-Sharief_No._I.

Francisco, Slinger (Mighty Sparrow). "Abu Bakr." In *We Could Make It Easy If We Try*. U.S. Virgin Islands: BLS Records BLS1011LP, 1991, LP.

Henry, Barnet (Preacher), and Leston Paul and the New York Connection. "Abu Baka Take Over." In *Abu Baka Take Over*. Brooklyn, NY: J. W. Productions JW-LPD-038, 1991, LP.

Joseph, Fitzroy (Brother Ebony). "Abu Bakr Take Over." 1991. In *Best of Straker's: Ah Feel to Party* (Disc 1). Boston, MA: Rounder Records CD 5066/67, 1996, CD.

Marley, Damian "Jr. Gong." "Road to Zion." Featuring Nas. In *Welcome to Jamrock*. Universal Records/Tuff Gong/Ghetto Youths United B0005413-02, September 12, 2005, CD.

Rawlins, Weston (Cro Cro). "Say a Prayer for Abu Bakr." In *Still de Best*. Brooklyn, NY: Straker's Records GS 2338 A, 1991, LP.

Rudder, David. "Hoosay." In *Rough and Ready*. Barbados: Lypsoland CR 016, 1991, LP.

Siddīq, Khāled. "My Grandfather Was a Muslim (Official Lyric Video)." YouTube, November 20, 2017. https://youtu.be/4rPGC1XpiWw.

———. "On Deen (Part II)." YouTube, April 10, 2018. https://youtu.be/aXDcEa8PoPc.

———. "Road to Palestine." YouTube, May 14, 2017. https://youtu.be/ATon83aCocM.

Tijani, Sayeed (Tijani Concious). "Baye Niasse (Boom Baye)." YouTube, January 2, 2015. https://youtu.be/WBmzY6Cw5aU.

———. "Fulani Woman." In *A King No Castle*. MediaLight Productions, Salaam Entertainment, March 25, 2015, MP3.

III. INTERVIEWS, LEGAL DOCUMENTS, AND PAMPHLETS

Ahamad, Anesa. "Transcript of B.B.C.'s Interview with Dr. Anesa Ahamad-Khan (1995)." Interview by BBC. In *The Call: Journal of the Ahmadiyya Anjuman Ishā'at-I-Islam Inc. Trinidad & Tobago* 21, no. 12 (April 28, 1996/Dhul-Hijjah 10, 1416): 2.

Anti-Terrorism Act. Act 26 of 2005, Amended by 15 of 2014. *Laws of Trinidad and Tobago* 12:07 (2014): 6–56.

"Bomb Stopped Children's Song." *Trinidad and Tobago Express*, August 16, 1983, 5. Reprinted in *Al-Aḥmadiyya: Journal of the Ahmadiyya Anjuman Ishā'at Islam (Lahore) UK* 5, nos 7/8/9 (July-August-September 1983): 35–36.

The Constitution of The Republic of Trinidad and Tobago. 1959. Act 4 of 1976, Amended by 12 of 2007. *Laws of Trinidad and Tobago* 1:01 (2007): 16–130.

Goring, Michael. "The Story of Hosay: Dancing the Moon." Interview by TriniView.com. June 27, 2005. http://www.triniview.com/hosay/2706051.html.

Hindu Marriage Act. Act 13 of 1945, Amended by 6 of 1993. *Laws of Trinidad and Tobago* 45:03 (1993): 4–14.

Hydal, Mustapha K., ed. "Ahmadi Murdered in Guyana." *The Call: Journal of the Ahmadiyya Anjuman Ishā'at-I-Islam* 2, nos 9/10 (May–June 1986/Ramadaan-Shawwal 1406): 5–6.

Marriage Act. Act 13 of 1923, Amended by 159 of 2013. *Laws of Trinidad and Tobago* 45:01 (2013): 6–25.

Muslim Marriage and Divorce Act. Act 7 of 1961, Amended by 6 of 1993. *Laws of Trinidad and Tobago* 45:02 (1993): 5–14.

Orisa Marriage and Divorce Act. Act 22 of 1999. *Laws of Trinidad and Tobago* 45:04 (1999): 5–16.

Tillerson, Rex W. "Department of State Public Notice 9944: E.O. 13224 Designation of Shane Dominic Crawford, aka Asadullah, aka Abu Sa'd at-Trinidadi, aka Shane Asadullah Crawford, aka Asad, as a Specially Designated Global Terrorist." *Federal Register* 82, no. 63 (April 4, 2017): 16466–16467.

Tufail, S. Muhammad, ed. "A Recipe of Violence." In *Al-Ahmadiyya: Journal of the Ahmadiyya Anjuman Ishā'at Islam (Lahore) UK* 5, nos 7/8/9 (July–August–September 1983): 3–4.

"Vocal Recording in Trinidad and Tobago." Port of Spain, Trinidad: Carnival Institute of Trinidad and Tobago, National Carnival Commission of Trinidad and Tobago, October 20, 2016.

IV. NEWS ARTICLES

"Abdhur Rahman Slade Hopkinson—The Forgotten Poet." *Guyana Times International*, January 25, 2013. https://www.guyanatimesinternational.com/?p=23815.

"AgCoP: The Jamaat Al Muslimeen Threat Memo Is True." *Trinidad and Tobago Express*, July 29, 2015. http://www.trinidadexpress.com/20150729/news/ag-cop-the-jamaat-al-muslimeen-threat-memo-is-true.

Arnot, Chris. "The Loose-Tongued Ambassador: Interview [with] David Dabydeen." *The Guardian*, April 1, 2008, 11.

Bakr, Abu. "The Former Foreign 'Friends' of Gaddafi Are Now Positioning Themselves to Do Business with His Inheritors." *Stabroek News*, February 27, 2011, 9.

"Canada Criticises Kadir Motion." *Stabroek News*, May 2, 2019, 10, 21.

"CIOG Slams Lawyer over Demand Woman Remove Hijab for Cross-Examination." *Stabroek News*, June 22, 2013, 8.

Coghlan, Tom. "Sun, Sea, and Jihad: Fears over ISIS in the Caribbean: Trinidad." *The Times*, London, April 30, 2016, 30.

Cottee, Simon. "ISIS in the Caribbean." *The Atlantic*, December 8, 2016. https://amp.theatlantic.com/amp/article/509930/.

"Court Awards Judgment for Muslim Cleric Who Was 'Wrongfully' Detained." *Kaieteur News*, April 27, 2013. https://www.kaieteurnewsonline.com/2013/04/27/court-awards-judgment-for-muslim-cleric-who-was-wrongfully-detained/.

"Desperate Measures; Suicide: When It Comes to People Taking Their Own Lives, Guyana Leads the World." *The Economist*, September 13, 2014, 44.

"El-Shukrijumah New Al-Qaeda Operations Chief—FBI." *Stabroek News*, August 7, 2010, 8.

Fraser, Mark. "Another Trini Discovered Fighting in Syria for ISIS." *Trinidad and Tobago Express*, October 22, 2014. http://www.trinidadexpress.com/news/Another-Trini-discovered-fighting-in-Syria-for-ISIS-280140192.html.

"Full Interview: *Dabiq* with Abu Sa'd at-Trinidadi." *CNC3*, August 2, 2016. https://www.cnc3.co.tt/press-release/full-interview-dabiq-abu-sad-trinidadi.

"GIT Condemns Actions of Islamic State of Iraq." *Stabroek News*, August 26, 2014, 9.

"Guyana Signs Air Services Agreement with the State of Qatar." *Guyana Civil Aviation Authority*, September 26, 2019. https://gcaa-gy.org/guyana-signs-air-services-agreement-with-the-state-of-qatar/.

Hopkinson, Abdur-Rahman Slade. "Be Careful with Details about Islam, Reader Urges." *Globe and Mail*, August 23, 1979, 7.

"Jamaat Al Muslimeen: We Are No Threat." *Trinidad and Tobago Express*, July 29, 2015. http://www.trinidadexpress.com/20150729/news/jamaat-al-muslimeen-we-are-no-threat.

Joseph, Francis. "Burka-Clad Women Can Sit on Jury." *Trinidad and Tobago Guardian*, February 26, 2010. http://www.guardian.co.tt/archives/news/general/2010/02/25/burka-clad-women-can-sit-jury.

"Kadir Had Links to Iran—U.S. Prosecutors." *Stabroek News*, July 25, 2010, 9.

Lacey, March. "Trinidad Group Denies Link to New York Bomb Plot." *New York Times*, June 10, 2007, A3.

"Libya Joins Guyana." *New Amsterdam News*, September 12, 1981, 2.

McClane, Daisann. "Pop Music: In Trinidad, 'Calypso Diplomacy' with a Beat." *New York Times*, March 31, 1991. www.nytimes.com/1991/03/31/arts/pop-music-in-trinidad-calypso-diplomacy-with-a-beat.html.

Mosendz, Polly. "General Warns of ISIS Fighters Entering U.S. through Caribbean." *Newsweek*, March 13, 2015. http://www.newsweek.com/general-warns-isis-fighters-entering-us-through-caribbean-313807.

———. "Jamaican Teenager Accused of Trying to Join ISIS Weeks after U.S. General Warns of Radicalized Caribbean Natives." *Newsweek*, April 13, 2015. http://www.newsweek.com/jamaican-teenager-accused-trying-join-isis-weeks-after-us-general-warns-322002.

"'My Concert Is for All'—Sami Yusuf Tells Guyanese." *Kaieteur News*, September 28, 2013. http://www.kaieteurnewsonline.com/2013/09/28/my-concert-is-for-all-sami-yusuf-tells-guyanese/.

"A Nation Challenged: President Bush's Address on Terrorism before a Joint Meeting of Congress." *New York Times*, September 21, 200, B4.

Powers, Martine. "Caribbean Nationals Join Forces with ISIS." *Miami Herald*, October 15, 2014. http://www.miamiherald.com/news/nation-world/world/americas/article2838599.html.

"Qatar Petroleum Takes Stake in Total's Guyana Assets." *Stabroek News*, July 30, 2019, 10.

Robles, Frances. "In Caribbean, Racing to Foil Flow of Jihad." *New York Times*, February 22, 2017, A1.

"Sami Yusuf Concert Stirs Controversy in Guyana." *Caribbean Muslims: News, History, Religion and Culture*, September 20, 2013. https://www.caribbeanmuslims.com/sami-yusuf-concert-stirs-guyana/.

Shabazz, Malik. "Black Muslims Speak: The 12 Principles of Guyana's Black Muslims." *The Clarion*, July 31, 1965, 7.

———. "Black Muslims Speak: The Role of Guyana's Black Muslims," *The Clarion*, December 31, 1965, 7–8.

Sulzberger, A. G. "Lawyers Dispute Suspects' Intent in J.F.K. Bomb Plot Trial." *New York Times*, July 1, 2010, A29.

"Sympathy Motion for Abdul Kadir." *Stabroek News*, April 29, 2019, 6.

Tracy, Thomas, Kerry Burke, and Larry McShane. "Woman Fatally Stabbed in Queens Home, Abusive Husband Found Hanging from Tree in Suspected Murder-Suicide." *New York Daily News*, January 1, 2018. http://www.nydailynews.com/new-york/queens/queens-woman-found-stabbed-death-home-article-1.3731590.

"US Condemns Kadir Motion: Guyana Gov't Says Regrets Interpretation Placed on It, Restates Commitment to Fight Terrorism." *Stabroek News*, April 30, 2019, 3, 21.

"The 'Werther Effect' in Juvenile Suicide in Guyana." *Kaieteur News*, June 8, 2014. http://www.kaieteurnewsonline.com/2014/06/08/the-werther-effect-in-juvenile-suicide-in-guyana/.

V. SECONDARY SOURCES AND SCHOLARSHIP

Abbas, Sadia. *At Freedom's Limit: Islam and the Postcolonial Predicament*. New York: Fordham University Press, 2014.

Abrahams, Roger D. "Joking: The Training of the Man-of-Words in Talking Broad." In *Perspectives on the Caribbean: A Reader in Culture, History, and Representation*, edited by Philip W. Scher, 115–128. Chichester, UK: Wiley-Blackwell, 2010.

Abu-Lughod, Lila. *Do Muslim Women Need Saving?* Cambridge, MA: Harvard University Press, 2013.

Addoun, Yacine Daddi, and Paul E. Lovejoy. "The Arabic Manuscript of Muhammad Kabā Saghanughu of Jamaica, c.1820." In *Caribbean Culture: Soundings on Kamau Brathwaite*, edited by Annie Paul, 313–341. Kingston, Jamaica: University of the West Indies Press, 2007.

———. "Muhammad Kabā Saghanughu and the Muslim Community of Jamaica." In *Slavery on the Frontiers of Islam*, edited by Paul E. Lovejoy, 199–218. Princeton, NJ: Markus Wiener Publishers, 2004.

Adebayo, A.G. "Of Man and Cattle: A Reconsideration of the Traditions of Origin of Pastoral Fulani of Nigeria." *History in Africa* 18 (1991): 1–21.

Afroz, Sultana. "*As-Salaamu-Alaikum*: The Invincibility of Islam in Jamaican Heritage." *Wadabagei* 10, no. 2 (Spring-Summer 2007): 5–39.

———. *Invisible Yet Invincible: The Islamic Heritage of the Maroons and the Enslaved Africans in Jamaica*. London: Austin & Macauley Publishers Ltd., 2012.

———. "Invisible Yet Invincible: The Muslim Ummah in Jamaica." *Journal of Muslim Minority Affairs* 23, no. 1 (2003): 211–222.

———. "The Manifestation of *Tawhid*: The Muslim Heritage of the Maroons in Jamaica." *Caribbean Quarterly* 45, no. 1 (1999): 27–40.

———. "The Moghul Islamic Diaspora: The Institutionalization of Islam in Jamaica." *Journal of Muslim Minority Affairs* 20, no. 2 (2000): 271–289.

———. "The Unsung Slaves: Islam in Plantation Jamaica." *Caribbean Quarterly* 41, nos 3/4 (September-December 1995): 30–44.

Agamben, Giorgio. *Homo Sacer: Sovereign Power and Bare Life*. Translated by Daniel Heller-Roazen. Stanford, CA: Stanford University Press, 1998.

Ahmed, Leila. "The Veil Debate—Again." In *On Shifting Ground: Muslim Women in the Global Era*, edited by Fereshteh Nouraie-Simone, 153–171. New York: The Feminist Press at the City University of New York, 2005.

———. *Women and Gender in Islam: Historical Roots of a Modern Debate*. New Haven, CT: Yale University Press, 1992.

Aidi, Hisham D. *Rebel Music: Race, Empire, and the New Muslim Youth Culture*. New York: Pantheon Books, 2014.

Alexander, M. Jacqui. *Pedagogies of Crossing: Meditations on Feminism, Sexual Politics, Memory, and the Sacred*. Durham: Duke University Press, 2005.

Ali, Amir. "Islam in Trinidad." *Muslim World* 15, no. 1 (January 1925): 72–73.

Alsultany, Evelyn. *Arabs and Muslims in the Media: Race and Representation after 9/11*. New York: New York University Press, 2012.

Arberry, A.J. *Aspects of Islamic Civilization: As Depicted in the Original Texts*. 1964. Reprint, New York: Routledge, 2010.

Asad, Talal. "The Idea of an Anthropology of Islam." 1986. Reprint, *Qui Parle* 17, no. 2 (2009): 1–30.

Austen, Ralph A. *Trans-Saharan Africa in World History*. New York: Oxford University Press, 2010.

Bahadur, Gaiutra. *Coolie Woman: The Odyssey of Indenture*. Chicago: University of Chicago Press, 2014.

Bakhtin, Mikhail. *Rabelais and His World*. 1965. Translated by Helene Iswolsky. Reprint, Bloomington: Indiana University Press, 1984.

Baksh-Soodeen, Rawwida. "Issues of Difference in Contemporary Caribbean Feminism." *Feminist Review* 59 (Summer 1998): 74–85.

———. "Power, Gender and Chutney." In *Matikor: The Politics of Identity for Indo-Caribbean Women*, edited by Rosanne Kanhai, 194–198. St. Augustine, Trinidad: University of the West Indies School of Continuing Studies, 1999.

Baptiste, Jeanne P. "More Than Dawud and Jalut: Decriminalizing the Jamat al Muslimeen and Madressa in Trinidad." In *Islam and the Americas*, edited by Aisha Khan, 269–294. Gainesville: University Press of Florida, 2015.

Baugh, Edward. "A History of Poetry." In *A History of Literature in the Caribbean*. Vol. 2, *English- and Dutch-Speaking Regions*, edited by A. James Arnold, 227–282. Philadelphia: John Benjamins Publishing Co., 2001.

Bayoumi, Mustafa. "Racing Religion." *CR: The New Centennial Review* 6, no. 2 (Fall 2006): 267–293.

Benjamin, Walter. "Doctrine of the Similar." 1933. Translated by Knut Tarnowski. *New German Critique* 17 (Spring 1979): 65–69.

———. "On the Concept of History." In *Walter Benjamin: Selected Writings*. Vol. 4, *1938–1940*, edited by Howard Eiland and Michael W. Jennings, translated by Edmund Jephcott and Others, 389–400. 1940. Reprint, Cambridge, MA: Belknap Press, 2006.

Berg, Herbert. "Black Muslims." In *Routledge Handbook of Islam in the West*, edited by Roberto Tottoli, 123–136. New York: Routledge, 2014.

Bhabha, Homi K. *The Location of Culture*. London: Routledge, 1994.

Birbalsingh, Frank. "The Indo-Caribbean Short Story." *Journal of West Indian Literature* 12, nos 1/2 (2004): 118–134.

Birth, Kevin K. *Bacchanalian Sentiments: Musical Experiences and Political Counterpoints in Trinidad*. Durham: Duke University Press, 2008.

Bowen, W. Errol, and Slade Hopkinson. "Slade Hopkinson on Slade Hopkinson: In an Interview with W. Errol Bowen." *Caribbean Quarterly* 23, nos 2/3 (1977): 66–76.

Brathwaite, Edward Kamau. "Nation Language." In *The Postcolonial Studies Reader*, edited by Bill Ashcroft, Gareth Griffiths, and Helen Tiffin, 309–313. New York: Routledge, 1995.

Braziel, Jana Evans. "'Caribbean Genesis': Language, Gardens, Worlds (Jamaica Kincaid, Derek Walcott, Édouard Glissant)." In *Caribbean Literature and the Environment*, edited by Elizabeth De Loughrey, Renée K. Gosson, and George B. Handley, 110–126. Charlottesville: University of Virginia Press, 2005.

Brereton, Bridget. *Race Relations in Colonial Trinidad, 1870–1900*. Cambridge: Cambridge University Press, 1979.

Brown, Edward G. 1906. *A Literary History of Persia: From Firdawsi to Sa'di*. Abingdon, Oxon, UK: Routledge, 2009.

Byrd, Jodi A. *The Transit of Empire: Indigenous Critiques of Colonialism*. Minneapolis: University of Minnesota Press, 2011.

Caillois, Roger. "Mimicry and Legendary Pyschaesthenia." 1935. Reprinted in *The Edge of Surrealism: A Roger Caillois Reader*, edited by Claudine Frank and Camille Naish, 89–103. Durham: Duke University Press, 2003.

Cainkar, Louise, and Sunaina Maira. "Targeting Arab/Muslim/South Asian Americans: Criminalization and Cultural Citizenship." *Amerasia* 31, no. 3 (2005): 1–27.

Carter, Marina, and Khal Torabully. *Coolitude: An Anthology of the Indian Labour Diaspora*. London: Anthem Press, 2002.

Castor, N. Fadeke. *Spiritual Citizenship: Transnational Pathways from Black Power to Ifá in Trinidad*. Durham: Duke University Press, 2017.

Césaire, Aimé. "Calling the Magician: A Few Words for a Caribbean Civilization." 1944. Reprinted in *Refusal of the Shadow: Surrealism and the Caribbean*, edited by Michael Richardson, translated by Krzysztof Fijalkowski and Michael Richardson, 119–122. London: Verso, 1996.

Chan-Malik, Sylvia. *Being Muslim: A Cultural History of Women of Color in American Islam*. New York: New York University Press, 2018.

Chickrie, Raymond. "The Afghan Muslims of Guyana and Suriname." *Journal of Muslim Minority Affairs* 22, no. 2 (2002): 381–399.

———. "Islamic Organizations in Guyana: Seventy Years of History and Politics, 1936–2006." *Journal of Muslim Minority Affairs* 27, no. 3 (2007): 401–428.

———. "Muslims in Guyana: History, Traditions, Conflict and Change." *Journal of Muslim Minority Affairs* 19, no. 2 (1999): 181–195.

Chickrie, Raymond, and Bibi Halima Khanam. "Hindustani Muslims in Guyana: Tradition, Conflict and Change, 1838 to the Present." In *Indentured Muslims in the Diaspora: Identity and Belonging of Minority Groups in Plural Societies*, edited by Maurits S. Hassankhan, Goolam Vahed, and Lomarsh Roopnarine, 109–140. New York: Routledge, 2017.

Coovadia, Imraan. *Authority and Authorship in V. S. Naipaul*. New York: Palgrave Macmillan, 2009.

Cottee, Simon. "The Calypso Caliphate: How Trinidad Became a Recruiting Ground for ISIS." *International Affairs* 95, no. 2 (March 2019): 297–317.

Curtin, Philip D., ed. *Africa Remembered: Narratives by West Africans from the Era of the Slave Trade*. Madison: University of Wisconsin Press, 1967.

Curtis, Edward E., IV. *The Call of Bilal: Islam in the African Diaspora*. Chapel Hill: University of North Carolina Press, 2014.

———. "Why Muslims Matter to American Religious History, 1730–1945." In *The Cambridge History of Religions in America*, edited by Stephen J. Stein, 393–413. New York: Cambridge University Press, 2000.

Darroch, Fiona. *Memory and Myth: Postcolonial Religion in Contemporary Guyanese Fiction and Poetry*. Cross/Cultures 103. Amsterdam: Editions Rodopi, 2009.

Dayan, Joan (Colin). *Haiti, History, and the Gods*. Berkeley: University of California Press, 1995.

———. "Paul Gilroy's Slaves, Ships, and Routes: The Middle Passage as Metaphor." *Research in African Literatures* 27, no. 4 (Winter 1996): 7–14.

de Bruijn, J.T.P. *Persian Sufi Poetry: An Introduction to the Mystical Use of Classical Poems*. Surrey, UK: Curzon Press, 1997.

de Kruijf, Johannes Gerrit. "Guyana Junction: Globalisation, Localisation, and the Production of East Indianness." PhD diss., Utrecht University, 2006. Repository Universiteit Utrecht. (ID 10-1874-12290).

———. "Muslim Transnationalism in Indo-Guyana: Localized Globalization and Battles over a Cultural Islam." *Focaal—European Journal of Anthropology* 50 (2007): 102–124.

Descartes, René. *Discourse on the Method of Rightly Conducting One's Reason and of Seeking Truth in the Sciences*. 1637. Translated by Ian Maclean. Reprint, Oxford: Oxford University Press, 2006.

Diouf, Sylviane A. "African Muslims in the Caribbean." *Wadabagei* 11, no. 1 (Winter 2008): 83–95.

———. *Servants of Allah: African Muslims Enslaved in the Americas*. 1998. Reprint, New York: New York University Press, 2013.

Diptee, Audra A. *From Africa to Jamaica: The Making of an Atlantic Slave Society, 1775–1807*. Gainesville: University Press of Florida, 2010.

Dobronravin, Nikolay. "Literacy among Muslims in Nineteenth-Century Trinidad and Brazil." In *Slavery, Islam and Diaspora*, edited by Behnaz A. Mirzai, Ismael Musah Montana, and Paul E. Lovejoy, 217–236. Trenton, NJ: Africa World Press, Inc., 2009.

Donnell, Alison. "V. S. Naipaul, a Queer Trinidadian." *Wasafiri* 28, no. 2 (2013): 58–65.

Earle, Gilbert. "Mohammedans in Trinidad." *Muslim World* 14, no. 1 (January 1924): 40–42.

Edwards, Bryan. *The History, Civil and Commercial, of the British West Indies*, Vol. 2. 5th ed. London: T. Miller, 1819.

Enayat, Hadi. *Islam and Secularism in Post-Colonial Thought: A Cartography of Asadian Genealogies*. Basingstoke, UK: Palgrave Macmillan, 2014.

Erickson, John. *Islam and Postcolonial Narrative*. Cambridge: Cambridge University Press, 1998.

Fadda-Conrey, Carol N. "The Passage from West to South: Arabs between the Old and New World." In *Arabs in the Americas: Interdisciplinary Essays on the Arab Diaspora*, edited by Darcy A. Zabel, 19–28. New York: Peter Lang, 2006.

Falk, Erik. "'To Say Profitably': Dabydeen's Exoticist Aesthetic." In *Talking Words: New Essays on the Work of David Dabydeen*, edited by Lynne Macedo, 84–100. Kingston, Jamaica: University of the West Indies Press, 2011.

Fanon, Franz. *A Dying Colonialism*. 1959. Translated by Haakon Chevalier. Reprint, New York: Grove Press, 1965.

———. *The Wretched of the Earth*. 1961. Translated by Richard Philcox. Reprint, New York: Grove Press, 2004.

Fernández Olmos, Margarite, and Lizabeth Paravisini-Gebert. *Creole Religions of the Caribbean: An Introduction from Vodou and Santería to Obeah and Espiritismo*. New York: New York University Press, 2011.

Figueira, Daurius. *Jihad in Trinidad and Tobago, July 27, 1990*. Lincoln, NE: Writers Club Press, iUniverse, 2002.

Flood, Finbarr Barry. "Bodies and Becoming: Mimesis, Mediation, and the Ingestion of the Sacred in Christianity and Islam." In *Sensational Religion: Sensory Cultures in Material Practice*, edited by Sally M. Promey, 459–493. New Haven, CT: Yale University Press, 2014.

Garvey, Marcus. "Speech by Marcus Garvey: The Work That Has Been Done." 1937. Reprinted in *The Marcus Garvey and Universal Negro Improvement Association Papers*. Vol. 7, edited by Robert A. Hill, 788–794. Berkeley: University of California Press, 1990.

GhaneaBassiri, Kambiz. "Islam in America: The Beginnings." In *Routledge Handbook of Islam in the West*, edited by Roberto Tottoli, 109–122. New York: Routledge, 2014.

Glissant, Édouard. *Caribbean Discourse: Selected Essays*. Translated by Michael Dash. Charlottesville: Caraf Books/University Press of Virginia, 1999.

Gomez, Michael A. *Black Crescent: The Experience and Legacy of African Muslims in the Americas*. New York: Cambridge University Press, 2005.

Gopinath, Gayatri. *Impossible Desires: Queer Diasporas and South Asian Public Cultures*. Durham: Duke University Press, 2005.

Graham, William A. *Beyond the Written Word: Oral Aspects of Scripture in the History of Religion*. New York: Cambridge University Press, 1993.

Hall, Stuart. "Cultural Identity and Diaspora." In *Theorizing Diaspora: A Reader*, edited by Jana Evans Braziel and Anita Mannur, 233–246. Malden, MA: Blackwell Publishing, 2003.

———. "The Local and the Global: Globalization and Ethnicity." In *Culture, Globalization and the World-System: Contemporary Conditions for the Representation of Identity*, edited by Anthony D. King, 19–39. Minneapolis: University of Minnesota Press, 2007.

Hamid, Ahmed, and Wazir Baksh. "Islam in Guyana." In *Islam and Muslims in the American Continent*, edited by Amadou Mahtar M'Bow and M. Ali Kettani, 353–421. Beirut: Center of Historical, Economical and Social Studies, Hariri Foundation, and Hekmat A. Kassir Foundation, 2001.

Haniff, Nesha Z. *Blaze a Fire: Significant Contributions of Caribbean Women*. Toronto: Sister Vision, Black Women and Women of Colour Press, 1988.

———. "My Grandmother Worked in the Field: Stereotypes Regarding East Indian Women in the Caribbean." In *Matikor: The Politics of Identity for Indo-Caribbean Women*, edited by Rosanne Kanhai, 18–31. St. Augustine, Trinidad: University of the West Indies School of Continuing Studies, 1999.

Harris, Wilson. "Epilogue: Theatre of the Arts." In *Caribbean Literature and the Environment*, edited by Elizabeth M. De Loughrey, Renée K. Gosson, and George B. Handley, 261–268. Charlottesville: University of Virginia Press, 2005.

———. "History, Fable and Myth in the Caribbean and Guianas." In *Selected Essays of Wilson Harris: The Unfinished Genesis of the Imagination*, edited by A.J.M. Bundy, 152–166. London: Routledge, 1999.

———. "A Note on the Genesis of *The Guyana Quartet*." In *The Guyana Quartet*, 7–14. London: Faber and Faber, 1985.

Hartman, Saidiya V. *Lose Your Mother: A Journey along the Atlantic Slave Route*. New York: Farrar, Straus and Giroux, 2007.

Hassankhan, Maurits S. "Islam and Indian Muslims in Suriname: A Struggle for Survival." In *Indentured Muslims in the Diaspora: Identity and Belonging of Minority Groups in Plural Societies*, edited by Maurits Hassankhan, Goolam Vahed, and Lomarsh Roopnarine, 183–228. New York: Routledge, 2017.

Hassankhan, Maurits S., Goolam Vahed, and Lomarsh Roopnarine, eds. *Indentured Muslims in the Diaspora: Identity and Belonging of Minority Groups in Plural Societies*. New York: Routledge, 2017.

Henry, Paget. *Caliban's Reason: Introducing Afro-Caribbean Philosophy*. New York: Routledge, 2000.

Hill, Joseph. "Sovereign Islam in a Secular State: Hidden Knowledge and Sufi Governance Among 'Taalibe Baay.'" In *Tolerance, Democracy, and Sufis in Senegal*, edited by Mamadou Diouf, 99–124. New York: Columbia University Press, 2013.

Hock, Hans Heinrich, and Brian D. Joseph. *Language History, Language Change, and Language Relationship: An Introduction to Historical and Comparative Linguistics*. 2nd ed. Berlin: Mouton de Gruyter, 2009.

Hopkinson, Slade. "'Dream on Monkey Mountain' and the Popular Response (A Few Questions)." *Caribbean Quarterly* 23, nos 2/3 (1977): 77–79.

Hosay Trinidad. Produced by John Bishop and Frank Korom. Watertown, MA: Documentary Educational Resources, 1999. Documentary, 45 min.

Hosein, Gabrielle Jamela. "Democracy, Gender, and Indian Muslim Modernity in Trinidad." In *Islam and the Americas*, edited by Aisha Khan, 249–268. Gainesville: University Press of Florida, 2015.

Hosein, Gabrielle Jamela, and Lisa Outar, eds. *Indo-Caribbean Feminist Thought: Genealogies, Theories, Enactments*. New York: Palgrave Macmillan, 2016.

Hulme, Peter. "Hurricanes in the Caribbees: The Constitution of the Discourse of English Colonialism." In *1642: Literature and Power in the Seventeenth Century*, edited by Francis Barker, Jay Bernstein, John Coombes, Peter Hulme, Jennifer Stone, and John Stratton, 55–83. Colchester, UK: University of Essex, 1981.

Jackson, Shona. "The Baptism of Soil: Rooplall Monar and the Aesthetics of the *Kala Pani* Modern." *Journal of Caribbean Literatures* 6, no. 3 (Spring 2010): 9–21.

———. *Creole Indigeneity: Between Myth and Nation in the Caribbean*. Minneapolis: University of Minnesota Press, 2012.

Jagan, Cheddi. "Race, Class, Color and Religion." In *Cultural Identity and Creolization in National Unity: The Multiethnic Caribbean*, edited by Prem Misir, 79–90. Lanham, MD: University Press of America, 2006.

James, C.L.R. *Beyond a Boundary*. 1963. Reprint, London: Yellow Jersey Press, 2005.

Johnson, Sylvester. *African American Religions, 1500–2000, Colonialism, Democracy, and Freedom*. Cambridge: Cambridge University Press, 2015.

Kale, Madhavi. *Fragments of Empire: Capital, Slavery, and Indian Indentured Labor Migration in the British Caribbean*. Philadelphia: University of Pennsylvania Press, 1988.

Kanhai, Rosanne, ed. *Bindi: The Multifaceted Lives of Indo-Caribbean Women*. Kingston, Jamaica: University of the West Indies Press, 2011.

———, ed. *Matikor: The Politics of Identity for Indo-Caribbean Women*. St. Augustine, Trinidad: University of the West Indies School of Continuing Studies, 1999.

Kassim, Halima-Sa'adia. "Education and Socialization among the Indo-Muslims of Trinidad, 1917–1969." *Journal of Caribbean History* 36, no. 1 (2002): 100–126.

———. "Forming Islamic Religious Identity among Trinidadians in the Age of Social Networks." In *Crescent over Another Horizon: Islam in Latin America, the Caribbean, and Latino USA*, edited by María del Mar Logroño Narbona, Paulo G. Pinto, and John Tofik Karam, 225–251. Austin: University of Texas Press, 2015.

———. "Identity and Acculturation of Trinidad Muslims: An Exploration of Contemporary Practices." In *Indentured Muslims in the Diaspora: Identity and Belonging of Minority Groups in Plural Societies*, edited by Maurits Hassankhan, Goolam Vahed, and Lomarsh Roopnarine, 141–180. New York: Routledge, 2017.

Kempadoo, Kamala. *Sexing the Caribbean: Gender, Race, and Sexual Labor*. New York: Routledge, 2004.

Kersten, Carool. "Islamic Post-Traditionalism: Postcolonial and Postmodern Religious Discourse in Indonesia." *Sophia* 54, no. 4 (December 2015): 473–489.

Kettani, Houssain. "History and Prospect of Muslims in South America." *Social Indicators Research* 115, no. 2 (January 2014): 837–868.

———. "Muslim Population in the Americas: 1950–2020." *International Journal of Environmental Science and Development* 1, no. 2 (June 2010): 127–135.

Khan, Aisha. *Callaloo Nation: Metaphors of Race and Religious Identity among South Asians in Trinidad*. Durham: Duke University Press, 2004.

———. "Contours: Approaching Islam, Comparatively Speaking." In *Islam and the Americas*, edited by Aisha Khan, 23–45. Gainesville: University Press of Florida, 2015.

———. Introduction to *Islam and the Americas*, edited by Aisha Khan, 1–22. Gainesville: University Press of Florida, 2015.

———, ed. *Islam and the Americas*. Gainsville: University Press of Florida, 2015.

———. "Islam, Vodou, and the Making of the Afro-Atlantic." *New West Indian Guide/Nieuwe West-Indische Gids* 86, nos 1/2 (2012): 29–54.

———. "*Juthaa* in Trinidad: Food, Pollution, and Hierarchy in a Caribbean Diaspora Community." *American Ethnologist* 21, no. 2 (May 1994): 245–269.

———. "Muharram Moves West: Exploring the Absent-Present." In *Caribbean Popular Culture: Power, Politics and Performance*, edited by Yanique Hume and Aaron Kamugisha, 484–500. Kingston, Jamaica: Ian Randle Publishers, 2016.

Khan, Aliyah. "Indigeneity and the Indo-Caribbean in Cyril Dabydeen's *Dark Swirl*." *Studies in Canadian Literature/Études en littérature anadienne* 40, no. 1 (2015): 205–226.

———. "Protest and Punishment: Indo-Guyanese Women and Organized Labour." *Caribbean Review of Gender Studies* 12 (2018): 269–298.

———. "Voyages across Indenture: From Ship Sister to Mannish Woman." *GLQ* 22, no. 2 (2016): 249–280.

Khanam, Bibi H., and Raymond S. Chickrie. "170th Anniversary of the Arrival of the First Hindustani Muslims from India to British Guiana." *Journal of Muslim Minority Affairs* 29, no. 2 (2009): 195–222.

Korom, Frank. *Hosay Trinidad: Muharram Performances in an Indo-Caribbean Diaspora*. Philadelphia: University of Pennsylvania Press, 2002.

Kurzman, Charles, ed. *Liberal Islam: A Sourcebook*. New York: Oxford University Press, 1998.

Lee-Loy, Anne-Marie. "'. . . The Chinese Are Preferred to All Others': Nineteenth-Century Representations of the Chinese in Trinidad and British Guiana." *Asian Studies Review* 27, no. 2 (June 2003): 205–225.

———. "Saying No to Chineseness: The Possibilities and Limits of a Diasporic Identity in Janice Lowe Shinebourne's Fiction." *Journal of Chinese Overseas* 5 (2009): 291–309.

Levtzion, Nehemia. "Islam in the Bilad al-Sudan to 1800." In *The History of Islam in Africa*, edited by Nehemia Levtzion and Randall L. Pouwels, 63–91. Athens: Ohio University Press, 2012.

Levtzion Nehemia, and Randall L. Pouwels, eds. *The History of Islam in Africa*. Athens: Ohio University Press, 2012.

Logroño Narbona, María del Mar, Paulo G. Pinto, and John Tofik Karam, eds. *Crescent Over Another Horizon: Islam in Latin America, the Caribbean, and Latino USA*. Austin: University of Texas Press, 2015.

Lokaisingh-Meighoo, Sean. "Jahaji Bhai: Notes on the Masculine Subject and Homoerotic Subtext of Indo-Caribbean Identity." *Small Axe* 7 (2000): 77–92.

Look Lai, Walton. *The Chinese in the West Indies, 1806–1995: A Documentary History*. Kingston, Jamaica: University of the West Indies Press, 2000.

———. *Indentured Labor, Caribbean Sugar: Chinese and Indian Migrants to the British West Indies, 1838–1918*. Baltimore, MD: Johns Hopkins University Press, 2004.

Lorde, Audre. *Zami: A New Spelling of My Name*. Berkeley, CA: The Crossing Press, 1982.

Love, Erik. *Islamophobia and Racism in America*. New York: New York University Press, 2017.

Lovejoy, Paul E. "'Freedom Narratives of Transatlantic Slavery.'" *Slavery and Abolition* 32, no. 1 (March 2011): 91–107.

———. *Jihād in West Africa during the Age of Revolution*. Athens: Ohio University Press, 2016.

Mackey, Nathaniel. "An Interview with Kamau Brathwaite." *Hambone* 9 (1991): 42–59.

Maes-Jelinek, Hena. *The Labyrinth of Universality: Wilson Harris' Visionary Art of Fiction*. Cross/Cultures 86. Amsterdam: Editions Rodopi, 2006.

Mahabir, Cynthia. "Adjudicating Pluralism: The *Hijab*, Law and Social Change in Post-Colonial Trinidad." *Social & Legal Studies* 13, no. 4 (2004): 435–452.

Mahabir, Joy, and Mariam Pirbhai. "Introduction: Tracing an Emerging Tradition." In *Critical Perspectives on Indo-Caribbean Women's Literature*, edited by Joy Mahabir and Mariam Pirbhai, 1–21. New York: Routledge, 2013.

Mahmood, Saba. *Politics of Piety: The Islamic Revival and the Feminist Subject*. Princeton, NJ: Princeton University Press, 2005.

———. "Rehearsed Spontaneity and the Conventionality of Ritual: Disciplines of Ṣalāt." *American Ethnologist* 28, no. 4 (2001): 827–853.

Majid, Anouar. *Unveiling Traditions: Postcolonial Islam in a Polycentric World*. Durham: Duke University Press, 2000.

Mamdani, Mahmood. "Good Muslim, Bad Muslim: A Political Perspective on Culture and Terrorism." *American Anthropologist* 104, no. 3 (Sept. 2002): 766–775.

Marr, Timothy. *The Cultural Roots of American Islamicism*. New York: Cambridge University Press, 2006.

———. "'Out of This World': Islamic Irruptions in the Literary Americas." *American Literary History* 18, no. 3 (Fall 2006): 521–549.

Mbembe, Achille. *On the Postcolony*. Berkeley: University of California Press, 2001.

M'Bow, Amadou Mahtar, and M. Ali Kettani, eds. *Islam and Muslims in the American Continent*. Beirut: Center of Historical, Economical and Social Studies, Hariri Foundation, and Hekmat A. Kassir Foundation, 2001.

McNeal, Keith E. *Trance and Modernity in the Southern Caribbean: African and Hindu Popular Religions in Trinidad and Tobago*. Gainesville: University Press of Florida, 2011.

Mehta, Brinda J. *Diasporic (Dis)locations: Indo-Caribbean Women Writers Negotiate the Kala Pani*. Kingston, Jamaica: University of the West Indies Press, 2004.

————. "Engendering History: A Poetics of the *Kala Pani* in Ramabai Espinet's *The Swinging Bridge*." *Small Axe* 21, vol. 10, no. 3 (2006): 19–36.

Meisami, Julie Scott. *Structure and Meaning in Medieval Arabic and Persian Poetry: Orient Pearls.* New York: RoutledgeCurzon, 2006.

Mernissi, Fatima. *Beyond the Veil: Male-Female Dynamics in Modern Muslim Society.* Rev. ed. Bloomington: Indiana University Press, 1987.

————. *The Veil and the Male Elite: A Feminist Interpretation of Women's Rights in Islam.* Translated by Mary Jo Lakeland. Oxford: Basil Blackwell, 1991.

Mignolo, Walter D. "Delinking: The Rhetoric of Modernity, the Logic of Coloniality and the Grammar of De-coloniality." *Cultural Studies* 21, no. 2 (2007): 449–514.

Misrahi-Barak, Judith. "Looking In, Looking Out: The Chinese-Caribbean Diaspora through Literature—Meiling Jin, Patricia Powell, Jan Lowe Shinebourne." *Journal of Transnational American Studies* 4, no. 1 (2012): 1–15.

————. "Ryhaan Shah's Silent Screams of *A Silent Life*." In *Voices and Silence in the Contemporary Novel in English,* edited by Vanessa Guignery, 249–259. Newcastle upon Tyne, UK: Cambridge Scholars Publishing, 2009.

Mitchell, Michael. "The Magic of Your Making: Magic and Realism in David Dabydeen's Recent Fiction." In *Talking Words: New Essays on the Work of David Dabydeen,* edited by Lynne Macedo, 136–149. Kingston, Jamaica: University of the West Indies Press, 2011.

Mohammed, Patricia. "Changing Symbols of Indo-Caribbean Femininity." *Caribbean Review of Gender Studies* 6 (2012): 1–16. https://sta.uwi.edu/crgs/march2013/index.asp.

————. "The 'Creolization' of Indian Women in Trinidad." In *Cultural Identity and Creolization in National Unity: The Multiethnic Caribbean,* edited by Prem Misir, 45–57. Lanham, MD: University Press of America, 2006.

————. "From Myth to Symbolism: The Construction of Indian Femininity and Masculinity in Post-Indentured Trinidad." In *Matikor: The Politics of Identity for Indo-Caribbean Women,* edited by Rosanne Kanhai, 62–99. St. Augustine, Trinidad: University of the West Indies School of Continuing Studies, 1999.

————. "Island Currents, Global Aesthetics: Islamic Iconography in Trinidad." In *Islam and the Americas,* edited by Aisha Khan, 295–326. Gainesville: University Press of Florida, 2015.

————. "Like Sugar in Coffee: Third Wave Feminism and the Caribbean." *Social and Economic Studies* 52, no. 3 (2003): 5–30.

————. "A Symbiotic Visiting Relationship: Caribbean Feminist Historiography and Caribbean Feminist Theory." In *Confronting Power, Theorizing Gender: Interdisciplinary Perspectives in the Caribbean,* edited by Eudine Barriteau, 101–125. Kingston, Jamaica: University of the West Indies Press, 2003.

————. "Towards Indigenous Feminist Theorizing in the Caribbean." *Feminist Review* 59 (1998): 6–33.

————. "Unmasking Masculinity and Deconstructing Patriarchy: Problems and Possibilities within Feminist Epistemology." In *Interrogating Caribbean Masculinities: Theoretical and Empirical Analyses,* edited by Rhoda E. Reddock, 38–67. Kingston, Jamaica: University of the West Indies Press, 2004.

Mohapatra, Prabhu P. *The Politics of Representation in the Indian Labour Diaspora: West Indies, 1890–1920.* NOIDA, Delhi: Integrated Labour History Research Programme, V. V. Giri National Labour Institute, 2004.

Mottale, Morris. "V. S. Naipaul and Islam." *Caribbean Quarterly* 56, no. 3 (2010): 71–79.

Moynihan, Colin. "Life Sentence for Leader of Terror Plot at Kennedy." *New York Times,* February 18, 2011, A24.

Munasinghe, Viranjini. *Callaloo or Tossed Salad? East Indians and the Cultural Politics of Identity in Trinidad*. Ithaca, NY: Cornell University Press, 2001.

———. "Nationalism in Hybrid Spaces: The Production of Impurity Out of Purity." *American Ethnologist* 29, no. 3 (2002): 663–692.

———. "Redefining the Nation: The East Indian Struggle for Inclusion in Trinidad." *Journal of Asian American Studies* 4, no. 1 (2001): 1–34.

"Muslim Brotherhood of Guyana." *The Clarion*, March 14, 1966, 5.

Mustapha, Nasser. "Islam in the Caribbean." In *Encyclopedia of African-American Culture and History*. Vol. 3, 2nd ed., edited by Colin A. Palmer, 1132–1134. Detroit: Macmillan Reference USA, 2006.

Naipaul, V. S. "Two Worlds." Nobel Lecture, Stockholm, December 7, 2001. https://www.nobelprize.org/nobel_prizes/literature/laureates/2001/naipaul-lecture-e.html.

Nance, Susan. *How the Arabian Nights Inspired the American Dream, 1790–1935*. Chapel Hill: University of North Carolina Press, 2009.

Nash, Geoffrey, Kathleen Kerr-Koch, and Sarah Hackett, eds. *Postcolonialism and Islam: Theory, Literature, Culture, Society and Film*. New York: Routledge, 2014.

Nerlekar, Anjali. "Living Beadless in a Foreign Land: David Dabydeen's Poetry of Disappearance." In *Talking Words: New Essays on the Work of David Dabydeen*, edited by Lynne Macedo, 15–29. Kingston, Jamaica: University of the West Indies Press, 2011.

Niranjana, Tejaswini. *Mobilizing India: Women, Music, and Migration between India and Trinidad*. Durham: Duke University Press, 2006.

Oakland, Ross. "In Search of a Better Life Toronto's 200,000 West Indians Didn't Come for the Climate." *Globe and Mail*, January 10, 1981, F3.

Pantin, Raoul A. *Days of Wrath: The 1990 Coup in Trinidad and Tobago*. Lincoln, NE: iUniverse, Inc., 2007.

Pirbhai, Mariam. "The *Jahaji-Bhain* Principle: A Critical Survey of the Indo-Caribbean Women's Novel, 1990–2009." *Journal of Commonwealth Literature* 45, no. 1 (2010): 37–56.

———. "Recasting *Jahaji-Bhain*: Plantation History and the Indo-Caribbean Women's Novel in Trinidad, Guyana and Martinique." In *Critical Perspectives on Indo-Caribbean Women's Literature*, edited by Joy Mahabir and Mariam Pirbhai, 25–47. New York: Routledge, 2013.

Poynting, Jeremy. "'You Want to Be a Coolie Woman?' Gender and Ethnic Identity in Indo-Caribbean Women's Writing." In *Caribbean Women Writers: Essays from the First International Conference*, edited by Selwyn R. Cujoe, 98–105. Wellesley, MA: Calaloux Productions, 1990.

Prorok, Carolyn V., and Mohammad Hemmasi. "East Indian Muslims and Their Mosques in Trinidad: A Geography of Religious Structures and the Politics of Ethnic Identity." *Caribbean Geography* 4, no. 1 (1993): 28–48.

Puar, Jasbir. *Terrorist Assemblages: Homonationalism in Queer Times*. Durham: Duke University Press, 2007.

Puri, Shalini. *The Caribbean Postcolonial: Social Equality, Post/Nationalism, and Cultural Hybridity*. New York: Palgrave Macmillan, 2004.

Quijano, Aníbal, and Immanuel Wallerstein. "Americanity as a Concept, or the Americas in the Modern World System." *International Social Science Journal* 44, no. 4 (1992): 549–557.

Quraishi-Landes, Asifa. "Rumors of the Sharia Threat Are Greatly Exaggerated: What American Judges Really Do with Islamic Family Law in Their Courtrooms." *New York Law School Law Review* 57, no. 245 (2012–2013): 245–257.

Rampersad, Indrani. "Becoming a Pandita." In *Matikor: The Politics of Identity for Indo-Caribbean Women*, edited by Rosanne Kanhai, 140–143. St. Augustine, Trinidad: University of the West Indies School of Continuing Studies, 1999.

Rana, Junaid. *Terrifying Muslims: Race and Labor in the South Asian Diaspora.* Durham: Duke University Press, 2011.

Reddock, Rhoda. "Jahaji Bhai: The Emergence of a Dougla Poetics in Trinidad and Tobago." *Identities* 5, no. 4 (1999): 569–601.

———. "'Up against a Wall': Muslim Women's Struggle to Reclaim Masjid Space in Trinidad and Tobago." In *Islam and the Americas,* edited by Aisha Khan, 216–248. Gainesville: University Press of Florida, 2015.

———. *Women, Labour & Politics in Trinidad & Tobago: A History.* London: Zed Books, 1994.

Reis, João José. *Slave Rebellion in Brazil: The Muslim Uprising of 1835 in Bahia.* Translated by Arthur Brakel. Baltimore, MD: Johns Hopkins University Press, 1993.

Retamar, Roberto Fernández. *Calibán y otros ensayos: nuestra américa y el mundo.* La Habana: Editorial Arte y Literatura, 1979.

Rickford, John R. *Dimensions of a Creole Continuum: History, Texts & Linguistic Analysis of Guyanese Creole.* Stanford, CA: Stanford University Press, 1987.

Robinson, David. *Muslim Societies in African History.* New York: Cambridge University Press, 2004.

Rocklin, Alexander. *The Regulation of Religion and the Making of Hinduism in Colonial Trinidad.* Chapel Hill: University of North Carolina Press, 2019.

Rodney, Walter. *History of the Guyanese Working People, 1881–1905.* 1981. Reprint, Baltimore: Johns Hopkins University Press, 1982.

Ruhomon, Joseph. "India—the Progress of Her People at Home and Abroad and How Those in British Guiana May Improve Themselves." In *They Came in Ships: An Anthology of Indo-Guyanese Prose and Poetry,* edited by Joel Benjamin, Lakshmi Kallicharan, Ian McDonald, and Lloyd Searwar, 44–50. Leeds, UK: Peepal Tree Press, 1894.

Ryan, Selwyn D. *The Muslimeen Grab for Power: Race, Religion, and Revolution in Trinidad and Tobago.* Port of Spain: Imprint Caribbean Ltd., 1991.

Said, Edward W. *Covering Islam: How the Media and the Experts Determine How We See the Rest of the World.* 1981. Reprint, New York: Vintage, 1997.

———. *Culture and Imperialism.* 1993. Reprint, New York: Vintage, 1994.

———. *Orientalism.* 1978. Reprint, New York: Vintage, 1994.

Samaroo, Brinsley. "Early African and East Indian Muslims in Trinidad and Tobago." In *Across the Dark Waters: Ethnicity and Indian Identity in the Caribbean,* edited by David Dabydeen and Brinsley Samaroo, 201–212. London: Macmillan Caribbean, 1996.

———. "The First Ship: The Fath al Razak." In *In Celebration of 150 Years of the Indian Contribution to Trinidad and Tobago.* Vol. 2, edited by Brinsley Samaroo and Kenneth Ramchand, 1–14. Port of Spain: Historical Publications Ltd., 1995.

———. "Seeking a Space in the Politics: Muslim Efforts to Join the Political Process in British Guiana and Trinidad in the 20th Century." *Man in India* 93, no. 1 (2013): 201–211.

Santesso, Esra Mirze. *Disorientation: Muslim Identity in Contemporary Anglophone Literature.* New York: Palgrave Macmillan, 2013.

Sayyid, Salman. "Empire, Islam, and the Postcolonial." In *The Oxford Handbook of Postcolonial Studies,* edited by Graham Huggan, 127–141. Oxford: Oxford University Press, 2013.

Schamp, Jutta. "'Everything Is Illuminated': Trauma, Literary Alchemy and Transfiguration in David Dabydeen's *Molly and the Muslim Stick.*" In *Talking Words: New Essays on the Work of David Dabydeen,* edited by Lynne Macedo, 116–135. Kingston, Jamaica: University of the West Indies Press, 2011.

Scott, Jamie S. "Religion and Postcolonial Writing." In *The Cambridge History of Postcolonial Literature.* Vol. 2, edited by Ato Quayson, 739–770. New York: Cambridge University Press, 2012.

Seecharan, Clem. *India and the Shaping of the Indo-Guyanese Imagination: 1890s–1920s*. Leeds: Peepal Tree Press, and the Centre for Research in Asian Migration, The University of Warwick, 1993.

Shaheen, Basima Kamel. "Literary Form and Islamic Identity in *The Life of Omar Ibn Said*." In *Journeys of the Slave Narrative in the Early Americas*, edited by Nicole N. Aljoe and Ian Finseth, 187–208. Charlottesville: University of Virginia Press, 2014.

Shepherd, Verene A. *Maharani's Misery: Narratives of a Passage from India to the Caribbean*. Kingston, Jamaica: University of the West Indies Press, 2002.

———. *Transients to Settlers: The Experience of Indians in Jamaica, 1845–1950*. Leeds: Peepal Tree Books, 1994.

Singh, Sherry-Ann. *The Ramayana Tradition and Socio-Religious Change in Trinidad, 1917–1990*. Kingston, Jamaica: Ian Randle Publishers, 2012.

Spivak, Gayatri. "Can the Subaltern Speak?" In *Colonial Discourse and Post-Colonial Theory: A Reader*, edited by Patrick Williams and Laura Chrisman, 66–111. New York: Columbia University Press, 1994.

Stephanides, Stephanie, and Karna Singh. *Translating Kali's Feast: The Goddess in Indo-Caribbean Ritual and Fiction*. Amsterdam: Editions Rodopi B. V., 2000.

Sudhakar, Anantha. "Muslim, Interrupted." Review of *Chinese Woman: A Novel*, by Jan Lowe Shinebourne. *Small Axe Salon*, June 2011. http://smallaxe.net/sxsalon/reviews/muslim-interrupted/.

Thaiss, Gustav. "Contested Meanings and the Politics of Authenticity: The 'Hosay' in Trinidad." In *Islam, Globalization and Postmodernity*, edited by Akbar S. Ahmed and Hastings Donnan, 38–62. London: Routledge, 1994.

Thifault, Paul. "The Rhyming Irons of Abdur-Rahman Slade Hopkinson." *Anthurium: A Caribbean Studies Journal* 13, no. 2, article 3 (2016): 1–14.

Tiffin, Helen. "'Man Fitting the Landscape': Nature, Culture, and Colonialism." In *Caribbean Literature and the Environment*, edited by Elizabeth De Loughrey, Renée K. Gosson, and George B. Handley, 199–212. Charlottesville: University of Virginia Press, 2005.

Tinker, Hugh. *A New System of Slavery: The Export of Indian Labour Overseas, 1830–1920*. 2nd ed. London: Hansib Publishing, 1993.

Tiwari, Rampersaud. "The October 1896 Non Pareil Uprising: The Unknown Story." *Man in India* 93, no. 1 (2013): 29–43.

Trotman, David V., and Paul E. Lovejoy. "Community of Believers: Trinidad Muslims and the Return to Africa, 1810–1850." In *Slavery on the Frontiers of Islam*, edited by Paul E. Lovejoy, 219–232. Princeton, NJ: Markus Wiener Publishers, 2004.

Turner, Richard Brent. *Islam in the African-American Experience*. Bloomington: Indiana University Press, 1997.

Upstone, Sara. *Spatial Politics in the Postcolonial Novel*. Burlington, VT: Ashgate, 2009.

van der Veer, Peter, and Steven Vertovec. "Brahmanism Abroad: On Caribbean Hinduism as an Ethnic Religion." *Ethnology* 30, no. 2 (April 1991): 149–166.

Vásquez, Sam. *Humor in the Caribbean Literary Canon*. New York: Palgrave Macmillan, 2012.

Vertovec, Steven. "'Official' and 'Popular' Hinduism in the Caribbean: Historical and Contemporary Trends in Surinam, Trinidad and Guyana." In *Perspectives on the Caribbean: A Reader in Culture, History, and Representation*, edited by Philip W. Scher, 227–241. West Sussex, UK: Wiley-Blackwell, 2010.

Walcott, Derek. "The Antilles: Fragments of Epic Memory." Nobel Lecture, Stockholm, December 7, 1992. https://www.nobelprize.org/nobel_prizes/literature/laureates/1992/walcott-lecture.html.

———. "The Caribbean: Culture or Mimicry?" *Journal of Interamerican Studies and World Affairs* 16, no. 1 (February 1974): 3–13.

Ware, Rudolph T. *The Walking Qur'an: Islamic Education, Embodied Knowledge, and History in West Africa*. Chapel Hill: University of North Carolina Press, 2014.

Ware, Rudolph, and Muhammad Shareef. "Shaykh 'Uthman bin Fudi." In *Jihad of the Pen: The Sufi Literature of West Africa*, edited by Rudolph Ware, Zachary Wright, and Amir Sayed, 25–63. New York: American University in Cairo Press, 2018.

Ware, Rudolph, Zachary Wright, and Amir Sayed, eds. *Jihad of the Pen: The Sufi Literature of West Africa*. New York: American University in Cairo Press, 2018.

Warner, Marina. *Fantastic Metamorphoses, Other Worlds: Ways of Telling the Self*. Oxford: Oxford University Press, 2002.

Warner-Lewis, Maureen. "Jamaica's Muslim Past: Misrepresentations." *Journal of Caribbean History* 37, no. 2 (2003): 294–316.

———. "Religious Constancy and Compromise among Nineteenth Century Caribbean-Based African Muslims." In *Slavery, Islam and Diaspora*, edited by Behnaz A. Mirzai, Ismael Musah Montana, and Paul E. Lovejoy, 237–268. Trenton, NJ: Africa World Press, 2009.

Waters, Robert Anthony, Jr. and Gordon Oliver Daniels. "Striking for Freedom? International Intervention and the Guianese Sugar Workers' Strike of 1964." *Cold War History* 10, no. 4 (2010): 537–569.

Wilks, Ivor. "Abū Bakr al-Ṣiddīq of Timbuktu." In *Africa Remembered: Narratives by West Africans from the Era of the Slave Trade*, edited by Philip D. Curtin, 152–169. Madison: University of Wisconsin Press, 1967.

———. *Wa and Wala: Islam and Polity in Northwestern Ghana*. New York: Cambridge University Press, 2002.

Winer, Lise, ed. *Dictionary of the English/Creole of Trinidad & Tobago: On Historical Principles*. Montreal: McGill-Queen's University Press, 2008.

Winter, Aaron. "My Enemies Must Be Friends: The American Extreme Right, Conspiracy Theory, Islam, and the Middle East." In *Conspiracy Theories in the United States and the Middle East: A Comparative Approach*, edited by Michael Butter and Maurus Reinkowski, 35–58. Boston: De Gruyter, 2014.

Wood, Donald. *Trinidad in Transition: 10 Years After Slavery*. Oxford: Oxford University Press, 1968.

Wright, Zachary. "Introduction: The Sufi Scholarship of Islamic West Africa." In *Jihad of the Pen: The Sufi Literature of West Africa*, edited by Rudolph Ware, Zachary Wright, and Amir Sayed, 1–24. New York: American University in Cairo Press, 2018.

Wynter, Sylvia. "The Ceremony Must Be Found: After Humanism." *boundary 2* 12, no. 3–13, no. 1 (1984): 19–70.

———. "Novel and History, Plot and Plantation." *Savacou* 5 (1971): 95–102.

Yamamoto, Shin. "Swaying in Time and Space: The Chinese Diaspora in the Caribbean and Its Literary Perspectives." *Asian Ethnicity* 9, no. 3 (2008): 171–177.

Young, Robert J. C. "Postcolonial Remains." *New Literary History* 43, no. 1 (Winter 2012): 19–42.

Younger, Paul. *New Homelands: Hindu Communities in Mauritius, Guyana, Trinidad, South Africa, Fiji and East Africa*. Oxford: Oxford University Press, 2010.

INDEX

ABOUT THE AUTHOR

ALIYAH KHAN is assistant professor of English and Afroamerican and African Studies at the University of Michigan, Ann Arbor. She holds a PhD in literature and feminist studies from the University of California, Santa Cruz, and an MFA in fiction from Hunter College CUNY. Khan's writing appears in *GLQ*, the *Caribbean Review of Gender Studies, Studies in Canadian Literature/Études en littérature canadienne, The Rumpus, Agents of Ishq,* and *Pree: Caribbean Writing.*